THE ROUGH GUIDE TO

Travel Health

There are more than one hundred and fifty Rough
Guide travel, phrasebook, and music titles,
covering destinations from Amsterdam to
Zimbabwe, languages from Czech to Vietnamese,
and musics from World to Opera and Jazz

www.roughguides.com

Rough Guide Credits

Text editor: Olivia Eccleshall; **Series editor**: Mark Ellingham
Production: Michelle Draycott, Helen Ostick, Sharon Martins, Maxine Repath
Proofreading: Margaret Doyle, Russell Walton

Publishing Information

This first edition published January 2001 by
Rough Guides Ltd, 62–70 Shorts Gardens, London WC2H 9AH.

Distributed by the Penguin Group

Penguin Books Ltd, 27 Wrights Lane, London W8 5TZ
Penguin Putnam, Inc., 375 Hudson Street, New York 10014, USA
Penguin Books Australia Ltd, 487 Maroondah Highway,
PO Box 257, Ringwood, Victoria 3134, Australia
Penguin Books Canada Ltd, 10 Alcorn Avenue,
Toronto, Ontario, Canada M4V 1E4
Penguin Books (NZ) Ltd, 182–190 Wairau Road,
Auckland 10, New Zealand

Typeset in Bembo and Helvetica to an original design by Henry Iles.
Printed in Spain by Graphy Cems.

© Nick Jones, 576pp includes index
A catalogue record for this book is available from the British Library.

ISBN 1-85828-570-4

THE ROUGH GUIDE TO
Travel Health

by Dr Nick Jones

with additional contributions by
Pema Sanders and Dr Charles Easmon

Acknowledgements

This book could not have been written without the towering and unerring support of my family, friends and colleagues. Special thanks to Jo, my wonderful wife and travel companion, for her love, strength, commitment and belief in this project . . . I really couldn't have done it without you; and to Will for welcome distraction and inspiration.

To the Jones family, past, present and future.

Grateful thanks from the author also to all at Rough Guides, but especially Olivia Eccleshall, Kate Berens, Martin Dunford, Anna Sutton, Henry Iles, Roger Barnes and Niki Smith; to Pema Sanders for the homeopathy sections; to Dr Charlie Easmon; to Tom Edwards, Ian Williams, Marc Dubin, Nick Edwards, Peter Eltringham, David Leffman, Vicky Nicholas, Helen Ostick, Polly Thomas and Justin Wintle for contributing accounts of their experiences of illness abroad; to all at St Chad's Surgery; to Graham Purches, Jane Solomons and the rest of the "It's Your Life" team; to the miscellaneous contributions of Dr Ian Anderson, Dr Keith Barrow, Debbie Brooks, Jacqui Buchanan, the Camerons, David (candiru!) Carter, the Gibbons's, Chris Kingdon, the Knotts, Dr Stephen Rye, Dr James Spreadborough, Dr Eric Walker, Professor David Warrell, Sara Watkins, The Wellcome Institute, Dr Henry Wilkinson and Steve Williamson. Sincere apologies to anyone whom I may have inadvertently forgotten.

Contents

Introduction

Travel can be fraught with health hazards, even the most minor of which can seriously hamper your enjoyment of a trip. Caught up in the excitement of being away, it's easy to drop your guard in a way that you might not at home, whether it's a simple case of overindulgence in the local cuisine or pulling a muscle in the rush to catch a train. Jet lag can just as easily disrupt your itinerary as an explosive case of Delhi Belly. But perhaps the biggest danger to the traveller is the assumption that "it can't happen to me".

By looking at travellers' health from two perspectives – the prevention of illness before it happens and how to cope if things do go wrong – **The Rough Guide to Travel Health** strives to help you avoid the risk, or at least minimize the impact, of illness abroad. **Part 1**, "Being Prepared", steers you through the considerations you need to make before you set out, with detailed advice on the kinds of vaccinations you might require, plus recommendations on what to pack in your medical kit – homeopathic remedies are discussed as well as conventional Western medicines. This section also advises on precautions to take so you stay well while you're away, and how to cope with problems like motion sickness and fear of flying in the course of getting there. Detailed advice for travellers with specific needs completes the section, catering to those with diabetes or epilepsy, for example, as well as elderly or pregnant travellers.

Part 2, the "A–Z", is an alphabetical listing of the illnesses and other health risks that you may encounter on your travels, with descriptions of the kinds of symptoms you can expect as well as the best treatments. The section opens with step-by-step instructions on "Making a diagnosis", or assessing your symptoms to determine a likely cause. At the close of the A–Z is a comprehensive section on First Aid. A country-by-country listing of potential risks forms **Part 3**, "Where in the world?", while **Part 4** comprises a "Directory" of useful sources of further information – chief among them a list of the top 5 recommended travel health Web sites.

There are a number of "**routes**" into this book. It might help to read through the whole of Part 1 in the planning stages of your trip. If you're far from home and suspect you're coming down with a particular illness, you can turn direct to the A–Z for advice on treatment. If you're less certain what you've got, the section on "Making a diagnosis" will take you through some basic steps to find out the cause. Before you arrive at a particular destination, or on experiencing symptoms, you might look up the relevant part of the world in Part 3 for a short summary of potential health hazards.

Whether you're in the planning stages before your trip or you're away and feeling ill, it's not the intention of this guide to replace a visit to a doctor. We are confident, however, that this book can help you make a more informed decision about what to do next, no matter where in the world you're travelling.

Don't allow health problems to be anything more than a minor setback; make this book the first item you pack every time the travel bug calls.

The *Rough Guide to Travel Health* is written by Dr Nick Jones, a general practitioner in Bath, UK, who in the course of his extensive travels has gained first-hand experience of illness off the beaten track. Pema Sanders, a practising homeopath and lecturer in Brighton, UK, has provided welcome advice on homeopathic and alternative preventative measures and treatments, while Dr Charles Easmon, Director of Travel Screening Services at the Hospital for Tropical Diseases, London, gave a valuable second opinion.

Remember

This book is intended to be used as a guide only. Designed to offer sensible, generalized advice to the sick traveller, it should **not** be considered as a substitute for the opinion of a qualified doctor. If you are worried about your symptoms, do not hesitate in seeking medical advice.

1

being
prepared

Planning

Prevention of ill health for the traveller starts long before you reach for your travel sickness pills in the airport departure lounge. Before so much as investing in a bottle of sunscreen lotion, you need to plan your itinerary carefully, consider what insurance requirements you will need, decide whether preventative measures (eg immunizations and malaria prophylaxis) are necessary and assemble a basic medical kit for emergencies.

Start by asking yourself three basic questions: **where**, **when** and **how** are you going to travel? Don't be under any illusions: travelling can be physically, psychologically and emotionally draining, and your answers may have significant implications for your health, not just on the road but also when you return.

Where?

Where will your travels take you? Will you stay in the city or the country, the mountains, rainforest or desert? Will you be lounging on the beach or wading through paddy fields? Will you visit more than one country and, if so, how long will you spend in each? Will you stay in established tourist areas, in tried-and-tested accommodation, or are you venturing into the wild and remote hinterland? Consider what diseases and dangers might lurk behind the glossy tourist brochures and how you can best prepare yourself for them.

When?

When are you going? Consider what the weather will be like, and which time of year is therefore best suited to the type of activity you're planning. If you intend to visit more than one country, are you likely to encounter different climates and seasons, and how will this affect you? Are there specific seasonal health risks to consider?

How?

How will you get there – by air, land or sea? Are you travelling alone, as a couple or in a group? Will you be going on an organized tour or independently? Will your chosen activity need pre-booking, special equipment, or specific health, fitness and insurance requirements? Who will be there if you are ill and, if alone, how will you cope?

Your answers to these questions are **individual** and, as such, will help you to focus on your particular pre-departure needs. The information that follows will help you to prepare for problems if and when they arise. So, as a starting point, identify your individual requirements and read on….

Insurance

It's a common and ill-considered mistake to subscribe to the "it only ever happens to other people" school of thought. Without adequate medical insurance, you risk sinking large amounts of money for treatment if you do become ill abroad and, in some places, inferior medical care to what you know at home. You've a greater chance of good and speedy treatment if you're armed with a sound insurance policy.

Choosing a policy

Rough Guides now offer their own travel insurance, competitively priced and customized for our readers (see p.534). If you do decide to shop around, keep in mind you want a policy that covers your individual needs and try to stick to reputable firms or personal recommendations. Make sure you read your insurance documents carefully and you understand the restrictions and exclusions that apply. Always declare pre-existing ill health to your insurer or you may jeopardize payments if a claim is later made – many policies will not cover you for a **pre-existing medical condition**.

For details about Rough Guides travel insurance, see p.534

Don't base your final decision on **cost** alone. A policy that is dramatically less expensive than the competition may well have loopholes in its coverage. It's worth remembering that many of the big credit card companies have allied travel insurance policies if you pay for your trip by card. Policies can be taken out for a **single holiday** or on an **annual basis**, the latter being a better deal for frequent travellers.

INSURANCE

The E111 and reciprocal health-care arrangements

For citizens of EU countries, the E111 is available across Europe and entitles you to the same emergency medical care as the local population. This may be free of charge or discounted depending on where you are. An E111 is valid in the 15 member states of the EU – Austria, Belgium, Denmark, Finland, France, Germany, Gibraltar, Greece, the Republic of Ireland, Italy, Luxembourg, the Netherlands, Portugal, Spain and Sweden – plus Iceland, Liechtenstein and Norway. However, as cover is often limited, and does not include repatriation, it makes sense to take out a separate travel insurance policy as well.

A number of other countries have reciprocal health-care arrangements with the UK, which are not dependent on possession of an E111: Anguilla, Australia, Barbados, British Virgin Islands, Bulgaria, Channel Islands, Czech Republic, Falkland Islands, Hungary, Isle of Man, Malta, Montserrat, New Zealand, Poland, Romania, Russia, Slovakia, St Helena, Turks and Caicos Islands, NIS (except Latvia, Lithuania and Estonia) and Yugoslavia.

For full details obtain the "Health Advice for Travellers" leaflet published in the UK by the Department of Health and available free from most post offices and many doctors' surgeries throughout the UK.

All policies have **exclusions** and many are weighted against the elderly, those with chronic illness, or those pursuing what the insurer considers to be dangerous activities (bungee jumping, white-water rafting, skiing, hang gliding or other hazardous sports). If you fall into any of these categories, before buying a policy contact the national representative group for your given interest or disability, or a travel agent specializing in your specific needs, as many offer customized and competitive policies arranged with reputable insurers that would not normally be available to you on an individual basis. If your policy covers your **children**, clarify their definition of a child (under 12, 16 or 18).

Make sure your policy includes cover for **repatriation** (air evacuation) on medical grounds. Be sure to clarify emergency procedures as well, for example what to do in the event of an accident, and whether you will be required to pay for care initially and claim it back later. To be on the safe side, keep all receipts. Many insurers offer 24-hour telephone advice lines. Remember that most policies do not provide cover for your travel companion to return with you, nor do they extend to ongoing treatment on your return home.

Always carry your insurance policy documents and important emergency contact numbers in a safe, but accessible place. Back-up photocopies carried by your travel companion are a good idea.

Don't forget that as well as coverin g health-related emergencies a good travel insurance policy should also cover for cancellation costs, baggage loss or theft, and have a robust personal liability clause in case you are sued for injury to others or damage to their property.

Immunizations

Immunization confers immunity against contracting some serious, even fatal, diseases, although the protection afforded is rarely 100%. Many immunizations are given as a series of vaccinations over a period of time, so you'll need to visit your doctor or local travel clinic at least 2 months before your trip, sufficient time both for the immunity to develop and for you to get over any mild reactions.

Bear in mind that vaccination **recommendations change** all the time, with new epidemics and variations in environmental conditions. Generally speaking, no particular immunizations are required for travellers to the USA, Canada, Europe, Australia and New Zealand, while precautions are likely for non-European countries encircling the Mediterranean and for Africa, Asia, the Middle East and South America. Your doctor or local travel clinic will have the latest advice.

If more than 10 years have elapsed since your last tetanus and polio immunizations, you'll need a **booster** before you go.

Always keep a **personal record** of which vaccinations you have been given and when. In the UK, **tetanus, polio and typhoid vaccinations** are given free of charge. If you're immunized by your family doctor, hepatitis A is also free, as is hepatitis B if you work in health care. The charges for other vaccinations vary but can be significant, so it's worth shopping around a little. **Yellow fever** is currently the only vaccine that requires **certification**, and production of the certificate is a legal requirement for entry into a number of countries, even if you are only passing through (see Part 3). If you are exempt from vaccination for any reason, you will require written evidence of this from your doctor.

Vaccination and immunity

Immunity to a disease can be acquired in two ways. The most common method, known as **active immunity**, stimulates the body to make antibodies to the disease in response to a vaccination or by contracting the infection itself. This usually affords long-term protection. **Passive immunity**, on the other hand, is achieved by inoculation with preparations derived from the blood plasma of individuals who already have immunity to the disease. The duration of protection is shorter, although repeat immunization is possible.

Vaccinations themselves can be divided into three categories: **live**, **inactivated** or **extracts** produced by the micro-organism in question. The body produces antibodies in response to stimulation by the vaccination and these confer immunity to the particular disease.

Inactivated vaccinations are produced from dead disease-producing organisms. Achieving adequate immunity frequently requires a series of injections, and the duration of immunity can vary from months to years. **Extract vaccinations**, derived from cellular components of the germs, require an initial series of injections followed by periodic boosters.

Live vaccinations are a weakened form of the disease-producing organism and include the following:

+ Oral polio
+ Oral typhoid
+ Yellow fever
+ BCG (TB)
+ Measles
+ Mumps
+ Rubella

Generally they produce a long-lasting immunity from a single vaccination. Try to allow enough time to avoid more than 1 live vaccination being given at the same time. A gap of 3 weeks between injections is ideal, but if this is unfeasible, at least make sure the vaccines are injected into different body sites. **Pregnant women** and people who have a **weakened immune system** from concurrent illness should discuss their plans with a doctor beforehand. For more detailed advice on vaccinations and HIV, see p.94.

Reactions to vaccination

It's common to suffer **mild reactions** after vaccination, such as swelling, redness or discomfort at the injection site, slight fever and malaise. As a general rule, it's best to postpone immunizations if you are suffering from an acute illness, particularly one causing fever, because the vaccine itself may cause a fever and your body's response to vaccination may be undermined. Again discuss this with a doc-tor beforehand. Some vaccinations contain small amounts of antibiotics or are derived from egg proteins. If you know that you have specific **allergies**, always tell the doctor or nurse before any vaccination. Severe reactions to vaccination, such as anaphylaxis (see p.151), are very rare but can occur.

Vaccines containing egg proteins

If you're allergic to eggs or are a vegan, be aware that the following vaccinations are derived from cultures containing egg proteins. The first two are low risk, but reactions to the others can be severe.

+ Measles
+ Mumps
+ Influenza
+ Rabies
+ Yellow fever
+ Tick-borne encephalitis

IMMUNIZATIONS

Although currently the subject of considerable research, as yet no vaccination is available against malaria. Malaria prophylaxis, discussed on pp.63 and 282, needs advanced planning and the most up-to-date advice.

Each vaccination is dealt with separately on the following pages, with advice on how soon before your trip you should be vaccinated, the length of immunity conferred by each, and any possible side effects.

Anthrax

Only people who will be working with animals, animal products or in agriculture in high-risk areas are likely to need **anthrax** immunization. The vaccine is in very short supply, however, and you may encounter difficulty obtaining it. **Reactions** to the vaccine – lymph gland swelling, mild fever and itching – are rare.

▷▷See also Anthrax, p.156.

Cholera

The current vaccination against **cholera** confers only limited immunity (about 50% protection lasting 3–6 months), and immunization against it is not routinely recommended nor is it an international travel requirement. Consequently you may find it difficult to obtain. A more effective means of avoidance is scrupulous food and drink hygiene. Although certificates of immunization against cholera are not officially required, customs officers in some countries still demand them (perhaps as a lever to extract money from tourists) – if you anticipate being asked, obtain a certificate

11

Adult immunization regimes

The table below lists the vaccinations you might need before a trip, together with the recommended regimes of administration (travel vaccinations for **children** are dealt with on p.105).

Vaccine	No. of doses	Interval between doses	Length of immunity
Anthrax	4	3 weeks between first 3, then 6 months between 3rd and 4th	1 year
Cholera	2	1 month apart	6 months
Hepatitis A	1–2	Repeat after 6–12 months for full immunity	10 years
Hepatitis B	3	2nd after 4 weeks, 3rd after 6 months	3–5 years
Influenza	1	–	1 year
Japanese encephalitis	2–3	7–14 days after initial	uncertain

IMMUNIZATIONS

Meningococcal meningitis	1	–	3–5 years
Plague	2	2nd between 4 and 12 weeks after 1st	6 months
Rabies	3	2nd after 7 days, 3rd after 28 days	2–3 years
Tick-borne encephalitis	2–3	2nd after 4–12 weeks, 3rd after 9–12 months	3 years
Tuberculosis	1	–	15 years+
Typhoid (3 types of vaccination)	1	–	3 years
	2	4–6 weeks	3 years
	3 (oral)	–	1 year
Yellow fever	1	–	10 years

NB: *Diphtheria, whooping cough, polio, tetanus, measles, mumps and rubella (German measles) are normally given as standard childhood vaccinations.*

of exemption from your doctor. Discuss further with your doctor the use of the cholera vaccination if you'll be staying in an endemic area for a prolonged period without easy access to medical care; if you've ever had surgery to your stomach; or if you are a heavy user of antacids or regular anti-stomach ulcer medications.

A new oral vaccination is under development, and reportedly offers short-term but high levels of protection. However, at the time of writing availability is still very limited.

▷▷See also Cholera, p.170.

Diphtheria

The **Diphtheria** vaccination is a routine childhood immunization. If you are travelling to countries where diphtheria may still be endemic, and if your last booster was more than 10 years ago, you certainly should have a further booster before travelling to these regions. If for some reason you have never been immunized, you will require the full 3-dose course at monthly intervals before departure. **Reactions** are usually mild, consisting of redness and swelling around the injection site, malaise, headache and a transient fever.

▷▷See also Diphtheria, p.20.

Hepatitis A

The most common method of immunization against **hepatitis A** takes about 10–14 days for the body to produce enough antibodies to confer high levels of immunity. A further vaccine 6–12 months later gives up to 10 years' immunity. Adverse **reactions** to the vaccine, usually confined to the first few days, include soreness around the injection site and, less frequently, fever, malaise, fatigue, headache, nausea and loss of appetite.

You can also be immunized against hepatitis A via one of the **combined vaccines** (see below).

▷▷See also Hepatitis A, p.242.

Hepatitis B

Hepatitis B immunization in the UK is currently restricted to those at particular risk because of their lifestyle, occupation or close proximity to a case or carrier, although in some countries (eg France, the US) it is given as a routine childhood vaccination.

There are two types of immunization available, one long-lasting vaccine which stimulates the body to make an immune response and an immunoglobulin, which provides short-term but immediate protection. Again, the first type is the most commonly used in cases where the duration of protection required is between 3 and 5 years, after which a booster is recommended.

Hepatitis B vaccination is generally well tolerated; the most common **reaction** is soreness around the injection site, although, rarely, fever, rash, malaise and influenza-like symptoms can occur.

You can also be immunized against hepatitis B via one of the combined vaccines described below.

▷▷See also Hepatitis B, p.243.

Combined vaccines

New **combined vaccinations** against **hepatitis A** and **hepatitis B**, and hepatitis A and typhoid, are now available. These will save you money as well as reduce the number of needle pricks you have to endure. The first combined vaccine offers protection against hepatitis A for 10 years and hepatitis B for 5 years. The course comprises 3 doses of the vaccination, with the second dose being given 1 month after the first and the third 6 months after the first. A booster is recommended after 5 years. As this is a new product, little is known so far regarding side effects and interactions.

The second combination vaccine, **hepatitis A** and **typhoid**, is given as a single dose to adults at least 2 weeks before risk of exposure. A booster of hepatitis A vaccination may be given between 6 and 12 months after the combined vaccination to confer longer-term immunity. People at prolonged risk from typhoid should have a booster after 3 years. There is not enough data available so far to comment on its safety in pregnancy. **Side effects** are reportedly uncommon but include redness, pain and swelling at the injection site and malaise, headaches, nausea, muscle aches, itching and fever.

The main drawback with combined vaccinations is the disparity between the length of time before a booster is needed for the individual vaccine components. Things can get very complicated and confusing unless meticulous records are kept.

Influenza

The ever-changing nature of the **influenza** virus means that it's impossible to produce long-term immunity from a single vaccination. Thus the vaccine is tailored against the prevalent viral strain on an annual basis and recommended to those at highest risk from the disease: the over-65s, people with severe asthma or chronic chest problems, those with other chronic illnesses such as diabetes, heart disease or kidney failure, and anyone with a compromised immune system.

IMMUNIZATIONS

The vaccine is generally well tolerated but should be avoided if you are allergic to **eggs**. Because influenza epidemics occur in the winter months, supplies of the vaccine may be a problem if it's summer where you're setting out.

▷▷See also Influenza, p.252.

Japanese encephalitis

Immunization against **Japanese encephalitis** is recommended for travellers spending a month or more in Southeast Asia and the Far East. The risks of contracting it, although very low, are greater if you're travelling at the end of the monsoon season (roughly June–September) to rural areas where pig farming and rice growing coexist.

The duration of protection after the vaccination course (3 jabs) is not known, but a booster is recommended after about 2 years. A 2-dose course is estimated to give an 80% short-term immunity. Bear in mind that as this is not a commonly administered vaccination, your doctor may need to order it specially – allow some extra time for this.

Adverse effects include swelling and pain at the injection site and rare systemic allergic reactions such as breathing difficulties and itching. This reaction can be delayed for up to 2 weeks after the vaccine has been given, so it's recommended that an immunization course be *completed* at least 2 weeks before you travel.

▷▷See also Japanese encephalitis, p.263.

Meningococcal meningitis

The risk of acquiring **meningococcal meningitis** is greatest for people who will be spending a month or more in close proximity to the local population in an endemic area. High-risk areas include much of Africa, as well as

Nepal, Bhutan, Pakistan and the area around Delhi. Saudi Arabia requires immunization together with relevant documentation for anyone attending Mecca for the annual hajj.

The vaccine is a single dose and should be given at least a week before travelling. Immunity lasts 3 to 5 years in adults, less in children. It is important to note that the vaccine is effective only against meningococcal meningitis types A and C, and not type B (thus immunization does not mean that you are completely protected from all causes of meningitis).

Following vaccination, a high temperature is not uncommon, especially in children. A local **reaction** at the injection site can last for a few days. The vaccine should be avoided if you already have a high temperature or if you have previously suffered severe reactions to the vaccine. There is no definitive data regarding the safety of the vaccine in pregnancy, so it's best considered only if there is a true risk of infection, for example following an outbreak.

▷▷See also Meningococcal meningitis, p.295.

Plague

The risk of the average traveller being exposed to **plague** is very low, and routine vaccination is unnecessary. Adverse reactions are usually infrequent and mild after the first vaccination but are more common or severe after repeat doses. Redness and swelling around the injection site occur in about 10% of individuals. More general effects include malaise, headache, fever and swollen lymph glands. When possible, try to avoid cholera and typhoid vaccinations being given at the same time.

▷▷See also Plague, p.311.

Polio

There are two types of **polio** vaccination: the oral, live version and the inactivated injection. The oral version is routinely administered in childhood. If you have not had a booster within the last 10 years, it's advisable to have one before travelling to any area other than Australia, New Zealand, northwestern Europe and the USA. The full 3-dose course should be taken at monthly intervals if you have not been previously immunized. Because the oral immunization is live and remains so in the gut, it should be deferred if you have diarrhoea or are vomiting and avoided if your immune system is weakened or you are in close contact with someone who is immunosuppressed. In such cases, you may have the inactivated vaccine instead.

Oral polio and oral typhoid vaccinations must be separated by at least 3 weeks because of potential interaction.

▷▷See also Polio, p.313.

Rabies

Although rare, **rabies** occurs in all continents except Australasia and Antarctica and, once the symptoms appear, is almost always fatal. Immunization should be considered by anyone likely to be working with animals and by travellers spending prolonged periods in remote areas where medical treatment is not readily available.

The 3-dose **pre-exposure** vaccination provides a reasonable level of protection to anyone at high risk, although it's important to remember that if you're bitten by a rabid animal, you will still require some degree of **post-exposure** treatment. If you are bitten by a rabid animal and you have not had pre-exposure prophylaxis, you will require

IMMUNIZATIONS

19

immediate, more involved, post-exposure treatment (see p.320). Thus:

✚ Pre-exposure vaccine x 3 + BITE =
Post-exposure vaccine x 2 on days 0 and 3–7;

✚ No pre-exposure vaccine + BITE =
Rabies immunoglobulin (RIG) immediately +
post-rabies vaccine x 5 on days 0, 3, 7, 14 and 30
(a sixth is sometimes given on day 90).

Two doses of pre-exposure treatment 4 weeks apart give acceptable levels of immunity if post-exposure treatment is likely to be immediately available. The full course of 3 vaccinations should provide protection for 2 to 3 years. If you're at continuous risk, you should have a single reinforcing dose after 2 years.

A localized **reaction** to the vaccine is the most common adverse effect. Headache, fever, muscle aches, vomiting and itchy rashes have also been reported. If you're pregnant, avoid pre-exposure vaccination unless there are exceptional circumstances.

▷▷See also Rabies, p.317.

Tetanus

Tetanus vaccination is part of the normal course of childhood immunizations in most countries. Booster doses after injury are only necessary if 10 years have elapsed since the previous immunization. Any adult who has had 5 doses (that's the normal childhood course of 3 and 2 subsequent boosters) is considered to possess lifelong immunity.

Reactions to the vaccine include pain, redness and swelling around the injection site and, less commonly, malaise, headache, lethargy, muscle aches and fever.

IMMUNIZATIONS

Tick-borne encephalitis

Tick-borne encephalitis is transmitted to humans via the bite of an infected tick and causes death in about 1% of cases. A post-exposure preparation is also available in some countries. The prophylactic vaccine is recommended for travellers who'll be hiking, camping or working in the warm, heavily forested parts of central and eastern Europe and Scandinavia in late spring or summer. After the initial course, boosters are recommended every 3 years for those at continued risk.

Adverse **reactions** to the vaccine are very rare and include local swelling and pain around the injection site, fatigue, limb pain, fever, nausea and headache which may last up to 24 hours, as well as transient itchy rashes. The vaccine is contraindicated if you have an allergy to egg protein.

▷▷See also Tick-borne encephalitis, p.376.

Tuberculosis (TB)

Some countries have routine vaccination programmes aimed at children and teens for the so-called **BCG** (Bacillus of Calmette and Guerin) vaccination against **TB**. If you're unsure whether or not you've been vaccinated, a test ("Heaf" test) is available through your doctor to assess your immunity. If you have not been vaccinated and have no natural immunity, BCG vaccination is recommended for trips of more than 1 month to Asia, Africa or Central and South America, especially for anyone who is likely to be in close contact with native populations in these areas. Because it's a live vaccination, it should only be used with caution in pregnancy or by people with weakened immune systems. The vaccination should be given at least 3 months before departure.

▷▷See also Tuberculosis (TB), p.381.

IMMUNIZATIONS

Typhoid

Typhoid fever is spread by ingestion of food or drink contaminated with the faeces of people already infected. You are therefore at greatest risk in areas where there is poor sanitation or low standards of personal and food hygiene. Immunization is probably less important for short stays in good accommodation.

Two types of typhoid vaccine are routinely available, an injected and an oral form. The injected form provides a 3-year protection of between 70% and 80% after a single dose. The newer 3-dose oral vaccine offers similarly reliable levels of immunity but a repeat 3-capsule course is required after 1 year if you remain at continued risk of infection. The 3 capsules must be taken on alternate days on an empty stomach with a cool drink. Neither of the vaccines offers full protection, and the need for scrupulous attention to personal, food and water hygiene cannot be over-emphasized.

Reactions to the injected form are uncommon, mild and usually local to the site of injection. The oral vaccine may cause transient nausea, vomiting, abdominal cramps, diarrhoea and an itchy rash.

Antibiotics can interfere with the immune response to the oral vaccine, as can gastro-intestinal upsets. Also, because it's a live vaccine, don't take the oral form if you have a weakened immune function. Oral typhoid vaccination and oral polio vaccination should be taken at least 3 weeks apart as they may interfere with each other, impairing immunity. Avoid starting the antimalarial mefloquine within 3 days of completing the course of oral typhoid.

Neither typhoid vaccine should be given if you have a high fever or have suffered severe reactions to previous doses of the same vaccine. If you're pregnant, you should

IMMUNIZATIONS

only be vaccinated if there is high risk of infection (seek expert advice).

▷▷See also Typhoid, p.385.

Yellow fever

Yellow fever symptoms vary in severity, but the fatality rate in unimmunized, non-indigenous populations can exceed 50%. Immunization, which offers high levels of protection against the disease (approaching 100%), is recommended for anyone spending time in countries where yellow fever is endemic.

An **International Certificate of Vaccination** against yellow fever is compulsory for entry into some countries, and you should check with the relevant embassy before travelling. The certificate is valid for 10 years, beginning 10 days after the vaccination. Travellers who for any reason can't be vaccinated require a letter of exemption from a doctor if they intend to visit these countries and should seek further advice from the relevant embassy regarding entry.

A single dose of this **live vaccine** provides protection for up to 10 years. If another live vaccine is required, it should be given either at the same time in a different part of the body or separated by an interval of 3 weeks.

Only a few people experience mild **reactions**, including headache, muscle pains, fever, generalized itching and soreness at the injection site. Severe allergic reactions are rare but have been reported. Avoid this vaccine if you are suffering from high fever; if you have abnormal immune function; if you know from previous reactions that you're allergic to neomycin, polymyxin or egg protein; if you are HIV positive; and if you are pregnant unless there is high risk of infection. Infants **under 9 months** should not be vaccinated unless they are at particularly high risk.

▷▷See also Yellow fever, p.406.

IMMUNIZATIONS

23

Travel by air

Airports are stressful places at the best of times, so allow yourself plenty of time to check in, especially if you are a nervous flier, as time pressure only exacerbates other stresses. Once on board, the cramped, claustrophobic environment can contribute to further anxiety and feelings of motion sickness, as well as make relaxation or sleep during the flight more difficult. Flying itself can affect your body in a number of ways, and the physiological changes that take place can cause a deterioration in existing medical ailments.

Fitness to fly

Flying when you are unfit may endanger your life as well as potentially disrupt the flight. If you have any form of chronic or ongoing illness which might be affected by flying, consult your doctor for advice beforehand and check that your travel insurance policy covers you adequately. Below are general recommendations for specific conditions.

Asthma and respiratory illnesses

In-flight medical incidents relating to **asthma** are surprisingly common. If you are asthmatic, make sure that your symptoms are well controlled before departure and carry your normal inhalers with you on the plane. For those with severe or "brittle" asthma, discuss with your family doctor the possibility of starting a course of oral steroids 2 to 3 days before the flight.

▷▷See also Asthma, p.83.

If you suffer from chronic respiratory disease (eg emphysema or chronic bronchitis), or have recently had a severe chest or upper airway infection, you should not fly without first consulting a doctor. The use of supplemental oxygen may be helpful for sufferers of chronic lung disease, although this needs to be arranged beforehand with the airline and may incur extra cost. Do not fly under any circumstances if you have a suspected collapsed lung (**pneumothorax**) or have had chest surgery within the previous 4 weeks.

Broken bones and fractures

You shouldn't fly within 2 days of breaking a bone. Tell anyone applying a plaster cast that you plan to fly so they can give you a **split cast**, in case the limb swells during the flight. Passengers with above-knee plaster casts are usually required to buy an extra seat or travel first class to have sufficient leg room. Do not fly within 10 days of sustaining a skull fracture and then only after medical clearance.

Diabetes

Insulin-dependent diabetics should keep to "home time" with regard to insulin and meals, and always carry sweets or sugary drinks in case of a hypo. A slightly higher than normal blood sugar level is more acceptable than a low reading during the flight. If you've had previous problems with severe hypoglycaemia, always carry glucagon (a drug that causes a rapid elevation in blood sugar). Carry your insulin with you on the plane; if stowed in the hold it will freeze.

▷▷See also Diabetes, p.85.

Ear problems

Consider delaying your flight if you have suffered a recent ear infection, which may have left fluid behind the eardrum. Blockage of the eustachian tube as a result of nasal congestion or a sore throat can lead to ear discomfort and even perforation of the drum as the cabin pressure changes. In rare circumstances, an expanding air pocket behind the eardrum can cause permanent damage to the ear. If you have a cold, use steam and decongestants to help clear your nose and upper airways.

Heart and circulatory problems

If you suffer from angina, always carry your **nitrate spray** (GTN) or pills with you. The risk of most modern airports' customs area metal detectors affecting your cardiac pacemaker is minimal, but tell airport security that you prefer to be searched manually if in any doubt.

Do **not** fly if you:

+ suffer from poorly controlled **angina, heart failure** or **abnormal heart rhythms**.

+ have suffered an uncomplicated **heart attack** or open **heart surgery** within the past 4 weeks. Those who have suffered complications should wait at least 3 weeks and then fly only after medical clearance.

+ have suffered a stroke or **subarachnoid haemorrhage** (a type of brain haemorrhage) in the past 10 days.

+ have suffered a recent deep-vein thrombosis (**DVT**), unless you are well established on anticoagulant treatment.

+ suffer from **anaemia** (with a haemoglobin level of less than 7.5 g/l you definitely should not fly without oxygen, while with a level less than 10 g/l get medical advice).

+ have **sickle cell anaemia** and have suffered a sickle cell crisis within the past 10 days or have full-blown sickle cell disease. Carriers of the sickle cell trait are at only slight risk in pressurized aircraft but might run into problems on unpressurized flights (generally short-hop, low-altitude flights in small planes).

Neurological disorders

Do not fly if you have been diagnosed with a brain tumour without first speaking to your specialist. It is also inadvisable to fly if you have frequent fits – postpone your trip until your condition is controlled with medication. If your epilepsy is well controlled, keep to "home time" with regard to medications and avoid missing doses.

▷▷See also Epilepsy, p.88.

Pregnancy and babies

Avoid air travel altogether if you are more than 36 weeks

FITNESS TO FLY

pregnant. In cases of multiple pregnancy, previous premature deliveries, lost pregnancies, vaginal bleeding or increased uterine activity (contractions), flying is not advised beyond week 24. Some airlines may request certification from your doctor specifying the expected date of delivery. It's also worth checking with the immigration authorities or embassy of your destination, as some countries refuse entry to heavily pregnant women.

Full-term babies should not fly until they are at least a week old. Seek advice from your paediatrician before flying with a premature baby.

Scuba diving

Take particular care in adhering to the published diving recompression schedules – the length of time you must wait before flying depends on how deep you dived and for how long. You should not fly for at least 10 days after suffering even mild symptoms of "the bends" or "the staggers".

▷▷See also Scuba diving, p.122

Surgery

Allow 2 weeks after major surgery to the abdomen, and 4 weeks after chest surgery, before embarking on a flight. Flying should also be postponed after eye surgery until permitted by a specialist because of the damage an intra-ocular air bubble could inflict by expanding at altitude.

Gastro-intestinal problems

You should not fly if you have suffered recent bleeding from the gut, unless it is known to be caused by a haemorrhoid, as there is an increased risk of further bleeding.

Onboard conditions

Cabin air has a very **low humidity**, which contributes to **dehydration**. Apart from making you feel thirsty, dehydration causes headaches, nasal congestion, drowsiness and increases the risk of deep-vein thrombosis (DVT) in the legs. It may also cause contact lens discomfort and exacerbate the symptoms of jet lag. Minimize the effects of dehydration by resisting last-minute alcohol binges and top-ups to your sun tan, and increase your intake of water or uncarbonated drinks during the flight. Tea, coffee and alcohol all act as diuretics (which rid your body of fluids), further dehydrating your body, and are therefore best avoided.

In the fit and healthy, the reduction in **oxygen concentration** on board the aircraft has an insignificant effect, but

The Valsalva manoeuvre

The difference in air pressure inside and outside the eardrum is equalized by the eustachian tube, a narrow passage that runs between the inner ear and the back of the throat. In flight, if the tube is blocked through nasal congestion, the air pocket in the inner ear can expand to cause discomfort and even rupture of the eardrum.

If your ears become uncomfortable, most likely during take-off and landing when the pressure variations caused by altitude changes are most apparent, try the Valsalva manoeuvre to reopen your eustachian tube. Pinch your nose to seal the airway, close your mouth and breath out *gently* against the resistance. You'll hear a click in both ears as your eustachian tube unblocks.

Other methods of keeping the eustachian tube clear include sucking sweets, chewing gum, and yawning.

problems can arise for people who have compromised heart or lung function. It may be possible to arrange a personalized oxygen supply from the airline if you give them advance notice. As a rule, if you suffer from a heart or lung condition that causes shortness of breath at rest, prevents you from walking more than 50m on the flat or ascending 12 steps, don't fly without oxygen and think hard before flying at all. The reduction in oxygen saturation of haemoglobin, the oxygen-carrying molecule in the blood, can also provoke premature labour in late pregnancy, and may be dangerous to premature babies.

The reduced **cabin pressure** in flight causes the gas inside the body to expand. As a result, abdominal bloating and mild ear and sinus discomfort are common, while the expansion of air pockets inside the body can be dangerous soon after an operation or a fractured skull. Minimize the discomfort from bloating of the gut by wearing loose clothing and avoiding fizzy drinks and wind-producing foods before your flight. **Sinus** or **ear pain** occur more commonly when there is already congestion of your airways after a cold or hayfever.

Immobility and inactivity can lead to uncomfortable swollen ankles and, more dangerously, to a deep-vein thrombosis (DVT), a blood clot in the calf. If you can, walk around the plane every 2 or 3 hours or do some calf-stretching exercises while seated. Note that the legroom at the seats close to exits and those that face the bulkhead are often better than elsewhere on the plane, and it may be possible to reserve these in advance (some airlines have started to charge for this privilege).

A large proportion of the air within aircraft is **recirculated**, which may increase the risk of **airborne infection**. If properly maintained, the plane's air filters are capable of removing potentially harmful bacteria. It's far more likely

Plane disinsectization

In order to prevent the transportation of insects from country to country, and thus the spread of insect-borne disease, some countries practise aircraft disinsectization. This may be done by spraying insecticides while passengers are onboard, by spraying when the plane is empty, by treatment of the interior surfaces of the plane with insecticides or a combination of the three. Despite media concerns about this practice, a WHO report in 1995 concluded that, when performed appropriately, disinsectization does not present a significant risk to human health, although occasional allergic reactions can occur.

Few countries currently require aircraft to be disinsectized but most reserve the right to do so if a threat is perceived. If you want to know the likelihood that your flight has been disinsectized, check with your airline.

that the prolonged period in close proximity to other germy humans will lead to infection by standard person-to-person droplet method. While there is little that you can do to reduce the risk from other people, act responsibly if you are unwell with an infectious illness and defer your flight.

Fear of flying

Whole books have been written about the fear of flying (**aviophobia** or **aerophobia**), an unwieldy subject to cover in a few short paragraphs. A simple fear of the plane falling from the sky is usually exacerbated by other influences such as claustrophobia, fatigue, peer influence, lack of knowledge about how planes fly and which noises and sensations are normal, anxiety about your destination,

31

Tips for comfortable air travel

+ Wear loose, lightweight clothing.
+ Avoid or minimize your intake of tea, coffee and alcohol during the flight.
+ Refrain from last-minute alcohol binges or sunbathing before you fly.
+ Avoid spicy food before flying.
+ Drink copious quantities of water or uncarbonated drinks.
+ Get up and move around or, if this is difficult, do calf-stretching exercises.
+ Carry any medications you are likely to need in hand baggage, including insulin, inhalers and decongestants.
+ Remove contact lenses before flying; alternatively, keep moisturizing eye drops handy.

adverse media publicity or perhaps a previous traumatic experience. The physical conditions in the flight cabin also contribute to the dry mouth, tension headache and nausea often caused by fear.

It's quite normal to suffer a degree of anxiety when flying, but severe, debilitating aerophobia, like any other phobia, is almost always irrational. Flying is reportedly 25 times safer than driving. Often simply talking through your fears and anxieties with a friend or experienced traveller will help. Many of the courses for aerophobics focus on putting the risks of flying in perspective, with emphasis on how the plane flies and how the body reacts physiologically to fear and anxiety – the "knowledge is power" principle.

On the bright side, psychologists view aerophobia as one of the easiest phobias to cure, responding well to simple relaxation techniques, hypnosis and psychoanalysis, among a wide range of different treatments. Resources range from educative, self-help pamphlets to in-depth courses. There are a large number of sites to check out on the Internet (see Part 4).

There are various ways to minimize aerophobia:

+ Learn some self-relaxation techniques, which focus on controlling your breathing, progressive muscle relaxation and positive imagery.

+ Think more about your destination and less about the flight.

+ Avoid rushing to the airport (it's not helpful if you are in a high state of anxiety before you even check in).

+ Distraction before and during the flight is a good idea: wander around the airport shops, stretch your legs, buy a compelling book or magazine, listen to your personal stereo, write your journal or watch the in-flight movie.

+ Let the cabin crew know that you are an anxious flyer.

+ Don't be upset by turbulence – modern aircraft are easily capable of dealing with the buffeting. When turbulence strikes, imagine you're on a boat that's buffing the waves – in fact that's more or less what's happening, though the waves are air pockets.

While some **medications** help to take the edge off anxiety, it's always worth remembering that they're treating the symptoms rather than the cause of the problem. That said, they are particularly useful in cases of mild to moderate aerophobia. **Antihistamines** (see p.58) such as promethazine, which can be readily bought over the counter, are

Panic attacks

If you do feel panicky, you may start to hyperventilate (involuntary rapid, shallow breathing). This can lead to further symptoms of anxiety such as shaking, chest and throat tightness, nausea and dizziness. Often simple recognition of the problem and concentrating hard on taking slow, measured breaths and expelling the air from your lungs can reduce the panicky feelings. If this fails, breathing in and out of a paper bag controls hyperventilation and its consequent effects. Simply seal the paper bag with your hands around your nose and mouth and breathe in the air you have just breathed out into the bag. The higher concentration of carbon dioxide you inhale will slow down your breathing.

sedating and are also helpful for the treatment of motion sickness. Alternatively, your doctor may prescribe either **diazepam** or **beta-blockers**, the latter used primarily to treat angina and high blood pressure, although in low doses they are a useful treatment for anxiety without being overly sedating or addictive. Diazepam (also widely known as Valium) is losing favour because of its addictive potential, but in low doses it is highly effective in the short-term treatment of anxiety. It is sedating and can impair memory and judgement.

There are a number of **alternative treatments** you can use to treat anxiety associated with a fear of flying. **Bach Rescue Remedy** (one of a number of flower essence remedies widely available) calms you when tearful, moody, shocked or fearful. Put 5 or 6 drops in a glass or small bottle of water and sip periodically. Because of its alcohol content, always dilute it for children; you might also run into problems taking it into "dry" countries. **Lavender oil** is calming and helps to send you to sleep. Both Rescue Remedy and lavender oil are safe to use in pregnancy.

Jet lag

Jet travel allows us to cross time zones in a shorter time than our body's natural rhythms need to adjust. The natural rhythms most susceptible to the effects of **jet lag** are those of sleep, appetite and bowel habits; menstruation pattern can also be disturbed. Estimates vary, but jet lag is usually appreciable after journeys in which 5 or more time zones (a 5-hour or greater time difference) have been crossed. It's worse on eastbound flights after which time is ahead of your natural body clock.

The most common **symptoms** of jet lag are feelings of exhaustion, insomnia, poor concentration, disorientation, loss of appetite, nausea, mood swings, irrational anger, weakness, headache, blurred vision, dizziness and bowel disturbance (diarrhoea or constipation). The cramped, dry conditions of the aircraft, and the effects of alcohol and caffeine may exacerbate the symptoms. It can take up to a week for your body to readjust.

There are a few measures you can take to minimize its impact on arrival:

➕ If possible, sleep on the flight, especially if it's an eastbound journey. Although you might find antihistamines or a mild tranquillizer helpful in getting some sleep, it's better to avoid using sedating medications during the flight as they

increase immobility and may contribute to
dehydration. They are better used on arrival to
restore normal sleep patterns.

✚ Increase your fluid intake during the flight but
avoid carbonated drinks, alcohol and caffeine.
Equally, avoid dehydrating activities – alcohol
binges and sunbathing – before you fly.

✚ Take regular walks around the cabin if possible.
While seated, tense and relax your calf muscles
hourly.

✚ If you can, avoid strenuous activities or important
decision-making within the first few days of
arrival, although it's helpful to adapt normal
activities of daily living – sleeping and eating,
for example – to local time as soon as possible.

You can treat jet lag **homeopathically** using
Arnica or Jet lag (30C). A mixture of grapefruit (2
drops) and peppermint (1 drop) **essential oils**

Melatonin and jet lag

Melatonin is sold in health shops (not pharmacies) in the US
and via the Internet. Claims have been made about its useful-
ness in the treatment of jet lag. A natural hormone secreted by
the pineal gland at the base of the brain, it is thought to be
responsible for the body's natural clock. There seems to be little agreement on when or how it should be taken (dose and
frequency), and there is a paucity of data available on its toxi-
city or long-term effects. Furthermore its production in the US
is not regulated by the Food and Drug Administration and there
is therefore no quality assurance on the products being sold.

JET LAG

in a cool footbath (double the amounts if filling a whole bath) willhelp to revive you after a long journey, especially if you have to go straight to work from the plane. (Don't use peppermint if you are, or might be, pregnant.)

For every time zone crossed, allow 1 day to recover.

▷▷See also p.297 on motion sickness.

▷▷See also p.297 on motion sickness.

Staying well

Only a tiny minority of travel-acquired infections lead to death but they are, without a doubt, responsible for a large proportion of ill health. Most travellers' illnesses are trivial (even if it may not seem so at the time) and not life-threatening. However, being unwell on your holiday is miserable for both you and your companions. It disturbs plans, wastes time and money, and frequently makes you wonder why you bothered to leave home in the first place. This is a great shame when so many of the factors that can affect your health while you're travelling are ultimately avoidable, **either by immunization or drug prophylaxis, or by taking simple strides to minimize your risks.**

Road accidents

It is sobering to remember that, despite the vast numbers of weird and unpleasant illnesses lurking between the pages of this book, **road accidents** are responsible for more deaths and serious injuries in tourists than anything else.

Driving on unfamiliar roads or in hazardous conditions, badly maintained vehicles, local driving customs, poor driving, and driving while under the influence of alcohol or drugs are all factors that inflate the statistics. While it's impossible to eliminate all of these risks, there are measures you can take to minimize them.

If travelling by bus, always go with an established, reputable company. Where you sit on the bus is of lesser importance, though if you're really worried about the journey ahead, sit near an emergency exit.

If you are behind the wheel, drive defensively and accustom yourself to local conditions before attempting anything too ambitious. Stay alert by breaking long trips periodically, and avoid unnecessary night driving. Don't exceed the speed limit, especially when road conditions are unfamiliar. Even if local laws are more relaxed, drink-driving abroad is even more foolhardy than at home, where at least driving conditions are more familiar. As at home, designate a driver and make sure that they don't drink.

If you **rent** a vehicle, check the tyres (including the spare), brakes, headlights and seatbelts before leaving the garage forecourt. Also check who you should contact in the event of an accident or breakdown. If you are renting a cycle or moped, always wear a helmet and check the brakes before starting – moped accidents involving tourists, both minor and severe, are very common.

Fire and water

Perhaps surprisingly, **fire** is another significant cause of death and injury abroad. In many developing countries fire regulations are slack, if they exist at all. Ask about fire escapes and precautions when you arrive at a hostel or hotel if nothing is posted. Never smoke in bed and, especially in dry, hot climates, ensure that cigarettes are properly extinguished. Have a plan of escape in case of emergencies, bearing in mind that the best way to escape a fire and the potentially lethal effects of smoke inhalation is to crawl low under the smoke.

The heat and humidity may tempt you, but think twice before cooling off. **Drowning** accidents involving travellers, both in the sea and in fresh water, are relatively common – remember that **currents** in rivers as well as the sea can be extremely strong, and that you're much less buoyant in fresh water than in salt water. Be aware of your own swimming ability and strength, and avoid taking unnecessary risks. Ask about local water conditions – strong currents or other potential hazards – before taking the plunge. A number of **diseases** can be contracted by bathing, even stepping, in fresh water, and avoidance is your only means of protection. Don't forget more **visible hazards** like snakes, crocodiles and voracious fish. On the beach always wear sandals, which also provide protection against saltwater hazards such as weaver fish. Never swim directly after eating, when you feel unwell or when under the influence of alcohol or drugs. Never dive into water without knowing its depth (this can result in a broken neck and and commonly causes paralysis).

▷▷See Freshwater hazards, p.224; Saltwater hazards, p.328.

Food and drink

Most food- and water-borne illnesses are spread via the faecal–oral root; or more bluntly, the food that you eat or water you drink has been contaminated by faeces. Although the risk exists anywhere you go, you're most likely to contract food- or water-borne illnesses in places where economics keep hygiene standards low. The advice below is tailored mostly to travellers in developing countries.

Try to ensure that your food is cooked thoroughly and eat it straight away. Be especially wary of "street food", which may have been left to stand for a long time – not only is it an easy target for flies, but cooling allows the contaminating bacteria to multiply quickly. If you can, check that cooked foods are kept separate from the uncooked ingredients, eliminating the risk of one contaminating the other.

Meat in developing countries may not have been butchered or prepared using adequate standards of hygiene – always order it "well done" to reduce the risk of worm and other infections from undercooked meat. **Fish** goes off quickly, particularly in hot climates, so should be consumed as soon as possible after being caught. Avoid eating it in areas that are a long way from the sea. Some species of fish, notably those found around coral reef, are poisonous even after being cooked (see Ciguatera, p.171, and Scromboid

Tips for your tummy

+ Cook it, boil it, peel it or forget it.
+ No matter how expensive the meal, or how established the restaurant, you're never totally free from the risk of food contamination – food can still be improperly chilled or left out for too long and waiters and kitchen staff in even the most salubrious restaurants use the toilet and forget to wash their hands.
+ Be aware of eateries that appear quiet; their food is less likely to have been freshly prepared and may have been reheated frequently.
+ Avoid "Chef's Specials", which are likely to be yesterday's leftovers.
+ Avoid seafood when you are a long way from the sea, and think twice about shellfish in any circumstances.
+ Baby wipes (a travel essential) are a good way of ensuring that your own hands at least are clean before handling food.
+ Inspect the cleanliness of crockery and cutlery before use.

FOOD AND DRINK

poisoning, p.342). **Shellfish** are particularly prone to contamination because of the large amounts of potentially polluted seawater they filter during feeding.

Rice, the staple diet throughout much of the world, seems innocuous enough but can be contaminated by specific bacteria that survive boiling water by forming heat-resistant spores and, on cooling, multiply rapidly. The bacteria cause quite severe diarrhoea and vomiting so where possible avoid rice that has not been freshly cooked.

Unpasteurized milk, or products made from unpas-

Examples of illnesses linked to contaminated food and water

teurized milk, can transmit a variety of diseases and should be avoided, particularly by pregnant women. Pasteurized, long-life and boiled milk are all safe.

It's often not the food itself or the cleanliness of the hands preparing it that cause problems but the **water** used in washing and preparation that may be contaminated. This is particularly a problem with foods eaten raw, like salads or fruit. In areas of high risk, **salads** are probably best avoided unless you prepare them yourself. This being the case, wash the vegetables thoroughly in iodine (see below), soak in vinegar for 15 minutes then rinse with bottled or boiled

FOOD AND DRINK

water. Try to avoid fruit that you have not peeled or cut yourself.

If the local water is contaminated, so too is the **ice** made from it and cups or glasses washed with it. If in doubt, drink directly from the bottle. Water-borne infections can also be transmitted during teeth-cleaning and by water swallowed during showering.

Where **water** purity cannot be guaranteed, drink only bottled drinks (check that the cap seal is intact), boiled water (for at least 1 minute but ideally for 3) or water sterilized with an adequate purifying preparation. Iodine is the best form of chemical purifier and is readily available from camping shops and pharmacies. It's important to follow the packet instructions carefully, as heavily contaminated water will require stronger solutions. Iodine is not effective against all microbes. A variety of portable **water filters** are available on the market.

Insect-borne diseases

Many **insect-borne illnesses** are seasonal and often simply adjusting the timing of your visit to a region can reduce the risks. However, for most travellers, arranging their itinerary around the lifecycle of insect species is not a primary consideration. Only a handful of insect-borne diseases are preventable by drug prophylaxis or immunization (even then, the protection conferred rarely approaches 100%), which means that your only real protection against the vast majority is **bite avoidance**. Anyone who has tried to avoid being bitten by insects will be aware that complete success is practically unachievable. Unless you are obsessional to an extreme that could jeopardize the enjoyment of your trip, you may as well accept that you are likely to be bitten at some point. The following recommendations are more about risk limitation – the fewer the bites, the smaller your chance of contracting infection.

Wear long-sleeved shirts, long trousers and socks and use insect repellent containing **DEET** (see p.260) on any exposed areas of the body, particularly between dusk and dawn when the air is thickest with feeding mosquitoes. Do not wear **perfume**, **aftershave** or **sandals**. At night, sleep under a mosquito net and ensure it is securely tucked under your mattress. It's a good idea to carry your own net as those provided by hostels and hotels are often damaged and therefore useless. For extra protection, spray the net with an insect repellent such as **permethrin** (see p.259). Permethrin can also be sprayed on camping equipment, shoes and clothing – its repellent effect is retained even after clothing has been laundered. Insect coils can help, but some contain DDT and therefore should be used with caution.

Ticks and mites are slightly easier to avoid than flying insects. Wear light-shaded, tightly woven clothing so that ticks can be easily spotted before they attach themselves to your skin. Ticks tend to gravitate towards darker recesses of the body, with favourite hiding places being the scalp, armpits and genital area. Tuck trousers into socks to close off the easiest channel for a tick to access bare skin. Apply permethrin-based repellents and inspect your skin and clothing carefully at the end of each day as prompt removal can prevent infection. For removal of ticks, see p.260.

Never walk barefoot, especially in the tropics. Shoes provide protection against insect, snake and spider bites, as well as some parasites, which enter the body through the skin of the foot. Shaking your boots out before putting them on is a good habit to get into.

▷▷See also Bite prevention, p.259.

INSECT-BORNE DISEASES

Disease information

Freshwater-borne diseases

Any disease contracted by swallowing contaminated water, see p.43

Diseases spread through animal contact

DISEASE INFORMATION

Contact with animals

The average traveller is at relatively low risk from illnesses spread by animal contact – agricultural workers and vets are most vulnerable. Nevertheless, think twice before stroking that cute puppy or playing with a pet monkey. It's very easy for a playful bite or scratch to draw blood, potentially allowing the animal's saliva to make direct contact with your blood.

Sexually transmitted diseases

Sexually transmitted diseases are dealt with more fully in Part 2, but the best way to avoid them is obvious. The second best way is always to use a good-quality condom with any new partner.

▷▷See Sexually transmitted diseases, p.344.

CONTACT WITH ANIMALS

Environmental factors

Sun exposure, heat, cold, humidity, damp and altitude all have a direct effect on health but also indirectly contribute to disease risks. For instance, mosquito-borne illnesses are usually most common during or after the rainy season; colds, upper respiratory tract infections and asthma tend to be more prevalent in cold, wet conditions; and leishmaniasis occurs in dry, dusty conditions. You may be able to arrange your travel plans around the seasons to minimize risks.

▷▷See also Altitude sickness, p.150; Cold exposure, p.172; Sun exposure, p.364.

Violence

Travellers worldwide are often the targets of **violence**, especially if alone, elderly or female. Listen to what the locals or your guidebook tell you, walk tall, look confident and try to avoid potentially dangerous situations. Be particularly alert when travelling on public transport, particularly at night or when there are few people around. If at all concerned about your surroundings, avoid drawing attention to yourself by puzzling over your map in the street. Don't wear expensive jewellery or flaunt cash and credit cards, and keep expensive camera equipment hidden until you intend to use it. Go with your instinct: if the person who gets on the subway makes you nervous, you've nothing to lose by changing carriages. If you are confronted by a mugger, the safest bet is to surrender your valuables without resistance.

VIOLENCE

The medical kit

Deciding what medical provisions to take away with you and what to leave behind can be tricky and depends on where you're going, for how long and how cautious you choose to be. Some people travel with their rucksack half full of medications and therapeutic equipment, including drips and even bags of intravenous fluids, while others hike in solitude in remote regions without so much as a sticking plaster.

This section aims to provide the forward-looking traveller with a little more information and advice on the kind of medications and equipment that might be of use on a global trip. While it's not the intention of this book to encourage using potentially dangerous drugs inappropriately, when access to medical advice is difficult, it's often better to start treatment for potentially serious conditions than to wait for help.

In developed countries, many drugs are available only on **prescription** and are therefore only obtainable through a doctor. For long trips, your family doctor or travel clinic may be willing to prescribe one or two items of particular use (don't visit them with a "shopping list"). Perhaps more relevant and useful to the traveller is the knowledge that the same drugs can be bought directly **over-the-counter** in many, usually less developed countries, without a prescription. Unfortunately, it goes without saying that any drug can have both good and bad effects on your body, so always use them responsibly. A summary of recommended items to include in your medical kit is provided on p.70.

Some drugs are available only on prescription from your family doctor. Consider why this might be and don't use any drug without first weighing up the risks and benefits. Remember that drugs can interact with each other so always tell your doctor what other medicines you're taking. Never exceed the recommended dosages.

If you are **pregnant** (see p.112 on which drugs are safe in pregnancy), **breast-feeding**, have ongoing **medical problems** or take **other medications** (interactions between drugs can occur), it's best to seek qualified advice before taking any medication. Although side effects are generally uncommon, it's best to stop taking the medication if a reaction occurs. Although alcohol interacts with only a handful of drugs, avoiding alcohol if you're taking medications is a good general rule.

The following section covers drugs and medications that might be useful to the traveller in certain situations. It's worth re-emphasizing that drugs should always be used responsibly. If you experience doubts, side effects or the condition you are treating does not improve, always seek medical advice.

We've listed each drug by its **generic name** because this is how it will be known internationally; what's more, most drugs are cheaper if you ask for them in their generic form. Those marked with an **asterisk** may be available by prescription only.

Basic advice on children's preparations and doses is given on pp.103 and 106.

Painkillers (Analgesics)

Paracetamol (**acetaminophen** in the USA) is cheap, effective and safe in normal dosage (it's very **dangerous** if you exceed the recommended dosage, as even a relatively small overdosage can cause irreparable liver damage). It's useful for bringing down high temperatures, as well as for general pain relief. Side effects are rare and it is safe to use in pregnancy.

Adult dosage: 1–2 x 500mg tablets 4–6hrly to a max of 4g (or 8 tablets) a day.

Aspirin is cheap and effective but can cause indigestion and stomach ulcers. To reduce such risks, only take it after food. Aspirin has anti-inflammatory properties, and is therefore particularly useful for sprains, joint pains, etc. Like paracetamol, it also reduces high temperatures. You can take aspirin in conjunction with paracetamol, but it can interact with other drugs so always check the labels of your other medications or consult a pharmacist. Allergic reactions are relatively common, and asthmatics should avoid aspirin because it can exacerbate their symptoms. Equally, people who've had a stomach or duodenal ulcer, pregnant women, breastfeeding mothers, children under 12 and haemophiliacs should not use aspirin.

Adult dosage: 300–900mg every 4–6hr after food to a maximum of 4g a day.

Ibuprofen, **naproxen★** and **diclofenac★** are members of a group of drugs collectively known as NSAIDs (non-steroidal anti-inflammatory drugs). NSAIDs are excellent in the treatment of soft-tissue injuries and joint pains. Their side effects (gastrointestinal discomfort, diarrhoea, nausea and rashes are the most common) and limitations are generally the same as for aspirin. Ibuprofen is generally recognized as having the fewest side effects of the three but is also probably the weakest painkiller, whilst diclofenac is perhaps the strongest but also the most likely to cause side effects. NSAIDs should be avoided by asthmatics, pregnant women and by people with kidney problems (unless used under medical supervision).

Adult dosage (all after food): ibuprofen 1–2 x 200mg tablet 3 times a day; naproxen 1–2 x 250mg tablet, twice daily; diclofenac 1–2 x 25mg tablet 3 times a day.

Co-proxamol★, **co-dydramol★** and **co-codamol** all contain paracetamol and another painkiller – dextropropoxyphene in the case of co-proxamol, codeine phosphate in the other two cases. They are safe if the normal dosage is not exceeded although all can cause nausea, mild drowsiness and constipation.

Dosage: the same as for paracetamol, although because of the additional drugs present, they are generally regarded as stronger.

Antibiotics

Antibiotics specifically treat **bacterial** infections, by either killing or weakening the bacteria, in effect assisting the body's immune system. They do not have any pain-relieving properties, nor do they directly relieve any other symptoms. In most developed countries they are available on prescription only. There is great variation in the spectrum of action and cost of different antibiotics.

All antibiotics have some, usually mild, side effects, and allergic reactions are relatively common. A rare but serious side effect is pseudomembranous enterocolitis (see p.314), which manifests as severe, often bloody, diarrhoea and requires urgent medical treatment.

Your doctor may be hesitant about prescribing antibiotics on a purely prospective basis; there is growing concern over the increasing incidence of bacterial resistance through antibiotic overuse (see box, p.55). Always finish a course of antibiotics once you've started it as incomplete treatment can lead to a failure in eradicating the bugs and also breeds resistance. Take special care if you use the oral contraceptive pill, as many antibiotics reduce its efficacy (see Contraception, p.183). All antibiotics increase the risk of **thrush** so if you're prone to it consider getting some antifungal treatment at the same time.

Amoxycillin★ is probably the most widely prescribed broad-spectrum antibiotic worldwide. Derived from penicillin, it should not be taken by people with penicillin allergy. Among its many uses are the treatment of chest, ear, mouth and urinary tract infections. It's inexpensive and has minimal side effects, mainly consisting of nausea, diarrhoea and rashes.
Standard adult course: 1–2 x 250mg tablet 3 times a day for 5–7 days.

Co-amoxiclav★ contains amoxycillin and another antibiotic, clavulinic acid, making it much more expensive than amoxycillin but able to fight a broader range of bugs, including bacterial skin infections and infected animal bites. It has much the same range of uses and side effects as amoxycillin (diarrhoea is common). Again, it is not suitable for penicillin-sensitive people, and in rare cases, co-amoxiclav can cause jaundice.
Standard adult course: 1–2 x 250/125mg tablet 3 times a day for 5–7 days.

Flucloxacillin★ is another penicillin-based antibiotic particularly useful in treating skin infections like boils and abscesses, as well as wound infections. Common side effects are similar to those of co-amoxiclav.
Normal adult course: 1–2 x 250mg tablet 4 times daily for 5–7 days.

Antibiotic resistance

Many people wrongly look upon antibiotics as the panacea, the universal remedy. Since the discovery of penicillin by Alexander Fleming in 1928 and the subsequent development of therapeutic antibiotics in the 1930s and 1940s, doctors have contributed in no small way to this misapprehension.

It's not difficult to see how it happened. Before antibiotics, millions of people were dying from illnesses that had no effective treatment. Suddenly doctors were equipped with a useful and potent means of controlling these previously lethal diseases.

Soon antibiotics were prescribed for any infection and it's only in recent decades that the consequences of irresponsible, albeit perhaps ignorant, prescribing have become apparent.

Bacteria reproduce rapidly, and because of mutation, an ongoing evolving process, subsequent generations genetically differ from previous generations. Bacteria with weak characteristics do not survive while those with beneficial mutations survive longer and give rise to more offspring. Thus, using an incomplete course of antibiotics will kill the weaker bacteria but may allow the stronger ones to survive. This is "survival of the fittest" at its most basic level. Thus bacterial populations have evolved capable of resisting treatment with antibiotics.

To do your bit in preventing the evolution of so-called "superbugs", use antibiotics wisely and responsibly:

+ Decide whether your condition really needs antibiotic treatment. If in doubt, wait or seek medical advice.

+ With the help of this book, try to choose the antibiotic that is most appropriate for your complaint.

+ Always complete the suggested course.

+ If you have antibiotics left over, don't leave them in inexperienced hands; donate them to the local clinic.

ANTIBIOTICS

Erythromycin★ is the most commonly prescribed broad-spectrum alternative to amoxycillin. It's the main option for people with penicillin allergy and its uses are broadly similar to amoxycillin. In addition, it can be used to treat some diarrhoeal illnesses and legionnaires' disease (see p.266). Common side effects include nausea, vomiting, abdominal discomfort and diarrhoea. It should not be used if you have liver disease, and care should be taken when using it with other medications as it can interfere with the metabolism of other drugs.

Adult course: 1–2 x 250mg tablet 4 times a day before or with meals for 5–7 days.

Metronidazole★ is a versatile antibiotic used to treat mouth and vaginal infections as well as amoebic, protozoal and giardial infections. It can also be used in the treatment of pseudomembranous colitis. Side effects include an unpleasant taste in the mouth, nausea, vomiting, gastrointestinal disturbances, rashes and itching. **Avoid alcohol** during and for 2 days after a course (it causes a very unpleasant reaction consisting of extreme nausea and facial flushing). Metronidazole should only be used under medical supervision in pregnancy, breast-feeding and cases of liver disease.

The adult course is usually 1–2 x 200mg tablet 3 times a day for 5–7 days although longer courses are sometimes necessary for certain conditions.

Trimethoprim★ is a commonly prescribed treatment for urinary tract infections and may also be used to treat travellers' diarrhoea. It should be avoided in cases of kidney impairment, pregnancy and porphyria (a rare and complex illness). Side effects are uncommon but include nausea, vomiting, itching and rashes.

Normal adult course: 2 x 100mg tablet twice daily for 5–7 days.

ANTIBIOTICS

Loratadine is a newer drug, similar to chlorpheniramine in its range of action, but generally regarded as less sedating. It's not recommended in pregnancy nor if you're breast-feeding.

Adult dosage: 1 x 10mg tablet daily.

Promethazine can be used for the same purposes as chlorpheniramine and loratadine, but is especially useful as a preventative against motion sickness – and may even help when you are experiencing symptoms. It is sedating, so much so that it's used as a premedication for surgery by some anaesthetists – driving or using machinery are inadvisable when taking it. As with all antihistamines, it can cause dry mouth, blurred vision, constipation and difficulty passing urine.

Adult dosage: for long journeys, 1 x 25mg the night before; shorter trips, 1 x 25mg 1–2hr before. Maximum of 4 tablets over 24hr.

Cinnarizine is an antihistamine used primarily as a preventative for motion sickness. It is less sedating than promethazine. It can also cause a dry mouth and blurred vision.

Adult dosage: 2 x 15mg tablet 2hr before journey, then 1 x 15mg every 8hr.

Anthisan cream and **caladryl** lotion contain antihistamines and are particularly helpful in treating insect bites. They should not be used on broken skin or if you have eczema. They can cause allergic reactions and increased sensitivity of the skin to the sun.

Apply 2–3 times a day for up to 3 days.

ANTIHISTAMINES

Antidiarrhoeals

The priority in treating **diarrhoea** is preventing or counteracting **dehydration** (see p.194) – the so-called "blocking drugs" available on the market are of secondary value. Preventon of dehydration is particularly important in children and the frail elderly.

A number of chemical solutions are available commercially which replace the salts lost through acute diarrhoea. They can usually be easily obtained anywhere in the world, but be sure to follow the brand instructions carefully and rehydrate the sachets with boiled water only.

The following drugs should be used only in conjunction with other rehydration measures. Remember that these drugs treat your symptoms only and not the underlying cause. Playing strictly by the book, they should not be used unless the cause of the diarrhoea is known (their use in the treatment of dysentery or diarrhoea caused by pseudomembranous colitis can lead to serious complications). Never use these drugs if you have other symptoms such as fever, severe abdominal pain or if you're passing blood in your stools.

Antidiarrhoeals are relatively expensive and, although there

Homemade oral rehydration solution

To 1 litre of boiled water add half a level teaspoon of salt and 8 level teaspoons of sugar. A little fruit juice or mashed banana provides potassium, which is often depleted by serious diarrhoea and vomiting, as well as improving the taste. The amount you need to take depends on how much fluid you're losing but as a rough guide, drink 200–400ml after every loose stool until the diarrhoea settles.

are many different varieties, none appears to have an edge over the others. Over-zealousness can lead to constipation, so take it easy. They should not be used in treating children.

Loperamide is very commonly used and is a highly effective blocker. Side effects include abdominal bloating, pain and skin rashes.

Dosage: 2 x 2mg tablet initially followed by 1 x 2mg after every loose stool to a maximum of 16mg over 24hr for no more than 5 days.

Bismuth subsalicylate ("Pepto-Bismol") has a mild but direct effect on the bugs causing diarrhoea as well as slowing down gut activity and relieving nausea and indigestion. It is useful in high doses for mild to moderate cases of traveller's diarrhoea.

Dosage: 4.2g daily.

Laxatives

Increasing your dietary fibre (lentils, brown rice, beans, peas, fruit, etc) and fluid intake is the kindest way to alleviate constipation, but if this fails, then generally the simplest and cheapest **laxatives** are adequate for most travellers' needs.

Senna is known as a "stimulant laxative" as it promotes muscular contraction in the bowel to force out the gut contents. It is not recommended for anyone suffering nausea, vomiting, abdominal pain or bowel obstruction. Its side effects include abdominal cramps.

Dosage: 2–4 tablets at night (start with 2) until normal bowel function resumes.

LAXATIVES

Lactulose works by retaining fluid in the bowel thereby softening the stool. It should not be used in cases of bowel obstruction and can cause flatulence, cramps and abdominal discomfort.

Normal adult dosage: 15ml once or twice daily.

Antisickness drugs (antiemetics)*

These are extremely useful drugs but are available only on prescription. Ideally, they should be used only when the cause of the vomiting is known; however, many family doctors are sympathetic to the potential plight of the traveller and will issue a private prescription if requested. A rare but unpleasant side effect of most antiemetics is **dystonia**, a condition of acute muscle spasm, usually of the head and neck. It is unusual in short-term use, however, and usually settles without treatment.

Don't forget that **ginger**, **acupressure bands** and some antihistamines, notably **promethazine** (see p.59), can be used to treat sickness and do not require a prescription.

Domperidome, available in tablet or suppository form, is an effective treatment for nausea and vomiting. It is less likely than other antiemetics to cause dystonia or drowsiness. It must be used with care, however, in kidney disease, breastfeeding and pregnancy.

Dosage: 1–2 x 10mg tablet every 4–8hr until symptoms settle.

Metoclopramide is a cheap, effective and much used antiemetic. However, it has a greater tendency to cause dystonia than domperidome, particularly in children and young women. It may also cause muscle stiffness, tremor, drowsiness, restlessness and diarrhoea. It should be avoided if you are breast-feeding or suffer from epilepsy, and kidney and liver impairment. It can be used in pregnancy under medical supervision but, like all drugs in pregnancy, is best avoided if possible.

Dosage: 1/2–1 x 10mg 3 times a day.

Motion sickness

Motion sickness arises as a result of confusion between signals sent to the brain by the eyes and from the balance apparatus in the inner ear and not from gut problems. As such it responds to different drugs. The antihistamines promethazine and cinnarizine, already discussed (see p.59), and hyoscine are useful. Don't underestimate the use of acupressure bands, homeopathic remedies and herbal ginger-based remedies.

Hyoscine is effective, cheap and available both in tablet and patch form. Common side effects include dry mouth, blurred vision, dizziness, constipation and difficulty passing urine. It should be avoided if you suffer from glaucoma and used only with caution in pregnancy, breast-feeding and a number of rarer medical conditions (eg myasthenia gravis, paralytic ileus, pyloric stenosis and prostatic enlargement). Read the pack instructions carefully.

Adult dosage: 1 x 300mcg 30min before travelling and every 6hr if required.

Antimalarials

The type of **antimalarial medication** you take depends primarily on where you intend to go and for how long. Patterns of resistance can change rapidly, so always seek up-to-date advice. None of the antimalarials currently available offers complete protection against malaria, and avoiding being bitten by mosquitoes is your only guarantee. All measures of malaria prevention are therefore more about risk limitation. Side effects can be troublesome and the protection conferred is not instantaneous, so start the course in good time before entering an endemic area (at least 1 week for all except mefloquine, which should be started 2 or 3 weeks in advance). Because of the complicated life cycle of the malaria parasite and the long incubation period, all antimalarials should be continued for at least 4 weeks after you leave an endemic area. Doxycycline is the exception in that it needs to be started only 2 days before entering a malarial area and continued for 2 weeks after returning.

The controversy surrounding antimalarials is discussed in detail on pp.286–287.

Combination drugs containing **pyrimethamine** are occasionally used in malaria prophylaxis (**Maloprim**) and in the treatment of falciparum malaria (**Fansidar**). They have been largely superseded now and are only used when the first-choice drugs are contraindicated or unavailable.

Chloroquine is steadily becoming less effective because of increasing worldwide drug resistance. It can be taken alone, but is now more commonly used in conjunction with proguanil. Combined with proguanil, its level of protection in sub-Saharan Africa, where the risks are highest, is estimated to be around 70%. Check with your doctor if you have a medical condition that precludes you from taking it. Side effects include gastro-intestinal disturbances, headache,

ANTIMALARIALS

Homeopathic antimalarial system

There's no scientific evidence of its efficacy, but the following "prophylactic" system against malaria appears to work in the field. Treatment involves three separate remedies.

Starting about a week before entering a risky area, take 1 Malaria (30C) tablet per week throughout your stay and continue for 3 weeks after you leave the area. At the same time take Ceanothus (the spleen support remedy) in low potency (either 1x or 3x liquid dose or 5–10 drops daily in a small glass of water; or 1 5–7C tablet daily), and China officinalis, again in low potency (less than 12C), once daily.

This system is safe in pregnancy and for children (although give them a slightly smaller dose of Ceanothus, say 2–5 drops daily).

convulsions, visual disturbances, depigmentation or loss of hair, and skin reactions. Mild side effects are quite common, severe are rare.

Dosage: 2 tablets taken together once a week on a full stomach.

Proguanil is used almost exclusively in conjunction with chloroquine and is difficult to obtain in the US although used in the UK, Australia, New Zealand and many European countries. It can be used with care in kidney impairment and pregnancy but it's best to discuss these issues directly with your doctor. Side effects include mild stomach upsets, diarrhoea, mouth ulcers and (rarely) skin reactions and hair loss.

Dosage: 2 x 100mg once daily.

Mefloquine⋆, despite much adverse publicity, is increasingly recommended as chloroquine resistance grows worldwide. Of the antimalarials currently available, it gives the best level of protection, estimated at around 90% in high-risk areas, but it is expensive and its profile of cautions, reactions and side effects is pretty daunting. Reported side effects include: nausea, vomiting, diarrhoea, dizziness, loss of balance, headache, somnolence, sleep disorders, anxiety, depression, hallucinations, convulsions, ringing ears, visual disturbances, circulatory disorders, muscle pain and weakness, joint pains, rashes, itching, hair loss, malaise, fever, fatigue, loss of appetite, and disturbances in liver function, blood composition and heart conduction.

The serious consequences so often quoted in the media are, in practice, rare (see p.286, "The mefloquine (Larium) debate"). It should not be taken in early pregnancy (current evidence suggests that it is safe later on), if you are breast-feeding, nor if you have had serious psychiatric illness, convulsions, or hypersensitivity to quinine. It should also be avoided if you have liver or kidney impairment, heart conduction disorders and epilepsy. It is not recommended for children under 3 months.

Dosage: 1 x 250mg tablet each week on a full stomach. (A dose of half a tablet twice weekly may reduce the incidence of gastrointestinal side effects.)

Doxycycline⋆ is actually an antibiotic which is increasingly prescribed as an alternative to mefloquine and is also useful in areas where mefloquine resistance exists. It reduces the efficacy of the contraceptive pill, however, and should be used with caution if you have liver impairment. It should not be taken at all if you suffer from porphyria, or if you are pregnant or breast-feeding. Side effects include nausea, vomiting, diarrhoea, rashes (including hypersensitivity to sunlight – a fairly major problem in malarial zones), and it may cause vaginal thrush. More rarely, headache and visual disturbances, pancreatitis and pseudomembranous colitis can occur, all of which need medical attention.

Dosage: 100mg daily after food. Begin the course 2 days before entering a malarial zone and continue for 4 weeks after departure.

Antifungal treatments

Clotrimazole and **miconazole creams** are cheap and effective in treating most fungal skin infections.

Apply twice daily until 2 weeks after the lesions have healed.

Vaginal thrush (see p.374) is best treated with **clotrimazole** or **miconazole pessaries**.

Of the number of different makes of vaginal pessary to choose from, the most convenient is one-off treatment using a 500mg pessary of clotrimazole or 1.2g of miconazole, inserted last thing at night.

Tranquillizers

Many doctors are reluctant to prescribe **tranquillizers** because of their addictive potential. If you do take tranquillizers for whatever reason, avoid taking them for more than a week at a time.

Temazepam is frequently prescribed for sleep problems. Side effects include clumsiness, drowsiness and lightheadedness the next day.

Adult dosage: 1 x 10mg at night.

Diazepam can be used in the short term as a relief for anxiety (eg aerophobia). Its side effects are similar to temazepam.

Dosage: depends on the prescribing doctor but, in most cases, 2mg every 8hr is sufficient.

Altitude sickness

Note that nifedipine, dexamethasone and frusemide (below) should only be used under medical supervision.

Acetazolamide★ is a useful **preventative** for acute mountain sickness. It is not recommended for prolonged use, however, and if taken concurrently with the oral contraceptive pill, you stand an increased risk of blood clots (eg DVTs).

Dosage: 500mg nightly.

Nifedipine★ is normally used for the treatment of high blood pressure and angina, but it can be used as a **prophylactic** against mountain sickness, or as a **treatment** in acute episodes. Side effects include feeling faint (caused by low blood pressure), headache, flushing, dizziness, lethargy, nausea, ankle swelling (unhelpfully, these are all symptoms of altitude sickness as well) and rashes. It should not be taken if you are pregnant or if you suffer from porphyria. If you suffer from heart problems, discuss this with a doctor before using nifedipine.

Recommended dosage: 20mg 3 times a day.

Dexamethasone★ is a strong steroid used to reduce brain swelling in altitude sickness. It should be used in emergencies only and not for more than 2 days without medical advice. It buys time for descent only, and further ascent must not be attempted once the symptoms have settled. The side effects of steroids are numerous and can be serious, but short-term use is usually safe.

The standard starting dosage is 4mg 4 times daily – a high dose bearing in mind that this is a very strong steroid. It's important that you don't stop taking dexamethasone abruptly; rather reduce your dosage gradually, for example by 2mg every other day.

Frusemide★, a strong diuretic, is useful for acute episodes of altitude sickness when breathing is impaired by an accumulation of fluid in the lungs. Used as a short-term, emergency treatment, side effects are likely to be minimal although expect to pass urine more often.

Dosage: 40–80mg daily.

Other useful medical items

A few other items you might consider packing include:

✚ **Antiseptic cream** or lotion.

✚ **Steroid creams**: Hydrocortisone reduces local swelling and itching (eg insect bites). Although only a mild steroid, and, as such, available without prescription, hydrocortisone should be used with discretion because long-term use can cause thinning of the skin. Generally speaking, it should not be used for more than 14 days at a time. It should not be used for untreated bacterial, viral and fungal infections, and contact with the eyes should be avoided.

✚ **Magnesium sulphate paste** is not an antibiotic but it can be useful in treating boils and minor skin infections.

Suggested medical kit

Medications or equipment you might want to include:

+ **Painkillers** Paracetamol or ibuprofen
+ **Antibiotics*** Amoxycillin or erythromycin; also consider ciprofloxacin
+ **Antihistamines** Chlorpheniramine or loratadine
+ **Antidiarrhoeals**
+ **Oral rehydration fluid**
+ **Antisickness*** Metoclopramide or domperidome
+ **Motion sickness** Hyoscine or promethazine, acupressure bands
+ **Antimalarials** Dependent on latest recommendations for country of destination
+ **Skin creams** Clotrimazole, anthisan, savlon
+ **Antacids**
+ **Condoms**
+ **Sunscreen** Any factor 15+ that protects against UVA and B
+ **Sticking plasters/Band-Aids**
+ **Steristrips**
+ **Crepe bandage**
+ **Scissors**
+ **Tweezers**
+ **Thermometer**
+ **Antiseptic**
+ **Sterile gauze and cotton wool**
+ **Safety pins**
+ **Insect repellent**
+ **Aftersun lotion**
+ **Tampons**
+ **Baby wipes**
+ **Sterile syringes and needles**

(* available only on prescription)

+ **Antacids**: Most brands provide good symptomatic relief after hastily gobbled, fried or spicy foods. Follow the instructions on the bottle or packet. The absorption of some drugs can be impaired by concurrent use of antacids.

+ **Sunscreen or sunblock**: Broadly speaking, sunscreens should have a sun protection factor of 15+, protect from both UVA and UVB, and be water-resistant (see p.366 for more information).

Homeopathy

Homeopathy was developed around 200 years ago by a German doctor, Samuel Hahnemann (1755–1843), who challenged the medical wisdom of the time with his insistence on developing a more natural and gentle system of healing for his patients – an alternative to the heavy metals, strong herbal purges and bloodletting favoured by his contemporaries. He attracted a small band of followers, and by the 1840s homeopathy had spread to the US, where it became part of the so-called Popular Health Movement – a

rebellion against established medicine which gave
birth to herbalism, self-help homeopathy and the
novel concept of "health food" (hence Mr Kellog and
Mr Graham of breakfast-cereal fame). Meanwhile in
Europe, "vitalism" and "mesmerism", both forms of
spiritual healing, became de rigueur, while certain
circles headed to the mountains to "take the waters".
Since then there has been no turning back, and in
some countries, homeopathy has achieved equal status with so-called Western, or allopathic, medicine.

Throughout this book, homeopathic alternatives to many preventions
and treatments have been provided. Look for this symbol:

How it works

Coined by Hahnemann, the word "homeopathy" derives
from the Greek meaning "similar suffering". Central to it is
the idea that **"like cures like"**, meaning that a substance
capable of causing certain symptoms in a well person can
be used to cure the same symptoms in a sick person. For
example, the allopathic approach to treating diarrhoea is to
take a substance which causes constipation; to treat the
same complaint homeopathically, you take a very tiny dose
of something that has the power to cause diarrhoea if given
to a healthy person.

All homeopathic medicines are prepared by trained phar-
macists according to a method laid down by Hahnemann
himself. Usually they are sold in tablet form, occasionally as

liquids. Through a process known as "dilution and succussion", substances are diluted to the point where no material evidence remains; the idea behind this is to release the true healing nature and potential of the original substance. Many homeopathic remedies are derived from highly poisonous plants, snake venoms, heavy metals and chemical salts.

Various schools of homeopathy exist. All the suggestions for homeopathic treatment in this guide are according to **Classical** (also known as Unicist) homeopathy, favoured in India and much of the West, which uses only one medicine at a time – this means you choose a single remedy that fits most of your symptoms. **Complex** homeopathy, which you may also hear about, meanwhile involves the use of many different remedies, often mixed together in one pill or liquid.

Choosing the right remedy

Treatment in homeopathy is **individualized**. Thus, it's the symptoms that make your condition atypical that determine which remedy to choose. For example, if you have a cold, it's not the fact that you have a runny nose – which is common to all colds – that's important, but the nature of the discharge in your particular case (eg bloody, clear, profuse, purulent and so on).

Homeopathy also takes into account your **mental and emotional symptoms**. So, if you have diarrhoea, and you are restless and anxious in an uncharacteristic way, then this would form part of what's known as your "**symptom picture**", which would then be matched to a homeopathic remedy, or "**drug picture**". If a choice of **potencies** is available to you, there's a simple rule of thumb in deciding

Before you go

Think about seeing a homeopath, herbalist or acupuncturist before you set out on a long journey, especially if you have a background of (even niggling) health problems – sun headaches, irritable bowel syndrome, period problems or back pains – which you don't want to be suffering from when you're a long way from home.

Vaccinations, too, can be dealt with homeopathically. If you opt to take the recommended allopathic vaccines, you can take a homeopathic potency made from the actual vaccines (usually a single dose of 30C) to "offset" any side effects. You can also take a homeopathic prophylactic system for malaria.

▷▷See Malaria, p.65.

You might also want to invest in one of the many homeopathic first-aid kits on the market (see p.536 for a list of suppliers), most of which contain 30C strength tablets only.

which to use: if it's something like a cold, take a low dose (eg 6c); if you have a fever, a 30c dose is better – it has a deeper action.

What you are looking for in homeopathic first aid are the recent changes to normal habits, mood and body patterns.

Taking the remedy

Newcomers to homeopathy should start by taking 6–30c doses. If using low doses, take the remedy 5 or 6 times on the first day, then 3 times a day on subsequent days. If using a higher dose (**30c**), take the remedy twice a day for 1–4 days.

For remedies to work effectively, take them with a "**clean mouth**", ie don't eat, drink or smoke for 10–15 minutes before or after each dose. As remedies can be **antidoted** by peppermint and menthol, it's also wise not to take them too soon before or after brushing your teeth. Avoid the antidotes of camphor, eucalyptus, coffee and cannabis completely for the days during treatment and for 48 hours after afterwards. Tea, moderate amounts of alcohol and tobacco meanwhile, don't usually affect remedies.

Storage

It's important to **store** your medicines, as far as possible, away from other very strong energy sources. The effectiveness of your remedies will be prolonged if you avoid exposing them to:

+ **direct sunlight**

+ **strong heat** – it's not necessary to refrigerate
    remedies, but try to keep exposure to great heat
    to a minimum.

+ **strong smells** – especially those in chest rubs
    and decongestants, like camphor, eucalyptus,
    menthol and peppermint.

+ **x-rays.** Although unproved, exposure to airport
    scanners may reduce a remedy's lifespan, or alter
    it in some way. In most countries it's common
    and perfectly acceptable to ask for your
    homeopathic medical kit not to be x-rayed when
    you go through customs with your hand luggage.
    Obviously it's wise to make sure that all bottles
    are clearly labelled, preferably with a pharmacy
    label.

Homeopathic first aid

If you see no improvement after a day of taking remedies, stop, review the symptoms again and look for another remedy, or else seek medical advice. Don't continue to take a remedy that isn't working – in treating an acute illness using homeopathic first aid, the *right* remedy will work *quickly*.

+ mobile phones, TVs, computers, microwave ovens, CD players, even fuse boxes.

Although nowadays homeopathic remedy bottles display an expiry date, most remedies do not appear to lose their activity over time.

Homeopathic first-aid remedies

The list below outlines the most common remedies used in **homeopathic first aid for travellers**. Next to each is a brief description of the remedy's uses – look under the relevant illnesses in Part 2 for more detail on recommended dosages and the like. (The names in brackets show how each medicine may appear on the pharmacy label.)

+ **Aconite** (Acon.) For fevers, shock, panic and anxiety.
+ **Allium cepa** (All-c.) Made from red onions. Head colds.
+ **Apis mellifica** (Apis mel.) Bites and stings.
+ **Argentum nitricum** (Arg. Nit.) Fear of flying, and anxiety before travelling.

+ **Arnica** (Arn.) Bruises, shock and swelling after injury or surgery. Also useful for jet lag.

+ **Arsenicum album** (Ars. alb.) For diarrhoea and vomiting.

+ **Belladonna** (Bell.) Used for fevers, sun headaches and localized inflammations.

+ **Calendula** (Calend.) Promotes healing of grazes, and good for wounds that may be going septic. Also useful for nappy/diaper rash.

+ **Cantharis** (Canth.) Urinary tract infections.

+ **China officinalis** (Chin.) Use if going to malarial areas. Also used for tummy upsets and rehydration.

+ **Coca** Altitude sickness.

+ **Cocculus indicus** (Cocc.) Travel sickness and jet lag.

+ **Colocynthis** (Coloc.) Diarrhoea, colic and menstrual cramps.

+ **Eupatorium perfoliatum** (Eup. perf.) Febrile illnesses, such as dengue fever; also influenza and malaria treatment.

+ **Ferrum phos** (Ferr-p.) Colds and the first signs of mild inflammatory complaints (chest, throat).

+ **Gelsemium** (Gels.) Flu-like colds, shock.

+ **Glonoin** (Glon.) Pounding headaches, especially after spending too much time in the sun.

+ **Hypericum** (Hyp.) Helps heal injuries to areas rich in nerves (tongue, lips, fingers and toes); also very useful for a bruised coccyx, eg after a long bumpy journey.

66 Jungle fever in Nepal 99

*A*fter a day in the open air I had expected to sleep well. *That morning I'd turned my back on the culture shock that was Pokhara – a kaleidoscope of prayer flags, monks in saffron, women selling sugar cane while pulling heavily on handmade cigarettes, and naked, laughing children everywhere. It was a scorching February day as I headed for the hills, past parched rice terraces that had been transformed into a soccer pitch by a group of local lads. In the buzzing forests beyond, beneath flocks of green parrots, I encountered only a handful of people all day. As the light faded, I returned to Pokhara, where the pungent aroma of daal bhaat filled the air. The end of a wonderful day.*

That night, however, my whole body felt as if it was on fire. In the cold light of day I saw that I was covered in huge, burning red blotches. I trudged down to the chemist's stall and bought a bottle of India's answer to calamine lotion. Back at my hotel, Lila, the young Nepali woman in charge, took a closer look at me and recalled a disease she'd had as a child known as "jungle fever". After taking a shower, which spread the infection further, I reasoned: at least Lila's existence meant I hadn't come down with anything fatal.

The rest of the day passed in a blur of codeine and tea. The following morning I was supposed to be trekking with Shiam, a lad from the hotel, but I had another night without sleep, and Lila called the doctor. His diagnosis was quick and to the point a massive allergic reaction, probably to a plant in the forest. After several jabs of antihistamine, I slouched away and spent the day asleep. Some hours later I awoke to find my condition had worsened. The rash had now spread to my face, and the earlier marks were turning into huge, black bruises. Lila immediately phoned for an ambulance.

When it arrived, half of Pokhara jumped in for the ride, and off we all went to the hospital. This was grim – the corridors crammed with bodies and the doctor seemed baffled by my symptoms, but to be on the safe side he dosed me up a bit more.

Having missed the first day of my trek, I was determined to start the next day. As the sun rose over Macchapuchre, I set off with Shiam. By 9am the sun was blistering, and I was beginning to have regrets: my body ached and itched, and my face was hideously swollen and bruised. I decided to rest a while beneath an old tree. Passers-by, laden with supplies for mountain-top villages, glanced briefly at me and hurried quickly on.

Shiam had wandered off somewhere, and I was just beginning to drift off to sleep when he returned with an old man. The man sat down next to me and began to whisper mantras while blowing gently over my arms and legs. It felt odd, lying there helpless, the subject of a grizzled old man's incantations, but Shiam looked confident, so I relaxed a little. After a few minutes he got up, telling Shiam the disease would be gone by morning.

It was hard going but we made it, spending the night in a mountain-top village. I awoke to the sun dancing on the floor of our cabin. Over-awed by the Himalayas, I took a few minutes to realize that the pain had gone and my entire body was free of the bruises and blotches; indeed I felt, for the first time in days, remarkably well.

About a year later I was visiting Kew Gardens in London, where one of the hothouses contained an area filled with native Nepalese plants and flowers. I avoided going too close – medicine men are thin on the ground in London!

Helen Ostick, Cheshire UK

"JUNGLE FEVER IN NEPAL"

✛ **Ignatia amara** (Ign.) Emotional shock and loss.

✛ **Ledum pal** (Led.) Heals deep, or dirty, wounds and bites. Can be considered as an anti-tetanus remedy.

✛ **Mercurius** (Merc. viv. or Merc. sol.) Sore throats.

✛ **Natrum mur** (Nat-m.) Head colds and cold sores.

✛ **Nux vomica** (Nux-v.) Hangovers, colic and any form of overindulgence.

✛ **Opium** (Op.) Travellers' constipation.

✛ **Petroleum** (Petr.) Travel sickness (particularly if you are averse to the smell of petrol).

✛ **Phosphorous** (Phos.) Persistent, dry and tickly coughs, and nosebleeds.

✛ **Podophyllum** (Podo.) Diarrhoea, tummy upsets.

✛ **Pulsatilla** (Puls.) Thick mucousy colds and coughs, and homesickness.

✛ **Pyrogen** (Pyrog.) Septic wounds.

✛ **Rhus toxicodendron** (Rhus tox.) Strains and sprains, and overlifting. Also useful for herpes attacks, chicken pox, and for local skin allergies to certain plants, particularly poison ivy – from which it is derived.

✛ **Ruta graveolens** (Ruta grav.) Wrist and ankle sprains.

✛ **Silica** (Sil.) Useful for ejecting foreign bodies from the system – splinters, sea urchin spines, bee stings and the like.

✛ **Sol** For photosensitivity reactions, and herpes triggered by excessive sun exposure. Also used to prevent sunstroke and sun headaches. Use in the

Alternative first-aid kit

The following are a few alternative items that will make good additions to your medical kit:

+ **Bach Rescue Remedy**: will keep you calm in times of stress, and **Walnut Bach Flower Remedy** will help you adapt to changing circumstances, while the **crabapple** variety helps clear your system of drugs (all sorts – allopathic, recreational, alcohol, etc). Sip 2 or 3 drops diluted in a glass of water.

+ **Lavender oil**: not only relaxing and calming but stimulates healing and has anti-bacterial and anti-spasmodic properties. Apply undiluted to bruises, insect and animal bites, and minor burns. Mix 1 or 2 drops in your after-sun cream to treat sunburn. Place a couple of drops on your pillow and sniff regularly during a migraine – this also helps to calm you down and makes you sleep.

+ **Tea tree oil**: a powerful anti-viral, anti-bacterial and anti-fungal all in one. It's great for thrush, athlete's foot and other fungal skin infections, all commonplace in hot climates. Put 3 or 4 drops in a small bowl of warm water for applying or dunking. Dropped into hot water for inhaling, it can help to ease colds, chest infections. Mix a few drops with almond (or any base) oil to make a good chest rub. It's also available as a cream. If you're pregnant, don't use tea tree oil – use lavender instead.

+ **Grapefruit seed extract**: widely available in liquid or tablet form, it acts as an anti-parasitic and natural antibiotic. It can be useful during colds, flu and chest infections, as well as acting as a daily prophylactic or as a treatment against intestinal infections.
→

+ **Lactobacillus acidophilus**: these are the so-called "friendly bacteria" that repopulate your intestines after you've had diarrhoea or taken a course of antibiotics. We produce them naturally, but you can take a top-up, available in tablets, capsules and powder. Taking them during a course of antibiotics helps to prevent an attack of thrush afterwards.

+ **Calendula** cream: great for grazes, cuts and wounds. You can also buy it as a tincture (a solution of the drug in alcohol). Place 3 or 4 drops in a small bowl of water for bathing. A combined cream of Calendula and Hypericum (see p.77) is a good alternative.

200C potency, if obtainable, to reduce ill-effects of exposure to sunshine.

+ **Sulphur** (Sulph.) Useful for vaginal thrush and itchy fungal skin complaints.

+ **Tabacum** (Tab.) Sea sickness.

+ **Veratrum album** (Verat. alb.) For severe tummy upsets, dysentery.

Travellers with specific needs

The elderly, the disabled, families with children, pregnant women and sufferers of chronic illness all have specific needs to consider in the planning stages of a trip. The key is not to overextend yourself, to recognize your limits and plan your trip within them. Pre-considerations such as immunizations, travel insurance and a medical kit are particularly important.

The traveller with asthma

Although not an illness which exclusively affects travellers, asthma is increasingly common, easily treatable and yet potentially dangerous if untreated. Travel can increase your chances of exposure to some of asthma's many **triggers**: cold, damp, exercise, air pollution, altitude, dust, cigarette or wood smoke, air conditioning, upper respiratory tract infections, and anxiety. Given the right conditions, anyone can develop the symptoms of asthma. Smog in cities, crop-harvesting in arid, dusty countryside and local pollen-emitting flora all conspire to cause wheezes and coughs in the unsuspecting traveller.

Symptoms and treatment

The wheeze of asthma does not come from the throat but the chest, and is characteristically worse on breathing out. You may feel tight-chested and have a dry, tickly cough, which is usually worse at night and can be the only symptom. If symptoms are severe, it may be difficult to breathe or speak in complete sentences.

Mild asthma can be treated fairly easily using inhalers. People who have a history of asthma should already be aware of the correct technique and the necessary dosages. Asthma can be controlled either with a beta sympathomimetic inhaler alone (eg salbutamol or terbutaline), or in

Inhaler technique

If you've never suffered asthma symptoms before, it is unlikely that you will develop serious disease whilst abroad. This is not to say that mild symptoms would not benefit from treatment. The first-line treatment for wheeze is a beta sympathomimetic inhaler, which is cheap and available on prescription in most developed countries. Some people find it difficult to use an inhaler. It helps to think in terms of getting the drug where it will do its work, ie the lungs. Basically, you take a deep breath in and then breathe out all the way. At the end of expiration, place the inhaler between your lips and start a slow, deep inspiration; the inhaler should be discharged during the deep breath in. Hold your breath for at least 10 seconds to allow the drug time to act, then repeat the exercise. Seek medical advice if the symptoms persist.

combination with a steroid inhaler (eg beclomethasone or fluticasone). The former are more useful for the active treatment of symptoms, whereas the latter are regarded more as a preventative. During an asthma attack the beta sympathomimetics can be taken as 2 puffs every 4 hours if necessary. The steroid dose may be doubled (usually 2 puffs twice daily) to 2 puffs 4 times a day.

Being prepared

If you are an asthma sufferer, you should:

✚ Be aware of the signs and symptoms of worsening asthma. In particular, understand the importance of monitoring changes in your peak flow rate.

✚ Be aware of correct inhaler technique.

✚ Know how to regulate the doses of your inhalers during acute episodes (increase the frequency of both treaters and preventers).

✚ Carry dog-tag identification, relevant medical notes and oral steroids (such as prednisolone) if you are prone to severe attacks.

✚ Consider vaccination against influenza if you're flying to an area with high seasonal risk.

✚ Seek medical help sooner rather than later.

The traveller with diabetes

As a diabetic it's important to discuss travel plans with your doctor or diabetic nurse well in advance of your departure so that your diabetes can be optimally controlled before you leave. Ensure that you can recognize symptoms of high and, more importantly, low blood sugar and that you understand how your drugs or insulin work. Know what to do if your blood sugar goes too high or too low and how to adjust your treatment during illness (eg diarrhoea and vomiting or high fever).

Although not essential, you'd be wise to travel with someone who is aware of the problems associated with diabetes and able to deal with them. Either way it's essential to wear **dog tag or bracelet ID** (see p.537) if your diabetes is insulin-controlled.

Medications and insulin

Take ample supplies of insulin, medications and testing equipment with you, as they might be difficult to replace when abroad. It may be possible to obtain information as to equipment availability from the national diabetic association of wherever you're heading.

Always carry an emergency supply of sweets in case of hypos.

When crossing time zones, remain on your **home time** for insulin injections and carbohydrate intake until arrival. Thereafter, injections can be adjusted in 2-hourly increments until they are in line with local time. If the time between successive injections is extended rather than shortened, a smaller, interim dose may be necessary. If the time between injections is shorter, a small, temporary reduction in dose may be necessary (of the order of 4 to 8 units). It would be sensible to discuss such adjustments with your doctor before leaving. Use urinary sugar as a guideline. When making adjustments, underdose your insulin rather than overdose – in the short term, it's safer to have blood

MEDICATIONS AND INSULIN

sugar levels that are slightly too high rather than too low. If you use oral hypoglycaemic tablets, you don't need to alter your dose times when crossing time zones. It may take a few days to adjust fully to the local time and it is advisable to check urinary sugars regularly (at least twice daily) during this period.

Take care over the storage temperature of your insulin – extremes of heat and cold can shorten its shelflife. Keep your insulin in your hand baggage when you fly; never store it in the hold.

Managing your blood sugar

Strenuous **exercise** drops the body's blood sugar level so try to plan ahead and take a carbohydrate-rich snack 30 to 60 minutes beforehand. This may need to be repeated during periods of extended exercise.

Insulin requirements during **illness** increase (ie when your body is under stress) and it may be necessary to increase your usual daily dosage temporarily. Continue as normal during diarrhoeal and other illnesses but monitor blood or urinary glucose regularly and try to eat easily digestible carbohydrates. Be particularly wary of dehydration. Continue your insulin injections as normal if vomiting occurs but monitor your blood sugar regularly and seek medical advice.

Infections are a common complication of diabetes so be particularly vigilant when travelling, especially if your glucose levels are running high. Use antibiotics early if infection is suspected, and have a low threshold for seeking medical help. Carry the address and telephone number of your doctor at home in case you or someone else need to make urgent contact. Vaccination against **influenza** is highly recommended if you're travelling to an area with a seasonal risk.

Because long-term diabetes can impair pain perception,

minor blisters on your feet can develop into more severe ulcers without you knowing. For this reason, take particular care to inspect your feet regularly and carry plenty of dressings, antiseptic and protective "corn plasters".

The traveller with epilepsy

Once your fits are well-controlled by medication, epilepsy does not exclude you from very much, especially travelling. There are nevertheless a number of considerations to take into account before you go and while on the road.

Being prepared

It may be difficult and even dangerous to travel alone, especially if your epilepsy is poorly controlled. Even if your fits are infrequent, it's sensible to travel with someone who knows about your condition and how to deal with a fit if you have one.

Be aware of conditions or activities which may increase the **risk** of fits: missed medications, fatigue, heat, infections, dehydration, over-rehydration, alcohol, severe diarrhoea, recurrent vomiting, low blood sugar caused by missed meals, stress, menstruation and strobe lights.

Always inform your travel agent and airline that you have epilepsy from the outset. Some airlines require special medical certification for epileptics.

Although it might be easy to avoid potentially hazardous situations at home, it can be more difficult when you are on the move. Pay particular attention to railway platforms, hotel balconies, roads, cliff edges and around water, camp fires and barbecues. As a sufferer of epilepsy you will know

First aid for a fit

✚ Stay calm.

✚ Loosen any clothing from around their neck and, if possible, roll the casualty onto their side or into the recovery position to protect their airway.

✚ Otherwise, do not attempt to move someone who is fitting unless they are in immediate danger.

✚ Remove nearby potentially hazardous objects away from the person having the fit.

✚ Do not attempt to restrain them and do not attempt to force open their mouth.

✚ Cushion the head and, as the fitting subsides, help to keep their airway clear by placing them in the recovery position, if you were unable to do so earlier.

✚ Stay with them until the fitting stops.

✚ Most fits are self-limiting and over by the time help arrives, but if the fit continues for more than 5 minutes, call for medical help or use rectal diazepam if it's available.

✚ Valproate
 Aspirin
 Erythromycin
 Chloroquine
 Mefloquine

These anti-epileptics increase your vitamin D requirements.

MEDICATIONS

Travelling with immunodeficiency

Immunodeficiency essentially means that your body's ability to fight off infections is compromised and, as such, you are more vulnerable to infections of any kind. Examples of illnesses or treatments which lead to immunodeficiency include leukaemia, lymphoma and HIV infection; you're also at risk after a splenectomy, after chemotherapy, and if you are on high-dose steroids. Focus your plans for travelling abroad around this important and inescapable fact, as you will face considerable risks in developing countries where standards of hygiene are poor and medical care may be inadequate.

You must declare your illness to your insurer as failure to do so will invalidate any claims made arising from immunodeficiency. Never travel without a repatriation clause.

Finally, depending on the cause of your immunodeficiency and its extent, you should avoid, or seek expert advice before, "live" **vaccinations** (p.9) as these depend on the body being able to form an effective immune response. If in doubt, seek the advice of your specialist. Vaccination against **influenza** is highly recommended if you're travelling to an area with a seasonal risk.

Travelling with HIV

If you are HIV positive and planning a trip, a good starting point is Ronald Russo's article "On the Road with HIV... or How to Have a Healthy, Fun Vacation", published by Body Positive in June 1999 but accessible on the Internet (see p.542). While any traveller is at risk of infection, travellers with HIV are more susceptible because of their impaired immunity. It's best to avoid visiting developing countries where sanitation is poor and medical care may be limited through lack of expertise or funding.

As HIV depletes the ability to fight off infection, it stands to reason that travellers with HIV are at higher risk of contracting an illness than most travellers. There is an increased frequency and severity of most illnesses with HIV but particularly gastrointestinal infections, TB, syphilis and leishmaniasis. Generally speaking though, if you are in good health and with a CD4 count (the white cells in the blood which protect against infection) greater than 200, you do not need to take special precautions, although remember that a previously healthy CD4 count could drop while you are away.

For those with CD4 counts below 200 it would be unwise to make an unnecessary trip to areas with poor sanitation. It is best to discuss the risks with your doctor before booking a long trip.

Be obsessional about the standard food and drink precautions (see pp.40–44) and, in particular, avoid unpasteurized dairy products.

Medications

Complex drug treatments have been developed which retard the progress of HIV. While your choices are very limited, carrying the drugs with you can present logistical problems. A doctor's letter stating your need for the drugs may allay the suspicions of customs officials, but if they suspect that you have HIV, this in itself can cause problems in some countries.

HIV vaccination advice

The UK Department of Health has issued the following advice on the vaccination of anyone with HIV infection:

✚ Anyone who is HIV positive, with or without symptoms, can receive the following live vaccines: measles, mumps, rubella (MMR), oral polio (although inactivated vaccine may be a better option for anyone with symptoms).*

✚ It is also safe to be given the following inactivated vaccines: cholera, diphtheria, haemophilus influenza type b, hepatitis A, hepatitis B, influenza, meningococcal, pertussis, pneumococcal, inactivated polio, rabies, tetanus, injected typhoid.

✚ If you are HIV positive, you should not receive BCG (TB), yellow fever (insufficient evidence on safety) and oral typhoid.

These are not a standard requirement for travelling although those with HIV may lose previous immunity to these illnesses.

Always carry enough supplies from home with you because replacements may be difficult to find, not to mention expensive. Some anti-HIV drugs increase sensitivity to UV light, so it is important to use high-factor sunscreen and avoid strong sunlight where possible.

Vaccinations

"Live" vaccinations (see p.9) should be avoided altogether (exceptions are listed in the box above). After inactivated immunization there may be a transient increase in the level of HIV in the blood and a consequent decrease in the CD4 count. With HIV, you've a greater chance of getting a reaction to immunization, as well as a weaker response, or lower level of immunity.

Visa requirements

While most countries officially do not deny entry to HIV travellers who are not intending to work or study, rather ambiguously, you could be refused entry on account of carrying a "communicable disease". Although you do not have to declare that you are HIV positive, the medications in your luggage might give the game away. No countries insist on **screening** for HIV in casual travellers, although many (including the USA) will require a test for longer term immigrants such as students and those seeking work. They'll refuse entry if the test is positive. If you are planning to work or study abroad, contact the appropriate embassy to clarify their policy on HIV tests.

A useful resource for country-by-country restrictions or visa requirements is the **aidsnet Web site** (see p.542).

Insurance

The normal insurance clause concerning pre-existing illness can present a problem. It's important to declare your health status because if you do not, and a problem arises, the insurance company may refuse to cover you. It's worth shopping around, however, because some companies are now revoking that particular clause. The importance of adequate cover for rapid repatriation in the event of an emergency cannot be overstated. Contact groups such as Body Positive in the UK will have the latest recommendations, and the Internet is packed with all sorts of useful Web sites for HIV-related issues (see p.542).

Sex

Sexual encounters with a new partner while travelling are common, yet despite the considerable risks to themselves and others, some people still don't use condoms. Although not offering complete protection, proper use of good-quality condoms greatly reduces the risk of contracting, and passing on, sexually transmitted diseases. **Act responsibly** if you have sex with a new partner, male or female, and always use high-quality condoms, preferably brought with you from home.

Discrimination

Some cultures remain prejudiced against HIV because of enduring associations with sexual behaviour and drug taking. It is possible that you will suffer discrimination when seeking medical help. There is not very much that you can do about this other than to anticipate it and ensure that your insurance cover will bring you home if the going gets rough.

▷▷See also HIV, p.247.

The elderly traveller

Age is no longer an obstacle to exotic travel. In fact, many people do not have the opportunity to travel seriously until retirement or the children have left home. However, there

Checklist for disabled travellers

It may help to consider your own case in context of the following:

✦ Travel to and from destination
✦ Mobility when you are there
✦ Ability to self-care: washing, dressing, etc
✦ Medications
✦ Equipment
✦ Extra costs
✦ Access to medical help
✦ Special diets
✦ Additional support required

All in all, the simplest, and perhaps safest, option is to travel with an organized group. This is especially relevant for the first-time traveller, as you instantly have access to help and support, and much of the planning and other pre-considerations are done for you. There are many companies that specialize in holidays for people with disabilities – see p.544 for more information.

If, on the other hand, you opt to go independently, there are plenty of resources available – a good starting point will be the national association for your particular disability (see Part 4). They should be able to put you in touch with specialist travel agents, insurers, reciprocal organizations in your destination. There are also a number of more generalized organizations such as the Access-Able Travel Source in the US, the Holiday Care Service in the UK, and Disability Net, who can provide independent advice (see p.544 for contact details). Always remember that facilities for the disabled in your destination country may be inferior to those at home and perhaps even non-existent. Even if you choose to travel without the help of a specialized travel agent, it's important to inform the airline of your disability (if relevant to flying) when you book.

Don't overlook the possibility of loss of, or damage to, **vital equipment**, such as wheelchairs, hearing aids, spectacles, splints, etc. Will replacements be easy to find or will you have to carry spares with you? Make contingency plans just in case.

The **extra cost** of a holiday for someone who is disabled is difficult to avoid. There may be less choice in **accommodation** and the budget end of the market is less likely to have the necessary adaptations which you may require. The same will apply to **eating out**. You might also have to rely on more expensive means of **transport** such as taxis or tourist buses because of a lack of alternatives.

Travelling with children

Children often make brilliant travelling companions, simply because they bring with them none of the "baggage" – anxieties and fears – which occupy adults on a trip. But it can be a very different experience without careful **planning and forethought**.

For ease and convenience, **package tours** are difficult to beat if you have children. Many travel firms organize holidays that go out of their way to accommodate the needs of both the children and their flagging parents, with organized activities for older children and creche facilities on hand for the younger ones, freeing up time for the parents to do what they like.

More ambitious trips need to be planned bearing in mind the age of the child, the mode of travel, the accommodation and the destination. Remember that the kinds of things that might interest you when travelling are unlikely to similarly impress children, and a bored child can ruin your enjoyment, so give careful thought to your itinerary, incorporating activities that will interest every family member. If possible, try to maintain some degree of **routine** as children of all ages are happier if there is some semblance of predictability to the day, even if it's only meal times.

Perhaps the most difficult age group to travel with are the 1- to 10-year-olds. They are mobile, past breast-feeding and need constant supervision and entertainment. They will be unable to carry their own luggage but will greatly add to yours. They are inquisitive, constantly exploring and testing their environment (frequently sucking unwashed fingers), which means that they will be at greater risk of injury, cuts, bites, stings, infections and more. They are also more prone to diarrhoeal illnesses, overheating, dehydration and sunburn. A number of the more exotic infections, such as Dengue or Japanese encephalitis, more commonly, or more seriously, affect children.

Potential hazards

For toddlers especially, potential **hazards** lurk around every corner. Children are closer to the ground and less wary of the potential dangers. Play often takes place in long grass and other environments favoured by snakes and other creepy crawlies. While deaths from scorpion bites are rare

POTENTIAL HAZARDS

they most commonly occur in children under 2. Always ensure that shoes or sandals are worn, even on the beach and when paddling.

Animals are an irresistible draw to children, yet animal behaviour can be unpredictable, especially when startled. Keep a close eye on children when animals are around and discourage them from approaching animals when they are on their own.

The importance of avoiding significant **sun exposure** at a young age cannot be overemphasized, as studies have shown that excessive sun early in life predisposes to skin cancer as you get older. Aim for indoor activities in the middle of the day when the sun is hottest, and be sure to cover up exposed skin as much as possible and apply high-protection sunscreen liberally and regularly when they're outside (see p.366). Encourage hat-wearing at all times and T-shirts when playing in the water. Fluid intake should be increased, and rest periods in the shade should be frequent.

Challenges en route

Plane, bus and rail travel come with their own challenges, since children can be difficult to entertain for long periods in confined spaces, toilet facilities may be inadequate and food choices limited. Although generally speaking, inquisitiveness and excitement predominate, children can feel frightened and panicky in a closed and controlled environment such as an aircraft cabin. Aisle seats are a good idea because they allow for greater mobility. Carry plenty of small toys, books or puzzles to keep young minds occupied. Reveal new toys at intervals, hourly for example, to combat boredom. Some of the medications used for motion sickness (eg antihistamines) can be usefully sedating.

Motion sickness commonly affects children over 2 and is more of a problem at sea and on the road than in the air. Encourage children to lie down on boats as this reduces the effects of seasickness. Place travel cots parallel with the direction of travel. Good ventilation helps, as do plenty of distractions. Antihistamines, acupressure bands and ginger can be used as preventative measures. (See p.63 for more on motion sickness.)

Extra baggage is unavoidable and obviously depends on the age of the child, but consider the following:

✚ Toys, books and puzzles

✚ Food (bring along a few favourites)

✚ Bottles, sterilizing equipment and formula milk if appropriate

✚ Nappies

✚ Wipes

✚ Changing mat

✚ Travel cot

✚ Children's medications

Immunizations and medications

Travel vaccinations for children, like those for adults, need to be planned well in advance of departure. Try to arrange your trip around the normal childhood vaccination programmes.

Avoid using **prescription medicines**, unless instructed to do so by a doctor, or medicines bought over-the-counter abroad for children. Stick to what you know and pack the medicines you might normally use at home.

If you suspect your child is significantly unwell, seek

OTHER CHALLENGES

medical advice at once. Deterioration can be rapid in children so the "wait and see" tactic mustn't be applied in the same way as for adults.

Children usually respond extraordinarily well to
homeopathic remedies and can be safely treated with
the same potencies as for adults.

Health risks for children

Children are more prone to **stomach upsets** because of their less robust immunity. **Diarrhoea** can present a real threat to children, as they are more susceptible to **dehydration** than adults. Use an oral rehydration solution (to both prevent, and treat, dehydration) – never use blockers or ciprofloxacin. Don't starve them but offer (don't force) bland food such as dry biscuits, freshly boiled rice, potatoes or bread. If the diarrhoea persists or the child is showing signs of dehydration despite the use of rehydration solution, seek medical help urgently.

Worm infections are common in children because of their tendency to run around barefoot and their fondness for digging in sand and soil and handling food with mucky fingers.

Malaria is even more dangerous for children than adults. Observe the normal anti-insect-bite measures (see p.43–45), and if you can, stay out of moderate to high-risk malarial areas altogether with children under 2. Insect repellents containing **DEET** are the most effective,

Children's vaccinations

The country-by-country requirements are the same for children as they are for adults – your doctor will have access to the latest recommendations.

Vaccine	Minimum age	Course
Hepatitis A	1 year	2 doses, months 0 and 6 to 12 (for 10-year protection)
Hepatitis B	No lower limit	3 doses, at month 0 and either months 1 and 2 or 1 and 6
Japanese encephalitis	No lower limit	3 doses at day 0, day 7 and day 28
Meningococcal meningitis	2 months	1 dose
Rabies	No lower limit	3 doses at day 0, day 7 and day 28
Tick-borne encephalitis	No lower limit	2 doses at weeks 0 and 4–12
Typhoid (oral)	6 years	3 doses; 1 capsule on days 0, 2 and 4
Typhoid (injected)	18 months	1 dose only
Yellow fever	9 months	1 dose only

Note: BCG can be given at birth if the risk of exposure to TB is high.

Signs of dehydration in children

+ Dry mouth and tongue
+ Skin loses elasticity
+ Eyes become sunken
  (as does the "soft spot" on the top of babies' heads)
+ Weak, rapid pulse
+ Lethargy, drowsiness

although advice regarding the strength of solutions safe to use on children is contradictory. Several studies have concluded that it is, by and large, a safe compound, the dangers

Medical kit for children

+ Paediatric paracetamol
+ Calamine lotion
+ Paediatric antihistamine syrup (of which there are many varieties, most not suitable for children under 2), useful for motion sickness, allergies or insect bites
+ Antihistamine cream
+ Rehydration solution sachets
+ A plentiful supply of plasters and antiseptic
+ Polythene bags –
  useful on long journeys in case of motion sickness
+ Baby wipes
+ Thermometer
+ Nappy/diaper rash cream

*Always store medications in child-proof
containers out of reach of inquisitive hands.*

Antimalarial recommendations for children

Age	Weight	Chloroquine/ Proguanil	Mefloquine
0–5 weeks	–	1/8 adult dose	No
6–52 wks	Up to 10kg	1/4 adult dose	No
1–5 yrs	11–19kg	1/2 adult dose	Not under 2yrs then 1/4 adult dose
6–11 yrs	20–39kg	3/4 adult dose	1/2 adult dose (6 to 8 yrs), 3/4 adult dose 9–11 yrs

The same cautions, limitations and side effects for these drugs detailed in the Medical kit (see pp.63–67) apply to children. Doxycycline should not be given to children under 12.

of which have been exaggerated by the media. The ill-effects caused by DEET do not appear to be dose-related although the general consensus is still to avoid unnecessarily high concentrations. Always follow the manufacturer's instructions.

▷▷For more on DEET, see p.260.

The kind of antimalarial your doctor prescribes is principally dependent on where you are travelling. Remember to start your child on the course at least a week before entering a malarial area and to continue it a month after you return. No antimalarial is 100% effective, so suspicious symptoms whilst travelling, or for up to a year after returning, deserve a medical opinion.

▷▷See Malaria, p.279.

Nutrition

Feeding your child abroad requires meticulous organization and an obsession with all things clean and sterile. Travelling with an infant needs careful planning around feeding schedules as a hungry child is likely to make life difficult for everyone.

Although travelling with a child young enough to be breast-fed is hard work, **breast-feeding** is safe, convenient and guarantees adequate nutrition. Try and respect local customs regarding the social acceptability of public breast-feeding. Breast-feeding mothers must drink plenty of fluids in hot climates.

Bottle feeding, on the other hand, can present a number of difficulties. First, you have to carry enough of your child's formula milk to last the trip unless you can be certain of obtaining it at your destination. Sterilization of the bottles and teats needs at least as much attention as you would give at home, which may mean carrying lots of unwieldy equipment. Remember that bottled water is not sterile and feeds should always be made up from boiled water. In countries where the local water is unreliable, boil bottled water. Refrigeration of made-up bottles can also present a problem – try to cool the bottles as quickly as possible and store them at low temperature, although it is best to make up fresh bottles in response to demand – if need be, carry the sterile bottles of cooled water with you and add pre-measured powder only when you need it. As for adults, a child's fluid requirements increase in hot climates, which means that bottle- or breast-fed infants may need top-ups of boiled (bottled) water.

When buying bottled water, use still water as opposed to carbonated for young children and always check that the cap seal is intact. Some mineral waters contain high concentrations of some chemical elements and it is worth noting that for children the sodium concentration should be no higher than 15mg/100ml, the potassium no higher than 2mg/100ml and the nitrates no more than 5mg/100ml. If you're feeding your child with ready-prepared jars of baby food, you may have to take a supply with you unless you can be sure of finding suitable substitutes abroad. Older children should follow the usual food guidelines as adults – see p.40. Take particular care with locally made fruit beverages, ice cream, milk shakes, ice in drinks and seafood. Also note that children can contract botulism from inadequately processed honey (see p.165). It's a good idea to take along a few familiar items of food from home for treats, bribes, in the event of illness or if local offerings are refused.

Women travellers

Although sexual equality is rapidly becoming a global phenomenon, there are some important practical issues that the woman traveller should consider before leaving home. **Personal safety** should be at the top of the list of priorities.

Do some research into where you are going beforehand. Are you likely to be hassled for money or sexually harassed? Developing countries may have a different opinion of the position of women in society than what you're used to – this may in fact mean they have more respect for women, just different expectations. The pervasive, male-dominated culture in some countries can make life difficult for Western women. Such difficulties can arise even if you are travelling in a group or with male companions. Carry a rape alarm at all times (although remember that a rape alarm doesn't confer instant protection – it's only useful if there is someone around to hear it) and always be aware of cultural assumptions about yourself. Avoid wearing jewellery that will attract attention, and dress appropriate to local customs. Hitch-hiking is never recommended, especially if you are travelling alone. Women may be perceived as easier targets by pickpockets and thieves, so look confident, purposeful and streetwise.

Menstruation

Travelling any great distance, especially flying, can disturb the body's natural patterns and rhythms, and **menstruation** is no exception. Periods can become erratic although regularity will be maintained if you take the combined oral contraceptive pill (see Contraception, p.181). A poor diet with significant weight loss, or strenuous physical activity, may lead to missed periods (the number 1 cause of a missed period is, of course, pregnancy). If you are due to have a period at a particularly difficult or inconvenient time, and you are not taking the contraceptive pill, using a drug called **norethisterone**, available on prescription only, can delay your period. It is a progestagen which is one of the hormones used in the contraceptive pill, and therefore the limitations and side effects are similar. The dosage is 5mg to be taken 3 times daily from 3 days before your period is due to start, to the day before you wish it to start. There are a number of contra-indications and side effects (although rare) and these should be discussed with your doctor beforehand. You should not delay your period using norethisterone for more than 14 consecutive days.

Period pains are no more likely to affect you travelling than they are at home. If you suffer from bad period pains regularly, however, discuss pain relief with your doctor before leaving home. NSAIDs (see p.52) are particularly effective, while paracetamol or co-proxamol can offer some relief.

It's worth remembering that menstruation is considered unclean in some cultures, and it can cause offence to enter a place of worship when you have your period.

It can be difficult to find **tampons** in some countries (particularly in isolated, rural areas), so take enough with you from home. Always wash your hands before changing a tampon to reduce the risk of infection.

Gynaecological problems

▷▷See also Urinary tract infections, p.391.

Pelvic inflammatory disease (PID) is a common complication of chlamydia and gonorrhoea infections. It is usually, although not invariably, acquired sexually. An ongoing, chronic form can cause considerable internal scarring and may seriously affect your fertility. Acutely, the common symptoms are pain on intercourse, vaginal discharge which may be bloody or purulent, fever and lower abdominal pain (usually unilateral) which is partially relieved by lying on your back with your legs flexed.

Prompt treatment is necessary to prevent septicaemia and reduce the likelihood of long-term complications. Ideally, medical input should be sought as you should have the nature of the infection confirmed before commencing treatment, and you may require both intravenous fluids and antibiotics. In an emergency, if medical help is difficult to access, commence a combination of oral metronidazole 400–500mg 3 times a day and doxycycline 100mg daily (or erythromycin) for 7 to 14 days. Ciprofloxacin 500mg as a single dose is effective against gonorrhoea.

If you have had surgery for **breast cancer** which involved removal of the lymph nodes, you must be careful to avoid insect bites on the relevant arm. The local swelling caused by a bite will normally dissipate quickly via the lymph system but if this has been disrupted by surgery, the swelling will remain and there is an increased risk of secondary infection. Cover up and use DEET liberally.

▷▷For Thrush, see p.374.

Pregnant travellers

A normal **pregnancy** lasts for 40 weeks (averaging 269 days from conception), and is frequently accompanied by a number of unwelcome physical symptoms. Breast tenderness, urinary frequency and fatigue are particularly common in the first 3 months. Nausea and vomiting can occur from as early as 2 weeks after conception but usually subside after 3 months. Week 9 of the pregnancy is reputedly the worst in this respect. Drugs are best avoided (a good rule of thumb in pregnancy) although some doctors might use promethazine if the symptoms are particularly severe. The main danger if vomiting is frequent or persistent is dehydration, which, in some rare cases, can be severe enough to merit hospital admission. If you have severe sickness, you may wish to defer your trip until the symptoms settle. Other common problems in pregnancy include swollen ankles, back pain and constipation. "Pica", the abnormal desire to eat sometimes unusual foods, can occur.

PREGNANCY

The **safest time to travel** in pregnancy is between weeks 14 and 28. In the early weeks of pregnancy there is a risk of miscarriage or ectopic pregnancy. Neither of these are brought on by travelling itself but both require medical input and you need to consider how you'd cope if the worst happened while you're away. Prematurity is a risk in late pregnancy and no airlines will allow you to take an international flight after 36 weeks' gestation. Don't travel at any stage in your pregnancy if your blood pressure is high, if you have experienced vaginal bleeding at any point, if your previous pregnancies have had complications, or if you are diabetic, epileptic or severely anaemic.

It's safe to use homeopathic remedies at any
stage during your pregnancy.

It's worth remembering that in the later stages of pregnancy, some countries may require written evidence from your doctor of your expected date of delivery – without it, they may refuse entry. Check with the relevant embassy before departure.

Insurance is dependent on individual company policy, but most companies do not surcharge premiums because of pregnancy although often will not cover you if you travel too close to your due date. Should you become pregnant after taking out insurance, most policies cover cancellation of your trip due to pregnancy provided you have a letter from your doctor.

PREGNANCY

Vaccinations in pregnancy

The following vaccinations are safe provided you are more than 12 weeks' pregnant:

✚ injectable typhoid

✚ hepatitis A and B

✚ diphtheria

✚ rabies

✚ meningococcal meningitis polysaccharide

Avoid the following live vaccinations at any stage in your pregnancy, although yellow fever and oral polio can be considered after the first 12 weeks if the risks of exposure are high:

✚ Yellow fever

✚ Oral typhoid

✚ MMR (measles, mumps, rubella)

Miscarriage, ectopic pregnancy and prematurity

The early part of pregnancy is the most risky time and **miscarriage** is, sadly, a frequent occurrence (miscarriages are estimated to occur in 1 in 5 pregnancies). It is very rare for a miscarriage to occur after the 14th week of pregnancy. The most common reason for miscarriage is an abnormality in the developing fetus rather than anyone doing anything wrong. Furthermore, there is nothing medically that can be done to avert a miscarriage and there is little evidence supporting the usual advice of bed rest. Travellers therefore should be at no greater risk of miscarriage than anybody else but it is important to ask yourself what would happen if you have a miscarriage when you are travelling. The bleeding can sometimes be severe, even life-threatening, so urgent medical input may be required. An operation to clear the uterus from any debris left behind (a dilatation and curettage, or "D&C") may be necessary. If your blood group is rhesus negative, you will require an injection of an immunoglobulin ("anti-D" or "Rho-GAM", eg) to prevent the formation of antibodies against your baby's blood group and thus avoid potential problems in subsequent pregnancies. Apart from the physical effects of miscarriage such as heavy or continuous blood loss, the psychological distress and feelings of guilt can take a long time to overcome. Although unfounded, you may blame yourself if you have taken unnecessary risks or pushed yourself too hard in the time leading up to the miscarriage. Try and avoid thinking in terms of "if only I hadn't...", which only results in even more distress.

Ectopic pregnancy occurs when the fertilized egg embeds itself and starts to grow somewhere outside the uterus (usually the fallopian tube, the canal that conducts the egg from the ovary to the uterus). It occurs in about 1 in 200 pregnancies, and you are at increased risk if you have had previous ectopic pregnancies, pelvic infections (PID) or gynaecological surgery. It usually manifests as intense, usually one-sided lower abdominal pain, followed by bleeding. The condition is life-threatening, so if you suffer severe, lower abdominal pain within the first 12 weeks of pregnancy, seek medical help urgently.

The bottom line is don't veer too far off the beaten track (or more pertinently, from medical assistance) in the first few weeks of pregnancy, as the chances of a problem arising that will require medical attention are higher during

Drugs in pregnancy

It's best to avoid taking any **drugs** in pregnancy if possible. Below is a list of medications mentioned elsewhere in this book, showing which are safe in pregnancy and which are not.

Safe in pregnancy:
+ Chloroquine
+ Proguanil
  (provided you take it with a folic acid supplement)
+ Amoxycillin
+ Erythromycin
+ Paracetamol
+ Some antihistamines (read the label closely and bow to the manufacturer's advice during pregnancy)

Avoid in pregnancy:
+ Mefloquine (Lariam)*
+ Doxycycline
+ Ciprofloxacin

this period. Consider the expense and expertise of the medical services that are going to be available to you as well as the potential risks of a blood transfusion should it be required. Always carry a letter from your doctor or (preferably) a copy of your pregnancy records.

Prematurity, or early labour, occurs much less often than the problems associated with early pregnancy but even so, no airline will let you fly if you're more than 36 weeks. As pregnancy proceeds, the frequency of medical monitoring increases, so stay close to your hospital or doctor's surgery in the final weeks.

✚ Trimethoprim (theoretical risk in the first 12 weeks)

✚ Co-amoxiclav

✚ Ibuprofen (and the other NSAIDs)

✚ Acetazolamide

✚ Nifedipine

✚ Diazepam

✚ Iodine preparations for water purification

The manufacturer advises avoidance of pregnancy when taking mefloquine and for 3 months after treatment, although studies have shown no harmful effects in humans. If travel to a chloroquine-resistant malarial area cannot be avoided, it may be an option in the later stages of pregnancy but seek expert advice.

If you're taking a potentially hazardous medication and find that you're unexpectedly pregnant, seek medical advice immediately.

Insect repellents containing DEET (see p.260) can be used in pregnancy, although those of weaker concentration are recommended.

Specific health risks in pregnancy

Diet is an area of concern in any pregnancy but while travelling you are less in control over what you eat and its origins. It's easy to become paranoid and either not eat anything or so restrict your diet to "safe" foods (dry biscuits, bananas and the like) that the nutritional value is compromised. As at home, aim to eat a balanced diet, avoiding unpasteurized milk and cheese, pate, raw eggs, liver and any undercooked meat. In countries where you have concerns about basic hygiene or the water purity, steer clear of fruit or vegetables that cannot be peeled.

Listeriosis, which can result in damage to the growing fetus and even still birth, is caused by the bacteria *listeria monocytogenes*, high levels of which are found in some foods. Foods to be avoided include cheese (especially camembert, brie and blue-veined varieties), pate, and ready-cooked and chilled meals unless reheated until piping hot. Sheep can carry listeria so avoid direct contact (during lambing in particular) while pregnant.

Toxoplasmosis causes a mild flu-like illness in pregnant women but can lead to significant abnormalities in the newborn. The bacteria causing toxoplasmosis can be found in raw meat, goats' milk and cat faeces. Avoid eating undercooked meat, unpasteurized goats' milk or cheese and vegetables that have not been adequately cleaned. Like listeriosis, sheep can carry toxoplasmosis therefore close contact should be avoided.

Malaria can be very dangerous in pregnancy, both to mother and baby, and unless your trip is vital, you should avoid travelling to high-risk areas. If there is no option but to travel to a malarial area, then effective prophylaxis is important: chloroquine and proguanil can be taken without concern (although take 5mg daily of folic acid in conjunction with proguanil). Mefloquine, however, must only be used where other options have been exhausted and then only after careful consideration and expert advice.

Diarrhoea presents no significant increased risk in pregnancy although it is important to avoid dehydration (see p.194). Ciprofloxacin, used in some instances to treat diarrhoea, must be avoided in pregnancy. Always remember to wipe yourself from front to back to avoid spreading infection to the vagina and urinary tract.

Advice for pregnant travellers

✚ travel light
✚ allow extra time in transit (don't rush)
✚ allow for increased frequency of toilet stops
✚ stay close to medical care

Constipation is a fairly common problem in pregnancy. Some laxatives (eg lactulose) are safe to use if you're pregnant (read box labels closely), but it's best to treat the problem by increasing your fibre and fluid intake.

Thrush is common during pregnancy, especially in hot climates. Wear loose-fitting clothes and if symptoms occur, use anti-fungal creams or pessaries (both are safe in pregnancy).

Pregnancy alone carries a five-fold increase in the risk of **DVT** (see p.30) and it is important to bear this in mind before you expose yourself to other risk factors like long periods of limited mobility (flying, bus or rail travel), altitude and dehydration.

Pregnancy and leisure pursuits

Think carefully before you partake in any vigorous exercise or activity if you're pregnant. Travelling to high **altitudes** will increase the risk of DVT, put more stress on the cardiovascular system and often remove you from quick access to medical care. **Scuba diving** can cause decompression sickness in the fetus and therefore should be avoided. **Snow skiing** accidents are often caused by other people, so regardless of your own competence as a skier, there is always a risk of trauma which could be damaging to the fetus. **Hot tubs and saunas** should be avoided in early pregnancy because they can raise your core temperature, which

PREGNANCY AND LEISURE PURSUITS

Drugs to avoid when breast-feeding

+ Alcohol (large amounts may affect the baby and reduce their milk consumption)

+ Antihistamines (these penetrate milk but are not known to be harmful, although some manufacturers advise avoidance)

+ Aspirin

+ Diazepam and temazepam

+ Ciprofloxacin

+ Combined oral contraceptive pill

+ Oral steroids (eg dexamethsone)

+ Ibuprofen (high doses or prolonged course)

+ Mefloquine (Lariam) – may be harmless but not enough data yet.

+ Metoclopramide

+ Metronidazole

+ Propranolol (high doses)

+ Senna

+ Tetracycline antibiotics (eg doxycycline)

+ Vitamins A and D (high doses)

increases the risk of birth defects. **Jacuzzis** and **spas** should be viewed with equal caution because of the risk of acquiring infection.

Breast-feeding

In general breast-feeding is convenient, safe and hygienic when you're travelling. Make sure that you keep well hydrated by drinking plenty, or your milk flow might be disturbed. Also remember that some drugs penetrate breast milk and are therefore best avoided.

The active traveller

Happiness for some is two weeks' grilling themselves on the beach, but for others, activity holidays hold greater appeal. If your trip involves any kind of physical activity, make sure that you are in good physical shape and up to the job before you go. While a high level of fitness is rarely required, a little forward thinking and gentle training will help you make the most of your holiday.

Concentrate on the parts of your body that will see the most action – **snow skiing** puts particular strain on the knees and should not be undertaken if you have weak or injured knee ligaments. Snow skiing also carries the inherent environmental risks associated with altitude (see below and p.150) and cold (see p.172). Avalanches are a particular hazard if you ski off-piste. Remember too that the adverse effects of the sun (p.364) are multiplied by altitude and by glare of the snow, so protect your skin with high-factor sunscreen, your lips with lip balm and your eyes with good-quality sunglasses.

Climbing and **hill walking** are hard on the knees and ankles and may involve ascent to high altitudes, which in itself can cause significant health problems (see p.150). Other common health issues include gastrointestinal upsets (p.226), sun exposure (p.364), muscle and ligament sprains (p.415) and backache (p.159). Dry mountain air may also cause nosebleeds (p.421). Remember that you may be a long way from medical help with very limited options for rapid evacuation. Always carry the necessary, good-quality equipment to suit your requirements (including a medical kit), and always be wary of environmental dangers such as landslides and avalanches.

Seawater sports expose you to a host of saltwater hazards (see p.328), while the glare of the sun on the water makes a high-factor (water-resistant) sunscreen essential (see p.364).

Freshwater sports like canoeing or whitewater rafting carry the risk of infections from the water itself including all of the water-borne diseases (see p.43), leptospirosis (p.275) and schistosomiasis (p.336).

Strong currents can present a significant hazard when swimming in the sea or in fresh water. Remember that your buoyancy is less in fresh water so you might find swimming harder work.

Scuba diving

Scuba diving can be physically strenuous and requires moderate degrees of respiratory and cardiovascular fitness, and any disease or illness which affects your heart or lungs may therefore put you at risk when diving. Do not dive if you suffer from angina, abnormal heart rhythms, severe asthma, chronic lung disease or if you have had a punctured lung in the past. If you are epileptic, diabetic, suffer from sickle cell disease, or simply have doubts about your general level of fitness, seek expert advice. If you suffer from panic attacks, anxiety or claustrophobia, then scuba diving is not for you. A rapid ascent during a panic attack underwater is very dangerous.

Because of the pressure changes that take place when you dive, air pockets in the body contract on your way down and expand on surfacing. This can lead to "**squeeze**", a painful condition caused by the sinuses and nasal air passages being blocked and can result in damage to the eardrums. Don't dive if you have a cold or severe nasal congestion. Always breathe in a steady, measured rhythm into your scuba gear. Never hold your breath as you surface because the expansion of the gas in your lungs will cause a pneumothorax, which can be life-threatening.

Decompression sickness ("**the bends**" or "**the staggers**") is caused by surfacing too rapidly after diving at depth for prolonged or repeated periods. Bubbles of gases such as nitrogen and helium lodge in the tissues, causing a variety of symptoms which can occur minutes – or hours – after a dive. Mild decompression sickness may cause skin mottling, itching, and joint pains. More serious effects include neurological impairment (blindness, partial paralysis and abnormal sensation), breathing difficulties and chest pain. Oxygen should be given as an emergency treatment, although most cases will require specialist treatment in a decompression chamber. Avoid decompression sickness by adhering strictly to **diving decompression tables**. The same tables enable you to calculate when it's safe to fly after scuba diving.

The returning traveller

Unless you are suffering suspicious symptoms, there is little value in seeing your doctor routinely on returning from a trip. Many travel-related illnesses have long periods of incubation and may not become apparent for weeks or even months after you return.

View any subsequent illness with high suspicion, however. Of particular significance are **diarrhoea**, **fever**, **jaun-**

" My Right Foot **"**

It was my first backpacking holiday as such – a fantastic three weeks in Malaysia. From Kuala Lumpur to Taman Negara Rainforest, on to the East Coast (Mersing), nine days on Tioman Island and finishing with a visit to Singapore. For a first-timer I was quite proud of myself – no lost or stolen gear and no sickness to report. Until, that is, I got home...

A few days before I left Tioman I noticed a small hard lump underneath the big toe of my right foot. Being a novice to the tropics and ignorant of the possible dangers, I put it down to excessive use of unfamiliar footwear (flip flops are not big in Bristol). Besides, it didn't hurt and it certainly wasn't going to spoil my holiday.

One night, two or three weeks after my return, I lay awake for several uncomfortable hours, constantly scratching the aforementioned lump. By the morning I awoke to find a small inflammation, almost like an infected vein, had developed across the top of my foot. My work colleagues displayed a deflating mixture of disinterest and unhelpfulness, so I visited my local chemist, explained the situation and walked away with some athlete's foot ointment (ME, an athlete?).

For the next few days I watched as this inflammation spread, now accompanied by a distinct tingling feeling. With the ointment making no impression I decided that my only course of action was to visit my doctor. Again, my first visit proved fruitless and I walked away with a second ointment

dice, **weight loss** and **rashes**. There are between one and two thousand cases of malaria imported into the UK each year. Anyone who suffers a fever after returning from a malarial area should be tested for the disease.

If you are treated medically **abroad**, ensure that you

(containing exactly the same drug as the earlier, and considerably cheaper, chemist's version).

My unease persisted so I sought the advice of a medically qualified friend who claimed to have some knowledge of tropical illnesses. He felt that I may have contracted something more serious and suggested another visit to my own doctor. This time I mentioned that I had recently returned from Malaysia (by now some six weeks ago) and he seemed slightly more interested in my concerns (by now growing at a serious rate).

A call to the local infectious diseases clinic proved fruitless (the two doctors there were both off sick!) and it took another four days before a doctor in Birmingham diagnosed hookworm infestation over the phone. I was then whisked back into the surgery, where my foot was duly photographed for a medical journal and I was asked to come back later that evening so that I could be paraded around a room of medical students.

Eventually I was given the correct prescription and within three days the worm had died. By that time it had been moving around inside my foot for nearly three weeks and had caused me considerable angst and discomfort. I was left with a feeling of betrayal by the attitudes of my so-called "carers" at home and still maintain a healthy distrust of medical opinion. Ironically, my original speculation about over-using my flip flops turned out to be the exact opposite of the truth!

Tom Edwards, Bristol, UK

obtain written details (preferably in your own language) of the diagnosis and treatment received so that you can pass these on to your home doctor. You may also need to keep copies (especially receipts) for insurance purposes.

It can be one thing recognizing the possibility of imported infection yourself, but quite another convincing your **doctor**. Exotic illnesses are unlikely to be prominent in the thoughts of many family doctors unless you put them there. Always tell your doctor where you have been, how long you were away, when you returned and what risks you may have subjected yourself to. Also tell your doctor directly if you have a particular concern about a specific disease.

If you are a **blood donor**, you must inform the transfusion service that you recently travelled abroad and whether or not you received any medical treatment while away.

Aspirin. Photo © Randy Faris/Corbis

Making a diagnosis

You're in a foreign place and you don't feel well. In fact you feel awful. Maybe it was the satay you bought off the street yesterday, the mosquito you were bitten by a month ago or the fellow traveller you had a fling with one drunken, abandoned tropical evening. You know how to say "two beers please", but you don't know the words for "doctor" or "hospital", let alone "is your equipment sterile?" Your guidebook tells you just enough to make you seriously paranoid and your fellow travellers offer advice along the lines of "Maybe it's…. You can die from that!"

Away from the familiarities of home, detached from the people who would normally care for you and your customary means of summoning medical help, the feeling of isolation can be devastating. To top it off you now have to choose between attempting self-diagnosis and treatment, cutting your losses and bolting for home, or battling it out with potentially expensive, and perhaps poorly equipped, local medical help.

This book is designed to prepare you for the eventuality of being ill abroad by providing an A to Z of diseases, with information on their avoidance and treatment as well as the areas of the world where they pose the greatest risk. However, there is no point reading it cover to cover and being conversant with every germ in the book if you don't know what to do when you are ill on a **practical level**. Cutting through all of the other anxieties that will go through your head, what you really need to know is:

+ Is my life in danger?
+ What can I do about it?
+ Do I need medical help now?

When to wait and when to seek urgent help

Time is both a good assessment tool and, in the majority of cases, a healer. In terms of infectious disease, however, there are arguably only 2 illnesses that will not wait: meningitis and falciparum malaria. If either of these is suspected, put the book down and get help immediately. This is not to say that many of the other infectious diseases are not dangerous or even life-threatening, but there are relatively few that will lead to serious problems within the first 48 hours.

Initial assessment

Proper assessment of an illness involves extensive training and experience, and while a book can never replace a doctor, it can help you to follow a logical train of thought with respect to your symptoms and make a more informed decision about what further help or treatment may be necessary.

The first step is to look at the **risks** to which you have been exposed. Keep it simple, and don't go chasing the minutiae until you have excluded the most likely cause.

Consider first **where** you have travelled and the possible diseases to which you may have been vulnerable as a consequence. Reading through Part 3 will give you an idea of the geographical distribution of the various diseases. Next, consider whether you may have exposed yourself to added risk through your **accommodation** (eg no mosquito nets) or **activities** (eg whitewater rafting or swimming in polluted water).

Food- and water-borne illnesses are extremely common, especially if you've been slack in observing basic precautions. Most travellers to hot countries suffer **insect bites**, so if you are feverish, always consider the possibility of malaria as well as other common insect-borne diseases like dengue or yellow fever. Ask yourself if you did all you could to avoid illness in terms of **immunizations** and the adequacy of your **malaria prophylaxis**.

You may be more vulnerable to, or have put yourself at increased risk from, diseases as a result of other **high-risk activities.** Contact with **animals**, walking **barefoot** in the tropics, contact with **fresh water** in areas where there is schistosomiasis, and **sex** with a new partner would all fall into this category.

Some **pre-existing illnesses** will increase your disease susceptibility. Being HIV-positive or diabetic, for instance, increases your chances of contracting infections and often results in a more severe illness. The elderly and the very young may have increased susceptibility to some illnesses.

It's worth remembering that a "disease" is simply a specific group of **symptoms** arising from a particular cause. Looking at your symptoms, ask yourself if there is an obvious likely cause. This is a simple enough question in principle but not always easy to answer. Consider the nature, severity, timing and associations of your symptoms and any familiarity they may have with previous illness.

The next stage in assessing an illness is to perform an **examination** in order to confirm or deny your working diagnosis. Examining yourself may not be practical, so enlist sensible help if necessary. Obviously training and experience are big factors here but there are a few basics that might help the novice.

SKIN

You can tell quite a lot by looking at someone's skin. Rashes are common, but it's very difficult to describe in words what a rash looks like. Itchy rashes usually mean a viral or fungal infection, or an allergy. Localized red, painful, swollen, warm areas usually mean a bacterial infection. The most important thing to exclude is a **purpuric** or **petechial** rash which does not pale on pressure (see the glass test, p.297). Its presence means that there has been bleeding under the skin, a sign of septicaemia (eg meningitis), a viral haemorrhagic fever (eg yellow fever) or some rickettsial infections (the "spotted fevers"), all of which are serious and require urgent attention.

Jaundice is a common finding in a number of diseases such as malaria or hepatitis. The yellowing of the skin is due to a build-up of **bilirubin** in the blood, a chemical secreted by the liver to aid the digestion of fats in the gut. Jaundice is usually fairly obvious in Caucasians but less easy to see in dark-skinned people. If in doubt, look at the whites of the eyes in natural light.

DEHYDRATION

Dehydration is a common, potentially serious, yet easily resolvable problem following diarrhoea and vomiting or during high fever. Thirst is the obvious symptom. Your mouth and tongue may be dry, your skin may lose its suppleness and you may have a headache. Your urine output will be reduced and the urine itself will be dark and strong-smelling. Severe dehydration may result in a complete cessation in urine output, drowsiness or loss of consciousness (all of which require urgent medical input).

TEMPERATURE

High temperature, or **pyrexia**, is most commonly associated with infection but may also be caused by severe sunstroke. Having an even slightly raised temperature can make you feel unwell, while high pyrexia causes headache, nausea, skin flushing and intense sweating accompanied by the feeling of being cold.

To assess degree of temperature, place a thermometer under the tongue and hold it there for 3 minutes. Normal body core temperature is 37°C or 98°F. Generally speaking, although you may feel unwell, temperatures below 39°C or 102°F are unlikely to be caused by significant illness, but temperatures higher than this need to be taken more seriously. Watch for patterns or recurring fevers (eg malaria, dengue fever).

In a malarial area (or after having travelled through a malarial area), treat any fever above 39°C as malaria until proved otherwise.

PAIN

The presence, degree and whereabouts of pain are important diagnostic signs. **Headache** is often pretty non-specific, being associated with many different illnesses from a simple hangover to something a lot more serious (see p.237). If headache is severe and accompanied by high fever, neck stiffness and photophobia, seek urgent medical help in order to exclude meningitis. Headache is particularly common in cases of fever, dehydration and heat exhaustion, but is most often simply tension-related.

Chest pain in the young is almost always caused by muscular or joint sprains, however **heart attacks** are still the commonest cause of death at home or abroad in people over 50. Cardiac pain tends to be worse on exertion, central, dull (crushing) and often spreads to the neck, back or down the arm. It is frequently accompanied by shortness of breath or nausea. If suspected, seek urgent medical help. Inflammation of the lining of the lungs (**pleurisy**) often follows a chest infection and tends to be sharp and worse on cough or breathing in deeply.

Abdominal pain is common yet rarely clear cut because of the vast number of potential causes. It is considered in more detail on p.136.

URINE

Examination of the urine by the naked eye is usually fairly fruitless. If it is dark but normal coloured, you are likely to be dehydrated. If there is blood in the urine consider a urinary tract infection (p.391) or schistosomiasis (p.337). If it's painful to pass urine or you have to go very often, urinary tract infection or sexually transmitted disease (p.344) are the likely candidates.

STOOLS

Diarrhoea and constipation are both extremely common problems for the traveller and can be symptomatic merely of the body's readjustment to time zone changes, or alterations in diet and water quality. Look for blood or mucous in the diarrhoea and for signs of worm infestation (sometimes fragments of the worm are visible in the stool). Pale yellowish stools may be a sign of liver inflammation, while pale stools of a whitish hue may be caused by constipation. Dark, black, tarry stools may be a sign of bleeding from stomach inflammation or a stomach ulcer. Flatus of an "eggy" nature is considered to be associated with giardiasis, but this is obviously very subjective and so somewhat unreliable.

48 hours

This is a fairly arbitrary timescale but, unless you think that you might have meningitis or falciparum malaria, **48 hours** is not an unreasonable period to rest, treat your symptoms and drink plenty of fluids. During this time many illnesses will settle spontaneously, while in others symptom patterns may become clearer. Don't be dogmatic about clock-watching, however, and if your condition is deteriorating rather than improving, seek help earlier.

If after 48 hours your condition has worsened, seek medical help. If there is no improvement, be guided by the severity of your symptoms and whether you have a hunch about the likely cause. Self-treatment may be a possibility but is best avoided unless you have a good idea of the diagnosis. It is at this point that you might consider requesting **laboratory tests** to confirm or deny your suspicions. In cases of high fever, for instance, a single blood test can confirm the presence or absence of malaria. This is often most easily done by visiting a doctor or a clinic, but in some countries you can go directly to a laboratory and ask for a specific test. It may save you time and money (a negative test is just as important as a positive).

Abdominal pain

Diagnosis of **abdominal pain** is not an exact science, and it's therefore only possible to offer some general guidelines here. If you suspect anything serious, seek medical attention immediately.

Start by asking yourself the following questions:

+ Does the pain spread anywhere else (to your back, your shoulder, down your legs, etc)?
+ What is the nature of the pain (constant or intermittent, dull, burning, crampy, stabbing, etc)?
+ Is there anything that makes the pain better or worse (lying still, bending double, opening your bowels, vomiting, etc)?
+ Do you have any other symptoms, such as fever, vomiting, diarrhoea or pain when passing urine?

Some gentle prodding may reveal masses or areas of particular tenderness, which can help to identify the specific organs involved.

Appendicitis

In theory, it should be a cinch to diagnose **appendicitis**, but in practice it's much more of a grey area, mainly because the symptoms can vary and mimic many other, less severe conditions.

It is caused by an inflammation of the appendix, a finger-like, vestigial pouch at the junction of the large and small bowel. Little is known about what triggers it to become inflamed, but untreated it can lead to **peritonitis**, a life-threatening inflammation of the abdominal lining.

Early **symptoms** are usually pain and recurrent vomiting. Initially the pain may vary in intensity but often starts centrally, migrating after a few hours to a more localized area in the right lower side of the abdomen when it usually becomes severe and unremitting. You'll feel most comfortable when lying still. Coughing and vomiting are particularly painful. You may also have a fever and, less commonly, diarrhoea. Your abdomen may be tender to even the lightest touch and exhibits a phenomenon known as **guarding**, an involuntary tensing on mild probing.

If you suspect appendicitis (or peritonitis), view it as an emergency and seek urgent medical help. Surgery to remove the appendix is the only treatment.

Stomach pain

Pain originating from the **stomach** tends to be central and just below the ribcage. It may be burning, sharp or aching in nature and is usually accompanied by nausea, vomiting and loss of appetite. The pain tends to be constant although it can vary depending on whether the stomach is full or empty. Acid can escape from the stomach up into the gullet causing an unpleasant burning sensation at the back of the throat (so-called **reflux**) which is usually worse after meals and at night. Stomach pains are often aggravated by spicy food and alcohol. The common causes of stomach pain are gastroenteritis, gastritis (inflamed stomach lining) and ulcers.

Large bowel (colic)

Pain originating from the **large bowel**, or colon – called "**colic**" – can be felt anywhere over the abdomen and tends to be cramp-like and gripey in nature. It's usually intermit-

❝Around the world with appendicitis❞

Colombia is perhaps not the best place in the world to go down with appendicitis. Fortunately, at the time, I was indirectly an employee of the United States Information Agency, the public-relations-and-propaganda arm of the State Department – and this status made a huge difference in how I fared.

Having stored all my worldly goods and given up my accommodation, I was loath to admit to my sister taking me to San Francisco airport that I was feeling rather worse than could be accounted for by first-time international travel jitters. As I learned later, I had typical onset symptoms: queasiness, pain around the navel drifting subsequently to the lower right abdomen.

By the time I got to Miami for my connecting flight, I desperately needed to lie down (temporary relief at best). I was incapable of appreciating the psychedelic interior decor of the long-defunct Aero Condor aircraft, nor the matching sunrise over the Caribbean. I barely pecked at the breakfast more sumptuous than any served me in the air since: massive portions of eggs, sausages and tropical fruit.

After ten hours in the air (plus the time zone change), I was distinctly green at the gills on arrival in Bogota; my first words to the embassy official who had come to greet me were "I'm pretty sick", news he didn't exactly appreciate. I think, until I was actually in hospital, he reckoned I was a malingerer.

The driver shuttling me across town to a clinic opined: Es la altura ("It's the altitude" – Bogotá is nearly 8000 feet up). Curled up in the back, in my painfully acquired university Spanish I weakly retorted that I'd lived at this altitude for two months fairly recently and it was not the altitude.

In the consulting room the doctor had me supine, on the table, while he donned gloves, stuck a finger up my rectum, and turned hard left (a classic diagnostic technique). As he peeled me off the ceiling and waited for my howls of agony to subside, he confirmed that it was not the altitude.

I was in a posh hospital (the embassy's designated care facility) almost instantly, in a private room, where an orderly whose vocabulary didn't include "soap" and "warm water", in either Spanish or English, shaved the necessary (and various unnecessary) regions with sadistic glee and a blunt razor. The surgeon appeared, a jolly, fluent-English-speaking, Harvard-educated chap named Rafael Samper – quite possibly, reflecting in hindsight, a relative of the last Colombian president but one. I was transferred onto a gurney and down the hall to the theatre.

I dreamed I was a koi in a pond under the moonlight; the moon became the light fixtures of the corridor as I came to on the return journey, and realized that I had traded one sort of pain for another. I was given the choice of two analgesics: oral tablets which didn't do much, and a stronger injection which was the only thing that would permit sleep through the night for the next four days. Dr Samper appeared next day, grinning and brandishing my appendix, double the normal size, in formaldehyde.

I was a very lucky boy; rupture had not been far off. Ironically, by flying 6000-plus miles in agony to a Third World country, I had secured far better medical care than if I had remained enrolled at university and been seen to at the student hospital.

Marc Dubin, London

tent, but can be severe, and often makes you double-up. It can spread to the lower back. Common causes of large bowel pain include wind, constipation, diarrhoea (indicative of a vast range of illnesses), gastroenteritis and irritable bowel syndrome.

Liver pain

Liver pain is characterized by a dull ache in the upper right area of the abdomen. It can be sharp, intermittent and radiate into the back and sometimes the shoulder. Nausea and loss of appetite are common. The stools can turn pale, the urine dark, and your skin may become jaundiced. The symptoms are often exacerbated by eating fatty foods or drinking alcohol. Some common causes of liver pain include gall stones, hepatitis and malaria.

Bladder or kidney pain

Originating in the central, lower abdomen, **bladder pain** tends to be dull and constant. It's often accompanied by the need to urinate frequently and a feeling of inadequate emptying, localized pain on passing urine, a weak stream, which is occasionally bloody or foul-smelling.

Pains from the **kidneys** occur in the small of the back and are usually one-sided. Kidney **infections** are usually preceded by the bladder symptoms above. Kidney **stones**, often marked by excruciating pain, can be caused by dehydration, especially if you have suffered from them in the past. You might see blood in the urine and feel grit when you are passing urine.

Common **causes** of bladder or kidney pain are cystitis, kidney infections and kidney stones, sexually transmitted infections and schistosomiasis.

Pelvic pain (women)

Benign **ovarian cysts** are a common problem and tend to cause most pain in the middle of your cycle when you're ovulating. Although usually short-lived, the pain can be extreme and may be partially relieved by curling up into the fetal position. Pain relief, such as paracetamol or ibuprofen, is the best treatment. **Uterine pain** – painful periods or premenstrual pains – usually respond well to NSAIDs. If you know this might be a problem for you, consider the combined oral contraceptive pill which often reduces the severity and menstrual blood loss. **Bladder infection**, or **cystitis**, frequently causes central, lower abdominal discomfort but is usually accompanied by other symptoms. Pain from **thrush** is uncommon.

▷▷ See also Thrush, p.374; Urinary tract infections, p.391; and Women travellers, p.109.

PELVIC INFLAMMATORY DISEASE

Pelvic inflammatory disease (PID) is caused by bacterial infection within the pelvic cavity (usually the uterus and fallopian tubes) and is often linked to sexually transmitted infections such as chlamydia or gonorrhoea. The most common symptom is a constant, dull but sometimes severe, pelvic pain which may spread to the back. The discomfort may be partially relieved by lying in the fetal postion. Vaginal discharge (often bloody) and fever are common accompaniments. Short-term complications of PID include **septicaemia** and the formation of a **pelvic abscess**, while there's a long-term risk of internal scarring increasing the risk of **infertility** and **ectopic pregnancy**. If PID is suspected, seek medical help to establish the exact identity of the offending organism. **Treatment** is centred around bedrest, adequate fluid intake and a 1- to 2-week course of antibiotics (doxycycline together with metronidazole is a common combination). Intravenous antibiotics may be needed.

Rarer causes of abdominal pain

There are a multitude of rarer causes of abdominal pain, many of which you are just as likely to experience at home as abroad, but a few are worth mentioning briefly here.

The chickenpox virus causes **shingles**, which can occur at any age but is more common and severe in the elderly. The pain can be quite severe and is often described as "burning". The accompanying rash occurs as a crop of blisters which is always localized and one-sided. You cannot catch shingles from someone who has shingles but you can catch chickenpox from shingles unless you have already had it (most people catch chickenpox in childhood) and therefore have natural immunity.

Pancreatitis, or inflammation of the pancreas, is usually caused by gallstones or severe alcohol abuse, although a rarer cause is scorpion envenomation. The pain is very intense, central and radiating to the back, and is usually accompanied by vomiting and shock. Pancreatitis is life-threatening and if suspected you should get medical help urgently.

Aortic aneurysm is a weakening, leading to expansion, of the main artery leading away from the heart and is very rare in anyone under 50. Although usually insidious in onset, acute cases may have pain that is severe and central, and often a pulsing mass can be felt or visualized in the centre of the abdomen. If suspected, get medical help at once.

Musculoskeletal abdominal pain is not uncommon after exercise and can be difficult to differentiate from potentially more serious causes. There should be no bowel disturbance, vomiting or fever and the pain should respond well to simple pain relief such as paracetamol.

ABDOMINAL PAIN

Abortus fever

▷▷See Brucellosis, p.167.

Acute mountain sickness

▷▷See Altitude sickness, p.150.

African trypanosomiasis

(Sleeping sickness)

African trypanosomiasis occurs throughout sub-Saharan Africa: in West and Central Africa where it is known as **Gambian trypanosomiasis** and in East Africa where it is known as **Rhodesian or East African trypanosomiasis**. There has been a particular preponderance of the disease in recent years in Uganda, the United Republic of Tanzania, Mozambique, Angola, the Democratic Republic of Congo (Zaire) and Sudan. It is caused by a parasite transmitted between humans (or from animals to humans) by the daylight-biting **tsetse fly**, which proliferates in the savannah and around fresh water. The more popular name for the disease, **sleeping sickness**, is derived from the effects on the central nervous system caused by the parasite.

Up to 20,000 cases of the disease are reported to the WHO each year, although as this is a disease that mainly affects rural areas, it's likely that the majority of cases go unreported. It's estimated that around 66 million people in sub-Saharan Africa are currently at risk from the parasite and the Rhodesian form may be a particular risk for tourists on safaris in East Africa. Epidemics among the indigenous populations have been linked to a sudden downturn in socio-economic conditions, for example after the onset of war or famine.

There is no vaccination against African trypanosomiasis and bite-avoidance is your only protection.

SYMPTOMS

The Rhodesian form of the disease tends to run a more rapid course than the Gambian, although the symptoms are broadly similar. The bite site may become painful and inflamed, resembling a **blind boil** ("papule"). First signs of illness occur after 3 weeks or so and include **rapid pulse rate**, **high fever**, **headache**, **weakness**, **joint pains** and **itching**. The liver, spleen and lymph glands (particularly in the neck) become enlarged, with the parasite weakening your body's immune system so that you become more susceptible to other infections. As the disease progresses, the parasite invades an increasing number of organs, with brain involvement in the final stages of disease leading to **behavioural changes**, **lethargy**, **frequent sleeping** and **apathy**. Untreated, the torpor increases to the point where the sufferer lapses into a coma.

DIAGNOSIS AND TREATMENT

Blood tests can detect the presence of the parasite or antibodies to the parasites, as can a biopsy of the inflamed lymph glands. A lumbar puncture may be necessary to determine whether the central nervous system has been affected.

If tests show you've got the disease, you'll need to be admitted to hospital for further treatment, usually with **intravenous drugs** such as suramin or melarsoprol (the choice depends on how advanced the disease is), the latter of which can have some unpleasant and even dangerous side effects. Cure cannot be assumed until 2 years after

AFRICAN TRYPANOSOMIASIS

treatment and there may be persisting neurological impairment.

AIDS

▷▷See HIV, p.247.

Alcohol

Alcohol is likely to figure at some point in most peoples' time abroad. Unfortunately the initial feel-good factor doesn't last, and alcohol is actually a depressant. It also reduces inhibitions and the ability to assess risks – even small quantities can impair the brain's higher thought functions.

Alcohol has no respect for sexual equality: it affects women more than men. This is because a higher percentage of a woman's body is fat, therefore containing less fluid than the male, so that for a given quantity of alcohol consumed, the blood alcohol concentration will be higher in a woman than in a man. From a health perspective, a man should not drink more than 4 **units** a day, a woman, not more than 3 (see box below).

Alcohol may quench a thirst in the short term, but it will increase your thirst later on – think how dry your mouth

One unit of alcohol

✚ a half pint of normal-strength beer or lager

✚ a small glass of wine (about 75ml – a bottle usually contains between 9 and 11 units)

✚ a single bar measure/shot of spirits (25ml)

feels the morning after you've overindulged. **Dehydration** of the brain is the source of your hangover, which will be much worse and the result of fewer alcohol units if you're already dehydrated, for example after heavy exercise, sun bathing or a bout of diarrhoea. Alcohol exacerbates the effects of jet lag and mountain sickness.

Consider what else besides alcohol is in your exotic beverage. **Home-brewed concoctions** will contain the local water, as will any ice cubes. Standards of hygiene in the brewing process may also be suspect. Local-made "fire waters" can contain methanol, which can cause headache, breathlessness, increased sensitivity to light and even blindness.

Remember, too, that alcohol doesn't interact well with some **drugs**, such as antihistamines or tranquillizers. Never mix alcohol and the antibiotic **metronidazole** – it can induce a severe, unpleasant reaction.

Hangover prevention and cure

If you don't want the fuzzy head, don't drink. If on the other hand you're set on having a heavy night, try to **eat** beforehand as food in the stomach will slow down the speed at which alcohol reaches your blood. Before going to bed, drink at least a pint of **water** (bottled if the water quality is suspect – this is the moment when many people forget) or other non-alcoholic fluid and again, try to eat something.

Next day, ibuprofen or paracetamol will take the edge off your **headache**. Rehydration solution or commercial hangover preparations will help to rectify the balance of chemicals in the blood. If **nausea** is particularly crippling, domperidome or metoclopramide (see p.62) usually work well.

66 Alternative treatment in Tobago 99

I rely on homeopathy at home, but an experience while I was in Tobago researching the Rough Guide proved its efficacy to me without doubt. After a couple of months haring from hotel to restaurant to plantation tour in the heat of the day – when everyone else was sensibly cooling off in the shade or cloistered in an air-conditioned office – my usually healthy system had been showing firm signs of rebellion. I'd succumbed to colds and niggly little ailments, all of which had been dealt with via the pouch of remedies that my homeopath and best friend had packed for me back in England.

It had poured from the minute I'd arrived in Speyside, a tiny fishing village in the island's remote southeastern tip. Though tap water in Tobago is normally safe to drink, the supply is easily contaminated away from larger towns, particularly after heavy rain, when the taps tend to produce a rather off-putting stream of tan liquid. So bottled water had been the order of the day. One night, though, after a power cut-induced bout of rum drinking, I woke in the early hours and downed a couple of glasses straight from the tap. The next morning, with the skies clear and the sun out in blistering force, I packed up, intending to check several hotels and

Made from "the nut that makes you vomit", **nux vomica** (1 30c tablet taken before you go to sleep; see p.80) is an ideal homeopathic remedy if you've got non-stop, empty retching after a night of overindulgence. If you are very restless or fretful about your hangover, chilly, weak and experiencing diarrhoea, try **arsenicum** **album**. **Bach** **Flower** **Remedy**

Ciprofloxacin★ is a powerful antibiotic that's particularly effective against the common bacterial causes of travellers' diarrhoea (salmonella, shigella and campylobacter), and can also treat chest and urinary tract infections. It's less commonly prescribed in the UK, however, because of its expense and increased incidence of side effects, which include nausea, vomiting, abdominal pain, diarrhoea, headache, dizziness, sleep disorders, itching and increased sensitivity to the sun. Tendon inflammation is an uncommon side effect, but if it occurs, discontinue the drug and rest your limb until the symptoms resolve. It may also impair the performance of skilled tasks and enhance the effects of alcohol. It should be avoided if possible in pregnancy, while breast-feeding, and by people with epilepsy, liver or kidney impairment. Like erythromycin, it can interact with a number of other drugs, so be sure to inform your doctor if you're taking anything else.

Adult course: 1–2 x 250mg tablets twice daily for 5–7 days.

Fusidic acid★ and **framycetin sulphate★** are antibiotic creams used to treat localized skin infections (impetigo, infected hair follicles, etc). Rarely, they can cause local redness, itching and swelling.

Adult dosage: apply 3 times daily for up to 5 days.

Chloramphenicol★, either eye drops or ointment, can be useful if you're prone to recurrent conjunctivitis and is generally well tolerated with minimal adverse effects.

▷▷See Eye problems, p.210.

Drops should be applied every 2hr until 48hrs after the eye has settled. Ointment should be applied to the inner surface of the lower eyelid 3–4 times a day for 5 days. If the problem persists, seek medical advice.

ANTIBIOTICS

Gentamycin★ drops are an effective treatment for outer ear infections (common in hot, tropical countries). **Gentisone HC** combines the antibiotic with a mild steroid to reduce inflammation. Occasional local skin reactions can occur.

Dosage: 2–3 drops applied 3–4 times daily for up to 14 days.

Antihistamines

The unsung heroes of the rucksack, **antihistamines** have multiple uses, are relatively cheap and are generally available **without a prescription**. They work by suppressing the body's allergic ("histamine") response and their range of action includes the relief of hay fever, skin rashes, itching, insect bites and motion sickness. Their principal side effect is drowsiness, so take care if you're driving or doing anything that requires co-ordination or concentration. Other side effects include headache, slowness of movement, difficulty passing urine, dry mouth, blurred vision, gastrointestinal disturbances (usually constipation) and occasional rashes. Antihistamines should be used with caution if you have epilepsy, prostatic problems, glaucoma and liver disease. They also interact with a variety of other drugs (alcohol among them) so be sure to read the pack instructions carefully. They should be avoided if you suffer from porphyria.

Chlorpheniramine is cheap and effective in treating allergies, itch and insect bites. It's relatively sedating compared to the newer antihistamines (eg loratadine, fexofenadine and mizolastine).

Adult dosage: 1 x 4mg tablet every 4–6hr to a maximum of 24mg over 24hr.

ANTIHISTAMINES

restaurants in the course of my journey back to the west coast. Assuming my queasy stomach and feeling of horror at the thought of breakfast could be put down to the rum, I made a start on the narrow, snaking road that winds along Tobago's south coast, every twist and turn being answered by a rolling, rising nausea inside. Stopping off at my first hotel, I only just managed to resist christening the toilet as I peeked into the bathroom; by the second, I made my excuses while the owner chattered on about the size of the pool, and headed for the bushes. Trying to maintain your composure when you're drenched in cold sweat and can think only of the next convenient place to barf uncontrollably didn't seem very feasible after that. Feeling painfully weak and confused from the vomiting and lack of food, combined with the mid-day heat, my journey back to the next hotel is a bit of a blur, though I do remember that it was punctuated by several increasingly unpleasant stops for roadside relief. When I finally arrived, I reached for a dose of arsenicum, the homeopathic remedy derived from arsenic; half an hour later, I was amazed to find that whatever nasty had been lurking in the Speyside water had lost its grip – I was even able to sip some tea, and was back on the road, none the worse for wear, by the following morning.

Polly Thomas, London

is always helpful if you need a little rescuing, while the **Crabapple** variety is especially good if you're feeling guilty about the night before – it removes not only the toxins but also the self-critical mind-set. The Chinese herbal remedy **Poh Chi** can also help relieve symptoms.

Allergies

Everyone has different susceptibilities to **allergens**, the substances that stimulate your body's defence mechanisms and trigger an allergic response. Some of the **signs** of an allergic reaction are itching, a skin rash and swelling, runny eyes and nose, sneezing, wheezing and cough.

Any **antihistamine** (eg chlorpheniramine or loratadine) will help to relieve the irritant symptoms (see pp.58–59). Topical antihistamine, calamine lotion or steroid creams can relieve skin itch and redness provided it's not widespread. Severe allergic reactions need medical input and perhaps a course of steroids.

If you've ever suffered a severe reaction to anything, and future avoidance cannot be guaranteed, see your doctor about carrying **injectable adrenaline** with you, which may save your life in anaphylaxis.

Common allergens

+ Pollen
+ House dust
+ Insect bites and stings
+ Drugs (eg penicillin)
+ Foods (eg nuts, dairy products, shellfish)
+ Chemicals (eg rubber, nickel or cobalt in jewellery, and miscellaneous in washing powders, deodorants)

Altitude sickness

(Acute mountain sickness, or AMS)

150 **Altitude sickness** is a serious and potentially life-

Anaphylaxis

Generally speaking, allergic reactions are usually mild and an irritation rather than a serious threat to health. Nevertheless, a thankfully rare but life-threatening reaction can occur known as anaphylaxis. Essentially the reaction of the body to the specific allergen is so strong that the airways swell to the point of becoming blocked and the blood pressure plummets. A dramatic and rapidly progressive event, the condition manifests as shortness of breath, wheeze, a bluish tinge around the lips, nausea, vomiting, diarrhoea and swelling of the tongue and face.

Anaphylaxis is an emergency of the first order. If you suspect it in a companion, do the following:

✚ Remain call and call for help.

✚ Lay the patient down with their head lower than the rest of their body to maintain blood flow to the brain.

✚ Ensure their airway is clear.

✚ If they've had severe allergic reactions in the past, they may be carrying injectable adrenaline. Don't delay – give it immediately.

✚ If they stop breathing, commence CPR (see p.411) until help arrives.

threatening illness which can affect anyone who normally lives at low altitude and ascends above 10–12,000 feet (roughly 3500 metres). Factors affecting the severity of symptoms include the altitude reached, your rate of ascent, and the degree of exertion and therefore level of fitness. If you have suffered previously from altitude sickness, you're more likely to experience it on subsequent expeditions.

Symptoms usually occur after about 6 hours but may be

latent for up to 36 hours. In cases of mild altitude sickness, you may experience headache, shortness of breath, malaise, weakness, loss of appetite, nausea, vomiting, rapid heartbeat and dizziness. Insomnia is also common. Increasingly severe symptoms – the result of an accumulation of fluid, and consequent swelling, of the brain and lungs – include an intense, constant headache, lassitude and confusion, difficulty breathing, coughing, frothy blood-stained sputum and a bluish tinge to the lips, nails and skin (known as cyanosis). Left untreated, severe cases can lapse into unconsciousness and die within hours.

To **minimize the risk** of altitude sickness:

✚ Don't attempt to climb above 3000m unless you're in good physical shape.

✚ Ascend slowly (no more than 300m a day at altitudes over 3000m). If possible, give yourself time to acclimatize at altitude.

✚ Stay hydrated by drinking at least 3 litres of non-alcoholic fluids a day.

✚ If mild symptoms develop, descend a little from the altitude you have reached and rest a day or two.

✚ Although offering no guarantees, drugs with a prophylactic effect against altitude sickness include acetazolamide (500mg nightly) or nifedipine (20mg 3 times a day); (see p.68).

✚ Remember that temporary relief of symptoms is not a green light to restart ascent – take time out for your body to acclimatize.

Don't dawdle at the onset of progressive or severe symptoms – prompt and rapid descent is the only effective what **activities** are ill advised. Remember that by doing them, it may not be just yourself you are subjecting to risk. Scuba diving and rock climbing are definitely out, while other activities must be viewed in the context of fit frequency and severity. Water sports can be safe provided someone who is aware of your epilepsy accompanies you. Treat horse riding and cycling with the same caution, and always wear protective headgear. There is no international consensus regarding **driving** restrictions for people with epilepsy: generally a licence may be granted after a fit-free period of 2 years but your travel insurer may impose further restrictions.

As an epileptic, you're likely to pay a heavy premium for your travel **health insurance**. Rates will vary and it is important to shop around. Preferable rates are often available through your national epilepsy association.

Most of the travel **immunizations** available are perfectly safe for epileptics, although seek expert advice about anti-malarials (chloroquine and mefloquine are not recommended). The influenza vaccination affects the metabolism of phenytoin. On p.90 is a list of drugs relevant to the traveller which may interact with anti-epileptic medication.

Medications

Although flying itself should not increase your risk of fits, disturbed sleep and taking your medications irregularly can. Try and keep to "home time" when taking your medications, but if dose times need to be adjusted, do so gradually. Carry spare medication in your hand luggage, and write down clearly and store in a safe place the name of your medication (the precise preparation – this is one instance where the trade name can be important), the strength of dose you take and its regularity in case you need to replace it while you're away. It

MEDICATIONS

may not always be possible to obtain the drug you take, so if you are travelling to countries where this may be the case, carry plentiful supplies or have a reliable contingency plan for obtaining medications from home. Some drug export companies can arrange to send supplies abroad for you (contact your national epilepsy association).

Drugs relevant to the traveller that may interact with anti-epileptic medication:

✚ **Carbamazepine***
Alcohol
Co-proxamol
Doxycycline
Erythromycin
Chloroquine
Mefloquine
Oral contraceptive pill

✚ **Phenytoin***
Aspirin (and possibly other anti-inflammatories)
Antacids
Metronidazole
Trimethoprim
Doxycycline
Ciprofloxacin
Fansidar (sometimes used in the treatment of
    falciparum malaria)
Maloprim (occasionally used for malaria
    prophylaxis)
Oral contraceptive pill

MEDICATIONS

treatment, although drugs dexamethasone, frusemide and nifedipine may buy some time (see p.68). Oxygen should be given if available.

If you fly into a higher altitude destination to which you're not acclimatized, it's not uncommon to experience some of the milder symptoms mentioned above. Don't attempt to ascend further or do anything strenuous for at least 2 days and resist the temptation to drink alcohol as this can exacerbate the symptoms. If your condition deteriorates, seek medical help without delay.

A useful homeopathic remedy to treat the classic symptoms of breathlessness, palpitations, exhaustion and insomnia associated with altitude sickness is **Coca** (30c), taken once a day. If symptoms are severe, descend at once and take the remedy 3 or 4 times a day thereafter.

▷▷See also Hill-walking and Climbing, p.121.

American trypanosomiasis

(Chagas' disease)

American trypanosomiasis, also known as Chagas' disease after the Brazilian physician who discovered it, occurs in South and Central America from Mexico in the north to Argentina and Chile in the south, although there have been reports of the disease as far north as Texas and even Virginia in the USA. It's estimated that around 20 million people worldwide are infected, resulting in 50,000 deaths each year.

Chagas' disease is caused by a protozoa that is spread from infected vertebrates by **reduviid bugs** ("assassin bugs" or "kissing bugs"). Blood sucked from the infected host contains the protozoa, which multiplies in the bug's gut and is then defecated onto the skin when the bug feeds again. The protozoa can only penetrate broken skin. While transmission via insects is by far the most common method of disease spread, the infection can also be acquired via blood transfusion and from mother to child at birth or through breast-feeding.

There is no vaccination available so the best ways to avoid contracting the disease include staying away from the adobe huts whose wall cracks and roofs are a habitat favoured by the bugs, and heeding the standard advice on avoiding insect bites (see p.259).

SYMPTOMS

Localized **swelling** around the site of the bite (and perhaps around the eyes) and **fever** usually occur within the first 10 days. An **itchy rash** and swelling of the lymph glands, liver and spleen may also occur in the early stages. The heart, brain and intestinal tract may be affected constituting potentially serious, even fatal, complications. A delayed chronic form of the illness occurring months or even years after the original infection may affect the heart, brain and gut, again with potentially fatal consequences.

DIAGNOSIS AND TREATMENT

A **blood test** will determine whether or not you've got the disease. A few **drugs** have been shown to be effective in treating the initial symptoms but **hospitalization** and medical supervision are necessary. The prognosis depends on age and the severity of infection. Mortality is highest in people who acquired the disease congenitally, in the very young and those with compromised immunity for other reasons (eg HIV).

Amoebiasis

The humble amoeba is found worldwide, but the infection **amoebiasis** itself is common only in countries with poor sanitation. It is spread via the faecal–oral route from contaminated food or drinking water, although it can (rarely) be spread by intimate person-to-person contact. In most cases the disease is restricted to the gastrointestinal tract, but it can reach the liver causing hepatitis and abscess formation.

Prevention focuses on avoiding potentially contaminated food or water. Observe the usual hygiene measures, although bear in mind that amoebae are only killed by boiling water for at least a minute and are unaffected by iodine.

SYMPTOMS

Most people suffer only mild illness between 2 and 4 weeks after exposure. In more severe cases, commonly referred to as **amoebic dysentery**, symptoms such as diarrhoea with blood and mucus, severe abdominal cramps, fever, nausea, weight loss and general malaise can occur. These may persist or recur over a period of weeks or months. A liver abscess causes a prolonged fever and intermittent upper, usually right-sided, abdominal pain.

DIAGNOSIS AND TREATMENT

A **stool sample** may show the gastrointestinal disease, although sometimes more than one sample is required. An **ultrasound scan** will detect the presence of an abscess on the liver.

Cure requires a 7-day course of **metronidazole** at a dose of 800mg 3 times daily. You must not drink alcohol during the treatment. Be particularly diligent in your personal hygiene, especially hand washing, as it's relatively easy to reinfect yourself. As the infection is spread via the faecal-oral route, remember that intimate sexual contact may pass it on and is best avoided until the infection is cleared.

▷▷See Metronidazole, p.56.

AMS

▷▷See Altitude sickness, p.150.

Ancyclostomiasis

▷▷See under Worms, p.396.

Anthrax

Anthrax occurs worldwide in epidemics, but the hotspots are Africa, Central Asia, South America, the former USSR and the Far East. Transmitted to humans via bacterial spores from infected sheep, goats, cattle, horses or pigs, it almost exclusively affects people in close contact with animals or animal products. Travellers may come into contact with anthrax from handling wool, hide, bones and the like in areas where there is an outbreak, although generally risk is very low. Of the **three distinct kinds** of anthrax, the most common is cutaneous anthrax, which occurs after handling affected animals or animal hides. Pulmonary anthrax and intestinal anthrax, affecting the lungs and the gut respectively, both carry a high mortality rate but are far rarer.

A **vaccination** is available against anthrax but difficult to obtain and only recommended for those at high risk.

SYMPTOMS

Initial symptoms of **cutaneous anthrax** show themselves between 1 and 5 days after exposure, and include ulceration of the skin, usually at the point of contact. The ulcers are dark red in the centre, and although itchy, rarely painful. Local lymph glands may become swollen and tender and lymphangitis may be apparent. Accompanying symptoms may include fever, headache, nausea and loss of appetite. Left untreated, **septicaemia** can develop, which is always dangerous, even life-threatening.

Pulmonary anthrax (the result of inhaling the bacterial spores) manifests as a dry cough, high fever and chest discomfort. **Intestinal anthrax** (from eating the meat of affected animals) causes diarrhoea, vomiting and fever.

DIAGNOSIS AND TREATMENT

Swab cultures taken from the skin lesion, or **sputum** if chest symptoms are present, will reveal the presence of disease.

A mild skin infection can be treated by a 2-week course of **oral penicillin** (500mg 4 times daily) or **erythromycin** (same dosage). More severe infections require hospital admission and intravenous or intramuscular antibiotics.

Ascariasis

▷▷See under Worms, p.400.

Babesiosis

▷▷See Human babesiosis, p.249.

Cowboy First Aid. Photo © Henry Diltz/Corbis

Back pain

Back pain is a common enough problem at home, but the traveller often faces additional risks – heavy or awkward luggage, cramped, prolonged bus or plane journeys, hostile mattresses – which can lead to back discomfort or exacerbate existing problems. Don't underestimate the impact of back pain – it can severely affect your travel plans. Not only can the pain be debilitating, it can take days, even weeks, to resolve.

In truth, the vast majority of back injuries are minor. Strained or damaged back muscles go into **spasm**, causing pain and stiffness. Time is essentially the healer, although it's important to take adequate pain relief and keep mobile as lying still for too long will increase spasm and prolong the symptoms. Standard **painkillers**, like paracetamol and ibuprofen, are usually sufficient to manage the pain although co-proxamol is often recommended by doctors for stronger relief. Helpful, too, are hot water bottles or hot towels (heat increases the blood flow to the muscles, helping to relieve spasm), gentle massage or in some cases cold compresses (cold helps to reduce inflammation, especially around joints if they're involved). Most episodes of simple back pain will settle within 4 weeks.

Severe back pain, particularly if the pain goes down one or both legs (**sciatica**) or if accompanied by numbness, weakness or tingling in the legs, implies that one of the discs (which essentially act as "shock-absorbers") between the vertebrae is bulging, impinging on the nerves as they leave the spine (a "**slipped disc**"). It commonly occurs after lifting excessively heavy weights. The standard treatment is bed rest until the pain subsides, pain relief and then gentle mobilization – simple stretching **exercises** are best. Walking on the flat and swimming are also helpful, but take

Lifting technique

To lift a heavy object safely:

+ Ask yourself first if you're being realistic in attempting to lift the object.

+ Stand close to the load with your feet well apart.

+ Bend at the knees to pick it up, keeping your back straight, and lift by straightening your legs.

+ Turn using your feet rather than twisting your back.

+ To put the load down, again bend your legs rather than your back.

BALANTIDIASIS

care not to proceed too rapidly. If symptoms persist or if at any stage you have problems controlling your bowels or bladder, seek medical help urgently.

To treat back pain homeopathically, try **arnica, hypericum** or **rhus tox.** (see pp.77 and 80).

Balantidiasis

Although the organism that causes **balantidiasis** can be found worldwide, the disease tends to occur only in the tropics and is usually passed to humans from animals (pigs, guinea pigs, rats and monkeys). Humans can also act as carriers, and infection can occur as a result of drinking water contaminated by infected animal or human faeces. The risk to travellers in general is low, but always wash your hands after handling animals in areas that have experienced outbreaks, and observe the standard food and water hygiene measures.

SYMPTOMS

Diarrhoea alternating with **constipation** is common. For the most part, however, infection is mild, even unnoticed, and the symptoms usually resolve spontaneously after a week or 2. Occasionally the illness can be severe, especially if you're already physically weak, causing rectal bleeding and severe abdominal cramps similar to dysentery.

DIAGNOSIS AND TREATMENT

Diagnosis can usually be made by microscopic examination of the **stool**, although several samples may be required as the bacteria are only passed intermittently.

Treatment is usually unnecessary unless symptoms are severe, but tetracyclines (eg doxycycline) or metronidazole can be used.

Bang's disease

▷▷See Brucellosis, p.167.

Barmah Forest virus

The **Barmah Forest virus** was first isolated in mosquitoes in the north of the Australian state of Victoria in 1974, although it wasn't until 1986 that it was linked to illness in humans. Occurring in sporadic outbreaks throughout Australia, it is less common but shares many similarities with **Ross River virus**. Risk to the traveller is low unless passing through an epidemic area.

▷▷See Ross River virus, p.327.

Bartonellosis

(Oroya fever)

Bartonellosis originates in the Andes of southwest Colombia, Ecuador and Peru – its common name, Oroya fever, refers to a town in the Peruvian Andes. You are most at risk in certain narrow valleys on the range's western slopes between 1000 and 3000m – outside these geographically isolated areas, the risk to travellers is negligible.

The bacteria responsible are transmitted by sand flies, which usually bite between dusk and dawn. There's no vaccination, so if you find yourself in an area of high risk, your only **protection** is insect-bite avoidance (see p.259).

SYMPTOMS

The disease has **two phases**: an initial, acute illness characterized by **loss of appetite**, **thirst**, **bone pains**, **fatigue** resulting from anaemia and **high fever**. The fever is particularly high at night and may last for up to 6 weeks. This phase is followed by **wart-like eruptions** on the skin, which are particularly dense on the face and limbs, and bleed easily. They do heal without scarring, although sometimes this takes up to 12 months. Victims of bartonellosis are unusually susceptible to **salmonella septicaemia**, especially in the second week of the illness, so prompt treatment or medical attention is important.

DIAGNOSIS AND TREATMENT

Blood tests will confirm the presence of the organisms. While there's no vaccine to prevent the disease, the bacteria are killed by **penicillin**. Amoxycillin is generally used although oral chloramphenicol may be required if salmonella is suspected.

Bedbugs

Uncommon in developed countries, **bedbugs** are usually associated with areas of deprivation, poverty and low standards of hygiene. Small (up to 5mm long), crawling insects inhabiting bedding, furniture and walls, they feed on blood, usually at night, with their bites often showing a linear pattern. By day they seek shelter in dark recesses. Rooms that have a bedbug infestation are said typically to have a musty, sweet odour. Bedbugs are not known to transmit any diseases to humans.

SYMPTOMS AND TREATMENT

Many bites will go unnoticed, but some appear as small, hard, pale **lumps**. An itchy, allergic reaction can develop into **wheals**. The wheals subside leaving red spots, which can remain for several days.

Bedbugs can be eradicated by spraying their likely daytime residences with **permethrin**. Oral **antihistamines** or topical **hydrocortisone** can speed up recovery from a bite.

Bilharzia

▷▷See Schistosomiasis, p.337.

Blood transfusions

Most of us give little thought to the matter of **blood transfusion** with only the small likelihood of ever needing one. It is only when faced with the prospect (if we are well enough) that we become alarmed at the thought of having someone else's blood pumping around our body and contracting a serious, potentially life-threatening virus (HIV or infective hepatitis, eg).

Blood groups

If you know your blood group, make a note of it before you go away and carry it with your passport and insurance documents in case of emergencies. There are four basic blood groups, of which blood group O rhesus negative is known as the "universal donor" because it can be given to someone with any other blood type – O negative people can be valuable travel companions!

Thus:

✚ Group A can receive A and O.

✚ Group B can receive B and O.

✚ Group AB can receive A, B and O.

✚ Group O can receive only O.

✚ If you are rhesus positive, you can receive both rhesus positive and negative blood.

✚ If you are rhesus negative, you can receive only rhesus negative blood. Rhesus negative blood is especially rare in the Far East.

In most developed countries, the technology and screening regulations are sufficient to keep these risks to a minimum. However, in the developing world, confidence in the screening process is less founded. Furthermore, the sterility of equipment used to transfuse the blood (needles, syringes, etc) cannot be guaranteed.

If you're in an emergency situation and need a blood transfusion, you'll probably have little choice about what happens next. However, your condition may be stabilized sufficiently to request **air evacuation** from a country where blood and blood products, or transfusion equipment, are suspect. Your insurance policy may also have arrange-

BLOOD TRANSFUSIONS

ments for getting adequately screened blood and sterile equipment to you if need be. If not, you can minimize the risk from unsterile equipment at least by carrying your own (see p.536 for a list of suppliers). All you can do about the blood itself is cross your fingers.

If you're concerned about blood transfusion abroad, check out the Blood Care Foundation, an organization that specializes in supplying screened blood directly to you anywhere in the world (see p.548 for contact details).

Botulism

Outbreaks of **botulism**, a form of food poisoning caused by bacteria commonly found in the soil, can occur anywhere in the world but are very rare. You can become infected by eating poorly cooked or reheated contaminated food, often from improperly processed canned goods. Person-to-person spread does not occur. Travellers are not necessarily at any higher risk than anyone else, although contamination of food or poor packaging may be more common in developing countries.

Children are at particular risk of contracting botulism from eating honey contaminated with the bacterial spores – avoid giving honey especially to babies under 1 year old. Don't buy cans of food that have been damaged or are bulging and don't eat the contents of any can that gives off an offensive odour.

SYMPTOMS

Nausea, vomiting and diarrhoea usually occur between 12 and 36 hours after eating contaminated food. Double or blurred vision, dry mouth, difficulty speaking or swallowing, weakness and shortness of breath may follow, all signs that botulism is affecting your nervous system. Gradual-onset muscle paralysis may develop leading to respiratory difficulties and even death.

DIAGNOSIS AND TREATMENT

Lab tests can identify the toxin produced by the bacteria in the blood and bacteria in the stool sample.

Hospitalization is necessary as severe cases may need to be hooked up to a ventilator. An injected anti-toxin may be given in some instances.

Brazilian purpuric fever

Brazilian purpuric fever was first recognized in Promissao in the state of Sao Paulo in 1984. Since then there have been sporadic outbreaks in a number of towns in Sao Paulo State. Cases resembling it have also been reported in Australia. Little is actually known about the bacteria that cause the disease nor its mode of spread, but it almost always affects children under 10.

SYMPTOMS

Characteristically, the illness begins with a severe, pustular **conjunctivitis**, or pink eye. In a few cases, a high fever, vomiting, abdominal pain and a purpuric rash occur, and other symptoms resembling infection with meningococcus (see p.295). Untreated, life-threatening septicaemia can develop.

DIAGNOSIS AND TREATMENT

The bacteria can be detected in **cultures** grown from blood or spinal fluid.

Chloramphenicol drops or ointment may help the conjunctivitis, but seem ineffective in preventing the more progressive symptoms from taking hold. **Oral amoxycillin** (sometimes in conjunction with oral chloramphenicol) can prevent progression to septicaemia.

Brucellosis

(Abortus fever, Bang's disease, Malta fever, Undulant fever)

Brucellosis occurs in epidemics throughout the world and is usually acquired by drinking unpasteurized milk (pasteurization kills the offending organism) from infected cattle, although it's also spread by goats and sheep in the Mediterranean (Malta especially) and the Middle East, and by pigs in North America and the Far East. People working closely with animals run the risk of the organism entering their body via their respiratory tract or through skin abrasions.

SYMPTOMS

After an incubation period of 1–3 weeks (sometimes longer), the onset of symptoms can be acute for some, insidious for others, and include **malaise**, **headache**, **night sweats**, **loss of appetite**, generalized **weakness** and **aches and pains**. The fever tends to undulate for a week or so during which time the lymph glands become swollen. The liver and spleen may also swell.

A **chronic** form of brucellosis may persist for several months following an acute attack, the symptoms of which are **muscle aches**, a tendency to **tire easily**, with bouts of **fever** and **depression**.

DIAGNOSIS AND TREATMENT

A **blood test** will determine whether or not you have the disease, which can then be treated, ideally in hospital, using high-dose **antibiotics**. Relapses of the illness can occur.

Buruli ulcer

Buruli is a rare, but serious, skin infection confined for the most part to Benin, Cote d'Ivoire, Gabon, Ghana and Uganda (it's named after a Ugandan region in which there were many cases in the 1960s), although isolated outbreaks have been recorded in Asia, Australia and South America. To date, relatively little is known about the disease, although the causative bacteria (related to those causing TB and leprosy) have been identified, as has the disease prevalence among women and children living near wetlands or rivers in tropical or sub-tropical rural areas. Its mode of spread may be via scratches or cuts on the skin. You're only likely to be at risk of the disease if you're planning to live basically in rural, wetland communities in the endemic areas.

There is no specific vaccine against Buruli, although the BCG vaccine confers a degree of short-term immunity.

SYMPTOMS AND TREATMENT

What appears first as a painless, occasionally itchy, skin swelling, usually on the limbs, develops over the course of a month or two into a destructive **ulcer**. The ulcer may remain small and disappear spontaneously or progress rapidly, destroying large areas of skin and causing disfigurements.

Treatment with drugs has been disappointing to date. Significant ulceration requires radical surgical excision of the ulcer and skin grafting, although the procedure is much simpler and less damaging if the disease is suspected early.

Candidiasis

▷▷See Thrush, p.374.

Chagas' disease

▷▷See American trypanosomiasis, p.153.

Chancroid

▷▷See under Sexually transmitted diseases, p.349.

Chiggers

▷▷See Tungiasis, p.384.

Chikungunya fever

Chikungunya fever occurs in both sporadic outbreaks and large epidemics in Africa, the Indian subcontinent and Southeast Asia (Philippines, Thailand Cambodia, Vietnam, Myanmar, Sri Lanka). Its name is derived from Swahili and means "that which bends up", a reference to the sufferers' stooped posture caused by joint pains.

Chikungunya fever is a viral infection spread by mosquitoes. There is no preventative vaccination so the standard bite-avoidance measures (see p.259) are an essential part of reducing your risk of exposure.

SYMPTOMS

Symptoms closely resemble those for dengue fever, with fever, headache, nausea, a rash and rapid-onset joint pains.

The symptoms usually last between 3 and 7 days and, although unpleasant, the illness is not life-threatening. Residual joint stiffness can continue for weeks or even months afterwards.

DIAGNOSIS AND TREATMENT

Diagnosis can be made by a **blood test**, but no specific treatment is available. Paracetamol or ibuprofen may help to alleviate the fever and pains. Be sure to drink plenty to replace lost fluids during the fever.

▷▷See Dengue fever, p.195.

Chlamydia

▷▷See under Sexually transmitted diseases, p.347.

Cholera

Cholera is a dangerous diarrhoeal illness caused by bacteria which enter the body via contaminated drink or shellfish. Spread by person-to-person contact is rare. Cholera occurs in sporadic epidemics in areas with poor sanitation and is common after natural disasters and war. "Bengal Cholera" is a particularly violent strain with recent outbreaks in parts of Asia. Provided you take good care with food and water hygiene, the risk to travellers is small – the bacteria are killed in a few seconds in boiling water. The acid in your stomach also protects against the bacteria, so you're at greater risk if you're taking acid-suppressant treatment.

Cholera **vaccination** has proved unreliable (see p.11), and is no longer routinely administered in the UK. While a new oral vaccine may soon be available, it's likely to be restricted to people travelling to high-risk areas or during outbreaks only. Your doctor will be able to give you the most up-to-date advice before you go. Because of the unpredictable nature of epidemics, it's important to be vigilant with food and water hygiene at all times in any under-developed country.

SYMPTOMS

The vast majority of cases – around 90% – are mild to moderate and, as such, difficult to differentiate from any other diarrhoeal illness. In more severe cases, you might suffer recurrent vomiting and profuse, sudden-onset watery diarrhoea ("rice water" stools). Muscle cramps can be severe. Dehydration can occur rapidly, and shock (cold, clammy skin, high pulse rate, etc – see p.194) may follow.

DIAGNOSIS AND TREATMENT

Diagnosis can be confirmed by lab examination of **stool samples**.

Urgent treatment will be needed to prevent severe, life-threatening dehydration – lost fluid and chemicals need to be replaced via oral rehydration solutions (see p.60). The **tetracycline** group of antibiotics (eg doxycycline, 200mg on day 1, then 100mg daily for 6 days) help eradicate the infection, decrease stool output and considerably shorten the duration of the illness.

Ciguatera

Ciguatera poisoning occurs after eating reef-dwelling fish who have fed on a particular type of toxic plankton. The disease occurs in sporadic outbreaks throughout the Pacific and Caribbean. Unfortunately, affected fish are indistinguishable from other fish by inspection, smell and taste, and the toxin is not neutralized by cooking. Outbreaks are rare, but if you are aware of one locally, avoid eating large predatory, reef-dwelling fish – commonly affected species include red snapper, grouper, barracuda, coral trout, cod and amberjack. The toxin tends to accumulate in high concentrations in the head, liver, roe and gut, so these parts of the fish should be avoided in particular.

SYMPTOMS

Usually occurring 1 to 6 hours after eating (up to as long as 30 hours), the symptoms are commonly mild and predominantly gastrointestinal (**diarrhoea**, **vomiting** and **abdominal pains**) or neurological (**muscle aches**, **weakness**, **pins and needles**, **burning sensations** of the skin, **blurred vision**, **photophobia** and a **metallic taste** in the mouth). Symptoms can persist for as long as 2 weeks. Severe cases are rare.

DIAGNOSIS AND TREATMENT

Diagnosis is usually made on the basis of history, symptoms and clinical suspicion. There is no specific treatment, with **bed rest** and **basic pain relief** your best options. Severe cases sometimes require IV fluids to prevent dehydration.

Clonorchiasis

See Oriental liver flukes, p.307.

Cold exposure

The normally well-regulated core temperature of the human body will fall under extreme environmental conditions such as **cold, wet** or **windy weather**. Alcohol, physical illness and exhaustion can all compromise your body's

Keeping your body warm in extreme cold

✚ Wrap up, paying particular attention to your extremities (don't forget your ears).

✚ Keep dry.

✚ Keep active and moving.

✚ Consume high-energy foods (eg chocolate) and warm drinks.

✚ Find shelter in rain or high winds.

✚ Avoid alcohol, which dilates the blood vessels to the skin (eg flushing) so you actually lose heat.

✚ Avoid smoking (nicotine contracts your blood vessels and impairs blood flow to the extremities).

COLD EXPOSURE

natural ability to withstand the cold. Discomfort aside, cold exposure can harm the body in several ways, and in the extreme, it can be life threatening.

Frostbite

Frostbite occurs when the skin and the flesh just beneath the skin surface freeze, preventing the flow of blood so that the flesh in effect dies. The areas of the body most likely to be affected by frostbite are your **extremities**: hands, feet, ears and sometimes the face.

Initial **signs** of frostbite are localized numbness and often sharp pain, although frequently the victim is unaware of the problem. In mild frostbite the skin looks pale and has a leathery texture. As the freezing progresses, sensation disappears and the skin feels hard to touch.

Mild frostbite (the skin is still soft to touch) is best

treated by gradually warming the affected area by wrapping it and holding it against warm, more central body parts. Keep moving to improve blood circulation. **Severe frostbite** (when the skin feels hard, like meat from the freezer) needs medical input, as the dead flesh may need to be removed surgically. In an emergency situation, don't attempt to warm or defrost the affected area until you're out of the cold and in a safe place. It's better to let a limb stay frozen for several hours than to warm it only for it to freeze again. The affected area can be warmed by immersing it in warm water (remember that feeling is lost so you won't be able to gauge temperature). As the area warms, it can be very painful – strong pain relief may be necessary. Stay warm and rest. The thawed area must be treated gently and kept clean. Blisters may form after a few days (avoid bursting them) and the flesh may blacken. Because the area is numb, it is more prone to local damage from minor trauma and infection. Medical help should be sought urgently.

Hypothermia

Hypothermia is caused when the core body temperature falls below a critical level (defined medically as below 35°C). It's a significant cause of death in climbers, polar explorers and off-piste skiers.

Symptoms initially include the feeling of intense cold and uncontrollable shivering. As the body's temperature continues to drop, speech becomes slow or slurred and mental confusion, stumbling gait and lethargy become apparent. The sufferer feels cold to touch, the pulse slows and breathing becomes shallow. Shivering eventually decreases and the muscles become stiff. Eventually the victim will lapse into coma, and death usually occurs as a result of abnormal heart rhythms.

To **treat** hypothermia the victim needs to be gradually rewarmed by placing them in a warm environment, wrapping them in blankets (aluminium space blankets if they are available), huddling to transfer body heat and giving warm, sugary drinks (no alcohol). This process may take several hours. As the body temperature increases, there is a risk of abnormal heart rhythms and abnormalities of the blood biochemistry. For this reason, a doctor should oversee the treatment of severe hypothermia. Never assume that a victim of hypothermia is dead even if their pulse and breath movements are absent; always attempt to resuscitate them using CPR.

▷▷See CPR, p.411.

Snow blindness

Snow blindness describes damage to the conjunctiva of the eye caused by the glare of strong ultraviolet light reflected off snow. It's easily **avoided** by wearing good-quality sunglasses.

After the early **symptoms** of prolonged blinking and squinting in response to the glare, the eyes begin to water and feel painful, gritty and irritable. Vision may take on a pink hue. The condition resolves without treatment but recovery will be hastened by resting in a dark place, preferably with a blindfold and applying cool compresses to your forehead. Take pain relief as required.

Trenchfoot

Trenchfoot develops when the feet are exposed to moist, cold conditions for a prolonged period of time (usually a day or more). The condition was common in World War I (thus the name); more recently, a number of cases have been reported after rain-sodden outdoor rock festivals. The condition may also be caused by prolonged wearing of tight, rubberized boots in which sweat accumulates or into which water has leaked. Being cold and wet causes the blood vessels in the feet to constrict, which in turn causes a reduction in the blood supply to the tissues of the feet.

Early **signs** of the condition are usually itching, numbness and pain. Later the feet may swell and the skin may look discoloured. There is often a distinct "waterline" coinciding with the water level in the boot. Red blotches and weeping blisters may appear and can become infected.

Prevention involves changing into dry socks at the first possible opportunity. To **treat** trenchfoot, first remove the wet, constrictive boots and socks. Gently wash and dry the area before elevating and covering with loose, warm clothing. Use adequate pain relief and anti-inflammatory drugs. Do not attempt to burst the blisters or expose the area to extreme heat. Treat suspected secondary infection with appropriate antibiotics (eg flucloxacillin). If the pain, swelling or blistering is severe, seek medical help.

Colds and coughs

(Respiratory tract infection)

You can catch a **cold**, **cough** or **sore throat** (collectively known as upper respiratory tract infection, or URTI) easily enough at home, but travelling can not only increase your susceptibility to these kinds of infection but can also expose you to previously unencountered germs to which you have no natural immunity.

Coughs, colds and sore throats are generally amenable to over-the-counter symptomatic reliefs. Paracetamol or ibuprofen should be used for pain relief or to reduce a fever, and oral or nasal decongestants help to dry up a blocked nose. Don't forget steam inhalation, with or without additions such as menthol or eucalyptus oil, an old but effective remedy.

Note that the fact that you have a **cough** doesn't automatically mean you have a chest infection – it's usually caused by the nasal secretions dripping down the back of your throat and stimulating your cough reflex. **Chest infections** are generally pretty rare in the young, fit, non-smoker. Asthmatics should increase the use of their inhalers (see p.84) in the early stages of an URTI.

The vast majority of respiratory tract infections are **viral** in origin and, as such, are not amenable to treatment with antibiotics. If a doctor prescribes you an antibiotic it's because of a secondary bacterial infection (eg chest infection, sinusitis, tonsillar abscess, inner ear infection, etc) or because the illness is prolonged and showing no signs of improvement.

Chest infections

Signs of a chest infection are a productive cough (yellow or green sputum), wheezing, high fever, shortness of breath, chest pain, and systemic illness (loss of appetite, vomiting, etc). **Legionnaires' disease** is a special case and dealt with in more detail later in this section. Appropriate **antibiotics** for the treatment of a chest infection are amoxycillin, erythromycin, doxycycline and ciprofloxacin.
▷▷See Legionnaires' disease, p.266.

Sinusitis

Classically, following an URTI, an intense, localized, pain develops in the forehead, cheek or behind the eyes, signify-

COLDS AND COUGHS

Alternative treatments for a cold

To cure a cold homeopathically, choose arsenicum album if you have a watery, burning discharge which makes your eyes water, and prolific sneezing, but blowing your nose brings no relief. Allium cepa will treat a cold marked by massive sneezes and a constantly dripping nose. The discharge, often acrid, ceases on going outdoors and returns when you go in. It's not advisable for asthmatics. Aconite is good for the first stages of a cold, when you feel the first tickle in the back of your throat. The symptoms begin abruptly and are often worse around midnight. You feel feverish and restless. Use gelsemium to treat the more fluey type of cold, with aching and chills, hypersensitive skin and heavy legs. All you want to do is go to sleep. Natrum mur can help colds which seem to come on after stress, and which have a nasal discharge the consistency of uncooked egg-white. It's also a good remedy for people who get cold sores with their nose cold, and will help clear up both. For colds that start with

ing **sinusitis**. It's usually one-sided and worse on bending forward and blowing your nose. Nasal discharge may be minimal but is usually purulent if present. Sinusitis can be treated using the same antibiotics as for chest infections; decongestants and steam inhalation can also help.

Sore throat

Most **sore throats** will settle without antibiotics within a week of onset, but if pain persists, or you encounter difficulties swallowing, systemic upset, high fever or develop a red rash, then consider treating it with antibiotics – penicillin or erythromycin are the most commonly prescribed.

a sore throat, with bad breath with lots of thick saliva, take mercury. You may have a mouth ulcer and your nasal discharge is thick and yellow or green, often bloody, perhaps with a foul smell. Pulsatilla treats children's colds, or the riper stages of an adult cold, when you're especially congested at night and by day feel better for fresh air. Nasal discharge, which is thick and yellow or green, is often heaviest in the morning, and you may have bad breath. You may also feel tearful and needy. Remember when taking any of these remedies that decongestants such as eucalyptus, menthol and camphor will act as antidotes so should be avoided.

Vitamin C and zinc supplements are also useful (take up to 1 gram of vitamin C a day for 4 to 5 days; take your zinc supplement between meals, drinks and other supplements). Zinc and vitamin C lozenges are a good way of taking these two together. Frankincense aromatherapy oil burned in a vaporizer or blended with a carrier oil (like almond) and massaged into your skin will help to clear your chest.

If at any stage you are unable to swallow fluids, you must seek medical help urgently because you are at risk of becoming dehydrated. It's worth remembering that diphtheria can present with a sore throat. Sore throats are dealt with in more detail on p.359.

▷▷See also Diptheria, p.201.

Constipation

A number of travel-related factors can lead to **constipation**, from simply suppressing a natural urge to go while intransit, to avoiding unwelcoming lavatory conditions, to changes in diet and water. Sitting, inactive, for hours on end alone disturbs the natural rhythms of the bowel, but when coupled with dehydration, you're likely to arrive at your destination in a mild state of constipation. Drugs, such as some painkillers, often have constipation as a recognized side effect.

SYMPTOMS

Apart from the obvious difficulty in opening your bowels, constipation often leads to more generalized unpleasant feelings such as abdominal **bloating** and **discomfort**, **mood swings**, **bad breath** and an overall feeling of **wretchedness**.

TREATMENT

Constipation usually resolves itself but you can help things along by increasing your **fluid** intake, **exercising**, and altering your **diet**: eat plenty of fibre (bran cereals, whole-meal bread) and fruit (prunes, apples, oranges and bananas in particular). **Liquorice** and some of the sugar-free chewing gums are also good at getting things moving.

If necessary, **senna** is a cheap and effective bowel stimulant although occasionally, if the stools are very hard, a softener such as **lactulose** may be a kinder first option.

 To treat constipation homeopathically, choose from among the following 3 remedies. If you've no urge to "go" at all; if the stool feels "stuck" for days on end; if you start to pass the stool but it retreats back again; and if when they do pass they're small, hard black balls, then **opium** will get things moving (6c 3 times a day for 3–7 days, or 30c 1–2 times a day). Take **nux vomica** (same dosage as opium) if you have lots of urging with little success. You feel bloated and irritable, and that if you try just one more time something will happen; you're very sensitive to any pressure about the waist and have probably been overdoing it with new foods, spices or excess alcohol. **Alumina** (same dosage) is the best option if after much straining you do manage to pass a soft or normal textured stool, and you may have been eating unusual foods at unusual times of the day.

Contraception

No matter what your intentions, think carefully about **contraception** before you set out travelling, and arm yourself with whichever of the options below best suits your lifestyle. Holiday romances are extremely common and anxieties about **pregnancy** or **sexually transmitted diseases** (STD's) may be the last thing you want on the trip of a lifetime.

Aware of the potential local dangers, many travellers make the dangerous assumption that it's safe to pair up with fellow travellers. Even if you consider yourself to be fairly choosy about whom you spend the night with, don't assume that your partner has similar standards or has been conscientious about using condoms to safeguard against STDs.

Condoms

As a contraceptive, **condoms** are relatively safe if a good-quality brand is used properly – take some with you from home as the local brands may be inferior. Condoms' advantage over other contraception is they also offer some, if not complete, **protection against STDs**. It is worth bearing in mind that the latex in condoms deteriorates when exposed to heat so always keep them out of the sun. Contact with sun oil can destroy a condom in as little as 15 minutes.

Thai anti-AIDS poster. Photo © Eye Ubiquitous/Corbis

The pill

Despite a lot of media hype, **the pill** or **combined pill** (combined oestrogen and progesterone) are relatively free of side effects, both minor and major, and are the safest contraceptive in terms of accidental pregnancies available (failures are almost always due to a missed pill). The pill offers no protection against STDs so it should be used in conjunction with condoms in the event of sex with a new partner.

There are a number of instances in which the combined pill should be avoided, but most relevant to travellers are any arterial or venous thrombosis, any active liver disease (eg hepatitis) or history of jaundice, and an existing or possible pregnancy.

If you are travelling for any length of time, always take adequate supplies with you as your brand may be difficult to find abroad. Other considerations that you should take on board as a traveller are set out below.

MISSED PILLS

The traveller's often haphazard lifestyle, with few daily routines and overlong journeys sometimes across time zones, means the risk of forgetting or missing pills is high. In the absence of the pill pack instructions, which usually tell you what to do in the event of a missed pill, follow the advice below:

✤ If you are less than 12 hours late, don't worry. Take the delayed pill at once and the rest of the packet as usual. No extra contraceptive measures are necessary.

✤ If you are more than 12 hours late, take the most recently delayed pill at once, continue the rest of the packet as normal, discard any previously missed pills and observe "the

CONTRACEPTION

183

7-day rule", ie use alternative contraception (condoms) for the next 7 days; if there are more than 7 pills remaining in the packet, maintain the usual 7-day pill-free break before starting your next pack; if there are fewer than 7 pills remaining in the pack, omit the break and start your next pack on the day following the completion of your current pack. If you are in any doubt, use condoms for 7 days.

THE PILL, VOMITING AND DIARRHOEA

If **vomiting** occurs less than 3 hours after the pill was taken, you should take a replacement pill (from a spare packet) as the original will not have been in the stomach long enough to be absorbed. If the replacement pill does not stay down, take extra precautions from the onset of the illness and continue for 7 days after the illness ends. If this is within 7 days of the pill-free week, omit the break and start the next pack on the day following completion of the current pack. **Diarrhoea** is generally not regarded as a major problem unless it is particularly severe. If so, observe the 7-day rule (see above).

OTHER DRUGS

Many drugs, antibiotics in particular, can reduce the effectiveness of the pill. Take alternative precautions while on any course of antibiotics and for 7 days afterwards, following the rules above for the pill-free week.

TIME ZONES

It's particularly difficult to keep track of pill-taking on long-haul flights to completely different time zones. This problem may be even more difficult to work out during pill-free weeks and may lead to a pregnancy caused by a prolonged pill-free interval (this is the usual cause of pill failures). The easiest way around this is to have two watches, one set at home time, at least until you get used to the local time. Once established on local time, gradually re-adjust your pill-taking to your usual time (no more than an hour change each day). If confusion arises, err on the side of taking the pill early rather than late.

FLYING

A rare side effect of pill-taking is the development of a blood clot in the leg, lung or brain. There is a slightly increased risk of this during long-haul flights, but this does not mean that you cannot fly if you take the pill. Minimize the risk by staying hydrated during the flight (avoid excess caffeine and alcohol) and take some exercise while you're in the air (either leg stretches or a periodic walk around the plane).

ALTITUDE

High altitudes and the pill both increase blood thickness and predispose to clot formation in the blood vessels. The effect is additive and therefore, other forms of contraception should be considered if you are planning to trek or climb above 4000m (especially if you smoke). The use of acetazolamide as a preventative for mountain sickness (see p.68) also increases the risk of clot formation.

REGULATING MENSTRUATION

By taking the next packet straight away, and ignoring the pill-free week, bleeding can be averted. You may feel uncomfortable about skipping a period, but this is not dangerous. In fact, there is no reason why the pill should not be taken continuously for 3 packets with a bleed occurring on withdrawal of the last packet.

CONTRACEPTION

The mini pill

The mini pill (progesterone-only pill) is not the best contraceptive choice if you're travelling far afield, as its efficacy is highly dependent on taking it at a fixed, regular time. There is very little margin for error (within plus or minus 1 hour each day), which clearly presents practical problems crossing time zones. The mini pill is also less reliable than the combined pill and is generally prescribed little to women under 35 (unless they are breast-feeding).

That said, the mini pill has less effect on the clotting system than the combined pill, and, theoretically at least, is safer to use at altitude. The efficacy of the mini pill is also less affected by other drugs (eg antibiotics) than the combined pill.

If a mini pill is taken more than 3 hours late, other contraceptive precautions should be taken for the next 7 days. The mini pill is not recommended in cases of liver disease and should be avoided if you have hepatitis.

Injectable contraception

Injectable contraception is less commonly used than the pill although seems to be gaining popularity. It is an effective and safe method of contraception whereby an injection is repeated at 12-week intervals. For the first 2 or 3 doses, irregular and heavy menstrual bleeding may occur, but after that the recipient usually has no periods at all while she continues to have regular injections.

The injections therefore have both positive and negative implications for the woman traveller. First, the fact that the injections are given every 12 weeks means that there is less reliance on memory for full efficacy – all you have to remember is the date of your next injection. However, this

Emergency contraception

You are most at risk of becoming pregnant after unprotected sex in the first half of your menstrual cycle (highest risk on day 14). Many people are already aware of the availability of the "morning-after pill" and in some countries it is now available without prescription. But don't use it as a regular form of contraception. If you have sex infrequently, always carry condoms – a frequent or constant need for reliable contraception is perhaps best served by the combined pill (see above). Remember that no form of oral contraception provides protection against STDs.

Two types of post-coital pill are currently available, one containing progesterone only (Levonelle 2) and the other a combined pill containing oestrogen and progesterone (Schering PC4). Both must be started within 72 hours of unprotected sex and are more effective if the first dose is taken as soon as possible. Both involve 2 doses of tablets, with the second dose 12 hours after the first.

Although reasonably reliable if taken promptly, neither type of pill is 100% effective. Your period may be late after treatment (you may also experience a mild bleed within a couple of days after taking the pills), but if you miss it completely do a pregnancy test.

Neither type of pill should be taken if you have severe liver disease or porphyria. The combined type may cause nausea, vomiting and headache and should not be used if you have had a previous thrombosis or suffer regular migraines. If you vomit within 3 hours of taking the pills, you need to take a replacement dose as the pills will not have been adequately absorbed. As with the combined pill, the efficacy of both types of post-coital pill may be reduced by interactions with other drugs (eg antibiotics). Always read the pack instructions carefully.

Following post-coital contraception, always use condoms as contraception until your period arrives.

is a drawback if you plan to be away for more than 12 weeks or if you are away when the injection is due. Most people are unwilling to, nor should they, self-administer the injection, and are therefore reliant on someone else (usually a doctor or nurse) to do this. You may need to carry supplies of the drug with you and even consider needles and syringes if you're heading for wilder parts. The effects of the injections on menstruation are also important – if you decide to travel within 3 to 6 months of the first injection, you may find the irregularity and unpredictability of the bleeding difficult to manage.

Other advantages of injectable contraception are that it is unaffected by vomiting or diarrhoea, and that it has little or no interaction with other drugs. (As the injectable contraceptive contains the same hormone as the mini pill, it shares its advantages.) A disadvantage is that it offers no protection against sexually transmitted diseases, although using a condom at the same time will reduce this risk.

The coil

The coil (intrauterine device or **IUD**) is a good contraceptive, although there are drawbacks which can make it less popular with the traveller. It is generally not recommended for women who have not yet had children (primarily because it is very difficult to insert). It also quite often leads to heavier periods (less so with some of the newer coils) and has an increased risk of pelvic infection.

The cap

The cap, or **diaphragm**, is roughly as effective as condoms as a contraceptive. While the cap offers some protection against STDs, it is less effective than a condom in this respect. From a travel point of view, a cap may be harder to replace abroad.

Cramp

Cramp is a sudden and sometimes sustained spasm of a muscle. It has a variety of **causes**, including dehydration, stress, fatigue, heavy exercise and poor posture. It most commonly affects the calf muscles, is more common in older people and often happens at night in bed.

To safeguard yourself against cramp, remember to warm up adequately before **exercise** and spend 5 or 10 minutes stretching afterwards. Eating fruit such as oranges or bananas will ensure that the levels of important salts in your blood are maintained during exercise. Drink extra fluids beforehand and while you work out.

During an attack of cramp, massage the muscle and gently stretch. A warm towel, bath or shower increases blood flow, helping to relieve the spasm. Gently stretch the muscle (for calf cramp, sit on the floor with your leg straight, grip your foot and gently pull it toward you; alternatively, quickly lift up your toes as high as you can, then slowly, slowly lower them over the course of a few minutes). Take extra fluids to rehydrate. If the calf remains tender, or becomes red, hot or swollen, it is possible that you have a **DVT** (see p.30) and you should seek medical advice at once.

Crimean-Congo haemorrhagic fever

Crimean-Congo haemorrhagic fever (CCHF) occurs in sporadic outbreaks throughout Africa, Asia, the Middle East and Eastern Europe. The name was coined in 1969 when it was recognized that two outbreaks of disease, one in Crimea in 1944 and one in the Congo in 1956, were in fact caused by the same virus. Common among a wide range of domestic and wild animals, CCHF is a rare but serious disease in humans.

CCHF is a **virus** transmitted to humans by the bite of an infected **tick** or by direct contact with infected animal blood or tissues. To the average traveller, risk is only slight, but there is no reliable or safe vaccination for humans so try and avoid wild areas when ticks are most abundant (usually from spring to autumn), wear long trousers tucked into your socks, use insect repellents and examine skin and clothes for signs of ticks daily.

SYMPTOMS

CCHF's incubation period is short, usually between 1 and 3 days if acquired from a tick bite but longer if through contact with animal tissues. The symptoms tend take hold rapidly and include **fever**, **dizziness**, **headache**, **neck pain and stiffness**, **generalized aching**, **abdominal pain**, **diarrhoea**, **nausea and vomiting**, **sore eyes** and **photophobia**. Mood swings and agitation can follow, succeeded by depression and lassitude. Bleeding into the skin, the bowel, the bladder or from the mouth and nose can occur.

DIAGNOSIS AND TREATMENT

The diagnosis of CCHF can be confirmed by a **blood test**. CCHF can be a severe, even lethal illness so if suspected, seek **medical help** immediately. While there is no specific treatment, intensive medical and nursing care improves the outcome.

Cryptosporidiosis

Cryptosporidiosis is caused by a gut parasite, and although uncommon in anyone with a normally functioning immune system, it occurs throughout the world. The disease particularly affects children because their immune system is less robust. It's also a very common complication of AIDS.

The parasite's major natural reservoir is cattle and it's spread by the faecal-oral route, usually via contaminated water. Person-to-person spread is common through poor hygiene.

SYMPTOMS

Cryptosporidiosis causes a gastrointestinal upset. It can be severe and, if your immune system is already compromised, extremely dangerous. After an incubation period of between 2 and 10 days, the symptoms are acute in onset and consist of profuse, watery **diarrhoea**, cramp-like **abdominal pains**, **flatulence**, **vomiting**, **fever** and general **malaise**.

DIAGNOSIS AND TREATMENT

Diagnosis is usually made by lab analysis of a **stool sample**. There is no effective drug treatment for uncomplicated cryptosporidiosis, but the illness usually settles after 7 to 10 days. In the interim, you can take the standard measures for treating diarrhoea (see p.228). In severe cases because of immunodeficiency, specialist treatment can reduce the diarrhoea, although it won't eradicate the offending organism.

Culture shock

"**Culture shock**" is the term used to describe the rather lost feeling that many travellers experience when they arrive at a new and unfamiliar destination – even home, for the returning traveller who has been away for a long time.

It can be fuelled by poor **preparation** before your trip, sadness about leaving home, fatigue from the journey or jet lag, concurrent illness and your reception (or lack of reception) on arrival. Feelings of anxiety, perhaps even panic, are common, as well as a sense of isolation, disorientation, irritability, irrational anger, mild depression, mood swings and often tearfulness. The anxiety symptoms occur to a greater or lesser extent in most travellers but are often suppressed by the excitement of being somewhere new.

A first step in minimizing the impact of a new culture is to do a little **research** into your destination before you set out (the "knowledge is power" principle at work again): read as much as you can, check out relevant Web sites and speak to people who have been there before.

On arrival, give yourself time to rest, recuperate and emotionally **acclimatize** to your new surroundings. Avoid making rash or important decisions in the first few days. Try not to seek solace in alcohol or any other drugs, as these are only likely to have a depressant effect and make the situation worse.

Try to **involve** yourself early. Start by chatting to fellow travellers where you're staying and participating in group activities. Get out and about and make the effort to interact with the locals. Set about seeing some of the sights in the first few days in case you need reminding of why you made the trip initially. Take an interest in and respect the new culture and avoid clashing with, or resisting it – you'll

make yourself unpopular and feel more isolated.

Above all, recognize culture **shock** for what it is. The initial symptoms usually dissipate and are forgotten after the first couple of days. If your low mood or anxiety persist, try giving yourself a little more time before deciding to move on or return home.

Culture shock has a **positive** side. Exposure to a different culture and environment can be a rewarding and refreshing experience, often bringing into focus and adding new perspective and context to the stresses and problems left behind at home. Reflection, or perhaps the time to reflect, is a rare and under-isolated luxury to many in the Western world.

Cuts and abrasions

▷▷See First Aid, p.419.

Cystitis

▷▷See Urinary tract infections, p.391.

Dehydration

In its simplest terms **dehydration** is caused either by excessive **fluid loss** (eg diarrhoea, vomiting, fever, bleeding, sweating, etc) or **inadequate fluid intake**.

The average **adult** should drink between 2 and 3 litres of fluid a day, although requirements increase in hot climates and during strenuous exercise. Susceptibility to dehydration is much higher in young **children**.

Thirst is the most obvious **symptom** although other

signs to look out for include a dry mouth and tongue, a loss of skin elasticity (tested by pinching the skin), dark, strong-smelling urine with a drop in output, headache or backache and, in more severe cases, fainting, lapsing into consciousness and a weak but rapid pulse. Dehydrated children tend to be listless and quiet, with dry, sunken eyes and, in babies, a sagging, flaccid fontanelle, or "soft spot".

If the dehydration is the result of diarrhoea or vomiting, start simply by taking frequent sips of **boiled water**. As this is tolerated, gradually build up your fluid intake with diluted fruit juice or, better still, **oral rehydration salts** (see p.60). Aim at taking a cupful for every loose stool passed. Don't attempt to eat solids until you are comfortable with fluids – fluid intake is much more important.

If you're unable to take fluids orally and there are signs of dehydration, seek medical attention as intravenous fluids may be required.

Dengue fever

Outbreaks of **dengue fever** occur in most tropical and sub-tropical regions of the Far East, the Middle East, South America and Africa with periodic epidemics in the Caribbean and Pacific Islands, Australia and the southern United States. The past 20 years has witnessed a steady rise in prevalence of dengue, with the WHO estimating currently that around 50 million cases occur each year. The main reasons for this explosion are poor mosquito control, inadequate public health measures, expanding urbanization and population growth leading to deterioration in sanitation, and increased air travel allowing early spread of the virus.

Dengue fever is a virus spread by the Aedes species of

DENGUE FEVER

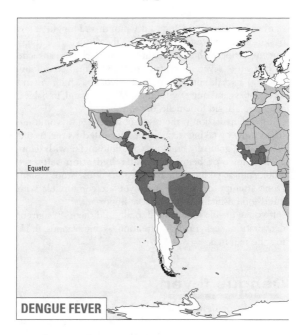

Equator

DENGUE FEVER

mosquito, identifiable by its black-and-white body and its penchant for biting shadowed areas of our bodies during daylight hours – usually in early morning or late afternoon. The mosquito is rarely found above elevations of 4000 feet (approx. 1200 metres).

You can't catch dengue from another person. A preventative vaccine is being developed, but for now your only means of avoidance is vigilant bite prevention (see p.259).

Although contracting the infection confers immunity, there are 4 separate subtypes of the virus, and it is unfortu-

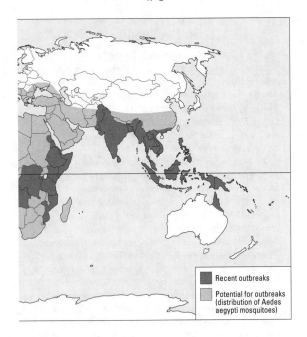

Recent outbreaks

Potential for outbreaks
(distribution of Aedes
aegypti mosquitoes)

DENGUE FEVER

nate that immunity to one does not extend to the other strains.

A rare but serious complication, which mainly affects children under 15, is **dengue haemorrhagic fever** (DHF). The predisposing factors to dengue haemorrhagic fever are mainly the particular viral subtype and epidemic strain, recurrent infections, age, general level of health, geographic region (a preponderance of cases are in Southeast Asia) and possibly genetic factors. It is particularly common in people who have suffered a previous attack with one of

197

"It can't happen to me"

After a gruelling 5 months backpacking through Southeast Asia, we finally reached Sumatra. The first night was spent in the bustling, grimy, tropical heat of Medan after which it was a relief to finally reach Bukit Lewang, home of the Orang Utan Rehabilitation Centre in the heart of the jungle. This was to be one of the highlights of our trip where we planned to base ourselves for a few days before moving on to the even more remote Lake Toba.

We reached our destination in the evening, after a six-hour journey by local bus which I was in no hurry to repeat. Little did I know I'd be making a premature return trip under even less comfortable circumstances. We woke early the next morning to make the 30-minute walk to see the orang-utans. As we set off, I found the intense heat and humidity even more stifling than before but couldn't account for my growing aches and lethargy. I finally collapsed on a rock by the river. Realizing this was not just another attack of Delhi-belly, my partner carried me back to our accommodation where I lay delirious for several hours. My body groaned with every movement, my head pounded as though it would explode and my fever soared. The grim reality of being in the backend of nowhere without medical help or even the ability to converse sensibly with the locals was hitting home. This was the classic "it can't happen to me" scenario.

My partner started to fret about malaria (even though I'd been taking antimalarials) and realizing that my condition was deteriorating, decided we needed to get back to Penang for medical attention (I was in no state to make any assessment of the situation).

I started vomiting into a plastic bag even before our taxi driver began to negotiate the dirt roads at breakneck speed. My fever hovered at an alarmingly high level and with fantastically poor timing I developed "explosive" diarrhoea.

On the outskirts of Medan, our taxi driver was stopped by the police and promptly arrested (we assumed because of speeding), leaving me lying on the pavement while my partner tried, with some difficulty, to seek alternative transport. We eventually managed to find a driver willing to take us to a hostel (for a hefty price of course). With electric fan by my bedside, polythene bags and a toilet close by, I rested while my partner booked our ferry to Penang. We needed to leave at 5am the next morning (too early for Sumatran taxi drivers) so had to walk for 45 minutes to catch the bus. Still suffering from sickness, diarrhoea and excruciating pain throughout my body, I thought I would never make it.

Some 6 hours or so later, I arrived in Penang feeling dehydrated, tearful and exhausted. Perhaps having momentarily forgotten his concern for my welfare, my partner asked if I could face the 30-minute walk to save on taxi fares! The next day I had a test for malaria at a local health clinic which proved negative. We were relieved by the negative result and the fact I was showing some signs of improvement, but my illness dragged on for several more weeks and in latter stages produced a new range of symptoms including a dreadfully itchy rash, intense fatigue and depression. We were becoming increasingly despondent at my lack of recovery and starting to contemplate a premature return home. It was not until we met several other travellers who had encountered similar symptoms and pursued medical opinion that we identified the cause of my illness: dengue fever. On reaching Singapore, several weeks later, my symptoms started to subside and I was able to remember why I had set out on my travels in the first place.

Joanna Gibbons, Bath, UK

"IT CAN'T HAPPEN TO ME"

the viral subtypes and who are then exposed to another, subtype. The victim may become shocked (pale, clammy faint and nauseous with a weak, rapid pulse and shallow, rapid breathing), and develop abnormal bleeding into the skin, and from the nose, mouth and rectum. This is a life-threatening complication and requires urgent medical attention.

SYMPTOMS

The **symptoms** of dengue fever are remarkably similar to malaria and usually appear between 5 and 8 days after being bitten. The onset is usually abrupt and includes high fever, malaise, headache (characteristically behind the eyes), joint pains and backache (hence dengue has been nicknamed "**break bone fever**"). Diarrhoea is fairly common after the first day and, although often being explosive in nature, it doesn't normally last more than a couple of days. A fine rash is likely to appear after a couple of days, initially affecting your torso before spreading to the extremities. It can be maddeningly itchy. The high temperature usually normalizes for a day or two before briefly recurring with the original symptoms. Abnormal bleeding can occur and will need medical assessment.

The acute illness does not normally last for more than 10 days, but the convalescence can be protracted, with severe fatigue and depression that may last for several weeks afterwards.

DIAGNOSIS AND TREATMENT

A **blood test** will reveal the virus or the viral antibodies. There is no specific treatment for dengue, and symptom control is your only option until the disease has taken its natural course. Get plenty of **bed rest** during the initial stages take steps to reduce the fever (see p.216). **Don't take** aspirin because it can increase the tendency to bleed. **Antihistamines** and **calamine** may ease the rash, and **loperamide** the diarrhoea. Seek medical help immediately if dengue haemorrhagic fever is suspected. Remember that anyone in a malarial area with the symptoms of dengue should also be checked for malaria.

You can treat dengue **homeopathically** using Eupatorium perf. (30c) 2 or 3 times daily for 5–6 days. Stop taking it on day 2 if there are no signs of improvement.

Diarrhoea

▷▷See Gastrointestinal upsets, p.226.

Diphtheria

Diphtheria is a bacterial illness spread from person-to-person. It can occur anywhere in the world but is rare in countries that have established childhood immunization programmes. (Significant outbreaks have occurred in the NIS in recent years following the collapse of such programmes.)

In countries without an immunization programme, asymptomatic carriers are often responsible for spreading the disease. The majority of people in developed countries have been immunized against diphtheria in childhood. If you have not received a booster for more than 10 years, however, and you're planning to visit a less developed country where the immunization programme may be sketchy or where there is an active epidemic, you should have a booster vaccination before you leave.

SYMPTOMS

After an incubation period of between 2 and 6 days, early symptoms are a **sore throat**, **fever** and **chills**. The **breath smells** very offensive and the **lymph glands** in the neck become very **swollen**. As the disease progresses, it becomes **difficult to swallow** because of pain and the presence of a **leathery membrane** over the tonsils and across the throat (a diagnostic feature of the disease). The bacteria causing diphtheria secrete a toxin, which can cause heart failure and paralysis. Diphtheria remains highly **infectious** for 10 days after the onset of fever.

DIAGNOSIS AND TREATMENT

Although a **lab culture** of throat swabs or blood can identify the bacteria, you can't really afford to wait around for test results – this is a potentially lethal disease and you need to seek urgent medical help. Intravenous antibiotics such as penicillin and erythromycin can be used to eliminate the bacteria, but an intravenous antitoxin also needs to be given to counteract the effects of the bacterial toxin.

Dracunculiasis

(Guinea worm infection)

Dracunculiasis has been eradicated from many regions of the world where it used to be prevalent. The vast majority of cases are now reported from southern Sudan, with occasional outbreaks in other sub-Saharan countries, and a few sporadic cases in Yemen.

The infection is contracted by drinking water contaminated with Cyclops water fleas that carry the guinea worm larvae. Once inside the stomach, the larvae penetrate through the intestinal wall, mature into adult worms and migrate to the peripheral tissues. The worm exits the body by boring through the surface skin (usually the feet but also from the genitalia, hands and breasts). It can take up to 3 weeks for the worm to fully emerge and it is during this time that embryos are shed into the water during bathing. Thus the cycle goes around again.

Dracunculiasis is largely restricted to poor, rural communities that are isolated from the well-beaten tourist tracks. Observe the usual water precautions in high-risk areas – boiling drinking water kills both the fleas and the larvae. No vaccination or preventative medication is available.

SYMPTOMS

The time from ingestion to emergence of the adult worms usually presents no symptoms and goes unrecognized. If the worm enters a joint during migration it can cause pain and swelling. The skin swells, blisters and ruptures when the thread-like worm exits, leaving an extremely painful ulcer which can take several weeks to heal. A more generalized allergic reaction to the emerging worm may take place causing nausea, vomiting, diarrhoea, swelling, wheeze and an itchy rash. Symptoms, both local and more generalized, can persist for prolonged periods when several worms are expelled successively.

DIAGNOSIS AND TREATMENT

The emerging worm, when visible, can be coaxed to release its larvae by repeated immersion in water over a period of days (the larvae look like a milky fluid). After a few days of this "milking" the worm will protrude sufficiently for gentle traction to be applied as it is carefully wound around a stick. It can take 2 weeks or more to

DRACUNCULIASIS

remove the worm in this way (the mature worms can be up to 1m long). Take care not to leave any residual pieces behind in the tissues since they can cause serious secondary infection. Taking a 5-day course of **metronidazole** 400mg twice daily can shorten the time it takes to extract the worm.

On the emergence of the worm a tetanus booster will be necessary if you're not up to date.

Ear problems

Infections of the ear are not uncommon especially after a cold, swimming or in hot, tropical conditions. Broadly speaking, ear infections can be divided into **2 types**: infections of the middle ear (behind the eardrum) and infections of the outer ear (outside the eardrum).

Middle ear infections are far more common in children than in adults, frequently following an upper respiratory tract infection. They are often bacterial in origin, although some are viral. Intense and acute, throbbing pain in the affected ear is the most prominent symptom. There is often a fever, as well as deafness and occasionally ringing in the ear. There may be a discharge, although this means that the drum has perforated and there will be subsequent relief from the pain. If this occurs, don't panic, the drum will usually grow back without any long-term damage although water entering the ears (eg through swimming) should be avoided for at least a month.

The mainstay of treatment is pain relief. The pain from an infected eardrum can be intense and children in particular will be very miserable and unsettled. Regular paracetamol is usually adequate. If the diagnosis is fairly certain, starting a 5- to 7-day course of antibiotics is appropriate (although not always necessary) and amoxycillin is generally regarded as the best option, but erythromycin (the first choice if you are allergic to penicillin) and co-amoxiclav are also effective. If in doubt, it's better to treat conservatively with painkillers alone.

Infections of the **outer ear** are also painful and the discomfort is often made worse by jaw movements. Discharge, deafness and visible swelling may also occur. The tragus (the hard bobble of flesh in front of the ear hole) and the ear lobe itself are often very tender. The frequent causes are inadequate drying of the ear after swimming, the presence of a foreign body or trauma (eg scratching or cleaning the ear with cotton buds). The causes of infections of outer ear can be bacterial (most commonly), fungal or viral. The best initial treatment is regular application of antibiotic eardrops, usually combined with a mild steroid to reduce inflammation. Apply 3–4 drops 3–4 times a day followed by gentle massage of the tragus to allow deeper penetration into the ear canal. A 2-week course is generally recommended. A course of systemic antibiotics, the choices being flucloxacillin, amoxycillin, co-amoxiclav or erythromycin, may be helpful as a supplementary treatment if the infection is severe. If symptoms persist despite these measures, it's best to seek medical help, as occasionally the residual debris in the ear canal will need to be removed by suction.

Reinfection is common in both inner and outer ear infections and it is sensible to avoid swimming for a month following the infection. Scuba diving is not recommended until the infection is fully healed and a doctor has checked for perforations of the eardrums.

EAR PROBLEMS

Fluid behind the drum

Fluid in the middle ear is not uncommon following a cold or an ear infection. The problem arises when the **eustachian tube** (the tube connecting the inner ear to the back of the nose), which allows pressure to equalize on both sides of the eardrum, becomes blocked. The sensation is frequently likened to being underwater – you're unable to "pop" the ears, causing a temporary reduction in hearing. Fluid trapped behind the eardrum can lead to significant discomfort when flying or scuba diving (activities which alter the pressure gradient across the eardrum).

The symptoms usually settle without treatment within a month, although it is best to avoid flying or scuba diving while the ear still feels blocked. Occasionally **nasal decongestants** and **steam inhalation** can help to alleviate the blockage.

 A **homeopathic remedy** that eases blocked ears when you're flying is Kali. mur. (1–4 6c tablets, depending on age), taken every 2 or 3 minutes on the way up and on the way down.

Earwax

We all produce **earwax** as part of the normal, natural cleansing process of the ear, but sometimes the outer ear canal can become blocked causing hearing loss. Do not attempt to remove earwax yourself; a good rule of thumb is not to put anything smaller than your elbow in your ear – resist using matchsticks and cotton buds as picking tools. Try softening the wax with some drops of warm olive oil: lie on your side and have someone place 2 or 3 drops of oil in your ear, then wait for a few minutes before plugging the ear loosely with cotton wool. If this fails to improve your hearing you might need to have your ears syringed (after adequate softening of the wax) by a doctor.

are a few points that the older traveller ought to bear in mind before setting out.

First, weigh up carefully the risks of travelling, particularly if you suffer from a chronic illness. Although you are not necessarily more vulnerable to the common travel illnesses, it will take your body longer to restore itself back to normal. Be aware of how particular climates or environments (altitude, heat, heavily polluted air, long flights) may affect existing medical conditions.

▷▷See also Altitude, p.150; Cold exposure, p.172; Fitness to fly, p.24; and Heat exposure, p.238.

The usual **pre-trip preparations** are particularly important for the mature traveller. Ensure you have the relevant immunizations and carry your personal medical details and any medications in a readily accessible place. Make sure that you have an adequate level of travel insurance and consider whether your levels of fitness are adequate for your planned activities – a foreign country is not the place to test your limits. Avoid over-extending yourself by building more time for rest breaks into your itinerary.

If you're 60 years or over and want to use homeopathic remedies during a trip, it's best to choose lower potencies.

Carry any necessary spares (spectacles, hearing-aid batteries, etc) with you, as these may be difficult to obtain at your destination. Inform your travel agent or airline beforehand if you are likely to require assistance boarding the aircraft or carrying luggage. You might consider taking low-dose aspirin daily to reduce the risk of a DVT (see p.30) when flying.

The elderly are regarded as more vulnerable by predators so it's important to look streetwise (see p.49) and avoid risky areas.

▷▷See also notes on influenza (p.252).

The disabled traveller

There is no reason why anyone with a disability, large or small, temporary or permanent, should be excluded from travelling abroad. True, the logistics may seem daunting and the planning must be thorough as well as flexible, but a positive, focused attitude goes a long way.

Be sensible and realistic in the planning stage. Acceptance and acknowledgement by all involved of your disabilities and limitations, coupled with a clear knowledge of what to expect at your destination, are crucial. You are the best judge of your abilities but be careful not to overestimate them in the excitement of a trip abroad. Don't forget how tiring travelling can be – mentally, physically and emotionally.

Much will depend on your specific disability and level of independence. How much help will be required at the airports, during the flight, in transit from the airport to accommodation and at the accommodation itself? Do you have specific requirements for accommodation, such as wheelchair access, ground floor rooms, an elevator, shower facilities or the ability of staff to speak your own language? Is it viable to consider travelling alone or will you need a helper to travel with you? If so, do you have someone who can travel with you or do you need help finding someone?

If you frequently have your ears syringed at home and are planning a prolonged trip, add it to your list of things to do before you leave.

Eastern equine encephalitis

Eastern equine encephalitis occurs in isolated outbreaks along the eastern seaboard of the US, Canada, the Caribbean and parts of Central and South America. It can occur all year around in the tropics but further north tends to be a summer illness, with the majority of cases occurring between May and August, often in swamp areas. The disease is extremely serious, but by the same token very rare among humans – it usually strikes birds and horses. The virus is spread to humans by mosquitoes. According to the American CDC, fewer than 10 human cases on average occur each year in the US.

Although a vaccine exists for horses, there is no preventative vaccine for humans.

SYMPTOMS

An abrupt-onset **high fever** is usually accompanied by headache, lethargy and vomiting. Progression of the disease leads to drowsiness, neck stiffness, fits and coma. The mortality rate of those severely affected is high and long-term effects in survivors are common, although adults tend to be more resilient than children.

DIAGNOSIS AND TREATMENT

Antibodies to the virus can be detected by lab analysis of a **blood sample**. There is no specific treatment other than **symptom relief**, intensive care and life support.

Ebola virus

Epidemics of the **Ebola virus** have made sporadic but devastating appearances since it was first recognized in 1976 after an outbreak along the Ebola River in Zaire. The disease affects humans, monkeys and chimpanzees with confirmed cases in the Democratic Republic of Congo, Gabon, Sudan and the Cote d'Ivoire. Healthcare workers in Africa should be on alert for the infection, but with outbreaks rare and generally restricted to isolated, rural areas, most travellers are unlikely to encounter the disease.

The virus is believed to be spread by direct contact with the blood, secretions, organs or semen of an infected human or animal, although its natural reservoir has yet to be pinpointed. Outbreaks have been known to spread rapidly in the rural hospital setting, where sterilization procedures and nursing standards may be inadequate.

SYMPTOMS

Within a few days after infection, a **high fever**, **sore throat**, **headache** and **muscular aches**, **stomach pains**, **diarrhoea** and **fatigue** become apparent. Around day 5, a non-itchy **pink rash** commonly spreads from the face to the rest of the body. Other symptoms include a dry cough, red and irritable eyes, vomiting blood and bloody diarrhoea. Within a week in severe cases abnormal bleeding, blindness, chest pain, shock and even death can ensue. Infection with Ebola virus is very serious but it is survivable, although why some people recover and others die is still poorly understood.

DIAGNOSIS AND TREATMENT

Early diagnosis is often difficult because the initial symptoms are non-specific. Once suspected, **blood tests** can confirm Ebola infection.

There is no specific treatment although an intravenous anti-viral agent called **ribavirin** may help. Hospital admission for supportive care is vital.

Echincoccosis

▷▷ See Hydatid disease, p.250.

Ehrlichiosis

Ehrlichiosis is a relatively recently recognized bacterial infection with outbreaks in parts of the eastern seaboard, south-central and midwest USA. It occurs in the same geographical areas, and is spread by the same **ticks,** as Lyme disease, although is far rarer. Incidence is highest in the summer months when the ticks are most active.

SYMPTOMS

Symptoms are very similar to those for Rocky Mountain spotted fever and Lyme disease. Onset is usually between 5 and 10 days after the initial tick bite, with common features including sudden fever, headache, rigors, muscle aches, nausea and vomiting. A generalized rash appears more commonly in children than in adults. Untreated, the disease can lead to serious complications such as meningitis and abnormal bleeding, and may adversely affect lung, liver and kidney function. Ehrlichiosis is a severe illness but is only rarely fatal.

DIAGNOSIS AND TREATMENT

Diagnosis is usually confirmed by a blood test. Early treatment, with either doxycycline or chloramphenicol, is necessary to prevent the disease's rapid progression, so if you suspect it don't wait for the lab results.

▷▷ See Lyme disease, p.278; Rocky Mountain spotted fever, p.323.

Eye problems

The dry atmosphere on long-distance flights, dusty, hot environments, swimming underwater, pollution, allergies and hygiene problems can all take their toll on your **eyes**. In most cases, simple moisturizing **eye drops** will provide relief. More of a problem, "**conjunctivitis**", or "pink eye", simply refers to inflammation of the thin membrane covering the white of the eye and the inner surface of the lids (the conjunctiva), and is symptomatic of a number of eye problems, from infections to allergies. The eye is red, itchy, irritable and watering. In infections there may be a sticky discharge, particularly after sleep. You may also be intolerant of bright lights. Conjunctivitis should not cause eye pain as such, nor impair your vision (other than from excessive tear production). If these symptoms occur, seek medical advice. Don't forget that most opticians will be suitably equipped to diagnose the cause of conjunctivitis.

While the risks to the average traveller of more serious eye diseases or injuries are only slight, impaired vision, eye pain and unequal pupils must always be assessed by a doctor.

Infections

Eye **infections** are relatively common especially among children. Conjunctivitis (see above) caused by infection is frequently one-sided, at least initially, although it's easy for the infection to spread to both eyes. Eye infections can be caused both by viruses and bacteria and it's difficult to differentiate between the two. There tends to be more discharge in the case of bacterial infections. Bacterial infections will also usually respond well to **antibiotic drops** or **ointment** such as chloramphenicol (see p.57), but be sure to avoid preparations that contain steroids (these can be dangerous if used inappropriately).

Sometimes the lids or roots of the eyelashes can become infected (**styes**). Mild infections are likely to resolve by themselves without treatment, but if the problem persists, antibiotics such as flucloxacillin, amoxycillin, co-amoxiclav or erythromycin will help.

Abrasions and foreign bodies

Grazes on the eye, or **corneal abrasions**, and **foreign bodies** embedded in the eye (eg dust, wood or metal splinters) cause the symptoms of conjunctivitis in the one eye. Although it is rarely possible to see abrasions with the naked eye, it is sometimes possible to see a particle in someone else's eye in a well-illuminated room as a dark speck in front of the pupil (try looking with a magnifying glass from the side with light coming from the opposite direction). Sometimes the particle will be loosely attached and may be freed by a simple eye bath using an egg cup and boiled, lightly salted water. More often than not the foreign body will be firmly embedded and medical help will be needed. Because of the risk of secondary infection, abrasions and removed foreign bodies need to be followed up with **prophylactic antibiotics**. Use a 5- to 7-day course to prevent infection. Resist the temptation of using local anaesthetic eye drops (eg amethocaine) because these slow down the healing process.

Allergies

Conjunctivitis is a common symptom in **allergic conditions** such as **hay fever.** Both eyes are usually affected and your nose tends to run with a watery discharge.

Antihistamines, such as chlorpheniramine and loratadine, and sodium cromoglycate eye drops are all helpful. Wearing spectacles or sunglasses may slightly reduce the amount of pollen reaching the eye.

Contact lenses

Contact lens wearers can be more prone to eye infections, and fastidious hand hygiene is important.

Lenses cause eye dryness at the best of times and the dry air in aircraft, at altitude and in hot, arid countries exacerbates the problem. Use moisturizing drops regularly. Carry spectacles in case you lose your lenses or are unable to wear them. Don't wear your lenses if you have inflamed eyes, ever.

Sub-conjunctival haemorrhage

This cumbersome medical phraseology simply means a painless bleed behind the conjunctiva caused by a ruptured blood capillary. The white of the eye looks bright red and although it usually occurs spontaneously, bleeds of this type are also associated with excessive coughing, straining, raised blood pressure and increased bleeding tendency (eg the viral haemorrhagic fevers, p.394). The condition, although it looks alarming, is benign and will normally resolve after a week or 2. No treatment is necessary for the bleed itself but consider whether you may be at risk from the possible underlying causes.

▷▷See also Brazilian Purpuric Fever, p.166; Cold exposure (Snow blindness), p.175; Loasis, p.222; Filariasis (Onchocerciasis), p.218; and Trachoma, p.379.

Doctor examining child, the Gambia. Photo © Liba Taylor/Corbis ▷

Fascioliasis

The liver fluke causing **fascioliasis** infects sheep, cattle and goats worldwide. It can be transmitted to humans who ingest food or water contaminated by the infected animals' faeces. The lifecycle of the fluke relies on the presence of a freshwater snail, which acts as an intermediate host to the larvae. Once swallowed by humans, the larvae penetrate the gut wall and migrate to the liver and biliary tract, where, after maturation, they begin to produce eggs. Misguided flukes have been found elsewhere in the body, such as the brain, the lungs and the skin.

Fascioliasis is a rare infection which can be easily avoided by observing the usual hygiene measures for drinking water (see p.40).

SYMPTOMS

Initial symptoms are non-specific – general **malaise**, intermittent **fever**, **weight loss**, **diarrhoea**, **abdominal pain** (mainly over the liver) and **itching** – and usually become apparent 2 or 3 months after infection. Once the flukes are in the biliary tract, they obstruct the flow of bile, causing **jaundice**.

DIAGNOSIS AND TREATMENT

The eggs can be identified in around 70% of cases by lab analysis of the **stool** once the flukes have reached the bile duct. More complicated blood tests can confirm the diagnosis.

A single dose of **triclabendazole** (10mg per kg body weight) is usually enough to eradicate the flukes, but a second dose may sometimes be necessary.

Fasciolopsiasis

(Giant intestinal fluke)

The **Fasciolopsiasis** fluke is commonly found in pigs and humans in south China, Taiwan, Southeast Asia (especially Vietnam and Thailand), Indonesia, India and Bangladesh. Humans are infected by eating raw water plants (eg water chestnuts or water caltrop) contaminated by larval cysts. The flukes are released from the cysts in the human intestine where they mature into adults, sometimes several centimetres long, after about 3 months. The eggs are shed in the stools and, on reaching fresh water, penetrate and develop into larvae in freshwater snails (similar to **paragonimiasis**) before escaping to form cysts on the plants. The average traveller is at low risk of contracting fasciolopsiasis, provided they observe adequate food and water hygiene measures.

▷▷See Paragonimiasis, p.309; Staying well, p.40.

SYMPTOMS

Most people show no signs of the infection, but in a few, severe cases, symptoms such as **abdominal pain** or discomfort, **loss of appetite**, **nausea**, **diarrhoea or constipation** can develop several months after ingesting the cysts. **Swelling** of the face and body can occur later on. **Anaemia** because of blood loss from the site of attachment of the flukes in the intestine is also possible. Heavy infection in children can cause malnutrition.

DIAGNOSIS AND TREATMENT

Microscopic examination of the **stools** shows the presence of the eggs. The disease can be treated with a single dose (15mg per kg body weight) of **praziquantel**.

Fever

(Pyrexia)

A **fever** is a complex physiological process characterized by a rise in the core temperature of the body. There are many causes for fever ranging from the innocuous viral sore throat to life-threatening nasties such as malaria. Identifying the root cause of a fever is not easy, especially in the tropics where most of the prevalent diseases cause a fever.

In a malarial zone, the presence of a fever means
malaria until proved otherwise!

Normal core body temperature is 37°C (98°F); generally anything over 39°C (102°F) is considered to be **high fever**. The most accurate way to take a reading is by placing a **thermometer** under the tongue or inside the rectum for no less than 3 minutes. A young child's temperature can be taken under the armpit, although the reading will be roughly half a degree centigrade lower than core temperature.

Fever leads to a general feeling of **malaise**, a sensation of feeling **hot then cold**, **sweating**, **shaking** (known as "rigors"), generalized **aches** and **pains**, **nightmares** and, in the extreme, **delirium**.

TREATMENT

Initial treatment should focus on reducing the body temperature. The treatment of specific infections is secondary and discussed elsewhere throughout this guide.

Measures to **reduce fever** include:

+ Taking regular paracetamol or ibuprofen
+ Increasing the intake of cool fluids – aim to drink at least 3 litres a day (more in hot climates) and avoid alcohol

+ Getting plenty of rest
+ Taking regular cool showers, or alternatively sponging down with cooled water
+ Minimizing layers of clothing even if you feel chilly
+ Fanning to reduce your body heat

Temperatures **below 39°C** are generally not dangerous – try to get your temperature down and if after 48 hours there's no reduction seek a doctor's help. A fever **above 39°C** should be taken more seriously. Take the steps above to reduce high temperature, but if in spite of these the high fever persists for more than 24 hours, seek medical advice. If at any time you develop symptoms of malaria or meningitis or you have a high fever and may have been at risk of either disease, seek medical help immediately.

Eupatorium Perfoliatum (30c 2–3 times a day for 5–6 days) is a **homeopathic remedy** used to reduce high fever in cases of simple flu as well as dengue and malaria. It will suit if you have chills spreading from the small of your back, a great thirst for cold drinks, but also nausea. You may feel restless and want to keep moving, even though motion doesn't actually help. (Discontinue taking the remedy after the second day if it's not having any effect.)

DIAGNOSIS

Fever is usually a sign of an **infection** but can also be caused by **heatstroke**. In determining the cause, consider the kinds of diseases to which you may have exposed yourself, any other symptoms you may have, and whether your condition is improving or deteriorating. If the fever is worsening, you'll need to seek medical input urgently. If the fever recurs in a cycle, for example every 48 hours, consider the possibility of malaria or dengue fever and

FEVER

take steps towards getting a lab test. Don't attempt strenuous physical activity for at least 2 weeks following a high fever, as it'll take at least that long to regain your strength.

▷▷See Making a diagnosis; p.132; Malaria, p.279; Meningitis, p.295.

Febrile convulsions

Febrile convulsions are an alarming complication of fever affecting some young **children**, usually between the ages of 6 months and 6 years. There is no specific "danger point" in a rising temperature at which they're more likely to happen, but only a small minority of children are susceptible to them (around 3%). Paediatric **paracetamol** is the mainstay of treatment to reduce temperature, but sponging them down or placing them in a lukewarm bath is also helpful to compensate for the fact that children's bodies are inefficient at sweating (a cooling mechanism).

See p.91 for the first aid treatment of a fit. Most febrile fits are self-limiting and rarely last longer than a couple of minutes. If the fit persists for longer, seek medical help urgently.

Filariasis

Widespread in the tropics, where they cause millions of people significant health problems, **filarial infections** are caused by parasitic worms and spread by biting insects. There are three distinct diseases caused by filarial worms: **onchocerciasis**, **filarial lymphangitis** and **loasis**.

Onchocerciasis

(Mal morado, River blindness, Roble's disease, Volvulosis)

Affecting more than 18 million people globally, **onchocerciasis** is a major cause of blindness in the developing world. The disease is found mainly in tropical Africa (95% of cases are in West Africa), but some cases also occur in tropical South and Central America and the Arabian peninsula. Onchocerciasis is caused by a worm parasite that is transmitted to humans via the bite of a **blackfly** generally found alongside stretches of fast-flowing water. The blackfly's bite deposits the larvae, which penetrate into the superficial tissues beneath the skin. A year elapses before the worm matures and starts to reproduce large numbers of tiny offspring – **microfilariae** – which migrate throughout the body. The adult worm can live for many years.

There is no effective vaccination or drug prophylaxis, so taking protective measures against insect bites in high-risk areas is crucial. Fortunately, even in high-risk areas, short-term travellers (staying less than 3 months) rarely acquire onchocerciasis.

▷▷See Bite prevention, p.259.

SYMPTOMS

The most prominent symptom caused by the large numbers of microfilariae produced by the mature adult worms is a widespread, red, maddeningly itchy **rash**. Skin nodules ("**bony bumps**") develop at the site where the adult worm is lodged. In Africa, the lesions are usually on the lower part of the body, while in the Americas they tend to be on the head, neck, shoulders or upper trunk. Other symptoms are caused by the microfilariae liberated around the body and include **fever**, **headache**, **lymph gland swelling** and **tiredness**. During migration, the microfilariae can lodge in the eyes, causing initial redness and irritation which if left untreated leads to **blindness** (hence the name "River blindness"). Such serious eye complications, however, are

FILARIASIS

219

only likely to affect people who are repeatedly infected over the course of many years.

FILARIASIS

DIAGNOSIS AND TREATMENT

Diagnosis is made either by the clinical picture or by a skin biopsy, which will reveal the presence of the microfilariae.

WHO trials of a drug called **ivermectin** have shown that a single oral dose once yearly is very effective at preventing the symptoms caused by the release of microfilarae. It doesn't kill the adult worm, however, and dosage must be continued annually until the worms die of old age – about 20 years. This and WHO's efforts to eradicate the blackfly breeding grounds have significantly decreased the incidence of onchocerciasis, giving high hopes for total elimination in the course of the next decade.

Filarial lymphangitis

(Bancroftian or Malayan filariasis)

Recognized as one of the world's leading causes of permanent disability, **filarial lymphangitis** is thought to affect more than 100 million people in sub-Saharan Africa, Egypt, southern Asia, the Western Pacific Islands, the northeastern coast of Central and tropical South America, and the Caribbean.

The disease is caused by infection with thread-like parasitic worms, which are spread from person to person (and in some strains, animal to human) by **mosquitoes**. The adult worms reside in the **lymph system**, liberating into the bloodstream microfilariae which the mosquitoes ingest during feeding. After a period of development in the mosquito, the larvae are deposited again during feeding and migrate via the bloodstream to the new host's lymph system.

There is no protective vaccination against filarial lymphangitis and your only means of protection is bite avoidance, although short-term, casual tourists are rarely affected.
▷▷See Bite prevention, p.259.

SYMPTOMS

Symptoms show themselves between 5 and 18 months after being bitten, as the parasitic worms slowly grow in the body's lymph system. The worms' presence in the lymph system causes a local inflammatory reaction, followed by scarring and consequent occlusion of the lymph channels. This in turn causes the accumulation of fluid (lymph) in the tissues and **swelling**. The swelling of the legs, in its extreme, can lead to a condition known as **elephantiasis**, so-called because of the skin's resemblance to an elephant's. The resulting disfigurement and reduced mobility are permanent. Scrotal swelling can also occur. Other symptoms include painful, **swollen lymph glands**, recurrent **fever**, skin **rashes**, **blindness** and a lung condition, **tropical pulmonary eosinophilia**, characterized by night-time coughing and wheezing.

DIAGNOSIS AND TREATMENT

A **blood test** will confirm the presence of infection. Diethylcarbamazine (2mg per kg body weight), taken 3 times a day for 3 weeks, is effective in killing the microfilariae and the adult worms. Reactions to the dead microfilariae and worms are common and can be severe, however, often necessitating additional treatment with antihistamines and steroids. It's hoped that shortly **ivermectin** (see opposite) will be licensed for the treatment of this type of filariasis.

FILARIASIS

Loasis

(Loa loa)

Loasis occurs in the forested areas of west and central Africa, particularly in Sudan and Cameroon. It is caused by the worm of the same name, which is transmitted to humans (its natural host) by the daytime-biting **tabanid flies**. Once the eggs are inside the body, they take about a year to mature into the adult worms, which move about freely under the skin and can measure up to 6cm long and 0.5mm in diameter. The females liberate microfilariae into the bloodstream, which are then taken up and transmitted to others by the feeding tabanid flies.

No vaccination against loasis is available, although risk to the average traveller is only slight. If you're likely to come into close, prolonged contact with the disease, speak to an expert about taking a weekly 300mg dose of diethylcarbamazine.

SYMPTOMS

Loasis very rarely causes serious complications, and the adult worms generally go unnoticed unless they pass through the bridge of the nose or the conjunctiva of the eye. You may feel the worm in your eye, even see it, and the irritation may continue for several days after the worm has moved on. Other signs of the worm are transient, soft, usually painless skin swellings known as "**Calabar swellings**" (named after a town in eastern Nigeria), which occur more commonly in the hotter months, appearing in close proximity to joints – they're thought to be caused by the migrating worms releasing a toxin in response to a minor local trauma. A localized, sometimes painful, swelling also occurs when the worm dies.

DIAGNOSIS AND TREATMENT

Diagnosis can usually be confirmed by a **blood test**. The

treatment is the same as for filarial lymphangitis (**diethyl-carbamazine**). When sighted in the eye or around the bridge of the nose, the worm can be removed by a doctor under local anaesthetic, but don't dawdle as you may have a window of only a few days.

Flu

▷▷See Influenza, p.252.

Foot problems

A number of factors can conspire against the traveller's **feet**, from ill-fitting hiking boots, extremes of heat and cold, unhygienic showers and swimming facilities, to perhaps a greater reliance than usual on walking. Resulting fungal infections, ingrowing nails, aches and sprains can all chip away at your trip enjoyment.

Athlete's foot is an itchy fungal infection that can cause intense irritation in hot conditions. You'll often see redness between the toes, accompanied by fluid-filled lumps (vesicles), fissuring and peeling of the skin. Treat athlete's foot with an antifungal cream such as clotrimazole and be sure to apply the cream for at least 2 weeks after the symptoms have settled – a common mistake is to stop using the antifungal too soon, resulting in recurrences of the condition.

Ingrowing toenails are a minor but nevertheless painful condition usually caused by incorrect trimming of the nail, although wearing ill-fitting shoes may also contribute. They usually affect the big toe, and the flesh surrounding the nail becomes red, swollen and painful. The problem often requires surgical treatment and, despite this, frequently recurs. **Preventing** a nail from ingrowing is simply a matter of cutting the nail straight across and **not** down to the peripheries (following the curve of the nail), allowing the nail to grow towards the centre rather than into the flesh at the edges. If you already have an ingrowing toenail, clip it in the same way – if you've caught the nail early, it may prevent the need for more radical action. **Secondary bacterial infection** is common and manifests as an angry, painful, red, and pustular swelling. It should be treated using antibiotics (flucloxacillin, co-amoxiclav or erythromycin). In addition, soak your foot in warm water, preferably containing antiseptic or salt. After the infection has settled, gently wedge a small piece of cotton wool under the edge of the nail to prevent it from cutting into the skin. Wear roomy shoes and keep your feet as clean and dry as possible. Seek advice from a doctor as to whether anything further needs to be done about the nail.

▷▷See also First aid (Soft-tissue injuries), p.415; Cold exposure (Frostbite), p.173; Cold exposure (Trenchfoot), p.175.

Freshwater hazards

Freshwater holds a range of **hazards**, from creatures to currents to a host of diseases. For the exhausted, overheated traveller, the temptation to cool off in the local lake or river can be quite strong, but before taking the plunge, consider the dangers lurking beneath the water's surface.

Currents and buoyancy

River currents can be deceptive, while **buoyancy** in freshwater is less than that of saltwater – a dangerous combination that increases the risks of drowning accidents. Even if you are a strong and experienced swimmer, exercise caution at all times and heed local advice. If you are rafting or canoeing always wear a buoyancy aid and a helmet.

Alligators and crocodiles

Alligators and crocodiles are potential hazards in the water-ways of southeastern USA (Florida and Louisiana especial-ly), tropical South America (mainly in the Amazon and Orinoco basins), tropical Africa, India, parts of Southeast Asia and Australia. Although not all species are dangerous to humans, alligators and crocodiles should always be treated with the utmost respect. It's worth remembering that some species are equally comfortable in fresh or saltwater.

Although they may appear sluggish on land, these decep-tive creatures are capable of moving extremely quickly over short distances. Never approach one, even if it appears to be asleep – they may just be laying in wait for their unsus-pecting dinner. They attack by attaching themselves to their victim with vice-like jaws and submerging, incapacitating their prey by breaking their neck in the course of spinning. All are most active at night and the majority of attacks occur during the rainy season.

For the average traveller, the risks of being attacked by a crocodile or alligator are small as long as you use common sense in areas where they proliferate, and heed local advice.

Fish

Tropical South American rivers hold the most dangers in terms of freshwater fish. **Electric eels** can inflict an elec-tric shock equivalent to 500 volts when touched, capable of killing an adult human. **Piranhas** attack their prey in shoals, inflicting considerable damage with razor-sharp teeth. They are most dangerous during the dry season when food is scarce. Also native to the Amazon region is the **can-diru**, a small eel-like fish which is parasitic to other fish and sometimes to humans. It swims up the urethra (opening to bladder) and lodges there or higher up in the bladder feeding on blood. This may result in blood loss and infection and may even be fatal. Removal is by surgery.

▷▷See also Cold exposure (Hypothermia), p.174; Leptospirosis, p.275; Schistosomiasis, p.337; and Staying well, pp.39–40.

Frostbite

▷▷See Cold exposure, p.173.

Gastrointestinal upsets

When people mention the words "travel" and "illness" in the same breath, chances are high that **diarrhoea** is really what they're talking about. Travellers' diarrhoea is a ubiquitous problem, and within the first 2 weeks of any visit to a developing country, the incidence among travellers may be as high as 50%. Bear in mind, however, that loose bowel movements, especially at the start of a trip, are fairly normal and usually settle spontaneously.

Travellers' diarrhoea can be symptomatic of a broad range of things, from a simple change in diet to severe diseases like typhoid or cholera. The vast majority of cases are mild and self-limiting, resolving themselves within 5 days without treatment, so before you panic, it might help to regard the condition as many experienced travellers do – as a sort of occupational hazard.

Prevention

As yet there's no **vaccine** targeting travellers' diarrhoea, but this may well change with interest being shown in promoting gut colonization of "friendly" bacteria to inhibit the growth of those more harmful. However, for the time being at least, your best bet is rigorous observation of the **food and drink hygiene** measures on pp.40–43.

Stomach acid acts as your body's own natural defence against the bugs that cause stomach upsets. If you have reduced stomach acidity because of recent surgery or taking regular heartburn medication, you will have less resistance. Ask your doctor about precautions before you travel.

The use of **antibiotics** prophylactically is a contentious area. They're best saved for targeted treatment rather than prevention (see p. 229). Studies have shown **bismuth subsalicylate** ("Pepto–Bismol"), in relatively high doses, to be an effective preventative. It overcomes the drawbacks of antibiotic resistance and side effects, but few people would choose to take high doses for prolonged periods – because of the cost, consistency and taste – so it's perhaps more of use for short trips or again as a treatment when symptoms arise.

Diagnosis

It's uncommon for diarrhoea to be an isolated symptom – at the same time you may experience nausea, vomiting, gripey abdominal pains (for more on abdominal pain, see p.136) and occasionally fever.

Blood mixed in with the stool may suggest a number of diagnoses, from simple haemorrhoids to dysentery to rarities like pseudomembranous colitis, a serious complication of antibiotic therapy (see p.314). In the case of **dysentery**, the diarrhoea is severe with watery, often bloody stools accompanied by fever (mild if amoebiasis is the cause but high in shigella). Potentially quite serious, it usually responds well to antibiotics (see p.229). In any case of bloody diarrhoea, try to submit a stool sample for lab analysis before you begin treating it.

▷▷See abdominal pain, p.136.

Diarrhoea's danger signs

In the event any of the following conditions apply, seek medical input:

✛ If your diarrhoea continues for more than 5 days.

✛ If blood is visible in the diarrhoea.

✛ If there are signs of dehydration.

✛ If abdominal pain becomes constant and unremitting.

✛ If there is high fever (above 39°C/102°F).

✛ If symptoms are particularly severe.

Treatment

It's amazing how many people try to continue travelling, even with quite debilitating diarrhoea. It's far better to **rest** up for a while. The majority of cases will settle within **5 days** without specific treatment.

However, it's very important to replace what's been lost. Solids are much less important than **fluids**: you can survive for weeks without food, not so without water. Bear in mind that you're losing fluids not just with the diarrhoea – fever, vomiting, and a hot climate will all contribute to **dehydration**. Remember, too, that **children** become dehydrated much more rapidly than adults.

▷▷ See Antiemetics, p.62; Dehydration, p.194.

Initially, boiled or bottled water may be adequate, but for persistent diarrhoea or vomiting, **oral rehydration fluid** (commercial or homemade – see p.60) is preferable as it replaces lost chemicals and salts as well as water. If vomiting makes it difficult to keep fluids down, take smaller amounts more often and try using an antiemetic drug (see p.62); antiemetic suppositories are useful if you're vomiting too frequently to keep the drug in

GASTROINTESTINAL UPSETS

the stomach long enough for it to work.

Bismuth subsalicylate ("Pepto-Bismol") offers effective relief in mild to moderate cases of travellers' diarrhoea (less than 3 episodes a day) without significant side effects.

The use of **antibiotics** for the treatment of travellers' diarrhoea is controversial. There's a weight of scientific evidence proving their efficacy backed up by the fact that they were issued to troops in the Gulf War conflict. On the flip side, antibiotics have side effects and sometimes these can be more severe than the condition they are being used to treat. This, coupled with the growing problem of antibiotic resistance (see p.55), emphasizes the need to target carefully the use of antibiotics for travellers' diarrhoea. Consider antibiotic use only in the following circumstances:

+ If lab stool analysis confirms a bacterial cause.
+ If there is blood mixed in with the diarrhoea.
+ If you have a high fever.
+ If the symptoms continue without signs of improvement for more than 48 hours or if you pass more than 6 stools over 24 hours.
+ If stopping, resting and treating conservatively is simply not a viable option.

There is no single antibiotic that can be used to treat all causes although **ciprofloxacin** covers the majority of bacterial causes (trimethoprim is also an option). There seems no firm agreement on the actual treatment regime but some studies have shown that a single 500mg dose may be as beneficial as a 3-day course. Short courses may have deleterious long-term effects by creating more resistant strains, so it is perhaps best to treat for no less than 3 days. It is not

GASTROINTESTINAL UPSETS

Alternative treatments for travellers' diarrhoea

 Arsenicum album (take 30c 5 or 6 times on the first day; continue, though slightly less often, for a day or two more if there is good improvement) is the best homeopathic remedy for an upset stomach caused by eating tainted food or water, ice cream, too many watery fruits, excess alcohol, and from any sudden change of diet. Choose this remedy if your stools are burning, dark and foul-smelling. You feel wiped out, anxious and perhaps fretful about being ill on holiday. You crave small sips of cold water, but vomit after drinking.

For basic over-indulgence in food (especially spicy or rich) and drink, which has triggered violent retching and vomiting so that you find it hard to stop, try **Nux vomica**. Your abdomen will feel tender and sore, worse on the pressure of a belt and from sudden movements, and you have a constant urge to go to the toilet, yet pass little despite much straining – it may feel as if the food is going the wrong way. You're irritable, short-tempered, and sensitive to light and noise.

Choose **Pulsatilla** if you are a lover of rich foods but suffer afterwards – the sensation is as though you have a heavy stone in your stomach and you feel sorry for yourself. Your stool is pale in colour or green, and may be mucousy.

China officinalis (dosage as for Arsenicum) can help treat diarrhoea after eating fruit, spoiled meat or fish, or drinking

effective against giardiasis or amoebiasis, which both usually respond to a 7-day course of metronidazole.

The use of **blockers** (such as loperamide, see p.61) may reduce the frequency of diarrhoea but can bung you up by reducing your gut motility, denying the organisms a means of exit. In the majority of cases, little harm will come from contaminated water or milk. Take this remedy if you feel bloated and burp prodigiously but without much relief. Your stools are dark, watery or yellow, smelly but painless. You're dehydrated, and hypersensitive to noise, touch, light, etc. (China can also help people suffering the effects of a loss of bodily fluids – sweat, tears, breastmilk and so on.)

Veratrum album is used for violent vomiting and diarrhoea. You may crave cold drinks and sour foods. You suffer profuse, watery, greenish or colourless stools, along with intense chills and cold sweating. Exhausted and limp, you experience crampy pains on defecating.

Podophyllum can help treat painless summer diarrhoea, where the stools are pale, thick and loose – like blended split pea soup. Your appetite is unaffected, but eating or drinking promotes a bowel rush. Your abdomen feels sore, especially over the liver area, but is relieved by rubbing.

The natural antibiotic properties of grapefruit-seed extract can help both as a preventative for diarrhoea, taken daily from the start of your trip, and as a treatment if you get ill. A 2- to 4-week course of acidophilus to rebalance your intestinal flora may help after an attack of diarrhoea, especially if you've taken antibiotics. It can also be taken during an attack. Aloe vera is a natural anti-inflammatory – drinking the juice during or after a stomach upset helps to heal the inflamed intestinal tract. Acupressure bands or ginger can also help to alleviate nausea and vomiting.

GASTROINTESTINAL UPSETS

using blockers cautiously, but they should **never** be overused, nor used to treat suspected dysentery. Since they don't kill the bugs responsible for the diarrhoea, recurrences are common. Blockers are perhaps most effective when used alongside antibiotics.

Rehabilitation

Eating solids during bouts of diarrhoea can trigger an episode, although small quantities of bland food will not cause any harm. Initially, concentrate on **fluid intake**. Start with sips of boiled or bottled water and, when tolerated, start on an oral rehydration drink or weakened fruit juice. In children, it is okay to continue breast-feeding, but cow's milk and dairy products may be poorly tolerated for a week or 2 after a bout of diarrhoea.

Once fluids are well tolerated, gently re-introduce **solids**. Keep it bland and small in quantity initially. Rice, pasta, potatoes, soup, bread, bananas and dry biscuits are reasonable starting points. Beans, lentils, chicken (boiled, grilled or roasted), boiled or grilled fish, and boiled eggs may be gradually introduced. Avoid rich, fatty, spicy or fried foods, dairy products, most raw fruit and alcohol in the first few days.

Persisting symptoms

There are a number of reasons why diarrhoea might persist. For continuing symptoms, you cannot expect to make realistic progress without sending a stool sample for lab culture. If no causative bugs are isolated (usually the case), **blood tests** can reveal the presence of bugs that may be missed on stool analysis. The possibility of **post-infectious lactose intolerance** or **irritable bowel syndrome (IBS; see p.262)** should also be considered (neither of these is likely if weight loss is apparent). Lactose intolerance is thought to be caused by the "friendly" bacteria in the gut essentially being flushed away by the diarrhoea. Their absence means that the gut cannot digest a sugar known as lactose (found in milk and dairy products). It may take a week or 2 for these bacteria to recolonize the gut and thus milk and dairy products are best avoided during this time.

Genital warts

▷▷See under Sexually transmitted diseases, p.350.

Giardiasis

Giardiasis can occur anywhere in the world, although the incidence is highest in areas where water supplies are not properly sanitized. St Petersburg in Russia is noteworthy for particularly high infection rates. Giardiasis is a common cause of **travellers' diarrhoea**.

Cysts of the giardiasis-causing protozoa can survive for longer than 3 months in water and are commonly found in streams and rivers. Infection is passed to humans by ingestion of contaminated water or food.

No vaccination is available so avoid drinking, or eating food off utensils that have been washed in, potentially contaminated water. Water boiled for 1 minute at sea level (or between 3 and 5 minutes at altitude) is generally considered sufficient to kill giardiasis. Chemical eradication (iodine, etc) is unreliable.

SYMPTOMS

The infection can go unnoticed but usually causes watery **diarrhoea**, **flatulence** (described as "eggy"), **nausea**, **weight loss** and **abdominal bloating** between 2 and 4 weeks after the cysts have been ingested. The symptoms generally last no more than 2 weeks and settle without treatment, although a minority of cases may continue to

❝Tummy trouble in Tibet❞

L ong dusty roads had led us independently to gather at the small Tibetan village of Tingri. There, in a dark, smoke-filled room, over butter-tea and noodles, we formed an alliance that was forged by a common goal. All three of us were chasing adventure, and so we set off on a two-week trek that would take us up into the heart of the Himalayas and to the head of the Rongbuck valley, a location that offered fine views of the north face of Everest. Although isolated, the valley had been a spiritual place and home long ago to a grand monastery. What remains of the original building today offers refuge to only a couple of monks, a nun and their big black mastiff.

We travelled light, supplementing what food we carried with staples acquired from locals along the way. We stayed in villages while passing through the lowlands, with yak herders in their tents as we gained altitude. It was a beautiful journey through a magical landscape and a foreign culture, but my health ensured that it was not a trip in paradise.

I had not been feeling well for a good part of our journey. I'd developed foul-smelling (sulphurous) burps, and my bowels weren't up to par either. One of my companions claimed that his mother was a physician, and this inherited characteristic allowed him to diagnose that I had giardiasis. He also had the drug to cure my ailment, or so he claimed. I popped a couple of pills, said a prayer, and continued on my way. I have no idea what he gave me, but whatever it was helped, temporarily.

A few days later I was feeling pretty bad again. I felt particularly under the weather when a drunken, Chinese-speaking and uniformed policeman confronted us in a lowland village demanding that we pay a permit fee for travelling through the area. I nearly lost all bodily control when he sent a sidekick off to fetch his rifle. Luckily his assistant never returned, and the man in uniform later apologized for his behaviour after sobering up.

We spent a night in that unfriendly place. I made countless trips to the "drop box", and experienced explosive diarrhoea all night. I was also vomiting with equal force, often barely making it out my bedroom door. I was throwing up into the dark night, then listening to starving dogs scavenge my vomit off the dust-covered ground. The lapping sound made me want to throw up all over again.

Another couple of demanding days brought us to the mouth of the Rongbuck valley. The surroundings were spectacular, but my physical condition dampened my appreciation of the scene. I tried to maintain a good humour, and a day's hike up the valley brought us eventually to the monastery. We were ceremonially welcomed by the resident monks, and offered salty yak-butter-tea and tsampa as refreshment, a rather simple fair that was well suited to my then delicate constitution. It was a setting clearly suited for monastic living, a location that naturally encouraged a lifestyle of profound reflection. And it was during our brief stay that my body had time to reflect on its physical state. Luckily for me, it decided to overcome its ailment, and I began to slowly feel better. With rest, and reasonably nourishing food, I gained enough strength to begin the journey out safely. Two weeks later I was in good health enjoying the numerous gastronomic delicacies that the Nepalese capital, Kathmandu, had to offer. My Tibetan journey had certainly provided much for me to reflect upon.

Ian Williams, Anchorage, Alaska

have problems for several months.

Lactose intolerance (see p.232) may occur after the infection. Caused by the body's inability to process the sugar lactose, found mainly in dairy products, this is usually a transient complaint, its main symptom being persistent diarrhoea.

▷▷ See Gastrointestinal upsets, p.226.

DIAGNOSIS AND TREATMENT

Giardial infection can usually be identified by microscopic examination of a stool sample, although frequently several samples need to be sent as the cysts are not expelled in every motion. A course of metronidazole (500mg twice daily for 7–10 days for adults) usually leads to effective eradication, although other treatment options are available.

Gnathostomiasis

Gnathostomiasis is a worm infection contracted by eating raw freshwater fish contaminated with the worm larvae. It usually affects domestic animals fed on raw fish but can also infect humans who eat raw fish in endemic areas. It's found mostly in Asia (particularly in Thailand and Japan), but outbreaks have occurred in Peru, Ecuador and Mexico.

There is no vaccination against gnathostomiasis. Avoid eating raw fish in risk areas.

SYMPTOMS

Once ingested the worm larvae migrate from the gut to other parts of the body. Lodging beneath the skin, they cause painful, itchy **swellings**. Elsewhere in the body, symptoms depend on which organs the migratory worms penetrate. Lung involvement results in a cough, bladder involvement results in blood in the urine and migration to the brain can cause meningitis (potentially life-threatening).

DIAGNOSIS AND TREATMENT
Blood tests may help in the diagnosis but surgical removal of the worm for identification is more reliable. Treatment involves the use of **anti-worm medications** such as albendazole and **surgery**.

Gonorrhoea

▷▷ See under Sexually transmitted diseases, p.346.

Guinea worm infection

▷▷ See Dracunculiasis, p.202.

Hansen's disease

▷▷ See Leprosy, p.273.

Headache

Most **headaches** are harmless, commonly caused by tension in the muscles at the back of the neck and covering the scalp. **Dehydration** and **heatstroke** are other causes that perhaps single out the traveller. Most diseases that cause high **fever** will cause a headache, so consider the likes of malaria and dengue.

Migraine, a term commonly used to describe severe headache, more accurately describes a headache with neurological symptoms – visual disturbances, flashing lights, sensitivity to light, unilateral tingling or weakness – and may also be accompanied by nausea, even vomiting. The pain is often localized and one-sided. You would be unfortunate to suffer your first migraine while travelling, but if you are prone to migraines, speak to your doctor before you travel about taking specific anti-migraine drugs with you.

Headaches are usually best **treated** by rest and simple pain relief such as paracetamol or ibuprofen. Consider a more significant underlying problem in the following circumstances:

+ High fever, a purple rash that doesn't whiten when a glass is pressed against it, neck stiffness, photophobia (signs of meningitis)
+ Severe, sudden-onset pains in the back of the head (may indicate a brain haemorrhage)
+ Lapsing levels of consciousness, weakness, double or blurred vision, profuse, unremitting vomiting, loss of co-ordination, pain on waking or worse on coughing (signs of a build-up of pressure around the brain)
+ High altitude (headache is one of the first signs of acute mountain sickness)

Heat exposure

Acclimatization to high temperatures such as those found in the tropics can take weeks or months and is characterized by an increase in perspiration and a lower salt loss in the sweat. **Heat exhaustion**, a mild version of heat stroke, can occur if you've not properly acclimatized and overheat, particularly if you're undertaking heavy exercise. The symptoms include giddiness, headache, nausea, weakness, fatigue and feeling faint. The body temperature may rise as high as 40°C leading to dehydration and delirium. It is a significant sign that sweating continues throughout. Get out of the sun and cool yourself down by tepid sponging, cool baths and fanning. Drink plenty to rehydrate and use paracetamol for the headache.

Heat stroke is more severe and is potentially life-threatening. It tends to occur in hot, humid climates affecting the unacclimatized, even without heavy exercise. Old age, diabetes and heavy alcohol consumption are recognized risk factors. The body temperature may rise above 41°C and you will experience headache, sensitivity to light, weakness, nausea and vomiting. Your pulse and breathing rates will both be rapid. Your skin looks red and you feel hot to the touch and dry (ie you're not sweating). Confusion, delirium and coma can follow. Heat stroke can be life-threatening and needs urgent medical treatment.

Prickly heat (sweat rash, heat rash, miliaria) is caused by inflammation of the sweat glands after prolonged exposure to high temperatures. It manifests as itchy or burning, red/pink pimples mainly affecting the head, neck, shoulders and sweaty areas of the body such as the armpits and groin and is usually caused by over-dressing or over-exertion in heat. It is more common in infants. It can be prevented by keeping cool, having frequent cool showers, using talc to keep the skin dry and cool and wearing light, loose-fitting clothing. If treatment is necessary simple soothing creams or low-strength hydrocortisone may be used.

HEAT EXPOSURE

Belladonna (1 30c tablet an hour for 3 doses, then no more than 3 doses over the rest of the day) is a useful homeopathic remedy to treat heat stroke if you have a hot, bright-red face, often with sparkling, lit-up eyes or dilated pupils. You may have fever, delirium, even hallucinations. Your headache is characteristically throbbing and made worse by lying down flat, tying up your hair, light and noise. You may feel better from sitting quietly propped up, or with your head resting on something. Choose **Glonoine** (same dosage) to treat violent waves of exploding, pounding headache, where your head feels tight and pulsating and your symptoms are exacerbated by the pressure of wearing a hat, drinking alcohol in the sun, or just from sun exposure itself. Often some relief is gained after vomiting.

Hepatitis

The word **hepatitis** simply means an inflammation of the liver, a vital organ in the upper right side of the abdomen, which, when it goes wrong, causes considerable systemic upset.

There are a number of causes of hepatitis, including drugs and alcohol, but by far the most common is the **hepatitis A** virus. Regardless of the root cause, the initial **symptoms** synonymous with hepatitis are malaise, nausea, loss of appetite, weight loss, aches and pains, fatigue and abdominal discomfort, followed after several days by jaundice. The urine usually turns dark and the stools pale. Infective hepatitis is likely to be accompanied by fever.

WARNING
NO SWIMMING

SWIMMING WITHIN 100 YARDS OF THE STORM DRAIN
OUTLET IS PROHIBITED. STORM DRAIN WATERS MAY BE
CONTAMINATED WITH HUMAN DISEASE CAUSING BACTERIA
AND VIRUS OR HAZARDOUS CHEMICALS WASHED DOWN
FROM URBAN AREAS.

ADVERTENCIA
PELIGRO
PROHIBIDO NADAR

ESTA PROHIBIDO NADAR DENTRO DE 100 YARDAS DE LA
SALIDA DEL DRENAJE. LAS AGUAS DEL DRENAJE QUE
VIENEN DA LAS AREAS URBANAS PUEDEN ESTAR
CONTAMINADAS CON BACTERIAS Y VIRUS, O DESPERDICIOS
QUIMICOS QUE PUEDEN CAUSAR ENFERMEDADES.

No swimming sign, Santa Monica Bay, California.
Photo © Joseph Sohm; ChromoSohm Inc./Corbis

Hepatitis A

The **hepatitis A virus** (HAV) is spread via the faecal–oral route, with water, shellfish and salads (washed in contaminated water) being the most common culprits. It's also frequently spread by person-to-person contact. HAV occurs worldwide, but you're most at risk of contracting it in the Middle and Far East, Central and South America, Africa and Eastern Europe. This is largely because of poor standards of hygiene and sanitation. The risk increases with the length of your stay and by visiting rural areas.

There are several **vaccination** options available for travellers to high-risk areas (see p.14).

SYMPTOMS

The **incubation period** of HAV can range from 10 to 50 days. It's usually a mild, and sometimes unrecognized (especially in children) illness. Adults tend to suffer more from the symptoms (see p.240). The period during which you are **infectious** ranges from early in the incubation period to about a week after the development of jaundice.

DIAGNOSIS AND TREATMENT

Antibodies to the virus can be detected in the **blood** about 4 weeks after infection. There is no specific treatment, but recovery is usually complete after 2 weeks, although more severe symptoms require a longer convalescence, with tiredness and lethargy being common features. In the interim, avoid fatty foods and alcohol as they can exacerbate the symptoms. Rest and a diet high in carbohydrates which are easily digested are encouraged. To avoid spreading the infection, intimate contact should be avoided during the period in which you are infectious.

Hepatitis B

Hepatitis B (HBV) is a global infection but areas of particularly high prevalence include Asia, Africa, South America, the Pacific Islands and the Caribbean. It's estimated that some 2 billion people worldwide are infected with HBV, with 350 million chronic carriers. Although it's spread by similar means to HIV and is no less dangerous, it has a much lower media profile. It is, in fact, estimated to be 100 times more infectious than HIV.

▷▷ See HIV, p.247.

HBV is **spread** mainly via infected blood and blood products, although the virus has also been found in semen. It can therefore be passed on through intimate contact, blood transfusions that have not been adequately screened, or the sharing of needles, razors or toothbrushes (which can cause gums to bleed) with an infected person. Body-piercing and tattooing using poorly sterilized equipment have also been implicated in its spread. The infection can be passed on in pregnancy from mother to baby. HBV is **not** passed on by ordinary social contact (kissing, hugging, shaking hands), sharing food and drinks or by using the same cutlery, toilet facilities and towels.

A **vaccination** available against HBV offers good protection but is generally only recommended for those at particularly high risk such as healthcare workers (who may be more likely to come into contact with infected blood). You might want to discuss the prophylactic use of HBV vaccination with your doctor before you leave if you think you might be at higher-than-normal risk. If you have sex with a new partner on your travels, a condom will offer some protection. As with HIV, however, avoidance is better.

HEPATITIS

"A souvenir from Thailand"

"I can't face those peanut butter sandwiches today!" I shouted to my friend who like me, was up a ladder picking fruit in Western Australia. "My stomach is feeling really strange. Maybe it has something to do with those apples we scrumped from the orchard last night," I joked. "Maybe," Sarah replied.

My friend and I had been in Australia for about a month. Prior to Perth we had spent two months on a beautiful island called Kao Tao, off southern Thailand. It was here that I had fallen in lust with a Thai resort owner. Unfortunately I had chosen to trust my Thai partner and we had made the crazy mistake of not using contraception on more than one occasion. It was not until eight weeks later, whilst settling in Australia, that the after-effects of these misjudgements began to materialize.

Initially I took very little notice of my symptoms, which included nausea, exhaustion and jaundice. However, after about a week I realized that the stolen fruit was not the cause and that something more sinister was afoot. I made an appointment with the doctor. After examining my abdomen the doctor told me that I could be pregnant and to return in a few days

SYMPTOMS

The time between exposure and first symptoms can be long, ranging from 6 weeks to 6 months. Initially, the symptoms of HBV mimic those of HAV (fever, malaise, loss of appetite, etc). Recovery from the acute illness is usuallycomplete after a month. However, after recovery from the initial symptoms, between 5% and 10% of affected adults and up to 90% of children become carriers of the virus. Some also develop a more serious **chronic form** of the illness causing a slow, *if I felt any worse. I did feel worse and I returned to the surgery for some blood tests. By this time I was very weak and my skin was banana yellow. I had been reading my travel guide books and had arrived at a self-diagnosis; I was convinced I had hepatitis A. When my blood tests came back, however, I was mortified. I had hepatitis B and was told by the doctor that I could develop cirrhosis of the liver in the future and could die within twenty years. My world collapsed.*

I returned home as soon as my symptoms had subsided enough for me to travel. On arriving home I had to face family and friends knowing that I had caught a disease through sexual contact. I also had to undergo two HIV tests and regular blood tests. Although the physical symptoms disappeared within months, the disappointment of having to cut short a journey of a lifetime and neglecting my own personal safety overwhelmed my thoughts for a long time. And although I am now immune to hepatitis B and am not a carrier, I don't know the extent of any long-term damage. As I embark on plans for my first trip abroad since my illness, I fully intend to take greater care of myself.

Vicky Nicholas, Salisbury, UK

gradual destruction of the liver, which can ultimately be fatal.

DIAGNOSIS AND TREATMENT

Blood tests can confirm the diagnosis but may not show positive for up to 8 months after the infection is acquired. The diagnosis can often be made simply by correlating the initial symptoms with a history of likely contact with HBV.

There is no specific treatment, although liver specialists have begun using a drug called interferon to some benefit (unlikely to be available in developing countries). Rest, plenty of fluids and a nutritious diet (high in carbohydrates) aid recovery from the initial acute illness.

Hepatitis C

Although a relatively newly discovered cause of hepatitis (first identified in 1989), **hepatitis C** (HCV) has a world-wide prevalence – WHO recently estimated that 3% of the world's population is affected by HVC, with 170 million carriers. A dangerous and difficult disease to treat, HCV occurs in high rates in some Mediterranean countries and Egypt in particular.

The infection is transmitted by similar means to HBV, but it appears to be less infectious via sexual contact. It's common among intravenous drug users, haemophiliacs and people who require frequent blood transfusions.

As yet no vaccine is available against HCV.

SYMPTOMS

The **incubation period** is usually 6–8 weeks but can vary between 15 and 150 days. The initial infection usually goes unnoticed, with acute symptoms similar to HAV-infection being rare. However, like HBV, a chronic form of HCV occurs in 60–80% of cases. This is slowly progressive and can lead to liver failure or liver cancer 30 or 40 years after the initial infection. It is still unclear as to whether all of those suffering from the chronic disease eventually develop terminal liver problems.

DIAGNOSIS AND TREATMENT

The infection can be diagnosed by the presence of HCV antibodies in the **blood**, although these can take several weeks to appear.

The only treatment currently available is a combination of **ribavirin** and **interferon**, which has been shown to be beneficial in some but not all cases. These drugs are expensive and likely to be in very short supply in developing countries. They should only be used in a hospital setting under expert supervision.

In cases of chronic liver damage, you'll need to curb alcohol intake and avoid some over-the-counter drugs (eg paracetamol) that may damage the liver further.

If you are a chronic carrier of HBV or HCV you should not donate blood, semen or organs, and you should inform your sexual partner and practise safe sex at all times.

Hepatitis D and E

Hepatitis D and E infections are rare. HDV infection only occurs in the presence of HBV infection and is transmitted via blood or blood products. Intravenous drug users are the most commonly affected group. HEV shows very similar symptoms to HAV and is transmitted in the same way.

Herpes (genital)

▷▷See under Sexually transmitted diseases, p.350.

HIV

There are two distinct types of **human immunodeficiency virus (HIV)** infection: HIV1, discovered in 1983, and HIV2, discovered two years later and generally regarded as being the weaker and slower-developing variant. Both result in **acquired immune deficiency syndrome (AIDS)**.

The WHO estimate that in 1999 alone there were some 2.8 million HIV/AIDS-related deaths. In 1998, 5.4 million people were infected with HIV (that's more than 10 people every minute), adding to a staggering global total of 34.3 million people living with HIV. Future predictions are equally alarming, with an estimated 7000 people between the ages of 10 and 24 being infected with HIV every day. Between 70% and 80% of HIV cases worldwide have been acquired through sexual intercourse, 5–10% at birth from an infected mother and the rest from drug-use and infected blood products. Ninety-five percent of the worldwide population infected with HIV, and a similar percentage of AIDS-related deaths, occur in the developing world, with women now comprising 43% of the total. Eighty percent of heterosexually acquired HIV in the UK is contracted abroad.

There is as yet no vaccination against HIV and it would still seem to be some years away. Therefore the advice for **avoidance** of HIV infection is clear: avoid contact with **blood products**, avoid **needle or syringe sharing** (don't forget dental work, acupuncture, tattooing and body piercing) and avoid **unprotected sex** with a new partner – bear in mind that using a condom alone won't afford total protection, and your only certain means of self-protection is abstinence.

▷▷See Blood transfusions, p.163.

HIV attacks the **white blood cells**, and by depleting their numbers reduces the body's ability to fight off infection and cancers. **AIDS** is medically defined by increasing susceptibility to specific infections and incidence of cancerous tumours. The time lapse from HIV infection to the development of full-blown AIDS varies and depends on a number of factors (age, mode of infection, genetics), but the mean delay is 11.2 years with death usually occurring between 18 and 24 months later. The long period without significant symptoms synonymous with AIDS means that many people infected with HIV are unaware that they are carriers. It also means that there is no way of knowing the true prevalence of the infection globally.

Initial infection with HIV is indistinguishable from any other viral infection and often not apparent at all. Roughly 50% of those infected will suffer a sore throat, joint pains or a rash.

HIV infection can be **detected** by a blood test but there is a lag period after infection of up to 3 months before the test will become positive.

A number of complex **treatments** are aimed at delaying the progression of HIV infection into AIDS by suppressing viral replication, but treatment can only be undertaken under strict medical supervision. There remains no cure for HIV infection or AIDS.

▷▷See also Travelling with HIV, p.92.

Hookworm

▷▷See under Worms, p.396.

Human babesiosis

Human babesiosis is a **tick-borne** protozoal infection common in animals but rare in humans – it tends to affect mainly those with a weakened immune system. Most reported cases are in North America (mainly northeastern coastal areas) and Europe. It is spread to humans by the same kind of tick that transmits Lyme disease and, although babesiosis is much rarer than Lyme, simultaneous infections have been reported. Rodents, wild animals and cattle usually act as the disease reservoir in the wild.

SYMPTOMS

Symptoms appear between 1 and 4 weeks after a bite and are mild, although they are much more severe, even life-threatening, in anyone who has low levels of immunity. In the more severe cases, human babesiosis **mimics malaria**, with high fever, rigors, nausea and vomiting, abdominal pain and muscle aches. Complications may cause a build-up of fluid on the lungs, anaemia, kidney failure and increased bleeding tendency.

DIAGNOSIS AND TREATMENT

The parasites can be seen in the **blood** cells using a microscope.

In most cases, the treatment is mainly aimed at **symptom relief**. For severe infections, **drugs** like chloroquine or pentamidine have been used with limited success. More recently combinations of quinine with an antibiotic, clindamycin, have proved promising.

Hydatid disease

(Echincoccosis)

Hydatid disease can be found all over the world but most commonly in the sheep- and cattle-raising areas of South America, South Africa, the NIS and the Middle East. Despite its wide geographic distribution, the disease is rare in humans and risks to the average traveller are low.

Eggs of the infecting **tapeworm** are transmitted to

humans by the ingestion of milk, vegetables or water contaminated by the faeces of infected animals or by direct contact with the animals (dogs, foxes, sheep and cattle usually) – stroking dogs whose fur has been contaminated is a major cause of human infection. The tapeworm larvae form cysts in the liver, lungs and other organs.

There is no vaccination so avoid potentially contaminated water and always **wash your hands** carefully after handling or stroking animals.

SYMPTOMS

Years can pass before any signs of the illness, and the symptoms themselves depend on the location and size of the cyst. Cysts in the liver may cause **abdominal discomfort**, **nausea** and **vomiting**. If a cyst **ruptures**, this will cause sudden pain, fever and even death from internal bleeding. Cysts in the lungs may cause a **cough** (sometimes containing blood) and **shortness of breath**. Pneumonia or a lung abscess can ensue after rupture of a cyst.

DIAGNOSIS AND TREATMENT

Blood tests may detect antibodies to the tapeworms, while a chest x-ray or an abdominal **ultrasound** may detect the presence of cysts in the lungs or liver. **Surgical removal** of the cysts remains the mainstay of treatment, but the **drug** albendazole can cause regression of the cysts in many cases.

Hypothermia

▷▷See Cold exposure, p.174.

HYPOTHERMIA

Influenza

The risk of exposure to **influenza** is determined by season (usually winter) in temperate countries, and the number of people with whom you mingle. Isolated cases of flu are rare: it almost always comes in epidemics. The last century saw 3 major flu epidemics: the "Spanish flu" in 1918–19 (causing a staggering 20 million deaths worldwide), the "Asian flu" in 1957–58, and the "Hong Kong flu" in 1968–69.

The influenza **virus** mutates frequently, which means that neither vaccination nor having suffered the illness once confers future immunity.

A **vaccine** tailored against the current prevalent epidemic is available but is usually recommended only for those at particularly high risk. Elderly people, severe asthmatics, diabetics, those with chronic heart, lung or kidney disease, and anyone with a compromised immune function should consider vaccination before they travel, depending on season and the likelihood they will be exposed to the virus through fellow travellers. The vaccine is between 70% and 90% effective, although maximum protection is not reached for up to 2 weeks.

SYMPTOMS

Highly **contagious**, influenza is spread by cough or sneeze droplets. It usually takes between 1 and 4 days from exposure for symptoms to appear. It can be passed on before the infected person experiences symptoms and for up to a week afterwards.

Many people think they have the flu when in fact they only have a heavy cold. There is no tell-tale symptom that defines influenza – it's usually a question of severity and the degree of debility (most people who've had flu never forget it).

Upper respiratory **symptoms** such as cough, runny nose and headaches predominate, in addition to high fever, loss of appetite, muscle pains and, often, extreme fatigue. Nausea, vomiting and diarrhoea commonly occur in children, less so in adults.

In most people, the symptoms resolve spontaneously over the course of 1 or 2 weeks. Serious, sometimes life-threatening, complications such as pneumonia are rare but occur more often in high-risk groups. A prolonged period of weakness, fatigue and depression may last for weeks or even months after the acute infection.

DIAGNOSIS AND TREATMENT

Flu is almost impossible to diagnose with any degree of certainty on clinical grounds alone. Although a firm diagnosis is usually academic (it will not change the treatment), **blood tests** can be used to identify the body's antibodies to the virus. In tropical areas (where epidemics are not seasonal), or in travellers returning from tropical areas, the diagnosis of influenza should never be made without first excluding other causes of high fever such as malaria, dengue and typhoid.

Antibiotics won't treat the flu itself, but should be used if secondary bacterial infections such as **sinusitis** or **pneumonia** are suspected. The use of expensive anti-viral medications is controversial; their effectiveness at treating the illness versus their considerable cost is the cause of ongoing debate in some countries.

Insects

Insects, as much of this book will tell you, are responsible for the spread of a vast number of human diseases. The **table**

INSECTS

INSECTS

Insect	Disease
Mosquitoes **Aedes**, a tropical species that have a black-and-white body and are daytime-biting. They are mainly urban-dwelling below 4500m. **Anopheles**, nocturnal-biting and mainly rural. **Culex**, dull, brown body.	**Chikungunya fever** (aedes) p.169; **Dengue fever** (aedes) p.195; **Filariasis** (anopheles, culex, aedes) p.218; **Japanese encephalitis** (culex) p.263; **Malaria** (anopheles) p.279; **Rift Valley fever** p.322; **Ross River virus** p.327; **Yellow fever** (aedes) p.405.
Ticks Ticks have 8 legs and tend to be small, flat, brown and round, but after a blood meal can swell up to corn-kernel size.	**Human babesiosis** p.249; **Lyme disease** p.278; **Relapsing fever** p.321; **Rocky Mountain spotted fever** p.323; **Tick-borne encephalitis** p.376; **Typhus** p.388.

Sand flies Small enough to pass through mosquito nets, and found mainly in arid areas. They have characteristically hairy wings, are low-altitude, noiseless fliers and bite mainly between dusk and dawn.	**Bartonellosis** p.162; **Leishmaniasis** p.268; **Sandfly fever** p.335.
Fleas	**Plague** p.311; **Tungiasis** p.384; **Typhus** p.388.
Lice	**Relapsing fever** p.321; **Typhus** p.388.
Mites Tiny, 8-legged creatures.	**Scabies** p.336; **Typhus** p.388.
Tsetse fly Found only in sub-Saharan Africa. Large (up to 1.5cm long). Painful, daytime-biting. Attracted to moving *Continues over*	**African trypanosomiasis** p.144.

INSECTS

INSECTS

vehicles and dark, contrasting colours. They are capable of biting through light clothing and are relatively impervious to the effects of insect repellent.

Reduviid bugs
(Kissing, cone nose or assassin bugs) Large, between 1 and 4cm long. Typically inhabit adobe or mud huts in Central and South America. Bite at night.

American trypanosomiasis p.153.

Black fly
Small, stumpy and black. Live near fast-flowing rivers in parts of the tropics. Mainly biting in the daytime.

Onchocerciasis p.218.

Tabanid fly
Large, fast, daytime biters.

Loasis p.222.

on pp.254–256 gives an idea of the extent to which flying insects, mites, ticks and the like are responsible for the spread of some key diseases. For more on the **specific diseases and the insects that cause them**, refer to the page numbers in the right-hand column.

▷▷For more on bite prevention, see p.259; see also Lice infestation, p.277; Malaria, p.279; Myiasis, p.301; Spiders and scorpions, p.360; Tungiasis, p.384.

Once bitten

While not all biting insects will cause you harm, many do act as the "vector", in essence the go-between between animals and humans who already have a disease and those who are about to get it. The risk of disease generally depends on the insect species (for example, only the *anopheles* type of mosquito can spread malaria) and the geographical area. Depending on the type of insect, the severity of the **local reaction** at the bite (or sting) site can vary. Swelling, redness and sometimes local heat often follow the initial pain. Later, the site may become irritable and the impulse to scratch may be irresistible. The process is self-limiting, although **antihistamines** (tablets or cream) will help relieve the symptoms. Local applications such as **calamine lotion** and **hydrocortisone cream** can also help.

Although rare, the proteins within the venom of the insect bite (or sting) can trigger a more **generalized allergic response**, with flushing, swelling, itching, a rash and wheezing. In severe cases this can lead to **anaphylaxis** (see p.151). In the majority of cases these symptoms are self-limiting, but oral antihistamines may help. More severe reactions, especially when breathing difficulties are encountered, require urgent medical help. Steroids are usually used

INSECTS

to treat severe allergic reactions, either as a one-off injection or a 5-day course of tablets.

Secondary bacterial infection at the bite (or sting) site is not uncommon and more likely in **tropical climates**. Usually scratching damages the skin and bacteria multiply within the wound. This can occur within the first 48 hours after a bite. Signs of infection are not immediately dissimilar from the initial local reaction – swelling, redness and heat are common – although you're more likely to experience local pain, rather than itching, with an infection. The presence of pus, red tracking up the affected limb (lymphangitis), local lymph-gland swelling and fever are also signs of infection. Treat with **antibiotics** such as penicillin, flucloxacillin or co-amoxiclav, or erythromycin if you have a penicillin allergy.

A number of **homeopathic remedies** can help treat bites and stings. **Apis mel** will treat an ant or a mosquito bite, a bee or a jellyfish sting (for bad pain, take a high potency every 15 minutes until it improves, less often thereafter). Choose this remedy especially for stings that are very hot, shiny red and puffy, with pain that burns or prickles (and worsens near heat – in sun, hot water, etc). If there is less puffiness, and the bite is hot and red but dry, and the pain more throbbing than stinging, choose **belladonna**. If there's twitching in the muscles near the wound, and the sting feels cold to the touch, take **ledum palustre** (30c 3 times on first day, twice on the second, once on the third). **Aconite** (1 30c dose, or a couple of 6c tablets over half an hour) is the best remedy if you're anxious and restless after the bite or sting. **Silica** (6 6c tablets in the course of a day) will help in removing retained bits of stings or bites, from bees, ticks and the like. **Rescue Remedy** drops (6 drops in a cup of water) can help reduce swelling and pain for more surface stings or bites. Sip the dilution to alleviate any accompanying anxiety.

INSECTS

Bite prevention

The first line of defence against catching something is **avoiding** being bitten in the first place. This may be next to impossible, but it helps knowing a little about how the insects behave, their preferred **habitat**, **times of day** and **seasons**. Most mosquitoes, for example, tend to be most active between dusk and dawn during and after the rainy season, and it's then that you'll need to be most vigilant. Similarly, sand flies only have a very limited flight range and therefore tend to bite people lying on, or close to, the ground. Ticks of course are unable to fly at all and usually attach themselves when you walk through long grass or vegetation.

Your next level of protection is appropriate **clothing**. Few insects are able to penetrate clothing, so expose as little skin to the air as possible during the times when they are most active. Tuck long trousers into your socks. Impregnating your clothing with **permethrin** greatly increases its protective properties.

Repellents are the next, and highly important, level of protection. Many preparations are available but the commonly accepted "gold standard" are those containing DEET (see below).

PERMETHRIN

Permethrin has very useful repellent and insecticidal properties with negligible effects on human health. It works best by being sprayed on clothing or mosquito nets – it bonds to fabric, does not cause staining and lasts for several washes before you need reapply it. Permethrin is less effective when applied to the skin because it's rapidly deactivated on contact. A few people suffer mild irritant reactions when it is applied to the skin.

INSECTS

Ticks and tick removal

Ticks are 8-legged external parasites of mammals, birds and reptiles and are found all over the world. After attaching to the host, they feed on blood. Some species are capable of transmitting diseases such as Lyme disease, typhus and Rocky Mountain spotted fever. Prompt removal of the tick can prevent these diseases from being passed on.

Removing ticks

When a tick attaches itself, it embeds its head below the surface of your skin. You need to take special care to remove the whole of the tick, head and all. Using tweezers, grasp the tick's head and pull gently (avoid twisting) until the tick dislodges. If it doesn't budge, try applying permethrin to the tick directly with a cotton bud, waiting for 15 minutes, then trying the tweezers again. Afterwards apply antiseptic to the area of the bite.

INSECTS

DEET (N, N- DIETHYL-M-TOLUAMIDE)

DEET is currently regarded as the most important constituent of an insect repellent in terms of determining its efficacy. Other factors that affect the level of protection conferred by a repellent are the type of formulation – dry, cream, ointment, roll on, etc - how often you apply it and how much you perspire, humidity and environment, and the species and feeding patterns of the insects.

The drawbacks of using a repellent containing DEET are generally minor: it may cause a local skin irritation and melts certain synthetics so can cause damage to watches, spectacles, clothing and shoes. Never apply it to your eyes, damaged skin or mucous membranes (nose, mouth, genitals). Although DEET is rapidly absorbed through the skin, it's also rapidly excreted and therefore does not accumulate.

It has been associated with rare neurological side effects and occasional fatalities, particularly in children. The exact role of DEET in these cases has never been firmly established and the media has in some cases sensationalized the issues. Current evidence suggests that the adverse effects were due to rare individual susceptibility rather than dose-related, and given its widespread usage, the general view is that the risk of serious side effects as a result of DEET application is extremely low.

Despite this, it is generally recommended not to use greater than 15% strength on children and 35% strength on adults. **Concentrations** higher than 35% are believed to be no more effective as a repellent and those less than 15% lose their efficacy. The lower the strength, the shorter the period of protection: an application of a 30–35% formulation should provide good protection for adults for 4–6 hours.

Using DEET in conjunction with permethrin on clothing and insect nets is a highly efficient way of repelling insects with minimal unwanted effects.

There is a very good article on DEET by Vernon Ansdell on the Medicineplanet Web site (see p.530) which puts the risks in perspective.

OTHER OPTIONS

Other repellents include citronella, Avon Skin-So-Soft, bath oil and lemon eucalyptus oil, all of which may provide limited protection against some kinds of insects. The majority of **insect coils** contain permethrin and are reasonably effective, although variables like drafts and room size are important factors to consider.

At night sleep under a **net** where possible in areas of high risk. Carry your own net (they're widely available on the market) or check closely nets provided by hotels as even slight damage can render them useless. Impregnate the net with permethrin for added protection.

Avoid wearing **aftershave** or **perfume** in high-risk areas as it's likely to attract the insects.

Alternative tactics to protect yourself include eating **garlic**, said to repel ticks and many other biting insects. Taking **B-complex** and extra B1 (thiamine) for up to 6 weeks before you set out and for the duration of your stay can also make you less attractive to local insect life. Speak to your homeopathic pharmacist about travelling with some **potenized histamine** if you've a tendency to get bitten by everything going and suffer over-reactions with lots of swelling.

Irritable bowel syndrome

Irritable bowel syndrome (IBS) describes a group of symptoms that affect us all to a greater or lesser extent at some time. The symptoms are usually brought on by stress, anxiety or even excitement. Irregular eating patterns or poor diet may also be contributing factors. It is not uncommon to develop IBS after an episode of travellers' diarrhoea.

IBS presents differently from person to person, but diarrhoea, flatulence, abdominal bloating and crampy abdominal pains are common. Other symptoms include constipation and nausea. Vomiting is rare and the presence of weight loss usually indicates another cause that will need further investigation.

Unfortunately there is no specific test that proves the presence of IBS, and because the symptoms are non-specific and may have other more serious causes, the diagnosis is usually only made when other possibilities have been excluded. Regular eating habits and a fibre-rich diet can help. Medications that can be used for **symptom relief** include mebeverine or peppermint oil capsules, both helpful antispasmodics (they relieve the crampy pains and frequency of diarrhoea), and refined fibre in the form of ispaghula husk benefits constipation and helps to restore normal bowel function.

Japanese encephalitis

Japanese encephalitis occurs seasonally throughout Southeast Asia, the Far East and the Pacific. Prevalent in areas where rice-growing and pig-farming co-exist, it is a viral disease spread by mosquitoes. Patterns vary from year to year and from country to country, but the disease tends to proliferate during and after the monsoon, when the mosquitoes are at their most active. The WHO reports at least 50,000 cases occur in Asia annually, accounting for some 10,000 deaths, with children most affected. Cases involving tourists, however, are extremely rare.

A **vaccine** against Japanese encephalitis is available (see p.17) and it is strongly recommended for anyone travelling to an endemic area, especially after the monsoon.

SYMPTOMS

Symptoms vary considerably from case to case but are often flu-like with sudden-onset headache, fever and vomiting. Weight loss is a prominent feature of the illness, and a stiff neck and intolerance to light can also occur. Fits are particularly common in children, while drowsiness can be a symptom. Mortality rates are as high as 40% in adults and higher in children, with long-term neurological impairment apparent in a high proportion of survivors.

DIAGNOSIS AND TREATMENT
Diagnosis can be made by a **blood test**. There is no specific treatment, although hospital admission for supportive and nursing care improves survival rates.

Jiggers

▷▷See Tungiasis, p.384.

Kala-azar

▷▷See under Leishmaniasis, p.272.

Lassa fever

Epidemics of **Lassa fever** occur mainly in the dry season in West Africa, particularly Guinea, Liberia, Nigeria, Sierra Leone and the Democratic Republic of Congo. It gets its name from the region in northeast Nigeria where the virus was first recognized in 1969.

The exact mode of transmission of the **virus** to humans is unclear, but it's likely to be via indirect contact with the saliva, urine or faeces of a species of **rat** that's found on much of the African continent. Lassa fever is highly **contagious** between humans – the virus infiltrates all bodily fluids and remains in the urine and semen for several weeks even after recovery.

Lassa fever poses little threat to most travellers, but health-workers in endemic areas may be at risk.

SYMPTOMS

Between 10% and 30% of people infected will show no sign of disease. For the remainder, there is believed to be an incubation period of 1–3 weeks before the gradual onset of symptoms. These include **high fever**, **vomiting**, **diarrhoea**, **cough**, chest and abdominal **pain** and generalized **weakness** lasting for several days. **Inflammation** of the eyes and throat is common, and the face and neck may also become swollen. After 3–6 days, more serious cases can experience shock, generalized bleeding, fluid on the lungs and brain swelling. Lassa fever is extremely dangerous in anyone who is severely affected, and survivors of the illness may face long-lasting, and sometimes permanent after-effects, such as hair loss, deafness and loss of co-ordination.

DIAGNOSIS AND TREATMENT

Clinically, there is little to differentiate Lassa fever from many other tropical causes of high fever, although throat inflammation with **white patches** on the tonsils is often a unique feature. Definitive diagnosis is made through a **blood test**

Caught early, **intravenous treatment** with the antiviral agent ribavarin can help but failing this, therapy is based around symptom control and intensive care.

Because of the long incubation period, cases of Lassa fever have been reported in returning travellers in Europe. Most cases have been reported in people who have spent considerable time in Africa rather than the casual tourist, but a fever in any traveller returning from the tropics, no matter how short their stay, needs to be fully investigated.

LASSA FEVER

Leeches

Although they also exist on dry land, **leeches** proliferate in tropical rainforests, where they're particularly active after the rains. They commonly attach themselves to trekkers wading through water. Aquatic leeches attack swimmers who ill-advisedly swim in tropical rainforest pools, and they are capable of crawling up into bodily nooks and crannies such as the mouth, nostrils and genitals.

Although unpleasant to many, leeches don't carry any serious diseases, and their main threat to health is secondary infection at the site of attachment.

Avoidance is not always easy when you're in their native habitat. Covering up any exposed skin and tucking trousers into socks helps, but most leeches can penetrate this kind of defence. Applying permethrin to your clothes offers some additional protection.

It's worth remembering that the leech, once satiated with your blood, will drop off of its own accord, although most victims would prefer to avoid the wait. Applying a lighted cigarette or match, vinegar, salt or chilli to the leech are most successful methods of **removal**, with direct tugging perhaps least effective since you risk leaving behind parts of the leech, increasing your chance of secondary infection. The resulting wound may bleed for a few hours (leeches have an anticoagulant in their saliva): clean it thoroughly with antiseptic and apply a sterile dressing.

Legionnaires' disease

This rare, but serious, infection occurs worldwide in sporadic epidemics. The name derives from the first outbreak in 1976 among members of the American Legion in a

Philadelphia hotel. **Legionnaires' disease** is spread by the inhalation of the disease-causing bacteria from infected water, for example through hot showers, air conditioning or steam rooms. Person-to-person spread never occurs.

According to the CDC there are between 8000 and 18,000 cases in the US each year, while the UK Public Health Laboratory Service reports an average of around 200 cases each year in the UK (between a third and a half acquired abroad). The elderly or those with pre-existing heart or lung diseases are most at risk of contracting the disease. For as-yet unknown reasons, men are more prone to infection than women.

Epidemics are rare but usually make the news. Think twice before travelling to a place that you know to have experienced a recent outbreak, as preventative measures may not be practical (as yet, no vaccination exists).

SYMPTOMS

The symptoms usually develop between 2 and 10 days after exposure, and although the infection may be mild, the characteristic picture is that of a **chest infection**, with high fever, headache, shortness of breath, cough (you may cough up blood), nausea and vomiting, muscle pains, mental confusion and weight loss.

DIAGNOSIS AND TREATMENT

Diagnosis can usually be made from a **blood, urine or sputum sample**.

Erythromycin (500mg 4 times daily) for 3 weeks can be used to treat the less severe forms of the illness. More severe cases require hospital admission for intravenous antibiotics and intensive care.

Leishmaniasis

The WHO estimates that around 12 million people (mainly indigenous) in 88 countries across the Mediterranean basin (mainly southern and eastern), central Asia, eastern Africa, China and Central and South America are currently infected with **leishmaniasis**. Female **sand flies** transmit this protozoal infection to humans, usually from dogs, rodents or, in India, other humans. Transmission of the dis-

LEISHMANIASIS: HIGH RISK AREAS

ease may also occur through blood transfusions, sexual contact with infected individuals and from mother to child.

The flies, which inhabit dry regions, normally bite at dusk, dawn and during the night. Because they are **low-altitude fliers** the best way to avoid sand flies is by sleeping above ground level (in a hammock if you can't get higher than the ground floor). Bear in mind they are small enough to pass through most mosquito nets. As yet there is no vaccination against leishmaniasis, although one is being developed.

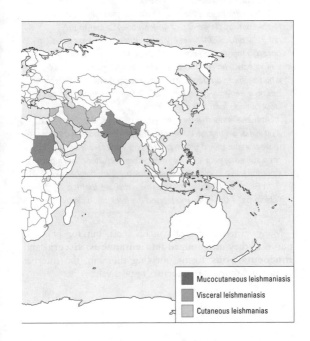

Mucocutaneous leishmaniasis

Visceral leishmaniasis

Cutaneous leishmanias

LEISHMANIASIS

66 Tropical acne 99

About a month after the hurricane had passed I was floating along a beautiful jungle river in Belize, camping each night on the riverbank. Spending a night in the rainforest is an incredible experience. As the light fades the air is filled with the shrill screeches of insects and the croaking and booming of frogs and toads. At dusk the biting insects increase their attacks, forcing you to cover up, burn leaves to create smoke or retreat into the tent.

Later, after dinner, the insect swarms gradually thinned and I rolled out my sleeping pad under a tree. Closer to the natural world here than in my tent, I thought. Indeed I was, because that's when the sand flies strike. I knew about these tiny insects who can't fly or jump far so you're most at risk when sleeping outdoors, without a mosquito net. And despite having a perfectly good tent, I didn't feel anything biting so slept outside for a few more nights.

At home a month later I noticed some tiny spots on my face, a bit like acne, though I'd never suffered from spots. A couple of weeks later they'd grown bigger, and were clearly active. I'd seen someone with leishmaniasis before and after checking the symptoms in a tropical medicine book my fears heightened.

In Belize and Guatemala this was a disease that the "chicleros" – the men who tapped the latex of chicle trees to

Many varieties of leishmaniasis exist, but for practical purposes they are grouped into **cutaneous**, **visceral** and **mucocutaneous** forms, affecting the skin, the internal organs and mucous membranes respectively.

gather the base ingredient of chewing gum – caught, but it was extremely rare for outsiders to catch leishmaniasis. By the time I'd got an appointment with a dermatologist the spots were about the size of a penny, looking like miniature red volcanoes, erupting with serum and turning green. By now small children were staring and pointing, asking their mums what was wrong with that man. The parents, not wishing to make a scene, told the kids to be quiet – but drew them away all the same. I now knew what it felt like to be a social leper – or perhaps even a real leper.

Strangers stared and colleagues were shocked. Telling them what the treatment involved horrified them further: a plastic drip tube was placed into my arm and on up to my main vein where it left my heart. For twenty days I had to go to hospital for a very strong dose of antibiotic delivered by the drip and each day I felt weaker than the day before. My whole body ached and at times I could barely move. Each joint in my body felt like it was being crushed in a vice and I was on massive doses of painkillers. I was completely unable to work for a week or so after the treatment ended. Today, more than a year later, the red lesions are still visible on my face and it will be several more months before they disappear entirely.

Peter Eltringham, Luton, UK

"TROPICAL ACNE"

Cutaneous leishmaniasis

(Aleppo boil, Aleppo button, Baghdad boil, Baure ulcer, Delhi boil, Oriental sore, Tropical sore)

It's estimated that between 1 and 1.5 million people contract **cutaneous leishmaniasis** each year. The sand flies' bites first appear as red patches, which gradually enlarge and ulcerate. The resulting nodules are painless but itchy, firm and may resemble burn marks. Multiple nodules may coexist in different areas of the body reflecting the insect's bite pattern. Without treatment, the lesions heal very slowly (sometimes over many years) and often leave permanent scarring.

Cutaneous leishmaniasis is usually identified from a **biopsy** of a skin nodule. Note that many doctors in developed countries will not think of investigating for leishmaniasis on the basis of the skin lesions alone, so if you suspect the illness, make sure your doctor knows where you have been and under what conditions you have been living.

A 10-day **intravenous course** of pentavalent antimony (sodium stibogluconate) is partially effective but side effects require specialist monitoring. **Relapses** are common and although the disease is not life-threatening, long-term scarring may occur.

Visceral leishmaniasis

(Dumdum fever, Kala-azar)

About 500,000 people contract **visceral leishmaniasis** each year, with 90% of cases occurring in India, Bangladesh, Nepal, Sudan and around the Mediterranean. Its local name "Kala-azar" is Hindi for "Black sickness" (the disease sometimes causes darkening of the extremities, face and abdomen). In the Mediterranean basin, up to 70% of cases are related to HIV infection.

Visceral leishmaniasis tends to affect young people, with an **incubation period** that ranges from months to years. Onset of **symptoms** is usually insidious, with a mild, intermittent fever and bouts of profuse sweating. As the disease progresses, weight loss, fatigue, poor appetite, nausea, abdominal pain and diarrhoea can develop. Over time the liver, spleen and lymph glands swell. Left untreated, the disease is usually fatal.

A **blood test** will identify the presence of visceral leishmaniasis. Again, an intravenous course of pentavalent antimony drugs can be used as **treatment** but side effects may be unpleasant. In resistant cases, it may be necessary to surgically remove the spleen.

Mucocutaneous leishmaniasis

(American leishmaniasis, Chiclero ulcer, Espundia, Forest yaws, Uta)

Occurring in South and Central America, **mucocutaneous leishmaniasis** has both short-term and long-term effects. The initially painful, itchy nodules, usually on the legs, are likely to resolve spontaneously within a few months. Years later, however, up to 40% of those infected can develop ulcers around the nose and mouth, which cause permanent scarring and disfigurement. Secondary infection of these lesions has serious consequences.

Diagnosis of mucocutaneous leishmaniasis is usually made from a biopsy of the ulcers, but blood tests may also help. Pentavalent antimony compounds can again be used as **treatment** but cure rates are unimpressive. Reconstructive surgery is often needed for facial deformities.

Leprosy

(Hansen's disease)

You may see cases of this misunderstood disease on your travels to some countries, but don't worry unnecessarily about catching **leprosy** – its low virulence makes it a weak bug, passed on only with difficulty, and transient contact with sufferers will cause you no harm. Contrary to commonly held misconceptions, it doesn't make your limbs drop off - these are outward signs, rather, of nerve damage and loss of sensation in the feet and hands, resulting in repeated injury to sufferers' limbs. Many living with the disease control their symptoms successfully with drugs. Meanwhile, a concerted campaign by the WHO has dramatically reduced the number of sufferers requiring medication worldwide. Eighty percent of cases live in just 6 countries: Bangladesh, Brazil, India, Indonesia, Myanmar and Nigeria, where poverty and overcrowding encourage its spread. However, it's not only the developing world that is affected – there are periodic reports of cases from the southern states of the US.

The disease is caused by a **bacteria** related to that causing TB, and is believed to be spread from person to person through coughing and sneezing. Prolonged contact puts you at greatest risk, while brief, transient contact with a case poses little threat. There is no preventative vaccination.

Leprosy can be subdivided into 2 different types depending on the degree of natural immunity exhibited by the victim. Although **tuberculoid** and **lepromatous** leprosy are caused by the same bacteria, they follow very different clinical courses.

SYMPTOMS

Although disfiguring, leprosy rarely causes fatal complications. The **incubation period** is long: between 2 and 5 years in the case of tuberculoid leprosy and 8 and 12 years for lepromatous cases. The effects of leprosy are long-term and principally involve the skin, the nervous system and the delicate membranes lining the upper respiratory tract.

Tuberculoid leprosy only affects the skin and the nerves. The **skin lesions** tend to be localized, well-defined, few in number and numb. They often look pale, particularly in dark-skinned people. Tuberculoid leprosy is commonly self-healing, and damage to the peripheral nerves is usually limited.

LEPROSY

Signs of **lepromatous leprosy** include a chronically **stuffy nose** and many ill-defined, pale **skin lesions** and nodules affecting the whole body. Unlike tuberculoid leprosy, the lesions themselves are not usually numb. Elsewhere, skin numbness has a slow, symmetrical onset in a "glove and stocking" pattern (the numbness is distributed over the hands and feet). The skin around the face thickens (giving a "lion-like" appearance) and hair is lost (the eyebrows in particular). Frequently the ability to sweat is also lost. The internal structure of the nose can be affected by the bacterial invasion, causing a gradual but progressive collapse of the bridge of the nose. The eyes can be affected either directly by the bacteria causing local inflammation, or as a result of a loss of sensation impairing the blink reflex.

DIAGNOSIS AND TREATMENT

Diagnosis is generally made on **clinical grounds** and is considered in anyone who is living or has spent long periods in endemic areas, who has skin lesions or unexplained numbness. A **skin biopsy** may confirm the diagnosis as can a **lepromin test**, which measures the body's reaction to the inoculation of killed bacilli. Leprosy responds well to prolonged treatment with a combination of **antibiotics**, with the risk of infecting others removed after just 2 weeks, but unfortunately the damage to nerve endings is permanent.

Leptospirosis

(Weil's disease)

Leptospirosis occurs anywhere in the world, but, in the tropics, outbreaks usually occur during and after the rainy season or heavy flooding. Dogs, pigs and rats are the main animal hosts to the microbes that cause it (the rat-borne infection is known as **Weil's disease**), and it's spread to humans who come into contact with water contaminated by the animals' urine – infection usually enters the body through skin abrasions. Certain occupational groups are at greatest risk (veterinarians, farmers, etc), though anyone who swims in contaminated water is also vulnerable. Whitewater rafting and canoeing are theoretical risks.

SYMPTOMS

Classically, severe infections have 2 distinct phases. It takes about 10 days from exposure for signs of the first phase to appear. Lasting up to a week, and resembling many other illnesses, symptoms include **fever**, **headache**, **malaise**, **loss of appetite** and **muscle pains**. Your eyes may be red and sore, your lymph glands swollen, and you may experience **rashes** and **nosebleeds**. Then follows a symptom-free lull of 1–3 days followed by the second phase, during which you may develop **meningism** (headache, stiff neck, drowsiness, vomiting, intolerance to light) and **jaundice**. Most people fully recover after a few weeks, although there's a small risk of developing abnormal heart rhythms, increased bleeding tendency, and heart, kidney or liver failure.

DIAGNOSIS AND TREATMENT

Since initial symptoms of leptospirosis are non-specific, successfully diagnosing it is often delayed until the more serious, second phase of illness. If you've had recent contact with potentially contaminated water and develop flu-like symptoms shortly afterwards, consider this diagnosis. A **blood test** can confirm or deny your suspicions.

Antibiotics, such as penicillin, erythromycin or tetracycline, are most effective if started early (before the fifth day of illness). Be sure to drink plenty of **fluids** so you stay hydrated during the acute phase of the illness. Complications of the second phase of the illness, though rare, may require hospital treatment.

Lice infestation

The **3 kinds of lice** that affect humans are head lice, body lice and pubic, or crab, lice. Ubiquitous throughout the world, **head lice** are spread from one head to the next by sharing of hats, clothing, combs and hairbrushes, or simply getting too close. They usually cause itching of the scalp and neck. Adult lice are rarely seen but diagnosis can usually be made by the presence of their eggs ("nits") tightly bound to individual hairs.

Body lice are far less common, with a greater incidence among poverty-stricken communities or in cases of self-neglect. They are spread by direct contact or by shared clothing, where they often bury themselves in the seams. Like head lice, body lice cause itching, but they're also responsible for spreading **louse-borne typhus** and **relapsing fever** in some parts of the world.

Pubic or **crab lice** are similarly uncommon. Spread by close (usually intimate) contact, they favour coarsely haired areas of the body – the pubic region and occasionally beards, underarms and the like. Crab lice cause itching, which is usually worse at night, and they're often visible to the naked eye at the base of the hair, with the nits attached further up.

TREATMENT

Aqueous (instead of alcoholic) lotions of **malathion** are

probably the most useful treatment against all lice infestations and are available without prescription. Shampoos are less effective than lotions for head lice. Leave the lotion on for 12 hours (apply it to the whole body in the case of crab lice). A further second treatment is recommended after 7 days. For head lice, it's recommended that all family members receive treatment and for pubic lice, it's important that your partner also has treatment. In cases of body lice, all clothes must be washed at a high temperature (or incinerated) at the same time as treatment.

Loasis

▷▷See under Filariasis, p.222.

Lyme disease

Lyme disease occurs mainly in rural areas of North America and Europe. Deriving its name from Lyme, Connecticut, where the first case was described in 1975, there has been a 25-fold increase in reported cases in the US over the past 15 years, although this may be largely attributable to increased public awareness.

The microbes causing Lyme disease are transmitted to humans via the bite of blood-sucking deer-ticks. The ticks are active in the spring, summer and early autumn, when they can be found in long grass and trees waiting for their host animal, **deer**, to pass by. If you go walking in areas where there are deer, observe the measures to avoid tick bites described on p.45. Infected ticks are unlikely to pass on the disease unless attached for more than 24 hours, so it's important to inspect your hair, skin and clothes for them every few hours.

A vaccine currently available in the US has met with controversy, but if you're going to be living in a high-risk area for any length of time you might want to enquire about it locally on arrival.

SYMPTOMS

Many people experience no symptoms at all, while in others a slowly spreading, red ringed ("bull's-eye") **skin lesion** develops at the bite site, any time from 3 days to 4 weeks after infection. There may also be **local lymph-gland swelling** and **fever**, generalized **aches**, **pains** and **tiredness**.

More serious symptoms are uncommon, frequently delayed by weeks or even months after the initial infection, and mainly affect the nervous system, joints and heart. These can manifest as weakness, paralysis, abnormal sensations, mild meningitis symptoms, joint pains and swelling, and palpitations.

DIAGNOSIS AND TREATMENT

A **blood test** can confirm the diagnosis in the later stages of the disease – early detection is unreliable. If you do manage to catch it early (on the basis of the bull's-eye skin lesion), a 2-week course of **amoxycillin** (250mg 3 times daily) or **doxycycline** (200mg once daily) should prevent further progression of the disease. The later stages of Lyme disease will need treatment by hospital specialists.

Malaria

Malaria has been recognized as a disease entity for a long time. References to a disease resembling malaria have been found in ancient Chinese and Hindu writings, while the

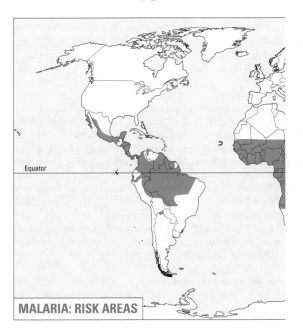

MALARIA: RISK AREAS

MALARIA

ancient Greeks noticed a connection between sporadic fevers, spleen enlargement and swamps. In the Middle Ages, it was thought to be caused by "miasma" (bad air or "*mal aria*") emanating from swamp areas, and by the seventeenth century Jesuits are known to have treated the disease using the bark of the South American cinchona tree – from which **quinine**, the medicinal substance that remains the cornerstone of malaria treatment derives.

Malaria remains widely **distributed** throughout the tropics and sub-tropics (see the distribution map above)

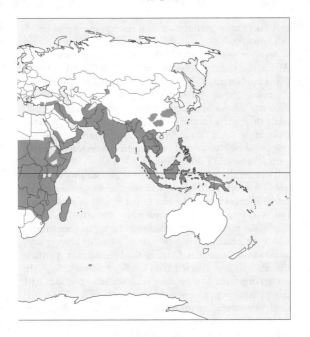

and continues to pose a serious threat to health. In 1997 the risk of contracting malaria existed in 100 countries, 92 of them affected by the dangerous **falciparum** variety (see p.285). The WHO estimates that there are between 300 and 500 million cases of malaria each year, with the result of more than 1 million deaths. The countries of tropical Africa account for roughly 90% of the total cases. The vast majority of malaria fatalities occur in young children in this area, although children who survive beyond 5 years have a high degree of immunity to the lethal effects of malaria. (This immunity wanes if re-exposure to malaria is infrequent.)

Areas of particularly **high risk** include sub-Saharan Africa, the Indian subcontinent, south and southeast Asia, Mexico, Haiti, the Dominican Republic, Central and South America, Papua New Guinea and Vanuatu and the Solomon Islands, although it must be emphasized that patterns of malaria outbreaks change every year. The major cities in Asia and South America can, for most intents and purposes, be considered malaria-free, whereas those in Africa, India and Pakistan cannot.

It's generally acknowledged that the mosquitoes responsible for the **spread** of malaria very rarely venture higher than 1500m (4500ft). The bite of the female *anopheles* **mosquito** transmits the malarial parasite to humans. Less commonly, the parasite can be transmitted from mother to baby across the placenta, via blood transfusions or among drug addicts sharing needles. Once in the bloodstream, the parasite multiplies in the red blood cells and liver cells – the **recurring** fever synonymous with malaria coincides with the parasitic reproduction in the blood cells. The drugs used in **malaria prophylaxis** disrupt the parasites' lifecycle and reproduction stages, although **resistance** to the drugs is growing on an alarming scale.

There are **4 subgroups** of the malaria parasite – *P. falciparum*, *P. ovale*, *P. vivax*, *P. malariae* – of which the falciparum form is the most dangerous and also the most geographically diverse, accounting for the vast majority of malaria-related deaths.

Prevention

Much debate surrounds the risks and side effects of **antimalarials**, which work by preventing establishment of the

Antimalarials under development

Two further drugs are currently attracting interest as alternatives in malaria prophylaxis. Malarone, a combination of atovaquone and proguanil, is currently licensed for the treatment of malaria but trials are still underway to prove its safety and efficacy as a preventative. Hopes are high in part because of its very low side-effect profile.

Savarine is widely prescribed as a prophylactic in many European countries, although at the time of writing it was not available in the UK, Germany, the US, Australia or New Zealand. It's a daily-dose combination drug containing chloroquine and proguanil.

 A Chinese remedy called quinhaosu, derived from the *Artemesia annua* plant, is attracting much research interest.

parasite in the blood and liver cells. Taking drug prophylaxis for any illness must be carefully assessed in terms of **risk versus benefit**, and this is particularly the case with malaria.

Although new drugs are being developed (see box above), the current **three mainstays** of malaria prophylaxis are chloroquine (with or without proguanil), mefloquine and doxycycline. Whichever antimalarial you choose, remember that none offers complete protection, so observation of the usual anti-insect bite measures (see p.259) is imperative, remembering particularly that *anopheles* mosquitoes tend to bite only between dusk and dawn. Anyone requiring **long-term prophylaxis** should take the **chloroquine/proguanil combination** (proguanil is difficult to obtain in the US), which can be used for up to 5 years (regular checks for eye damage are necessary). **Mefloquine** is licensed for up to 1 year. **Doxycycline,**

MALARIA

283

used in parts of the world where there is chloroquine and mefloquine resistance, is only effective against the falciparum variety of mosquito.

Chloroquine/proguanil should be started at least 1 week before entering a high-risk area, and mefloquine at least 2 weeks before entering, while doxycycline can be started just 2 days beforehand. All should be continued for 4 weeks after leaving.

More detail on the drugs used for malaria prophylaxis, their dosages and side effects can be found on pp.63–67 of the Medical kit.

People with **epilepsy** cannot take either chloroquine or mefloquine so in areas where chloroquine is first choice (ie no resistance) proguanil can be used alone, whereas in areas where chloroquine resistance exists, specialist advice should be sought (doxycycline is the likely candidate but its metabolism can be influenced by some anti-epileptic medications).

Avoid travelling to high-risk areas in **pregnancy**. If this is unavoidable, effective prophylaxis must be used because of the increased threat malaria poses in pregnancy to both mother and baby. In areas where there is no chloroquine resistance, chloroquine and proguanil may be used but **folic acid supplements** must also be taken at a dose of 5mg daily. In areas of chloroquine-resistance, mefloquine can be used but with caution: the manufacturer advises avoidance in the first 3 months of pregnancy even though no scientific evidence of harmful effects to the fetus has been demonstrated. Doxycycline should not be taken at any stage of pregnancy.

In the event conventional drugs are too daunting, a **homeopathic antimalarial system** is detailed on p.65. Note, too, that some homeopathic pharmacies can supply a **homeopathic potency of the allopathic drug** you have been advised to take. You can take this simultaneously in a low potency to offset side effects of the allopathic drug – it's not intended as a substitute. Homeopathic potencies can also help to clear the allopathic drugs from your system after you finish your course. A short course of the **Bach Crabapple Flower Remedy** at this point will have a similar detoxifying effect.

Recognizing the symptoms

The **incubation period** for malaria is usually between 9 and 16 days, though longer in rare cases. The symptoms for all of the subgroups are broadly similar and relate to the parasite's cycle of reproduction and subsequent destruction of the body's red blood cells.

Initially, malaria is very difficult to distinguish from many other febrile illnesses, especially those found in the tropics. Classically, victims go through three stages: a **cold stage** characterized by shivering and shaking, a **hot stage** in which you develop a high temperature (sometimes above 41°C), hot flushes and rapid heartbeat, and a third, **sweating stage** during which your temperature falls. Typically the fever recurs cyclically, every 1–3 days depending on the type of malaria. Common accompanying symptoms include a **cough**, **joint pains**, **loss of appetite** and **vomiting**, which coupled with the high fever can cause significant **dehydration**. As the disease progresses, **anaemia** and **jaundice** may occur as a result of the destruction of large numbers of red cells and the spleen (functionally a kind of filter for the blood) becomes enlarged early in the disease. (You'll feel it as a tender mass in the left side of your upper abdomen.)

By far the most dangerous form of malaria, **falciparum**

MALARIA

The mefloquine (Larium) debate

Key to the complex debate surrounding malaria prophylaxis is the matter of balancing the risks of contracting malaria against those of experiencing side effects from the preventative drugs. All drugs have side effects but much has been made of the sometimes severe and debilitating effects suffered by people who take mefloquine.

On the one side you have the manufacturers of Larium (the brand name for mefloquine) reassuring the public and playing down the side effects, while on the other a media-fed storm of perhaps unjustified anxiety and hysteria brews. Mefloquine has a number of heavyweight backers including the World Health Organization (WHO), the Center for Disease Control (CDC) in the USA and the Department of Health in the UK. Yet with increasing involvement of consumer groups, legal actions and questions being asked of governments, it's become an emotive issue.

It's important to remember that mefloquine is not always necessary. There are still malarial areas of the world where the parasite is sensitive to chloroquine (itself carrying a number of side effects) and mefloquine should really only be seriously considered in areas where chloroquine resistance exists. Refer to Part 3 to see if your destination is chloroquine-resistant or not, or check out the malaria Web sites or telephone helplines detailed in Part 4.

can cause considerable damage to the body in a number of ways, and death in about 2 percent of cases usually as a result of delayed treatment. **Cerebral malaria** is the most dangerous complication, and if untreated can be fatal. Typical signs of cerebral malaria include delirium, disorientation, a reduced level of consciousness, fits and coma.

Also bear in mind that if you have a previous medical history of fits, psychiatric illness or heart conduction defects, then you cannot take mefloquine anyway, so save yourself the agonizing.

SIDE EFFECTS

The risk of "serious" side effects, notably fits or psychosis, lies somewhere between 1 in 10,000 and 1 in 20,000. Less serious side effects, including headaches, dizziness, mood swings and insomnia, are reported to occur in up to 20% of cases, with women being slightly more at risk than men. Various numbers of studies have identified little or no difference between the incidence of side effects caused by mefloquine compared to a chloroquine/proguanil combination.

Most adverse reactions manifest within the first weeks of taking the drug, which is one reason why it's suggested that you start mefloquine at least 2 (preferably 3) weeks before departure – any side effects are likely to occur before you enter the malarial area in the majority of cases. A significant problem with mefloquine is that it stays in the body for a long time, so if you do experience mild side effects, it may take several days for them to settle. More serious psychiatric side effects, meanwhile, can remain for much longer and can be difficult to treat.

MALARIA

Recovery is followed by longstanding damage to the nervous system in up to 10% of cases.

So-called **"blackwater fever"** occasionally occurs as a result of kidney failure following the mass destruction of red blood cells and leading to the escape of haemoglobin (the oxygen-carrying molecule in the blood) into the urine. Other systems affected by falciparum include the gastrointestinal tract (nausea and vomiting), the liver (jaundice), and the lungs (an accumulation of fluid causing shortness of breath). In **children and pregnant women** (see below), a common complication is **hypoglycaemia** (low blood sugar).

Malariae malaria follows a recurring cycle of fever which over time becomes less severe although, in the absence of treatment, can continue for many years. The **ovale** and **vivax** forms cause similar illnesses which manifest as a periodic but irregular relapsing fever. The cycle may continue for up to 5 years despite drug treatment.

MALARIA AND PREGNANCY

All types of malaria can lead to miscarriage or premature delivery. Mothers often become very anaemic, and the baby is frequently underweight at birth. Pregnant women are particularly susceptible to the complications of falciparum malaria, including hypoglycaemia and the accumulation of fluid in the lungs. Although rare, malaria can be passed on to the baby who may suffer fever, anaemia and failure to thrive.

Diagnosis and treatment

A **blood test** can usually identify the parasites in the blood although occasionally more than one sample needs to be examined. On confirmation of the diagnosis, you must seek hospital treatment. The following are only guidelines in the event you suspect malaria but have no immediate access to medical help. Remember that **rehydration** and **reduction of the high fever** are also crucial.

Falciparum malaria is generally regarded as being chloroquine resistant, so treatment options revolve around

Purple jellyfish, California. Photo © Brandon D.Cole/Corbis

quinine, mefloquine, Malarone or a rarely used drug called halofantrine. For an **adult** able to swallow, oral treatment with mefloquine (20–25mg/kg body weight either as a single dose or 2 to 3 divided doses) or Malarone (4 tablets daily for 3 days) are the preferred options. If oral quinine is used, a 7-day course of 600mg 3 times a day has to be followed by Fansidar (a combination drug of pyrimethamine and sulfadoxine; 1 dose of 3 tablets) or a 7-day course of doxycycline 200mg daily. Anyone too ill to take tablets will need to be treated intravenously. **Pregnant women** should be treated with quinine alone.

Any fever occurring in the returning traveller requires the exclusion of malaria, particularly in the first 3 months. Although malaria can present later, this is rare and more likely to be the vivax, ovale or malariae types rather than falciparum.

For a **child**, the dose of mefloquine is calculated on the same basis as for adults. Malarone is not suitable for children weighing less than 11kg. For those between 11 and 20kg, 1 tablet should be taken daily for 3 days; for those between 21 and 30kg, 2 tablets should be taken daily for 3 days; and for those between 31 and 40kg, 3 tablets should be taken daily for 3 days. Children over 40kg in weight can tolerate adult dosages of Malarone. Quinine may be used at a dose of 10mg/kg body weight, 3 times daily for 7 days although the course must be followed by a single dose of Fansidar: 1/2 tablet for under-4s, 1 tablet for 5–6 year olds, 1 and 1/2 tablets for 7–9 year olds and 2 tablets for 10–14 year olds.

Vivax, **ovale** and **malariae** malaria are usually chloroquine-sensitive although resistance is emerging in some parts of the world. The **adult** starting dose for chloroquine of 600mg should be followed by a further 300mg dose after 8 hours, then 300mg daily for 2 days. **Children** follow the

MALARIA

““Once bitten... ””

My 1998 Rough Guide research trip to India was going well, despite the steamy rains of the late monsoon. I had travelled up from Chennai (Madras) to the huge central state of Madhya Pradesh. There I visited the jungle of the Kanha National Park, where I recall picking up a few mozzie bites and seeing a very sick forest worker, possibly a victim of malaria.

By the end of September I was in Bhopal, the state capital, scene of the Union Carbide factory disaster in 1984. It was while covering this surprisingly pleasant city that I started to feel a little run down and achey. I kept going but collapsed exhausted each night. I was about to leave for a remote hill station but by this stage my dramatically fluctuating temperature had alerted me to the possibility of malaria – I had only been taking chloroquine as prophylaxis – so decided to seek medical advice while still in a major city.

Luckily, the friendly hotel manager unhesitatingly called a doctor and arranged for me to be taken there by scooter. At the small surgery in the dark and wet backstreets I didn't argue about getting bumped up the queue and was soon being examined by Dr Dubey, a scholarly man with excellent English. He immediately suspected a chloroquine-resistant strain of malaria.

The ride back in the late monsoon rain past gaily coloured neon-lit mobile shrines, pumping out wild devotional music for the Durga Puja festival, was unforgettable, my heart oscillating between love for this amazing country and fear for my current predicament. The worst was confirmed by next morning's blood test: the presence of the falciparum parasite that can lead to cerebral malaria.

→

At first I wanted to run for the first plane home but Dr Dubey's calm authority and assurance that the disease was completely curable if treated promptly gave me courage, and by that evening I was hooked up to a quinine drip in an air-conditioned private room with TV at the small Hajela Hospital.

Events moved pretty fast and I was struck by the surreal sensation aroused by knowing I had a potentially fatal illness without feeling particularly ill. Thankfully I never got to feel any worse. I received expert treatment from Dr Dubey and colleagues. I also got a strong sense of being cared for in the emotional sense. The nurses popped in to chat in their limited English and even the thorough cleaning staff had smiles for me.

After three days I knew I was out of the woods, as a further blood test proved clear, and when discharged I felt healthier than I had in ages. Amazingly, the cost of six days' excellent treatment was barely £100. This included follow-up medication and some dreaded Larium pills, as prophylaxis for the rest of the trip.

Ironically, I'd previously spent long periods in India without any protection, fearful of potential side effects, when, in the end, I caught malaria on a much shorter stay. Looking back, I feel very lucky to have survived the ordeal, thanks to the swift diagnosis and available resources. I just hope the forest worker was as lucky.

Nick Edwards, Pittsburgh

same regime in the doses of 10mg/kg body weight initially, followed by 5mg/kg body weight for subsequent doses. Mefloquine can be used as an alternative if necessary.

For recurring malaria, a drug called **primaquine** is commonly and successfully used. Adult dosage is 15mg daily for 14–21 days, while children should be given 250mcg/kg body weight for the same period.

Malta fever

▷▷ See Brucellosis, p.167.

Marburg virus

Marburg virus was first recognized in 1967 in Marburg, Germany, among laboratory staff who had been in close contact with Ugandan monkeys. The virus occurs in small outbreaks across sub-Saharan Africa – Sudan, Kenya and the Democratic Republic of Congo – and appears to be passed between people by intimate contact, although the exact mode of infection remains unclear. It is a rare illness, even in these endemic areas, and the risk of the infection being passed to a casual traveller is very small.

SYMPTOMS

Marburg virus is a **viral haemorrhagic fever**. Although considered marginally less dangerous than **Ebola** with which it is compared, in severe cases Marburg virus causes potentially fatal bleeding. The virus remains in the body for a long time even after the symptoms have settled, so there's a potential risk of infecting others during that time.

▷▷ See Viral haemorrhagic fever, p.394.

DIAGNOSIS AND TREATMENT

A **blood test** will confirm the diagnosis. There is no specific treatment, although careful nursing and hospital care is vital to prevent further spread (known as "barrier nursing").

Meliodosis

("Vietnamese time bomb", Whitmore's disease)

The organisms causing **meliodosis** can be found anywhere in the world, but outbreaks occur mainly in Southeast Asia (it was relatively common among troops during the Vietnam War), the Far East and northern Australia. Isolated outbreaks have occurred elsewhere but are very rare.

The **bacteria** enters the body through skin cuts or abrasions, although transmission may also occur via contaminated water and inhalation. The disease is rare in humans (it affects animals such as goats, sheep, cattle and pigs), and those with a healthy immune system are unlikely to be severely affected. Diabetics and those with deep wounds or burns are more susceptible.

Meliodosis is a severe illness for which there is no immunization. Protect yourself by cleaning all wounds, even trivial, carefully and thoroughly in high-risk areas and observe the usual food- and water-hygiene measures (see p.40).

SYMPTOMS

Common symptoms are a **high temperature** with prostration, and occasionally drowsiness and delirium. Diarrhoea, vomiting and joint aches may also occur. Septicaemia with abscess formation in the vital organs such as the kidneys, lungs, liver and spleen often follows. Meliodosis can be life-threatening, so it's essential to seek medical help early if it is suspected.

DIAGNOSIS AND TREATMENT

Infection can be confirmed by a **blood test**. Treatment involves a 2- to 4-week course of **intravenous antibiotics** (ceftazidime is the current recommendation), followed by a 6-month course of amoxycillin or co-amoxiclav.

Meningitis

The word "**meningitis**" strikes terror into most people's hearts, although in fact it simply relates to inflammation of the membranes covering the outside of the brain (the *meninges*). The symptoms are usually serious but the outcome is dependent on the specific cause of the meningitis and how quickly it is treated. The most high-profile and feared of the many different causes is **meningococcal** meningitis, which is in turn divided into 3 subgroups – A, B and C – each showing signs of localized predominance (eg the commonest in the UK is group B, whereas the commonest in Africa are groups A and C). **TB**, **syphilis**, **leptospirosis**, a host of **viruses** and a number of other bacteria can all also cause meningitis (the bacteria that often affects children is now on the decrease thanks to the development of an effective preventative vaccine).

Sporadic **outbreaks** of meningococcal meningitis occur anywhere in the world, but they are more common and enduring in the belt of sub-Saharan Africa from Ethiopia in the east to Senegal in the west, particularly during the dry season. Epidemics often occur after war, drought and famine, when immunity of the population as a whole is low.

The bacteria causing meningococcal meningitis are spread from person to person by droplets after coughing or sneezing. A **vaccination** is available against the A and C strains but is ineffective against group B. All travellers should be immunized if they're headed to areas of high risk. If you plan to travel to Mecca for the annual **haj**, vaccination is **mandatory**.

SYMPTOMS

The majority of people infected with the bacteria causing meningococcal meningitis remain asymptomatic, and many become unwitting carriers. Because the number of people carrying the bacteria is far higher than the actual incidence of the disease, susceptibility to meningitis is likely to be more down to individual health and immunity rather than the bacteria itself.

When symptoms occur (usually after an incubation period of between 2 and 10 days), initially it's almost impossible to differentiate them from those of a common cold or any other viral infection. Progression of the disease can be alarmingly rapid, however, and can include the following:

+ Intense malaise
+ High fever
+ Severe headache
+ Intolerance to light
+ Vomiting
+ Irritability
+ Lapsing consciousness
+ Neck stiffness
+ A rash (in the case of meningococcal meningitis)

Untreated, meningitis can lead to septicaemia, convulsions, coma and death in over half of those affected. Early treatment is essential.

The **rash** in meningococcal meningitis indicates the presence of septicaemia and requires rapid medical attention. The rash looks purple and does not blanch on pressure (see box opposite). Initially it appears in clusters of tiny blood spots (like pinpricks) over pressure points or areas of friction (armpits, groin, buttocks, ankles, etc). These clusters will expand and the spots join together looking like fresh bruises. The rash may be difficult to see on dark skin.

MENINGITIS

The glass test for a "purpuric" rash

Press a glass against the spots. If they pale or disappear, it is not a purpuric rash. If they do not lighten, and there are other symptoms that suggest a diagnosis of meningitis, seek medical help rapidly. (Note that a purpuric rash does not necessarily mean meningitis – there are a number of other causes.)

DIAGNOSIS AND TREATMENT

If meningitis is suspected, don't consider self-treatment. Every minute counts, so get to a doctor or a hospital quickly. There the diagnosis can be confirmed by the presence of the bacteria in the cerebrospinal fluid taken from a **lumbar puncture**. Generally, if caught in time, meningitis responds well to intravenous antibiotic treatment, usually penicillin.

When isolated cases occur, close contacts of the case may need to be given **prophylactic antibiotics**. The need for prophylaxis depends on the type of organism causing the meningitis and the closeness of contact. In any event, take advice from the medical team treating the case.

Motion sickness

The chances are that if you travel with any regularity or for a prolonged length of time, at some point you'll experience the dismal symptoms associated with **motion sickness**. Children (over the age of 3) tend to be the most prone to the effects of motion sickness, and it's also one of the few illnesses that affects women more than men.

The **symptoms** – nausea, sweating, disorientation and dizziness – evolve from a discrepancy in the messages being sent to the brain from the eyes and the balance apparatus of the ears. This conflict of the senses usually arises in turbulent conditions when visual contact with the **horizon** is lost.

Although the scientific mechanism for motion sickness is well recognized and understood, there is a less predictable **psychological component**, with people who are fearful or anxious more likely to experience sickness than those who stay calm.

Prevention

Prevention of motion sickness is easier than treatment so if you've been previously affected or anticipate a rough journey, plan ahead and take preventative measures at least an hour before you set out. The main drug options on offer for the prevention of motion sickness revolve around various preparations of **hyoscine** and **antihistamines** (eg cinnarizine, promethazine, etc). There's little to choose between them in terms of efficacy, although their **side effects** differ slightly: while both types of drug can cause drowsiness (sometimes a welcome bonus), hyoscine can also cause a dry mouth and blurred vision, but has the advantage of being available as a skin patch as well as a tablet.

The standard drug preventatives are discussed in greater detail in Part 1.

▷▷See the Medical kit, p.63.

DRUG-FREE TACTICS

In addition to the specific preventative measures, there are several more generalized tactics:

+ Eat a light, easily digestible meal before setting out and nibble something bland like a dry biscuit or cracker during your journey.

MOTION SICKNESS

+ If you have a choice, position yourself in a well-ventilated environment, facing forward.

+ The best places for minimizing the effects of motion are over the wings on a plane, the front seat of a car, the front of a train, around the middle of a boat or ship (on deck if possible) and just forward of the midsection of a bus.

+ Avoid reading, particularly in a car or bus.

+ Avoid cigarette smoke, which may exacerbate nausea.

+ Keep your eyes fixed on the horizon or a stable point in the distance.

+ Keep still if possible, particularly avoiding head movements.

+ Sleep if you can; if not, try to distract yourself from your surroundings.

+ Try wearing acupressure bands on your wrists or take a ginger-based herbal remedy.

Treatment

If you start to feel sick **having embarked on your journey**, remember to keep your eyes on the **horizon** if possible, helping to reduce the inconsistencies between the messages the brain is receiving from the eyes and balance apparatus. Slowly sip a cool drink, try and relax taking slow, deep breaths and distract yourself. The antihistamine promethazine, although primarily a preventative, can also be taken to reduce the symptoms when they strike.

Tabacum is a good homeopathic remedy for sickness from rolling motion, and will suit you if you feel terribly faint, with a sinking feeling in the pit of your stomach – you'll probably be found up on the deck of the boat, in the fresh air, with your coat open and belt loosened. You look pale, may be covered with cold sweat, and have intense nausea followed by violent vomiting.

Increased salivating makes you want to spit. **Petroleum** is good for car, train and boat travel, especially for people who are really strongly affected by the smell of petrol. Take this if you feel the need to keep wrapped up and warm. Your nausea is eased by eating plain biscuits or crackers. **Cocculus indicus** is best for people who can't look out of moving vehicles, especially sideways. Your nausea can be worsened by virtually any external stimuli – light, noise, smell, etc. **Bach Rescue Remedy**, taken as a few drops every half hour or so in water, also helps take the edge off travel sickness.

Mycetoma

(Madura foot, Maduromycosis, Maduromycetoma)

Mycetoma is a chronic fungal infection relatively common in Africa, India and Sri Lanka, with sporadic cases also reported in Europe and North America. A rare but serious condition, usually affecting the skin, muscle and bones of the lower leg (sometimes the upper limb), mycetoma is caused by a number of soil fungi which probably enter the body through a puncture wound – yet another reason for wearing something on your feet and for cleansing all wounds (particularly any that breach the skin and superficial flesh, eg a thorn or nail).

There is no vaccination against mycetoma but it is extremely rare in travellers.

SYMPTOMS

Small, firm, painless nodules develop weeks or months often after an apparently innocuous injury. Slowly the nodules grow in size, becoming soft in the middle and eventually **ulcerating**. Straw-coloured fluid containing small granules (red, white, yellow, brown or black, depending on the type of fungus) drains from the deeper tissues. The process is progressive and will continue to invade deeper tissues unabated. Invasion into the joints will cause intense pain on movement.

DIAGNOSIS AND TREATMENT

The fungus is usually microscopically identified from the discharge. Drug treatment is generally disappointing and once the infection has taken hold, surgical amputation can be necessary.

Myiasis

Common causes of **myiasis**, which, in medical terms, means the invasion or infestation of bodily tissues or cavities by larvae of flying insects, are the tumbu fly and Lund's fly in Africa (mainly west and central), and the human botfly and New World screw worm fly in Central and South America and the Caribbean.

Tumbu flies commonly lay their eggs on drying laundry, with the larvae emerging and burrowing into the skin when the clothes are worn. Incubation usually takes less than 2 weeks. The boils created by the maturing maggots are often multiple – it's sometimes possible to identify the maggots' breathing tubes as two black dots in the boils.

Human botfly infestation most commonly affects cattle and humans. The fly captures a blood-feeding insect such as a mosquito and lays its eggs on it. The mosquito then transports the eggs to humans – as it feeds on the host's blood, the eggs hatch and start to burrow. The larvae tend not to migrate through the tissue but settle below the skin in the area where they originally penetrated. After what can be as long as 12 weeks the larvae exit by the same means as they entered and pupate in the soil.

📖 Uninvited travelling companions in Central America 📖

The trouble with the insects began as Hurricane Mitch was heading up the coast. The botflies – often found in the vicinity of large mammals – struck as I was helping to round up the horses at the tourist cabins where we were going to sit out the hurricane. I didn't notice anything at first. But a few days later, after the storm had passed, I saw and felt a number of small red bumps – similar to mosquito bites – on my arms and body.

It was only when the short, sharp stabbing pains began that I suspected the lumps might be what the locals called "beef worms" – a type of fly maggot that lives just under the surface of the skin, and is common on horses, dogs, and of course cattle. I'd heard about beef worms and their effects many times but had never suffered a bite – I was soon to find out what having them meant.

The female flies have an ingenious method of depositing their eggs. First she catches a female mosquito, lays eggs on the mosquito's body, then releases the mosquito which promptly heads for a source of blood – any large animal will do! Upon landing on its chosen victim the mosquito feeds, and the heat of the host's body triggers the botfly eggs to drop off the mosquito. The botfly larvae immediately hatches on the warmth and burrows under the skin.

The larvae grow by feeding on your flesh, and the stabbing pain begins. It's like having a thin needle stuck into a nerve, sending a short, but intense, flash of pain up to your brain. As the grub grows bigger it also grows spiky hairs around its body segments, making it difficult to remove by yourself. You *know for certain it's a beef worm when it pokes its breathing tube out of your skin.*

They're so common in the Central American lowlands (though tourists are rarely affected) that the locals all have their own method to get rid of them. These always involve blocking the breathing hole with something – wax, glue, tobacco – and waiting for a few hours until the larvae die. Then a really good squeeze brings the creature shooting out like a tiny rocket.

I went to some Maya friends of mine who simply pulled a few twigs from a tree in their garden and dabbed the resulting sticky white latex over the breathing holes. They then stuck more leaves over the latex and told me to come back in the morning, when all the larvae but one were duly squeezed out.

I had eight beef worms altogether, but I actually wanted to keep the one I had on my wrist, where it could easily be observed as it matured. Sounds gruesome, and indeed it was to some people who saw it, but I'd heard that the larva produces an antibiotic-type chemical preventing wound infection, so it was safe enough. I still had to keep it covered by a bandage to avoid offending delicate stomachs but most people were in fact morbidly fascinated.

For the next couple of months I gave request viewings of "my worm" in various bars and hotels as I travelled up to Mexico. It popped out in the highland town of San Cristóbal de las Casa, where these flies do not exist. I took it round the drugstore, dropped it into formaldehyde and it now sits on a bookshelf in my study. I'm thinking of encasing it in perspex for a paperweight.

Peter Eltringham, Luton, UK

"UNINVITED TRAVELLING COMPANIONS IN CENTRAL AMERICA"

The New World screw worm flies deposit their eggs on the edges of wounds and healthy mucous membranes (mouth, nose, etc), allowing the larvae to burrow into the flesh. Incubation usually takes about a week.

All forms of myiasis are rare in casual travellers, but your best means of protection against any of these insects is to take the bite-avoidance advice on p.259 when travelling in areas of prevalence.

SYMPTOMS

Regardless of the cause, the most common initial signs of myiasis are **itchy sores**, which develop into painful, often **oozing boils**. However, these lesions rarely develop into a significant health risk, as the maggots are essentially hitching a ride until they mature, after which they'll make their exit leaving no long-term effects.

DIAGNOSIS AND TREATMENT

There is no formal test for myiasis, but the maggots can often be seen through the air hole they create in the skin.

Applying Vaseline to the skin essentially cuts off their air supply and will force the maggot closer to the surface, making **extraction** easier. Maggots must be removed completely to reduce the risk of secondary bacterial infection.

Nutrition

During prolonged trips abroad, it's not uncommon to lose a few pounds. However, eating a **balanced diet** is important wherever you are and failure to do so can put your health at risk.

Aim to eat at least 5 helpings of **fruit and vegetables** a day (juice, tinned and dried fruit all count). A good tip from the mouth of a dietitian: "If in doubt when you're travelling, go vegetarian." In addition, there are 6 basic foodstuffs which you should include in your diet:

+ **Water:** the basic constituent of life, without which we die remarkably quickly. The average adult needs to drink at least 3 litres/day and larger quantities in hot climates or after heavy exercise (in which case it's worth remembering to add a pinch of salt which is lost in sweat).

+ **Carbohydrates:** Energy foods, particularly important if you are exercising vigorously. Examples include cereals (including rice), bread, sugar, potatoes and other root vegetables.

+ **Proteins:** Body-building food, particularly important after you have been ill and lost weight and in conditions affecting the liver. Examples include meat, dairy products, fish, eggs, lentils, beans, nuts.

+ **Fats:** Energy foods which act as building blocks for some of the important chemicals manufactured in the body. Eating too little of foods from this group is a much rarer problem than eating too much. Avoid fats if you are suffering from hepatitis. Examples include dairy products, eggs, nuts, any fried food, and red meat.

+ **Vitamins and minerals:** Important in the manufacture of various chemicals within the body and also vital factors in some metabolic processes such as releasing the energy from the food we eat. It is rare to be lacking in vitamins and minerals if you follow a balanced diet, particularly incorporating fresh fruit and vegetables. If you're going to be away for long periods of time and think you'll have trouble keeping a balanced diet, consider taking vitamin and mineral supplements.

NUTRITION

Onchocerciasis

▷▷See under Filariasis, p.218.

O'nyong nyong virus

Taking its name from an African phrase meaning "very painful and weak", **o'nyong nyong (ONN) virus** caused a major epidemic in the late 1950s in Uganda, Kenya, Tanzania and Malawi which affected an estimated 2 million people. In recent years, outbreaks have been rare and usually follow the rainy season, in East and West Africa and Zimbabwe. It is spread by the same mosquito responsible for the spread of malaria.

Risk to the casual traveller is very low unless passing through an area where there is an active epidemic. There is no preventative vaccination and the best means of protection is to observe the usual precautions for avoiding insect bites.

▷▷See Bite avoidance, p.259.

SYMPTOMS

The illness is indistinguishable from Chikungunya fever and Dengue fever (see pp.169 & 195; previous infection with Chikungunya confers immunity to ONN), with the main symptoms being **high fever**, **severe joint pains**, **headaches**, **swollen lymph glands** and occasionally a generalized **rash**. Recovery from the acute symptoms usually takes about 2 weeks, but joint pains can persist for longer. The infection can cause miscarriage in pregnant women.

DIAGNOSIS AND TREATMENT

There's no specific treatment for o'nyong nyong virus other than **symptom relief** and **rest**; however, no serious long-term effects have ever been reported following infection.

Oriental liver flukes

(Clonorchiasis, Opisthorchiasis)

There are 3 main species of **Oriental liver fluke** that affect humans:

+ *Clonorchis sinensis*, common in China, Taiwan, Korea, Japan and Vietnam, and carried by domestic dogs and cats.

+ *Opisthorchis felineus*, widespread in Eastern Europe (particularly Poland and the NIS), and carried by a variety of wild and domestic animals.

+ *Opisthorchis viverrini*, very common in Thailand (especially the north), and again mostly carried by dogs and cats.

Humans are usually infected after swallowing the larvae from raw, dried, smoked or pickled freshwater fish. The larvae reach the fish via a complicated life cycle (it all hangs on a water snail), whereby the habitat of the fish is contaminated by the faeces of human or dog carriers. Once ingested, the larvae migrate up the bile duct from the gut and mature into adult worms in the gall bladder over a 4-week period. Eggs from the mature flukes pass out of the body in faeces.

There is no preventative vaccination. Avoidance measures are simple: don't eat raw, freshwater fish in high-risk areas.

ORIENTAL LIVER FLUKES

SYMPTOMS

Oriental liver flukes affect millions of people but only a small number experience symptoms. **Liver discomfort** (the right upper aspect of the abdomen) is the most common symptom, occasionally accompanied by **bouts of fever**, **nausea**, **diarrhoea** (usually pale in colour) and **jaundice**. Advanced cases may suffer permanent liver and pancreatic damage.

DIAGNOSIS AND TREATMENT

The eggs are identifiable on microscopic examination of the **stool**. **Praziquantel** is an effective treatment at a dosage of 20–30mg per kg body weight of the person taking it, twice daily for 3 days.

Oropouche virus

Oropouche virus is a zoonosis with a **sloth** acting as the natural reservoir. It is transmitted to humans by midges, which breed in piles of the rotting husks of cacao beans. The disease has caused large epidemics in recent years in Brazil, Peru, Trinidad and Panama. Its incidence appears to be on the increase, and this seems to be related to the intense deforestation in these areas, which is altering the local ecosystems and bringing humans into closer contact with the disease vectors. There is no vaccine against the virus so the best means of avoiding the infection is to observe **precautions against insect bites** (see p.259). The risk to the traveller is low unless you plan on venturing into an epidemic area.

Symptoms include sudden-onset high fever with muscle and joint pains, intense headache, nausea and diarrhoea. In severe cases, symptoms of meningitis occur. **Diagnosis** is confirmed by a blood test. There is no **treatment** other than rest and symptomatic relief for the fever including drinking plenty of fluids. The presence of meningitis symptoms, however, requires urgent medical assessment.

Oroya fever

▷▷See Bartonellosis, p.162.

Paragonimiasis

(Oriental lung fluke)

Paragonimiasis occurs throughout the Far East, West Africa, south Asia, Indonesia, Papua New Guinea, and Central and northern South America. It's caused by a group of parasitic flatworms (flukes), whose eggs hatch in water and develop initially in freshwater snails, after which they move into crabs or crayfish where they develop into cysts. Humans become infected by handling or eating the crustaceans or when food preparation utensils have been contaminated. After the cysts are eaten, the immature flukes are released into the intestine, where they penetrate the wall and migrate to other tissues (usually the lungs, but sometimes abdominal organs or the nervous system). The adult worms develop after about 6 weeks and start producing eggs, which are subsequently coughed up in sputum.

Avoid eating raw, pickled or under-cooked freshwater crustaceans ("drunken crabs" – live crabs immersed in rice wine before eating – are a delicacy in some parts of Asia) if you're anywhere there might be a risk of infection.

SYMPTOMS

The symptoms are very similar to pulmonary TB, although up to a quarter of people affected show no signs of illness at all. The presence of the adult worms in the lungs causes a **mild fever** and a **cough** which, although starting off dry, becomes productive with **blood-stained sputum**. **Chest pain** often occurs and **night sweats** are common. As the infection becomes more longstanding, shortness of breath, weakness and weight loss occur. The lung flukes can survive for a number of years if left untreated. When they eventually die, the cysts close up, leaving long-term scarring (similar to TB).

DIAGNOSIS AND TREATMENT

The worm eggs are usually microscopically identified in the **sputum** or the **stool**. A drug called **praziquantel** (25mg/kg body weight, 3 times a day for 3 days) is the best treatment, although surgery may be needed to remove the cysts.

Paratyphoid

Paratyphoid is clinically the same as typhoid (see p.385), although it's a milder illness. It occurs sporadically in small epidemics across the world. Three subgroups of the salmonella bacteria cause paratyphoid and are spread by the faecal–oral route.

Common **symptoms** are identical to typhoid, though less serious, and occur between 1 and 10 days after eating contaminated food. They include general malaise, fever, headache, loss of appetite and sometimes a dry cough. Bleeding from the intestine, confusion and hearing loss are occasional complications.

Diagnosis is usually established by lab analysis of blood or stool samples. Amoxycillin can be used as **treatment** but resistance is common, after which the quinalone antibiotics such as ciprofloxacin are usually effective.

Plague

The word "**plague**" never fails to conjure up a sense of fear. The term "**Black Death**" arises from the dark appearance of bleeding under the skin, seen in advanced cases of plague septicaemia. Throughout history it has caused major epidemics which have significantly reduced the human population. There were 3 major epidemics in the sixth, fourteenth and seventeenth centuries, with an estimated total death toll of 137 million. As recently as the early part of the twentieth century, an epidemic killed 10 million people in the Indian subcontinent. In the 1980s around 9000 cases of plague were reported to the WHO, the majority occurring in Asia and Africa but with small foci in South America and even the southwest USA. In the 1990s outbreaks of plague have been reported in sub-Saharan Africa, Madagascar, Peru, China, Vietnam and India.

Plague often follows natural disasters such as earthquakes, which tend to increase the contact between wild and domestic rodents. The first sign of a plague epidemic is often the deaths of large numbers of rats. The disease is caused by a bacteria transmitted to humans by animals, usually via the bite of a rat flea. Wild rodents remain as the natural reservoir.

A plague **vaccine** is available but not routinely administered – it's used mainly for lab or medical personnel who may be at risk (see p.18). Its use in mass immunization of the population during an outbreak has not been properly assessed. Plague is a rare but serious disease which is unlikely to trouble the average traveller, but you should avoid areas where there have been outbreaks. Avoid contact with rats, live or dead, use insect repellent on your ankles and legs and an insecticide on your clothing and outer bedding. If your exposure risk is high, consider taking prophylactic antibiotics

(see below) – these should certainly be used if you have face-to-face contact with a known case of pneumonic plague.

SYMPTOMS

The initial flea bite often goes unnoticed. Symptoms can develop in a matter of hours (to a maximum of 17 days) and start with **high fever**, **headache**, **malaise**, **muscle aches** and **nausea**. In a very short time (often a matter of hours), the infection spreads to the lymph nodes, causing (very) tender swellings, known as **buboes**. The buboes can be very large (up to 10cm in diameter) and may form abscesses.

The infection gradually spreads to the blood, leading to **septicaemia** and more focused organ damage. Involvement of the lungs can proceed to **pneumonic plague**, which is highly infectious (by coughing and sneezing) and carries a particularly high mortality. The clotting system of the blood can be affected by the septicaemia, leading to an increased tendency to bleed.

DIAGNOSIS AND TREATMENT

Diagnosis can be made on the basis of a **blood test**. Because of the potential seriousness of plague and the risk of spread, treatment should be undertaken in hospital, under isolation. A course of **antibiotics** of the tetracycline group (doxycycline, for example) is usually effective.

Polio

The **polio virus** exists worldwide but most cases occur in Asia and Africa, where vaccination uptake is poor, and it is spread mainly via food and water.

Provided you have been **immunized**, the risk of contracting polio during your trip is almost non-existent. A

POLIO

◁ Puppy sitting on a road, Playa Tambor, Costa Rica. Photo © Martin Rogers/Corbis polio booster should be considered every 10 years, so check whether you're due before you go (see p.19). Otherwise, observe the normal food and water precautions to reduce your risk.

SYMPTOMS

People who've contracted the virus are most infectious for the week to 10 days before and after they develop symptoms. A staggering 95% of those infected will show no symptoms. In the remainder **fever**, **headache**, **nausea** and **vomiting** occur after a 1- to 2-week incubation period. The virus multiplies in the gut and enters the nervous system. **Neck stiffness** and a **unilateral tremour** sometimes occur. Paralysis results in roughly 0.1% of cases, and the risk increases with age.

DIAGNOSIS AND TREATMENT

A **blood test** can detect the antibodies to polio virus. Polio cannot be treated, although the majority of cases will recover without long-term effects. **Bed rest** is important in the early stages, and **physiotherapy** is vital for anyone who suffers paralysis.

Pseudomembranous enterocolitis

Pseudomembranous enterocolitis is a rare complication following treatment with antibiotics, when the bowel becomes inflamed as a result of colonization and overgrowth of bacteria. The symptoms can mimic some infectious diarrhoeal diseases. Although the infection can be passed on from person to person, this is rare and tends to occur mainly in hospital in patients with low immunity.

SYMPTOMS

Symptoms usually occur 4 to 10 days after taking antibiotics but can be delayed for up to 6 weeks. Severity of symptoms is variable and comprises **watery diarrhoea**, often a **mild fever** and **abdominal tenderness**. **Severe abdominal pain** and **bloody diarrhoea** can also occur.

DIAGNOSIS AND TREATMENT

Pseudomembranous enterocolitis should be considered in anyone who develops the above symptoms within 6 weeks of taking a course of antibiotics. If it's suspected and you are still taking the original antibiotics, stop the course. The diagnosis is usually confirmed by a **stool analysis** or by **sigmoidoscopy**. Ironically, a further 10-day course of the antibiotic **metronidazole** (400mg daily) usually cures the illness, although relapses are common.

Pyrexia

▷▷See Fever, p.216.

Q fever

Q fever was first identified in 1935 in Australia, where it was given the name "Query fever" because its cause was initially unknown; the microbes that cause it eventually were identified 2 years later. The illness occurs worldwide, although with a higher incidence in rural areas. Many people have a natural immunity to the microbes, which suggests that the infection is widespread but usually goes undetected.

The micro-organisms responsible are usually carried by sheep, cattle and goats and are found in particularly high concentrations in the placenta but are also present in the milk, urine and faeces. It's possible to become infected simply by breathing in the microbes from contaminated air, although ticks also carry the disease and may be responsible for a small number of human infections. Farmers, abattoir workers, vets and anyone else in close contact with animals are at greatest risk, with little threat posed to the average traveller. A **vaccine** against Q fever exists, but is not widely available – discuss it with your doctor if you plan to work with animals while you're away.

SYMPTOMS

After an incubation period of between 10 and 20 days, **headache, fever, shivering, muscle aches, loss of appetite, nausea** and **fatigue** are the prominent symptoms. A cough and sharp chest pains that are worse on taking a deep breath or coughing can also occur. Symptoms are usually self-limiting, lasting upto 2 weeks. Rarely, the illness can lead to heart, liver or brain complications.

DIAGNOSIS AND TREATMENT

Q fever is difficult to differentiate from many viral illnesses, and unlikely a doctor will consider it as a diagnosis unless you've had contact with the microbes that cause it – in which case a **blood test** can confirm you've got it. Symptoms will usually resolve themselves, although a 5- to 7-day course of **doxycycline** can speed up the process.

Rabies

Rabies is present in all parts of the world except Australasia and Antarctica. In some parts of India, 1 in 500 admissions to hospital is due to rabies, almost always secondary to a dog bite. It is estimated that around 2% of dogs in Bangkok are rabid, and the disease accounts for around 300 deaths in the city each year.

The virus is commonly carried by dogs, wolves, foxes, jackals, skunks, cats, bats, mongooses and even farm animals, but can be found in any warm-blooded animal. Cases of human rabies are most prevalent in the Indian subcontinent and Southeast Asia.

The virus is transmitted in the saliva of an infected animal, usually via a bite or by licking an open wound. Human-to-human transmission is very rare. Half of all people bitten by an infected animal will develop the disease.

A **vaccine** against rabies is available to travellers who may be at risk (see pp. 19–20). **Pre-exposure** vaccination is recommended if:

+ You are at particularly high risk of animal contact (vets, agricultural workers, etc).
+ You plan to visit remote areas where medical care is less accessible.
+ You plan to stay longer than a month in an area where dog rabies is common (the longer you stay, the greater your risk of exposure).

Completing the full 3-dose pre-exposure vaccination course usually confers good protection for up to 2 years (taking chloroquine at the same time as being vaccinated may reduce your antibody response and thus impair the development of immunity). However, if you are bitten by an animal in a high-risk area even after being vaccinated, you must still seek urgent medical attention – prior vaccination may "buy you time" to a degree but it's still important to start post-exposure treatment as early as possible.

RABIES

❝ Rats! ❞

Hanoi in the 1980s was very different to what it is today. I remember on my first walk-about seeing through the window of the city's central government-run pharmacy some highly toxic heart medicines displayed on a sun-baked shelf, which not only were years past their use-by date, but should have been refrigerated. It was a couple of nights later, after I'd been bitten by a rat and some thoughtful sod intimated I could have caught rabies, that I quietly started to panic.

At the dilapidated Thong Nhat Hotel, every room had its resident rodent, but mine was an especially famished little thug I wasted no time christening Rattus Vietcongus. After the rat's molestation of some biscuits and a banana, I began placing all foodstuffs under lock and key, not realizing that in doing so I transformed myself into the menu. Around 2am I awoke to the hitherto untried sensation of tiny teeth drilling into a finger I had carelessly left dangling outside the mosquito net. Although the same finger rapidly became a minor celebrity among a frankly covetous foreign press corps, none of their accolades could assuage my burgeoning

Vaccinated or not, always **avoid contact** with animals (domestic or wild) in high-risk areas. If you are bitten, **thorough cleaning** of the wound initially with soap and water followed by an application of alcohol or iodine reduces the chances of becoming infected.

The **post-exposure treatment** is discussed on p.320.

SYMPTOMS

It can take weeks, months or even years for the symptoms of rabies to develop, though the average incubation period is between 2 and 8 weeks. Early symptoms are non-specific and apprehensions. Duly I presented at the only dependable clinic in town, sited within the compound of the Swedish embassy. I'd had a rabies jab back home; now I needed a booster, but the doctor refused point blank to oblige. Consulting an ancient French textbook he assured me no-one had ever contracted rabies directly from a rat. "Dogs, bats and cats to be sure, anything that might nibble a dead rat, but actual rats? Never!" He was adamant, too, about the prohibitive cost of the injection (half a year's wages for the average Vietnamese at the time).

After a protracted dialogue I acquiesced. A week later, after 8 hours spent in an unsprung jeep grinding along a road consisting of nothing but unbroken rock, things started looking very black. When finally I reached the middle of nowhere, each fibre of my body began aching with dull pain – all except my brain, where the ache was rather more acute. Although the fever that ensued turned out to be unrelated, I recalled the doctor's earlier parting shot: "People always say about the East that life is cheap, but in most cases the opposite is true. Life here is expensive."

Justin Wintle, London

"RATS!"

include **fever**, **general malaise**, **loss of appetite**, **nausea**, **vomiting**, **diarrhoea**, **muscle aches**, **sore throat**, **cough** and **headache**. Odd behaviours such as **anxiety**, **agitation** and **aggression** may occur. Pain or pins and needles over the area of the bite occur in just under half of all cases. From the initial non-specific symptoms the disease can take one of two different courses. "**Furious rabies**" is characterized by hyper-excitability, muscle spasms and hydrophobia or fear of water. Insomnia and strange purposeless movements can occur spontaneously or in response to touch. Frothing of the mouth is accompanied by swallowing difficulties and vomit-

ing. The final stages of the disease are characterized by progressive muscle paralysis and breathing difficulties. "**Dumb
rabies**" involves gradual paralysis, which begins in the bitten
limb in half of all cases. The muscle spasms and hydrophobia
of furious rabies hardly ever occur. The paralysis spreads rapidly and is usually symmetrical.

DIAGNOSIS AND TREATMENT

Tests on the **blood** and **saliva** of the victim will show evidence of the virus, but if you are at high risk, it's unwise to
defer post-exposure treatment pending lab results. Once
symptoms develop, there is no cure.

The importance of thorough wound cleaning cannot be
over-emphasized. If you have been bitten in a high-risk
area, seek medical help urgently as the sooner post-exposure treatment is initiated, the better. If you have received a
pre-exposure course, you will need a further 2 rabies vaccinations on days 0 and between days 3 and 7 (in some cases
more doses are given). Without previous immunization, you
will need a dose of rabies immunoglobulin (RIG) as soon
as possible, followed by a course of at least 5 rabies vaccinations on days 0, 3, 7, 14 and 30, although this can be dis-
continued if it is later proved you were not at risk.

Bear in mind that in many developing countries RIG
may first of all be hard to come by, and second it will have
been derived locally from human neural tissue and may
carry a risk from other blood-borne infections such as HIV
or hepatitis B.

If you are bitten by an animal, don't forget the risk of
tetanus and bacterial skin infections in the panic over
rabies.

RABIES

Relapsing fever

Relapsing fever is a bacterial infection which derives its name from the relapsing nature of the untreated illness. There are two distinct varieties: louse-borne or tick-borne. The **louse-borne** variety is usually found in areas of great poverty anywhere in the world. Epidemics often occur after war or natural disaster. Clothing provides refuge for the lice. The **tick-borne** variety is found in Africa, southern Europe, the Middle East, Asia and the Americas (including the western US and Canada).

The risk of infection to the traveller is generally low, especially if the standard insect bite-avoidance tactics are observed (see p.259). Person-to-person spread of relapsing fever does not occur (unless via body lice).

SYMPTOMS

After an incubation period of 2–10 days, initial symptoms consist of an **abrupt-onset fever**, **rigors**, **muscle pains**, **headache** and **extreme weakness** lasting for up to a week. A **remission** period of similar length follows before the symptoms **relapse**. Without treatment, further periods of regression and relapse occur. A cough and swelling of the lymph glands, liver and spleen may develop, and in severe cases (particularly the louse-borne variety) jaundice and a purpuric rash. Each time the fever abates a dangerous drop in blood pressure can occur. Progression of the disease can lead to dangerous swelling of the brain and inflammation of the heart muscle.

Overall, relapsing fever is a dangerous, potentially fatal illness although there is usually a good response to treatment.

DIAGNOSIS AND TREATMENT

A **blood test** confirms the presence of the bacteria. The

usual methods for reducing high fever should be adopted such as regular paracetamol and drinking plentiful, cool fluids. Treatment with **antibiotics** such as tetracycline, chloramphenicol or penicillin must be conducted under medical supervision in case they react with the bacteria (a rare complication). The length of treatment with antibiotics is dependent on the type of relapsing fever.

Respiratory tract infection

▷▷See Colds and coughs. p.176.

Rift Valley fever

Over the past few years there have been a number of major outbreaks of **Rift Valley fever**, mainly in sub-Saharan Africa, although particularly violent epidemics broke out in Egypt in the late 1970s and Kenya and Somalia in 1997–98. Outbreaks are often associated with heavy rainfall and flooding.

Rift Valley fever is a mosquito-borne viral haemorrhagic fever (see p.394). The infection is also found in animals (cattle, sheep, goats and camels), and humans can also contract the illness through contact with the blood, meat or body fluids (perhaps from the milk) of infected animals.

Experimental vaccines have been used to protect veterinary and laboratory workers at high risk, and animal vaccines are available, but the average traveller is at very low risk and should simply take steps to avoid mosquito bites (see p.259) and not get too close to livestock in any area that has seen outbreaks.

SYMPTOMS

Rift Valley fever is difficult to distinguish from other causes of high fever, and can be mistaken for meningitis. After an incubation period of between 2 and 6 days, the **fever** tends to peak **twice**, the first episode lasting 2 to 4 days, followed by a brief remission before the second. **Headache, muscle pains** and **backache** are common, with **neck stiffness, vomiting** and **photophobia** occurring in more severe cases.

Severe cases of Rift Valley fever, although rare, may develop brain, blood, liver and eye complications within the first 3 weeks of the illness, and such progressions carry a high mortality rate.

DIAGNOSIS AND TREATMENT

Blood tests reveal the presence of antibodies to the virus. There is no specific treatment for Rift Valley fever, and most cases are relatively mild and self-limiting. Observe the usual methods to reduce fever, rest and drink plenty. In severe cases intensive medical care is needed.

River blindness

▷▷See under Filariasis, p.218.

Rocky Mountain spotted fever

(Choix fever, New World spotted fever, Pinta fever, Tick fever)

Rocky Mountain spotted fever (RMSF) is a **tick-borne** illness affecting 600–800 people annually across the USA, with cases most commonly occurring in the south-eastern states – Oklahoma, Tennessee, the Carolinas,

Georgia and Virginia are particular hotspots. It also occurs in parts of Central and South America. The risk is higher in the spring and summer when the ticks are most active. Children between the ages of 5 and 9 are most commonly affected, for the simple reason that they're more likely to indulge in pastimes that put them in contact with the ticks.

A form of typhus (see p.388), RMSF is caused by the rickettsial bacteria transmitted by the bite of dog ticks (in the eastern USA) and wood ticks (in the western USA). The longer the tick remains attached to the body, the greater the chance of infection. Careful removal of ticks is important (see p.260) to avoid leaving body parts in the skin and because the infection can be contracted from the body juices of a crushed tick coming into contact with broken skin.

There is no vaccination against RMSF so the best way to avoid the illness is to avoid being bitten by ticks (see pp.45 and 260). Person-to-person spread does not occur.

SYMPTOMS

Between 1 and 2 weeks after the tick bite, the symptoms are usually sudden in onset and include **high fever**, **chills**, **muscle pains**, **severe headache** and **vomiting**. The **eyes** may become **painful** and there may be **generalized swelling** of the body. A **crusted, raised lump** can develop at the site of the bite, while nearby lymph glands are likely to become swollen and tender.

The **rash** synonymous with the name begins between 1 and 10 days after the onset of the fever. Small red spots or blotches begin peripherally (hands, feet, wrists, and ankles) and spread up the limbs to the trunk (the face is usually spared). As the illness progresses the rash changes to look like bruising and blood blisters (which do not blanch under pressure, ie purpuric – see p.297).

Complications of RMSF can affect the brain, liver, kidneys and lungs, and the disease can be fatal without appropriate antibiotic treatment.

DIAGNOSIS AND TREATMENT

The diagnosis can be made initially on a high level of suspicion, connecting your high fever with a recent tick bite. If neurological signs are present, a **lumbar puncture** will be needed. Blood tests are usually only useful retrospectively, as the results can take a few days, by which time the RMSF should already have been treated.

If you suspect you might have RMSF, seek help early as the overall likelihood of complications is related to how fast you get treated. For adults the usual treatment is a course of a **tetracycline antibiotic** (eg doxycycline). This group should be avoided if possible in young children, for whom chloramphenicol is an alternative treatment.

Other spotted fevers

Elsewhere in the world there are several varieties of tick-borne spotted fevers caused by rickettsial bacteria. The kind of tick may differ from country to country but, broadly speaking, the symptoms, diagnosis and treatment are the same. RMSF remains the most dangerous, followed by Mediterranean spotted fever and Siberian tick typhus. Like RMSF, most of the fevers are seasonal, occurring in the summer when the ticks are most active. The fevers' names generally hold clues to the parts of the world where they are prevalent. Thus:

✦ Mediterranean spotted fever
✦ Kenyan tick typhus

ROCKY MOUNTAIN SPOTTED FEVER

✚ African tick bite fever

✚ Israeli spotted fever

✚ Astrakhan fever (Caspian Sea)

✚ Siberian tick typhus

✚ Indian tick typhus

✚ Japanese spotted fever

✚ Queensland tick typhus

✚ Flinders Island spotted fever (Australia)

Rodent-borne hantavirus infection

Rodent-borne hantavirus infection describes a group of viruses found throughout the world which are spread to humans via rodents, causing viral haemorrhagic fevers (see p.394). Usually transmitted by inhaling dried rat excreta, typically after brushing floors or beating carpets, the infection is rare, particularly among travellers, but to be safe avoid contact with rodents and their droppings. There is no preventative immunization. Person-to-person spread is unknown.

Hantavirus infections are rare but serious. Characteristically, the infection starts with **symptoms** of high fever, rigors and muscle pains. As with all haemorrhagic fevers, the infection affects the blood, leading to an increased bleeding tendency, with spontaneous bleeding from the nose, gums, rectum, etc, possible. A rare but recognized complication of hantavirus infection is shock, which can lead to kidney failure ("haemorrhagic fever with renal syndrome", or HFRS). Without treatment, this can be fatal. In the Americas, hantavirus infection may cause a build-up of fluid on the lungs, known as hantavirus pulmonary syndrome (HPS). Occurring within the first 10 days of the illness, HPS is a serious complication that also demands prompt medical attention.

Blood tests can identify antibodies to the virus. While there's no specific **treatment**, intensive medical care improves the chances of survival.

Ross River virus

(Epidemic Polyarthritis)

Taking its name from the river in northern Queensland where it was first identified, **Ross River virus** is endemic throughout Australia, with isolated outbreaks occurring in the islands of the South Pacific.

Ross River virus is spread by mosquitoes, and outbreaks tend to occur after flooding during the rainy season, when mosquitoes are most active. Direct person-to-person spread does not occur.

The disease can also infect domestic and wild animals, and the Australian kangaroo and wallaby populations are believed to be the natural reservoir for the infection (it is thought that this is the reason that Ross River fever has never been exported to any great extent).

There is no vaccination against the disease and your best means of protection against infection is by taking steps to avoid mosquito bites whenever possible (see p.259). The risk to travellers is generally low unless you visit an area where there is an active epidemic.

SYMPTOMS

Ross River virus causes a remarkably similar illness to Dengue fever (see p.195). After an incubation period of between 2 and 21 days, symptoms emerge as a **flu-like illness** with fever, chills, muscle pains, headache, lethargy and occasionally a rash. Painful, stiff and sometimes swollen joints, which are usually worse in the morning, may occur. The symptoms tend to be less severe in children. Although the acute illness resolves fairly quickly, the joint pains, tiredness and sometimes depression can continue for several months.

DIAGNOSIS AND TREATMENT

Blood tests show antibodies to the virus in the blood. No specific treatment is available, but rest and pain relief such as **paracetamol** and ibuprofen relieve the symptoms.

Saltwater hazards

There are plenty of fish in the **sea**, but **drowning** is by far the greatest risk to your health. The majority of potentially hazardous **maritime creatures**, from the majestic shark to the lowly, and seemingly innocuous, shellfish, are found in tropical or sub-tropical seas and only attack if provoked.

▷▷See Fire and water in Staying well, p.39; and Freshwater hazards, p.224.

Fish

The majority of injuries caused by fish are from accidentally treading on one with venomous spines or by handling those caught during fishing. Though widely feared, sharks are generally shy creatures and tend to stay well away from humans, making **shark attacks** very rare – accounting for fewer than 15 deaths a year worldwide. Sharks have very poor vision and hunt by smell and vibration, mainly feeding between dusk and dawn. When they do strike, it's usually territorialism or in response to some kind of commotion (which they interpret as a fish in trouble), blood, bodily

SALTWATER HAZARDS

waste or refuse thrown overboard from ships that has attracted them. Most attack humans only if they are hungry (although great whites tend to be less ruled by hunger and attack anything fairly indiscriminately). If you find yourself swimming in the presence of sharks, those that keep their distance are nothing more than curious; those that circle inwards or make sudden, erratic movements are more likely to attack. Don't hang around for the sake of curiosity; swim to safety without delay.

The bite of the **barracuda** and **moray eels** can also be severe, although the danger is usually restricted to divers exploring reefs. If a fish bites you, be sure to clean the wound thoroughly to prevent infection and check your tetanus immunization is up to date.

The **lesser weever** fish sting is particularly common in temperate climates. The fish lies buried off sandy beaches with its spiney dorsal fin pointing upwards. Its sting can be very painful but poses no other threat.

In tropical waters the sting from the venomous spines of a **stingray** can inflict serious injury, although it's almost always accidental through stepping on the tail in shallow water (stingrays are not aggressive). The tail can cause deep lacerations, while envenomation from the spines may cause local swelling around the wound. Rarely, more generalized symptoms can follow, such as sweating, excessive salivation, nausea and vomiting, cramps, convulsions and abnormal heart rhythms, which will need urgent medical attention.

You'd be unfortunate to become the victim of a sting from the spines of a **stonefish,** which can be agonizing (the pain is unresponsive to morphine). Well camouflaged as a stone on the seabed, the stonefish can be found around reefs and estuaries in Indo-Pacific waters. The potent venom may cause fits, paralysis and even death.

Other fish with fins or spines which can inflict harm (but

66 All in a day's dive 99

I was only minutes into the first dive of the day at Bougainville Reef when I looked down into the blue and saw the shark. In itself this wasn't too unusual; it's a rare thing not to see sharks while diving on the outer edge of the Great Barrier Reef. Despite their reputation, however, most reef species are timid and either keep a respectful distance or simply bolt away from you on sight. After all, a diver wearing fins is bigger than the average shark, and is more likely to be seen as a threat than a food source. True, some sharks are territorial and resent divers intruding on their patch. Rather than attacking immediately and risk getting injured, however, they try to warn you away with a formalized display of aggression, arching their backs, swinging their heads from side to side, and pushing their pectoral fins down. Back off and so do they. It's only when divers fail to recognize this behaviour and hang around that they get bitten.

But then there are a few types of shark that are plain pugnacious. As was this one, a two-metre-long silvertip, which was tearing up the reef wall towards me like a torpedo, mouth open, teeth out. I had just enough time to back up against the coral and think "Bloody hell, here we go" before the shark shot up in front of me, missed, banked tightly around and came in again. Not being armed with anything sharp, all I could do was grab my reserve air source and fire a cloud of bubbles into its face. Amazingly enough this mild

are unlikely to be fatal) include **rabbitfish** (spinefoot), **surgeonfish** (tang), toadfish and **scorpionfish** (zebrafish)**, sea urchins** and the **crown of thorns starfish**.

The **blue-ringed octopus**, found in shallow waters

defence worked instantly, and the silvertip sheered away, dropped into deep water, and was gone.

Such events are, thankfully, rare, and in nine years of scuba diving this is the only instance in which a shark has shown me anything more than superficial interest. I wasn't fated to get back to the dive boat unscathed, however. Towards the end of the dive I was watching a group of orange-and-white-striped anemone fish, which grow to about twelve centimetres in length and live in amongst the stinging tentacles of large sea anemones. A mucus coating prevents them from being stung, but their presence lures other fish over to the anemone to be killed and eaten by it, while they get the scraps. Curiously, anemone fish also change sex, from male to female, as they mature.

As their protector and provider, these fish are extremely proactive in defending their anemones. Unlike sharks, they don't worry about picking fights with larger animals either, and will fearlessly attack divers who approach too close. Again, often this is no more than a bluff, the fish just warning you away by swimming at you with a stilted, jerky motion. On this occasion, however, one struck without ceremony, hitting me first on the chest and then, with unerring accuracy, biting me hard on the neck just above my wetsuit. Surfacing, I found that it had taken out a chunk of skin about a centimetre across and half as deep, leaving me sore and bloody – and the victim of shark attack jokes once I was back on board the boat.

David Leffman, Queensland, Australia

around Australia, has a generally painless though venomous sting that can cause respiratory arrest. The gastropod inside a **cone shell**, found in tropical and sub-tropical waters, has a venomous barb that can also paralyze breathing. In both

SALTWATER HAZARDS

First aid for maritime stings

+ Where possible, seek medical help urgently.
+ Remove any obvious foreign material from the wound.
+ Wash the wound with fresh water.
+ Apply pressure and immobilize the area of the sting.
+ If the sting results in respiratory difficulties, start mouth-to-mouth resuscitation.
+ Many stings can be very painful so use strong pain relief if available.
+ As a general rule immersing the sting site in hot water (45°C/113°F) for 30 to 90 minutes is a good pain reliever for most types of marine sting, as it inactivates the poison.
+ There is a specific antivenin for stonefish stings but it may not always be immediately available.
+ All cuts, bites or stings originating from the sea have a high risk of secondary infection so the use of prophylactic antibiotics (eg flucloxacillin, co-amoxiclav) should be considered.

cases, there is no specific antivenin and if stung you may need to be ventilated in hospital until the venom wears off (see box above).

Certain species of **trigger fish**, **puffer fish** and **porcupine fish** are extremely toxic if eaten and should be avoided.

Sea snakes

Sea snakes are found in tropical and sub-tropical waters (none are found in the Atlantic, the Mediterranean or the Red Sea), although being air breathers they are usually found in shallow waters and quite commonly on some tropical beaches. Their venom is highly toxic (far more so than terrestrial snakes: up to 20 times more potent than cobra venom) but they only attack when they are provoked. Don't be alarmed if a sea snake comes up close when you are diving – they have a reputation for being curious and it is not a sign of aggression. Avoid provocation and swim upwards away from the bottom, where they are less likely to follow. Since their teeth sit at the back of their small mouths, they're only capable of inflicting a bite on particular parts of the human body – ears, webs of fingers and toes, behind the ankle).

Although most sea snake bites are "dry" (do not result in envenomation), if you are unlucky enough to be bitten, seek medical help urgently. The first-aid treatment is the same as for a land snake bite (see pp.356–357).

Jellyfish

Jellyfish stings are caused by the stinging cells, or **nematocysts**, on the tentacles which discharge on contact (they're actually triggered by movement). Even dead on the beach, many jellyfish can inflict a sting provided that the tentacles are still moist. Despite their reputation, the majority of species of jellyfish are harmless to humans. The main dangerous ones are described below.

The sting from a **Portuguese man of war** (or "bluebottle"), which populates mainly sub-tropical waters but is also found in the Atlantic Gulf Stream, is very painful and can cause other symptoms such as numbness, weakness, muscle pains, nausea and breathing difficulties (occasionally fatal). Shore "invasions" tend to occur after storms.

Box jellyfish ("sea wasps" or "stingers") are generally acknowledged as the greatest maritime hazard. They're found in the warm waters of the Indian and Pacific oceans,

First aid for jellyfish stings

Remove yourself from the water to prevent further contact with the tentacles. Resist rubbing the sting, as you will cause more venom to be discharged and the tentacles may embed in your hands.

If you think that you have been stung by a box jellyfish, call for help and stay calm and still. If it's available, vinegar applied liberally as quickly as possible will inactivate the nematocysts and prevent the discharge of further venom. Cold compresses can be used to relieve pain, and, for serious stings, pressure applied to the area of the sting reduces the spread of venom. If a limb is the most affected site, immobilize it after deactivating the stinging cells with vinegar. An antivenin exists but needs to be given quickly. Many beaches in northern Australia will have local supplies. Cardiopulmonary resuscitation may be necessary.

For Portuguese man of war, Irukandji and other less dangerous jellyfish, soak the area of the sting in vinegar or, if unavailable, salt water (fresh water may cause further discharge of venom). It may be possible to carefully remove the tentacles using forceps, or a knife (even the edge of a credit card). Reapply more vinegar or seawater. Use antihistamines, painkillers and cold compresses to relieve the swelling and pain. If you think you may have been stung by an Irukandji, seek medical help as the elevated blood pressure will need to be monitored and will respond well to treatment.

but the majority of reported deaths have occurred off north Australian shores in summer months (September to April). Their sting is very painful and their venom is more potent than that of a cobra. Severe envenomations can cause rapid death (within 5 minutes).

The **Irukandji jellyfish** is found predominantly off the coast of northern Australia, although there have been sightings in other parts of the Pacific. It usually inhabits deeper waters and thus reef snorkellers and divers are more at risk. The initial sting is only slightly painful but within 30 minutes severe back, limb and abdominal pains occur with nausea, vomiting, sweating and agitation. Dangerously high blood pressure and a racing pulse can also occur.

Coral

Like most wounds sustained in the sea, **coral** cuts can easily become infected, often because small particles of coral are left in the wound. **Cleanse** any wounds thoroughly, and if infection is suspected, treat with **antibiotics** such as flucloxacillin, erythromycin or co-amoxiclav. Remember that you're far more likely to cause permanent damage to coral than it is to you.

Sandfly fever

(Dog disease, Phlebotomus fever, Pym's fever)

Sandfly fever occurs across dry areas of the Balkans, throughout the Mediterranean littoral, the Middle East, Central and Southeast Asia, and Central America. It is a viral illness spread by sand flies, which tend to bite at night and are also responsible for the transmission of leishmaniasis (see p.268).

There is no preventative vaccine so observe the usual precautions against insect bites (see p.259). Bearing in mind that sand flies don't fly above 3 metres, sleeping above the ground floor is safest.

SYMPTOMS

Sandfly fever is very similar to **Dengue fever**: after an incubation period of between 3 and 8 days, there is an abrupt onset of **fever**, **rigors**, **headache** (usually behind the eyes) and **muscle** and **joint pains**. Although symptoms can be quite intense and are usually followed by a period of weakness and lethargy, complete recovery is the norm.

DIAGNOSIS AND TREATMENT

Diagnosis is usually made on the basis of **symptom assessment** alone although blood testing may pick up evidence of the viral infection. **Bed rest**, basic **pain relief** and measures to **reduce the high fever** are all helpful, but there's no specific treatment to shorten the course of the illness.

Scabies

Exclusively a human infection, **scabies** is caused by skin infestation of a mite. Although skin-to-skin contact is the commonest form of transmission, the infestation can also spread via inanimate objects such as clothing and bed linen. The pregnant female mite penetrates the skin and burrows for a few millimetres. The mite can burrow anywhere in the body but tends to seek out natural recesses such as between the **fingers**, **armpits**, the **groin** or in **skin creases**. Eggs are deposited in the burrow and hatch into larvae after 2–3 days, when they move out of the burrow and onto the surface of the skin. After a week or 2 of maturation and mating they begin the cycle again.

SYMPTOMS

The burrows are difficult to see with the naked eye and may go unnoticed for several weeks. Chemicals secreted by the burrowed mite cause an allergic skin reaction. This manifests as a more generalized **red, maddeningly itchy rash**, which is typically worse at night and in heat. Consequent scratching further damages the skin, and can in turn cause secondary infection and more itching. It's not uncommon for the itch to continue for a few weeks even after treatment.

DIAGNOSIS AND TREATMENT

Scabies should be considered as the possible cause for any severely itchy rash. Sometimes it is possible to see the burrows with a magnifying glass (the webs between fingers are a favourite haunt).

There are several different types of treatment, most of which are available without prescription. The most common are **malathion** or **permethrin lotions**, the latter perhaps being the more effective of the 2, but it should not be used in pregnancy or breast-feeding. Neither preparation is recommended for children under 6 months. The lotion should be applied to the entire body (especially finger and toe webs and under nails) and left for 12 hours in the case of permethrin and 24 hours for malathion. Reapply the lotion after hand-washing and going to the toilet. A second treatment may be necessary after a week. Any close contacts should also be treated – it's common to treat a whole family even if only one member has symptoms. **Antihistamines** and **calamine lotion** can be used to treat the persisting itch.

Schistosomiasis

(Bilharzia)

The WHO estimates that currently more than 200 million people in 74 countries are infected with **schistosomiasis** – and the disease is spreading. Don't underestimate schisto-

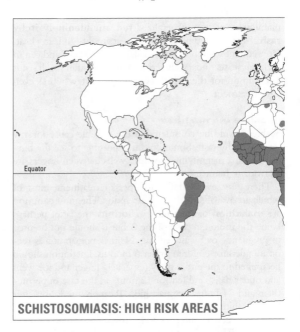

SCHISTOSOMIASIS: HIGH RISK AREAS

Equator

somiasis – it's the second most prevalent tropical disease after malaria and poses a **serious risk** to travellers, especially in Africa. London's Hospital for Tropical Diseases sees an average of 200 cases a year in returning travellers, an underestimate of the true figure as many more will be unaware that they have contracted the infection and therefore will not have sought help.

The infection is caused by 3 species of worms, or flukes, of the *Schistosoma* family: *S. haematobium*, which is geographically distributed throughout Africa, Arabia, the Near

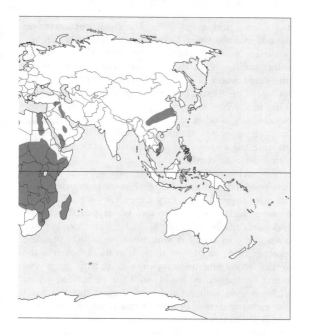

East, Madagascar and Mauritius and mainly affects the urinary tract; *S. mansoni*, which is mainly found in Africa and Mauritius but was transported by the slave trade to parts of South America, the Caribbean and Arabia and mainly affects the gut and the liver; and *S. japonicum*, which is found in China, Japan, the Philippines, Sulawesi and in a small focus on the eastern Thai border and which mainly affects the gut. (In Asia, this acute illness is known as **Katayama fever** after an area of Japan where it once proliferated.)

The worms reproduce in the bodies of small water snails,

and minute, fork-tailed larvae known as **cercariae** are released into the water. On contact with human skin, the cercariae penetrate and enter the blood stream. Schistosomiasis can also be contracted by **drinking untreated water** or eating food washed in it.

Once in the human body the cercariae mature into adult flukes in the liver. After mating, the worms migrate via the blood vessels to other parts of the body where the eggs are shed. The eggs pass through the walls of the bladder or intestine and are returned to the outside in faeces or urine – thus the cycle continues.

No vaccination is yet available although one is being developed. For the time being, prevention and control of the disease spread are mainly dependent on public health measures such as **education** and **water purification** in endemic countries. Generally speaking, schistosomiasis only poses a risk to travellers who bathe or indulge in water sports in rivers or lakes or those who do not observe the normal eating and drinking rules in endemic areas. No matter the temptation, avoid bathing in fresh water where schistosomiasis is found and bear in mind that the water you bathe or shower in may also be contaminated. River rafting down African rivers obviously presents the threat of infection, although fast-flowing water is generally considered safer than still. Swimming in the ocean or chlorinated swimming pools is considered safe. If you think you've been exposed, promptly remove your wet clothing and vigorously **rub your skin with a towel**, which although unreliable, may remove the cercariae before they have a chance to penetrate the skin.

SYMPTOMS

The majority of people infected with schistosomiasis will not experience any symptoms. Initial invasion of the cer-

SCHISTOSOMIASIS

340

cariae into the skin may cause an itchy rash, known as "**swimmer's itch**". This usually happens within the first 48 hours and may continue for up to a week. The first symptoms of the illness usually occur during the egg-laying phase, between 1 and 10 weeks after infection, and are non-specific. **Fever, swollen lymph glands, muscle aching, itching, diarrhoea, coughing and wheezing, weight loss** and enlargement of the **liver and spleen** are common. Later on, invasion of the eggs into the bladder and urinary tract causes bleeding and sometimes pain, which is why historically schistosomiasis has been called the disease of "menstruating males". If the gut is involved, abdominal pain and diarrhoea (sometimes bloody) are also common.

Most of the long-term damage to the body is caused by the reaction to retained eggs. Initial inflammation is replaced by permanent scarring. In particular, the ureters (the tubes carrying urine from the kidneys to the bladder) can become obstructed, leading to kidney damage and failure in the final, untreated stages of the disease. Damage to the heart, lungs, gut and central nervous system can result from the eggs escaping into the general circulation and becoming lodged in different organs.

SCHISTOSOMIASIS

DIAGNOSIS AND TREATMENT

The presence of blood in the urine in endemic areas points to the likely diagnosis, after which lab examination of the **urine, faeces** or **blood** usually detects the presence of eggs. Ultrasound of the liver and tissue **biopsies** can also be definitive.

Even in the advanced stages of the disease treatment can be very effective, but only if there is evidence of living worm activity. The damage from scarring caused by the worms may be less easy to rectify. Treatment should only be carried out under medical supervision. A short course of **praziquantel** is usually all that is necessary.

Scombroid poisoning

Scombroid poisoning occurs worldwide and is the commonest type of **seafood poisoning**. Certain fish with dark or red meat, such as mackerel, tuna, bonito, albacore and skipjack, contain large amounts of a chemical called histidine. As the fish spoils, bacteria change this chemical into **histamine**, which is unaffected by cooking and as such responsible for the symptoms of scombroid poisoning after the fish have been eaten. Contaminated fish are said to have a metallic, peppery flavour.

The risk of scombroid poisoning is higher in hot countries with poor refrigeration facilities where fish will spoil quickly. To be safe, stick to fish that is freshly caught.

Symptoms usually arise within 3 hours of eating the fish and mimic an allergic reaction. Common features are flushing, burning or tingling sensation in the mouth, abdominal pain, nausea and vomiting, headache, thirst, difficulty in swallowing, wheezing, hives and itching. There is no specific test for scombroid poisoning, and the **diagnosis** is usually made by connecting the symptoms with the ingestion of suspicious fish. **Antihistamine drugs** (eg chlorpheniramine and loratadine) will generally relieve symptoms, although severe reactions may require hospital admission. The symptoms are self-limiting and rarely last longer than 3 or 4 hours.

Snake venom, India. Photo © Jeffrey L. Rotman/Corbis

Sexually transmitted diseases

Sexually transmitted diseases, or **STDs**, can have significant effects not only on your immediate health, but also on your future health, on your fertility and on the health and fertility of your sexual partner. STDs are also a lot more common than many people think, especially in developing countries and countries where the sex industry plays a leading part in tourism – so-called "sex tourism". The highest global prevalences for syphilis, gonorrhoea and chlamydia occur in South and Southeast Asia and sub-Saharan Africa. The WHO estimates that there are approximately 333 million cases of STDs (AIDS excluded from this figure) worldwide each year, principally affecting the 15–30 age group.

The most obvious way to protect yourself from STDs while you're away is to abstain from sex with new partners. If this proves difficult then it follows that your risk of contracting something increases with the number of partners you sleep with – but remember it takes only one infected partner for you to wake up with an STD. Always keep in mind that your chosen partner may have been less choosy than yourself in previous sexual encounters. Using a **condom** will dramatically reduce the risks to many, although not all, STDs, so carry them no matter what your prior intentions. Use quality condoms brought from home – local brands may be less reliable.

Many people who contract an STD have no **symptoms**. However, when they occur, they can include:

✚ Unusual vaginal or penile discharge

✚ Pain, increased frequency or difficulty in passing urine

✚ Genital pain, itching or irritation

SEXUALLY TRANSMITTED DISEASES

+ Genital ulceration

+ Abnormal vaginal bleeding

+ Testicular pain

+ Lower abdominal pain

+ Pain during sex (dysparaenia)

If you suspect you have an STD, don't attempt to treat yourself – **see a doctor**. It's not uncommon for more than one STD to be passed on at the same time (particularly gonorrhoea in tandem with chlamydia) so there may be more than one cause for a single infective episode. A full medical work-up including swabs and blood results is therefore necessary. Any STD that causes genital ulceration increases the risk of transmission of **HIV**.

All STDs with the exceptions of herpes, HIV, genital warts and hepatitis B can be **treated** effectively with antibiotics. Always avoid sex until the treatment is complete. Untreated STDs are likely to be passed on and can cause longer-term effects, such as neurological impairment or cardiovascular problems in the case of syphilis, and infertility in the case of gonorrhoea. Syphilis, gonorrhoea, herpes and chlamydia can all affect the developing fetus or newborn baby.

Syphilis

Syphilis prevalence has increased globally over recent years, especially in inner cities where it is associated with sex workers and drug use. The WHO estimates that in 1995 there were 12 million new cases of syphilis. The incidence is particularly high in Africa and Southeast Asia.

SYMPTOMS, DIAGNOSIS AND TREATMENT

The presentation of syphilis has **3 stages**. Between 2 and 4 weeks after infection a hard but painless swelling, called a

chancre, develops on or just inside the genitals, or less commonly around the hands, the anus or the mouth. It usually heals after a few weeks. This is known as **primary syphilis**. Two or 3 months after the chancre has healed, **secondary syphilis** involves a fever, sore throat and joint pains. Lymph glands tend to enlarge and a non-itchy rash appears on the body and on the palms of the hands, the soles of the feet and around the mouth and nose. Wart-like lesions can appear around the perineum and ulceration occurs on the genitalia and in the mouth. This stage settles without treatment after several months, although don't be fooled into thinking that the infection has disappeared. Anyone with either primary or secondary syphilis is infectious. Late, or **tertiary syphilis**, appears years later as an inevitable result of the untreated initial infection and generally involves the skin and the bones. Swellings or ulcers can appear anywhere on the skin, and are also found in bones and some internal organs. The neurological and cardiovascular systems can be affected, causing potentially serious complications.

The **diagnosis** of syphilis is usually made by blood tests. All stages of the illness are amenable to **treatment** with penicillin (or erythromycin) following various regimens.

Gonorrhoea

Gonorrhoea is present throughout the world but, like syphilis, is particularly rife in South and Southeast Asia and sub-Saharan Africa. That said, it's far commoner than syphilis, with an estimate of 62 million new cases in 1995. Concomitant infection with chlamydia is common.

SYMPTOMS, DIAGNOSIS AND TREATMENT

A small percentage of men but up to 80% of women show

no symptoms and are therefore unaware of their need for treatment or of the likelihood that they can pass the disease on to others. **Men** usually notice a pustular discharge from the penis within 5 days of sexual contact with an infected partner. The tip of the penis may be sore, with pain on passing urine, and the frequency of passing urine is likely to increase. Sometimes the infection can cause scrotal pain. **Women** may notice vaginal itching or discomfort, a pustular vaginal discharge, increased urinary frequency and occasionally discomfort around the anus. The commonest complication in females is **pelvic inflammatory disease** (see p.141), which presents with lower abdominal or pelvic pain and fever. Scarring of the fallopian tubes can occur, leading to increased risks of ectopic pregnancy or infertility later on.

In both sexes, gonorrhoea can affect the rest of the body causing fever, malaise, muscle and joint pains, and a rash. Septicaemia, meningitis and hepatitis are rare complications.

The diagnosis of gonorrhoea is confirmed by lab analysis of the pustular discharge. There are several options in terms of treatment, but the penicillin group of antibiotics are now being superseded by the **quinolones** (eg ciprofloxacin) because of growing resistance.

Chlamydia

Chlamydia is globally very common and is believed to be the biggest single cause of infertility in the developed world. It also has a particularly high incidence in Africa, Southeast Asia and India. It is more common again than gonorrhoea with the WHO estimating that 89 million new cases occurred in 1995 alone.

As with gonorrhoea, many people who are infected with

chlamydia are asymptomatic and therefore unaware they risk transmitting it to others.

SYMPTOMS, DIAGNOSIS AND TREATMENT

If symptoms appear, they usually do so between 2 and 4 weeks after infection. Painless ulceration is apparent on the genitalia in about a quarter of those affected. A yellow-green vaginal discharge and pain on passing urine, with greater urinating frequency as well, are common in **women**. **Men**, too, can experience pain on passing urine as well as a whitish discharge from the penis and scrotal pain.

Lymphogranuloma venereum (LGV) is a particularly unpleasant variant of chlamydia infection, common in Africa, Southeast Asia and India. Initial painless ulceration is followed by pain and swelling of the lymph glands in the groin, which may develop into pus-filled abscesses. Although LGV is treatable using the same antibiotics as for other chlamydia infections, a chronic form of infection can develop causing extensive local scarring which may require surgery.

Like gonorrhoea, chlamydia can cause pelvic inflammatory disease in women (see p.141).

Diagnosis is usually made from swabbing the ulcers or discharge, although blood tests may also be useful. The standard **treatment** for genital chlamydial infections is a 1–3 week course of doxycycline or erythromycin, which should cure it. Sexual partners should also be treated whether or not they have symptoms.

Trichomoniasis

Trichomoniasis is the commonest STD worldwide with an estimated 170 million new cases in 1995. The microbe responsible can lie dormant for many years without causing symptoms. It has been implicated in facilitating the spread of HIV infection.

SYMPTOMS, DIAGNOSIS AND TREATMENT

It causes symptoms in approximately half of all infected **women**, mainly consisting of vaginal itching and burning, a frothy, greenish-yellow, often offensive-smelling discharge and burning pain on passing urine. In **men** the infection usually goes unnoticed but if symptoms do occur, they consist of penile itch or irritation and pain when having sex or passing urine.

Lab analysis and cultures of swabs usually confirm the diagnosis. Trichomoniasis usually responds well to metronidazole (400mg twice daily for a week) although resistance has been reported.

Chancroid

Worldwide prevalence of **chancroid** is less easy to estimate than other STDs because the disease is generally less understood. It is rare in developed countries but common elsewhere, particularly sub-Saharan Africa.

SYMPTOMS, DIAGNOSIS AND TREATMENT

Chancroid causes painful genital ulceration, usually within a week of infection. Localized painful swelling of the lymph glands also occurs. The symptoms are often less noticeable in women and mainly consist of pain during sex, on passing urine or defecation, rectal bleeding and vaginal discharge.

Diagnosis is usually made by culturing swabs taken from the ulcers or material drawn from the swollen lymph glands. Chancroid is best **treated** using erythromycin,

500mg 4 times a day for 7 days, although a single 500mg dose of ciprofloxacin can also be used.

Genital herpes

Genital herpes is extremely common and is usually caused by the **herpes simplex virus 2**. The **herpes simplex virus 1** causes cold sores but can affect the genitalia as well, especially after oral sex. Both are spread by direct skin-to-skin contact.

There is no cure for herpes and, once you're infected, you carry the virus for life. The symptoms of the disease are only apparent at initial infection and during flare-ups. You are infectious for a few days before blistering appears, during the blistering phase and for up to 2 weeks afterwards.

SYMPTOMS, DIAGNOSIS AND TREATMENT

Initial infection usually causes a flu-like illness accompanied by genital or perineal blistering which, after a few days, breaks down leaving a crop of painful ulcers. These usually last between 5 days and 3 weeks. Subsequent attacks occur infrequently, usually at times of stress, fatigue or during ill health. Recurring symptoms are usually milder (with less systemic upset) than the initial episode.

Since herpes is one of the few STDs that causes painful ulcers, it's usually easily diagnosed, although swabs and blood tests can also confirm the diagnosis. Although there is no cure for herpes, anti-viral drugs such as aciclovir can limit the length of each symptomatic episode.

Genital warts

Like herpes, genital warts are very common across the

world, and they appear to be on the increase. Infection is caused by the human papilloma virus (HPV).

The most apparent sign of HPV infection is the presence of genital warts, although the majority of infections are **asymptomatic**. Some strains of the virus lead to increased risk of cervical and other genital cancers later in life.

Diagnosis is usually fairly obvious from the appearance of the warts. Treatment should only be undertaken under medical supervision and usually involves freezing the warts or the topical application of **podophyllin** paint.

▷▷For detailed coverage of HIV infection, see p.247; for full coverage of Hep B, see p.243; see also Hep A, p.242, Hep C, p.246 and Hep D and E, p.247; Lice infestation, p.277; and Scabies, p.336.

Skin problems

During travel your **skin** will be subjected to all manner of attack from the tropical sun, marauding insects, chafing backpacks, itching infestations and weird infections. Your skin is your body's first line of defence to all of these potential hazards, but it is delicate and easily breached. Manifestations of more generalized illnesses – jaundice, an increased bleeding tendency and the like – are also commonly reflected in the skin, while skin infections are a frequent problem, resulting from an invasion of bacteria, fungi or a virus.

Belladonna can help treat small skin wounds that form large hot, red areas around them. It can also help subdue lymphangitis. If taking a low potency (under 30c) then repeat the dose up to 6 times in 1 day; seek medical advice if this doesn't show early signs of improvement. (If using 30c or 200c, take 3 tablets spread over 1 day.) **Silica** can be helpful in removing foreign bodies – deep splinters, sea urchin spines, shards of glass, etc. (Don't use this remedy if you have an IUD or any other artificial insertion in your body as it can promote expulsion.) Take up to 6 doses of a low potency over 1 day; for higher potencies, 1 or 2 doses in a day are enough. **Calendula** and **Hypericum** are also beneficial – see p.77.

BACTERIAL INFECTIONS

Bacterial infections often follow minor trauma to the skin – any **wound**, even the most trivial, can become infected, and there is particularly high risk of this in hot, tropical countries. Dirty, penetrating wounds, animal bites and coral cuts are highly susceptible to secondary infection by bacteria. Any cut must be cleaned using an appropriate antiseptic but if one is not available, boiled, preferably saline, water or alcohol are alternatives. If the wound is obviously dirty, a penetrating injury or an animal bite, it may be sensible to start a prophylactic course of **antibiotics**. Flucloxacillin, erythromycin or co-amoxiclav would all be appropriate choices. Always ensure that your **tetanus immunization** is up to date. If you are concerned that a wound has become infected (see box below), and especially if there are

Signs that a wound is infected

+ Local redness
+ Heat
+ Swelling
+ Pain
+ Pus (thick white/yellow)
+ Lymphangitis (see opposite)
+ Local lymph-gland swelling
+ Fever

signs of the infection spreading such as **lymphangitis**, **lymph-gland swelling** or **fever**, seek medical advice.

Impetigo (or "school sores") is a bacterial infection particularly common in children and highly contagious. Mainly affecting the face (around the mouth and nose), it erupts into well-defined sores which become honey-coloured, crusty scabs. The scabs can be unsightly but are usually painless. Scratching the sores can cause spread to other areas. Impetigo can be **treated** with antibiotics, either orally (usually flucloxacillin) or cream (fusidic acid). The sores usually take a week or 2 to clear up but beware of both recurrences and spread to other people. Cut your fingernails (long nails are a haven for bugs), bathe or shower daily and do not share towels, eating utensils and the like.

Folliculitis occurs when hair follicles become infected and can be a common problem in hot climates and for diabetics. It takes the form of a red, tender swelling (usually single, but occasionally in localized clusters). Often there is a central head of pus at the base of the hairstem. Folliculitis can occur anywhere on the body but is particularly common in the armpits and the groin. The infection is usually localized but can spread, and nearby lymph glands can be tender and swollen. It is often self-resolving but can be treated with magnesium sulphate paste (works by drawing out the pus) or a course of flucloxacillin.

An important sign to look out for in any bacterial infection involving a limb is **lymphangitis**, a single red trail up from the site of infection towards the trunk. This indicates the infection is spreading up the lymph vessels and needs antibiotic treatment. Failure to adequately treat a spreading infection can result in blood poisoning (septicaemia), which can be life-threatening.

FUNGAL INFECTIONS

Fungal skin infections are very common especially in hot, humid climates or if you wear tight-fitting, synthetic clothing. Generally, fungal infections can be distinguished from bacterial because they tend to itch rather than cause pain, they rarely cause swelling of the skin and they usually affect particular areas of the body. **Athlete's foot**, **ringworm**, **thrush** and **tinea infections** (eg "jock rot" or "jock itch") are all common examples of fungal infections.

Caused by a variety of different fungi, **athlete's foot** can lead to intense itching between the toes. The skin becomes scaley and cracked and often there are fluid-filled vesicles in between the toes. The symptoms are often made worse by wearing shoes that causes the feet to overheat (eg trainers/ sneakers).

Ringworm is not caused by a worm but by a variety of different, although related, moulds (including those that cause athlete's foot). The infection starts with an itchy, raised, slightly scaly red patch which, over the course of a few days, expands in size to form a red ring. Ringworm can occur anywhere on the body (often the arms and trunk), and spread elsewhere is not uncommon.

All of the above fungal infections respond well to treatment with anti-fungal creams such as **clotrimazole**. Continue applying the cream for 2 weeks after the rash has disappeared, as recurrences are common and usually mean the cream was not used for long enough.

VIRAL INFECTIONS

Viral infections, with one or two exceptions, tend to cause widespread rashes, whereas bacterial or fungal infections tend to be more localized. There is no specific treatment for most viral skin infections, although calamine, hydrocortisone and oral antihistamines can reduce itching.

SKIN PROBLEMS

▷▷See also Bedbugs p.163; Heat exposure (Prickly heat), p.239; Insects p.253; Myiasis, p.301; Scabies, p.336; Tungiasis p.384; Worms, p.396.

Sleeping sickness

▷▷See African trypanosomiasis, p.144.

Snakebites

You might take some comfort from the fact that less than 10% of the world's known 2500 **snake** species are venomous (simply meaning they inject poison via their fangs when they bite), with only about 5% dangerous to humans. Worldwide the estimated annual death rate from snakebites is 50,000, with Myanmar (Burma) and Brazil heading the league table for snake attacks. About 10,000 Americans are bitten by poisonous snakes each year, resulting in around 20 deaths. In the majority of European countries the average death rate from snakebite has been less than one a year for the past half century. Snakes are generally shy creatures who will, where possible, avoid human contact. Bites usually occur in self-defence when the snake is disturbed.

Eighty-five percent of bites are sustained below the knee and between 50% and 80% are "dry", meaning they do not result in **envenomation**. The effects of snake venom on the victim depend on the type of snake and degree of envenomation. It can attack the nervous system causing paralysis, inflict severe local tissue damage at the bite site, and interfere with the clotting system of the blood causing an increased bleeding tendency.

Venomous snakes can be divided broadly into **3 basic groups**: elapids, vipers and sea snakes.

The **elapid family** has roughly 250 members, among

SNAKEBITES

First aid for a snakebite

Remember that not all snakes who bite you are venomous. If your bite mark shows 2 rows of teeth as opposed to 2 small punctures, a non-venomous snake has bitten you. For venomous bites, all that first aid of a snakebite can hope to achieve is retard the effects of the venom, buying time for you to get to medical help for further treatment, and reduce the risk of other complications such as infection. Although the bite from a venomous snake is not usually the type of emergency in which seconds count, don't delay in seeking medical help.

There is precious little scientific evidence supporting the use of the more traditional remedies such as suction and cold compresses, and perhaps these methods belong more to folklore and the silver screen. They may perhaps help in situations where urgent medical help is unlikely to be available but generally they are more likely to increase the risk of local tissue damage and infection. The only certain method of improving the prognosis after snakebite is to immobilize the victim and the limb in particular. Like CPR, a cool head and a rapid, organized response are much more helpful than a chaotic panic.

Mark the time as the speed of the onset of symptoms is a useful indicator of the degree of envenomation. Call for help.

Carry the victim to a place of safety. If practical and safe, try to identify the snake concerned. If you manage to kill the snake don't immediately pick it up because the strike reflex may be preserved for a minute or two.

them cobras, mambas, kraits, coral snakes and all of the Australasian venomous snakes. Although snake venom is complex and has a range of effects on the body, as a general rule, elapid venom tends to affect the nervous system, causing muscle paralysis. Bites from some members of the

Place the victim in the recovery position to reduce the risk of vomit inhalation. Wipe the wound with a clean cloth to remove superficial venom.

Remove jewellery or tight-fitting clothing from around the bite site. If the bite is on a limb, immobilize it as far as is practicable. Tourniquets have lost favour because they can result in an increased local concentration on the venom, which may cause more severe local damage.

If you're tending someone who's been bitten, keep them warm and don't give them any food or drink (water can be given but only if dehydration is a risk).

You should get the victim as rapidly as possible to medical help, trying to avoid moving the affected limb and keeping it below the level of the heart. Antivenin is the only direct treatment for envenomation but it must be given under experienced medical supervision. After careful assessment, the doctor may decide that it doesn't need to be given (remember that a high percentage of bites are dry) and quite frequently bite victims are simply carefully monitored for signs of envenomation.

Sucking the venom out of a snakebite, cutting around a bite to prevent the spread of venom and applying ice to a bite are **not recommended** as first-aid measures.

While treatment against the initial envenomation is obviously your first concern, don't forget the possibility of tetanus (p.372) and skin infection (p.352) later on.

SNAKEBITES

elapid group do not cause any local swelling or reaction. Cobras in particular tend to "chew" in order to sufficiently envenomate the victim, so if bitten by a cobra, shake it off as quickly as possible.

The **viper family** includes the adder, pit viper, the several rattlesnake species, the bushmaster and the fer-de-lance. They have large venom glands, which give the head a triangular appearance, making it quite distinct from the body. Although the quality of its venom tends to be less potent than that of the elapids, it's produced in larger quantities. Viper venom tends to affect the clotting mechanisms of the blood, and causes local tissue swelling (within 2 hours generally).

Although **sea snakes** are the most venomous by some way, they are also timid and rarely bite. Their backward-pointing fangs and small mouths mean that they are poorly adapted to biting large creatures such as humans. The venom, however, can cause nerve and muscle paralysis.

A snakebite can be traumatic, both physically and psychologically. The physical sensation is often initially burning in nature before severe pain develops. The **symptoms** of envenomation depend on the type of snake but things to look out for are local swelling, increased bleeding tendency, shock caused by a drop in blood pressure, anaphylaxis, drooping of the eyelids (an early sign of nervous-system involvement) and muscle pains.

PREVENTION

The vast majority of snakes are not aggressive and will only bite when threatened. Avoidance measures are based more around common sense than hard science. When you're walking in snake country wear boots and long trousers, make a lot of noise and develop a habit of watching where you step or place your hands. If you see a snake, curb your curiosity and keep your distance.

Sore throats

Although the incidence of **sore throats** in travellers is no higher than in the general population, they are nevertheless very common and, as such, capable of taking a few days' enjoyment out of your trip. From the outset, it's important to recognize that the **majority** of sore throats are caused by **viruses** (estimates vary geographically from 60% to 90%) and so are not amenable to antibiotic therapy.

There is no certain way to differentiate between bacterial and viral sore throats by examination alone. Consequently, often what happens is that a course of antibiotics is unnecessarily prescribed. Most sore throats, regardless of their cause, will resolve spontaneously after about 5 days, and the best course of **treatment** is pain relief and increasing oral fluid intake.

It's difficult to be specific, but consider using antibiotics in the following circumstances:

+ Sore throats that go on longer than 5 days (although consider glandular fever).
+ If you are generally feeling very unwell (high temperature, loss of appetite, etc).
+ If you are having difficulty swallowing.
+ If your tonsils or the back of your throat look red, inflamed or pustular (you can sometimes see by examining your mouth with a torch).

Paracetamol or **ibuprofen** should be used for pain relief and to control high temperatures. Gargling with **salt water** or **soluble aspirin** may provide some additional relief. Increase your fluid intake. If antibiotics are used, a 7- to 10-day course of **penicillin V** or **erythromycin** is the standard recommendation. If symptoms persist for more than a week, and are not resolving after antibiotic use, consider **glandular fever** (a blood test can confirm the diagnosis). There is no specific treatment for glandular fever (a viral illness) other than symptomatic relief. It's notorious for requiring a long convalescence – sometimes as long as a year.

If at any time the pain or inflammation precludes swallowing fluids, seek medical help as intravenous antibiotics and fluids may be necessary. **Diphtheria** (see p.201) commonly starts off as a severe sore throat.

Spiders and scorpions

The ubiquitous **spider** is a common subject of phobias. **Scorpions** are rarer and more geographically localized, but nevertheless carry a fearsome reputation.

Spiders

The vast majority of spiders are harmless to humans, either because they are unable to inject enough venom to cause effect, or because their jaws are unable to penetrate human skin. As ever, however, there are exceptions to the rule, among which the following are most notable.

THE BLACK WIDOW

Various species of **black widow** are found throughout the USA, Central and South America, Africa, Australia, Asia and some parts of southern Europe. The female is bigger and more dangerous than the male. She is usually identified by a red "hourglass" shape on her abdomen. The **Australian redback**, or jockey spider, notorious for hiding under toilet seats and inflicting bites to sensitive parts, is a member of the black widow genus.

The black widow's bite is in most cases painless – **pain** commonly starts an hour later, closely followed by severe **muscle cramps**. A **burning sensation** or **numbness** on the soles of the **feet** are common; **other symptoms** include headaches, vomiting, dizziness, muscle spasms and intense sweating. Although unpleasant, the bite of a black widow is rarely fatal and only dangerous to the very old, the very young or those who develop a severe allergic reaction (anaphylaxis). The symptoms generally settle within a few days but in rare cases may persist for some weeks. Antivenin is available but rarely needed.

THE BROWN RECLUSE

Also known as the fiddleback or violin spider, the **brown recluse** is responsible for more bites than the black widow in the USA, where it's found in all states but predominantly in the south and midwest. Some 2–3cm in length and reddish–light brown in colour, often with a "violin" pattern on their back, these spiders are generally found in dark, dry recesses and attack only if disturbed – children are most likely to uncover them and as a result are their commonest victims.

The bite is often painless initially, but within a few hours a tender **blister** develops, characteristically with a "bull's-eye" appearance – a red centre with a bluish surround. **Other symptoms** of envenomation include fever, rigors, muscle weakness and a rash. The bite is rarely fatal, but sometimes scarring can occur at the bite site.

Because the initial bite is generally painless, it can be difficult to implicate the spider as the cause. For first-aid measures to **treat** the bite, see the box overleaf. Antibiotics may be useful later on if the bite site ulcerates.

SPIDERS AND SCORPIONS

THE AUSTRALIAN FUNNEL WEB

The **Australian funnel web** is generally considered to be the most dangerous type of spider in the world – but you only risk coming face-to-face with one in south and eastern coastal regions of Australia. The most feared of this species is the Sydney funnel web, found around Sydney under rocks and below houses in web-lined burrows, and in trees farther inland. It's also found in rainforested areas to the north.

The funnel web can be very aggressive and may inflict successive bites. Its venom is easily capable of causing human fatalities. There is usually intense pain initially at the bite site, after which the venom attacks the central nervous system, causing **tingling** and rapid-onset **breathing difficulties**. **Other symptoms** include a rapid, weak pulse, nausea, vomiting, abdominal pain, mental confusion and loss of consciousness.

First aid for spider bites

The vast majority of spider bites are not dangerous although pain can be intense with some species. Apply ice to the bite site and take antihistamines and pain relief. If the victim shows signs of allergy to the bite or shock, seek medical advice quickly. Generally medical advice should be sought for bites from black widow, redback and brown recluse spiders, although antivenin is rarely necessary.

First-aid measures for a funnel web bite are more complicated, parallel to those for a snakebite (see pp.356–357), and should focus on restricting the spread of the venom. Keep calm; if it's a limb that has been bitten immobilize it, and apply pressure and cold compresses. You must get the victim to proper medical facilities to receive antivenin.

Scorpions

Scorpions are found in a number of different habitats although most commonly in arid regions. They often shelter inside boots or shoes, so in areas where scorpions are found always check your footwear carefully before putting it on. Scorpions inflict a sting from their tail in self-defence, which in the vast majority of cases is painful rather than life-threatening. Despite this, it is crudely estimated that more than 5000 people die each year as a result of scorpion stings. Potentially lethal scorpions exist in the Indian subcontinent, North Africa, South Africa, the Middle East, North, Central (especially Mexico) and South America and the Caribbean.

The sting site is instantly very tender. Localized **swelling**, **redness**, **numbness** and **tingling** can follow. The pain may spread towards the trunk, being felt particularly acutely in the groin and armpits. With the spread, profuse **sweating**, generalized **swelling**, and **anxiety** can occur. The venom can also affect the central nervous system, causing **blurred vision**, **difficulty swallowing**, **loss of bowel control**, **shaking** and **breathing difficulties**. At its most severe, heart or respiratory failure are possible.

First aid for a scorpion sting follows similar lines to spider bites. Wash the sting site and apply cold compresses. If you suspect a bad sting, immobilize the victim and seek rapid medical help. Pain can be intense so use painkillers and antihistamines liberally. Antivenins to the dangerous species of scorpion are available but need to be given quickly.

St Louis virus

Named after the city where the first cases were recognized in 1933, **St Louis virus** outbreaks occur sporadically throughout the USA, especially in summer. Between 100 and 200 cases are reported annually, although this is likely to be an underestimate of the actual incidence as many cases go undetected. The virus, related to the one causing Japanese encephalitis, occurs naturally in birds and is spread to humans by mosquitoes.

SYMPTOMS

The majority of cases are **asymptomatic**. After a prolonged incubation period (usually 5–15 days), **flu-like symptoms** occur – high fever, headaches and lethargy. Severe cases can develop complications such as fitting, double vision and paralysis, and the disease can be fatal, especially among the elderly and the very young.

DIAGNOSIS AND TREATMENT

Examination of the **blood** or **cerebrospinal fluid** (via a lumbar puncture) confirms the diagnosis. There is no specific treatment for St Louis virus beyond **symptom relief** and supportive care. The large majority of cases fully recover within a few weeks.

Stomach pain

▷▷See under Abdominal pain, p.136.

Sun exposure

For many, the primary motivation for travelling abroad is to acquire a "healthy tan". But it is foolhardy to ignore the unrelenting statistics that link the effects of **sun exposure** with the increasing incidence of skin cancer. The evidence is there for all to see. In the UK, the incidence of newly diagnosed skin cancer appears to be doubling every 10 years, with more than 40,000 new cases in 1997. Skin cancer is perhaps the commonest form of cancer in the world, but, with the exception of melanoma, is rarely fatal.

Many find it difficult to take seriously the long-term risks when they're experiencing the short-term gains of both looking and feeling "well". It's also difficult to fully experience an activity-based holiday without potentially exposing yourself to large amounts of the sun. Although the real long-term danger of sun overexposure is skin cancer, it's worth remembering that it also leads to **premature ageing**.

You are most at risk of **sunburn** between 10am and 3pm, at altitude, in equatorial countries and anywhere there is a large amount of reflected light, for example in snow, on white sand and near water. Water provides absolutely no protection against UV light and reduces your awareness of burning – it's a good idea to wear a T-shirt (preferably dark) when swimming outside for extra protection. Pale-skinned, red haired, blue–green-eyed, freckled individuals are especially at risk to the adverse effects of sun exposure.

Drugs and the sun

Some medications can increase your susceptibility to sunburn. The most commonly prescribed drugs that can cause a photosensitivity reaction are:

+ Doxycycline (and other antibiotics of the tetracycline group)
+ Ciprofloxacin
+ The combined contraceptive pill (though rarely)
+ Thiazide diuretics (used to treat high blood pressure)
+ Sulphonylurea drugs (used to treat mature-onset diabetes)

SUN EXPOSURE

Prevention: UVA, UVB and SPF

Sunlight is **ultraviolet light** composed of different wavelengths, of which UVB and, to a lesser extent, UVA pose the greatest threat and are linked to the development of skin cancer. Apart from being the wavelength responsible for your tan, **UVB** – strongest in the summer and in hot climates – is also the one that causes burning. **UVA** is less seasonal but causes deep, long-term damage and is linked in particular to an increased risk of **malignant melanoma**, the most dangerous form of skin cancer.

To safeguard yourself, wear a **sunscreen** that protects against both UVA and UVB, is water-resistant, and has a sun protection factor (SPF) of at least 15. The **SPF number** is in fact a guide to the relative strength of the product in protecting the skin from **UVB light only** – many sunscreens indicate their relative capacity to block out **UVA light** by a **star system** (4 stars being the strongest). Theoretically, the SPF number increases your **burn time**, prolonging the time you can spend in the sun without burning by the factor quoted. There are, however, many variables involved, such as the time of day, time of year, amount of reflection, how cloudy it is and your skin type. The important point here is that SPF alone is not an accurate measure of the relative strength of your protection because it gives no indication of UVA protection. Thus a high SPF cream with poor UVA protection might actually be increasing your risks of damage by encouraging you to stay in the sun for longer.

SUN EXPOSURE

Remember that sunscreens will only protect the skin
to which they're applied – commonly neglected areas
are the back, the ears and the neck.

The most expensive sunscreen is not necessarily the most effective. Screens with a very high SPF are usually more expensive (and may well be used too sparingly as a result) and offer little more protection than a good-quality cream with an SPF of 15 and 4 stars of UVA protection. **Zinc oxide** or **titanium dioxide creams** are especially useful for more sun-sensitive areas such as the nose, lips, shoulders and ears.

Always use high-protection sunscreens on **children** (never less than an SPF of 15 with 4 stars); better yet, keep them out of direct sunlight in the middle of the day. It's estimated that as much as 80% of skin damage caused by the sun occurs before the age of 20.

Reapply your sunscreen at least every 2 hours for maximum protection and more often if you are swimming or sweating profusely.

Don't forget your **eyes**: ultraviolet rays can lead to cataracts in later life, and melanoma can also affect the back of the eye. Decent sunglasses will block the ultraviolet rays, protecting your eyes and eyelids – cheap ones may not. In high sunlight wear a brimmed cap or hat, which will reduce by half the amount of UV light reaching your eyes and the upper part of your face.

Use lip balm to prevent your **lips** from drying and to reduce the likelihood of cold sores, which are often triggered by excessive exposure to UV light.

If you're sun-sensitive or fair-skinned, a dose of **Sol** (200c) can help prevent sunstroke, sun headaches, skin reactions to the sun's rays, puffiness and heat exhaustion. Take 1 dose before you depart on your trip and a second halfway through. If you're going to be away for a while, try taking 1 dose a month for the first few months to help you acclimatize. In the event of an acute skin allergy to the sun, 1 dose a day for 3 days can help.

A false sense of security?

While it is still much better to use a sunscreen than to expose yourself unprotected to the sun, when all is said and done, it is sobering to remember that there is little scientific proof that its use w... protect against skin cancer in later life. What is fairly clear is that using sunscreens encourages people to stay out in the sun for longer than they normally would, exposing themselves to more UV light as a result. We do not yet know what the long-term effects of this will be.

Treatment

Sunburn is much easier to prevent than it is to **treat**. Skin feels hot, sore and stinging when it's already too late and the damage is done. It looks red and may be swollen. Blistering can occur, and after a few days the skin will peel and itch.

Taking a cool shower or sponge bath will provide initial relief but won't reverse the damage. It is important to increase your **fluid-intake** to counteract the drying effects of the burn. Commercially available "aftersun" lotions are also soothing (those containing aloe vera are particularly good); alternatively, vinegar is reputedly helpful. Anti-inflammatories and paracetamol can be used for **pain relief**. Don't burst blisters as this just exposes raw skin underneath and can lead to infection. Peeling cannot be prevented and is part of the natural healing process.

Deep burns tend to be relatively painless because of damage to the nerve endings. Characteristically, they are dry, firm to touch and may be brown, white or black in appearance. Damage of this nature requires urgent medical intervention.

▷▷See First aid of a burn, p.423.

Cold sores

Cold sores are something of a misnomer. Painful sores caused by a herpes virus, they have little to do with cold exposure. They are usually precipitated by ill health, stress or sometimes by prolonged exposure to sunlight. Cold sores look like a cluster of blisters and usually occur on the lips but can erupt inside the mouth or elsewhere on the face.

They will settle without treatment although if caught early (within 48 hours after the eruption) aciclovir cream applied to the lips 5 times daily for 5 days can shorten their duration. The bacteria causing impetigo (see p.353) can sometimes secondarily infect cold sores.

Teeth and mouth problems

The last thing you want when you're travelling is an emergency visit to the dentist, and in the developing world there are very real risks from poorly sterilized equipment. Have a **full dental check-up** before you leave if you're planning to be away for anything more than a couple of weeks.

Toothache most commonly occurs when decay of the tooth enamel causes exposure of a nerve. However, it also occurs as a result of mouth abscesses and gum infections and may originate from other problems in the head and neck.

Damage to tooth enamel requires a **filling**, and if this happens while you're away you'll have no option but to seek a dentist. Adequate pain relief in the interim is key and any of the painkillers described in the medications section can be used (see pp.51–53). Other helpful measures are dabbing the tooth with **clove oil** to deaden the pain or holding a heated pad or hotwater bottle (or, equally, a cold

pack) against the affected cheek. Wash your mouth out regularly with warm salt water and avoid direct contact between the tooth and very hot or cold food and drinks as well as sweets, soft drinks and spicy foods.

A **tooth abscess** is a result of infection entering into the gum or the roots of the teeth, usually through a damaged tooth or occasionally following sinusitis (see Coughs and colds, p.176). Apart from pain (sometimes intense and throbbing), the gum will swell and there may be an unpleasant taste in the mouth. A dental abscess requires a course of antibiotics, usually amoxycillin, co-amoxiclav or erythromycin although metronidazole can also be used. A dentist will not, as a rule, attempt any dental work until the infection is under control.

If your **tooth is knocked out**, gently rinse it and either keep it in your mouth (under the tongue or between your cheek and gum), in milk or in a wet cloth – don't allow the tooth to dry up. See a dentist as soon as possible, within 30 minutes if you can. For a **broken tooth**, apply a cold compress to the cheek over the area (not directly to the tooth itself) to reduce swelling, save the fragments in milk or a damp cloth and make your way to a dentist urgently.

Mouth ulcers and thrush

Acute **mouth ulceration** has several causes, although the commonest is usually a viral infection. **Herpes** in particular can cause a very painful oral ulceration. Some drugs (eg proguanil) cause mouth ulceration as a side effect. Apthous **ulcers** tend to affect the inside of the upper or lower lip and the tip of the tongue and usually occur when you are run down or unwell in some other way. Friction from dentures or a broken tooth can also result in ulceration. Left alone, mouth ulceration will almost always settle down

◁ Doctor signs, Erzincan, Turkey. Photo © Nik Wheeler/Corbis without treatment. In the meantime, avoid citrus fruits, spicy foods and vinegar. Clove oil, paracetamol or ibuprofen can help with pain relief, while there are also a range of antiseptic oral rinses available over the counter from pharmacies. Teething gel preparations bought over-the-counter are particularly effective against apthous ulceration on the lips or gums. Ulcers that don't spontaneously resolve after 2 weeks should be reviewed by a doctor or dentist.

Oral thrush is rare in healthy adults but common in infants, in the very old and those with diabetes or the immunosuppressed (eg AIDS sufferers). Regular use of steroid inhalers for asthma also predisposes to the condition. Your mouth will feel sore and, looking in the mirror, white plaque may be evident on your tongue and the roof of your mouth. Chlorhexidine-based oral rinses can be bought over-the-counter and are usually effective. Failing that, anti-fungal preparations like nystatin pastilles or suspension should resolve the problem.

Tetanus

(Lockjaw)

Spores of the bacteria that cause **tetanus** are found in soil, dust and manure anywhere in the world and enter the human body through an open wound. The wound needn't be great – a scratch or pinprick will do – but you're most at risk with a deep puncture wound. Any potentially contaminated wound must be cleaned thoroughly as standard procedure to prevent infection.

Most people will have been **vaccinated** against tetanus in childhood, conferring basic immunity, after which you should have a **booster** every 10 years. It is likely that any adult who has had 5 tetanus vaccinations will have lifelong immunity. Nevertheless, a repeat vaccination may be necessary if a wound is sustained if more than 10 years have passed since your last vaccination. For very dirty wounds, it may be necessary to temporarily boost your immunity with a vaccination of tetanus immunoglobulin.

Because of comprehensive immunization campaigns, tetanus infection is very rare in developed countries.

If it's been more than 10 years since your last tetanus vaccination, arrange a booster before you go travelling.

SYMPTOMS

First signs of tetanus follow an incubation period of between 5 and 20 days, and include **headache**, **fever**, **restlessness**, **irritability** and **spasms of the jaw muscles**. These spasms spread to the face (causing a characteristic grin-like expression), neck, limbs, and the muscles of the torso, which can result in breathing difficulties. Severe convulsions can occur. Rarer complications include bone fractures (as a result of the convulsions), heart-rhythm abnormalities, fluctuating blood pressure, blood clots on the lungs, pneumonia and coma. Tetanus is a dangerous, potentially fatal, but eminently avoidable illness.

DIAGNOSIS AND TREATMENT

Diagnosis of tetanus is usually made on the basis of the quite easily **recognizable symptoms** alone, although if need be the bacteria can usually be isolated from the wound. Treatment is complex and intensive involving **antibiotics**, **antitoxins** and **muscle relaxants**, and should always be undertaken in hospital.

TETANUS

Thrush

(Candidiasis, Moniliasis)

Vaginal thrush is a common condition caused by a yeast fungus, candida. The fungus itself is present in the vagina of about 20% of **women** without causing symptoms because other bacteria and the acidity of the vagina prevent their overgrowth. Thrush usually breaks out when this balance is somehow disturbed. Vaginal thrush is most common in fertile women, up to 75% of whom suffer from at least 1 episode before menopause. Although thrush is not usually caught from another person, it can be passed on by sexual contact. **Men** who carry it rarely show signs of the infection.

Conditions that increase the likelihood of symptomatic thrush include:

+ Pregnancy
+ Antibiotic use
+ Combined oral contraceptive pill
+ Tight-fitting, nylon underwear
+ Hot climate
+ Diabetes
+ Minor trauma, for instance, after scratching
+ Sexual intercourse with a carrier

SYMPTOMS

Common symptoms when they occur include vaginal **itch** or **soreness**, **discomfort during sex**, **pain on passing urine** and a white or yellow, inoffensive **discharge**. It's worth remembering that these symptoms can also be caused by some of the less innocuous sexually transmitted diseases (see pp.344–351), so if you are potentially at risk from these, see a doctor.

Although irritating and uncomfortable, thrush rarely causes complications in people who are otherwise fit and well. It can cause problems, however, in anyone who has a compromised immune system.

TREATMENT

You can successfully treat vaginal thrush with an **antifungal preparation**, in the form of either vaginal pessaries or cream bought over-the-counter in most countries. Clotrimazole preparations are generally effective, although there are a number of alternatives (including an oral course of antifungal treatment available only on prescription, fluconazole).

Avoid sexual intercourse during treatment, as a common cause of recurring thrush is reinfection from your partner, who may unknowingly carry the fungus. Note that condoms are often weakened by using an antifungal preparation.

Alternatively, insert plain **yoghurt** in the vagina (try putting it on a tampon if that's easiest), which will soothe any irritation. To treat thrush homeopathically, try **Sulphur** (1 30c tablet a day for 3–4 days) if your symptoms are mainly itching, worse in the heat or from sweating, and the whole area is red, hot and dry. Other things that can help include **tea tree oil** (1–3 drops in a shallow, warm bath) and **salt baths** or **calendula oil (or tea) baths**. **Dietary changes**, even if only for a few days, can also bring relief: avoid yeast-containing or yeast-encouraging foods, like sugar (this means biscuits, cakes, etc), bread (eat matzos or crackers instead), marmite or vegemite, quorn, mushrooms, wine and beer (spirits aren't so bad), fruits with "bloom" on their skins such as peaches, plums and grapes, and blue cheese. If you've a tendency to get thrush, see a homeopath before you go away about taking some potenized **Candida albicans** with you.

THRUSH

Protecting yourself against thrush

+ Wear loose-fitting, cotton underwear, particularly in hot countries, and change frequently if you're perspiring lots.
+ Avoid sitting for long periods in a wet swimsuit.
+ Avoid vaginal deodorants, bath salts and other possible irritants that may alter the natural balance of bacteria in the vagina.
+ Always wipe front to back after using the toilet.

Although **men** are often the unknowing carriers of thrush, occasionally it can cause the end of the penis to become red, swollen or blotchy (called balanitis). Clotrimazole cream usually clears up the problem within 1 or 2 weeks.

Oral infection from thrush is much less common and usually occurs in the old, the very young or in those with compromised immune function. For more on this see p.372.

Tick-borne encephalitis

Tick-borne encephalitis is a viral illness that occurs mainly in forested areas of northern, eastern and central Europe. A related illness known as Russian spring-summer encephalitis (RSSE) is found in Siberia, northeast China and Korea. The disease tends to be seasonal, occurring mainly between May and September (when the ticks are most active) and is caused by a virus, which is transmitted by a tick bite, closely related to dengue, yellow fever and St Louis encephalitis. Walking or working in wooded areas puts you most at risk, but the chance of contracting the illness from a single tick bite is very low. The illness may also be transmitted to humans in the unpasteurized milk of cows, goats or sheep.

An effective preventative **vaccination** is available (see p.21), although it often has to be specially ordered as required and can be expensive. Always observe the standard measures to prevent tick bites when walking through endemic areas (see p.260), and avoid unpasteurized cow, goat or sheep dairy products.

SYMPTOMS

A very small number of people who become infected with the virus actually develop symptoms (estimated at around 1 in 250). After an incubation period of between 1 and 2 weeks, symptoms classically occur in 2 phases: the first phase presents as a non-specific **flu-like illness** (headache, fever, generalized aches and pains) while the second phase, following between 1 and 3 days later, affects the central nervous system causing **encephalitis** (dizziness, tremour, fits, paralysis, psychiatric disturbance) and **meningitis** (see p.295). Although the disease is very rarely fatal, it can cause permanent damage to the nervous system.

DIAGNOSIS AND TREATMENT

Antibodies to the virus can be detected by lab analysis of the **blood**. There is no treatment other than **supportive therapy** and nursing care, although in most cases the illness is self-limiting and resolves without long-term complications. In Austria, where cases are more common, rapid administration of immunoglobulin can treat the illness (derived from blood, the locally produced immunoglobulin has high levels of the antibodies because of the high likelihood of previous exposure).

Toxocariasis

Toxocariasis is a ubiquitous worm infection of cats and dogs most commonly affecting puppies and pregnant bitches. The worm eggs are found in cat and dog faeces and usually find their way into humans via poorly washed hands or unrinsed vegetables.

The actual incidence of toxocariasis in humans is uncertain but is believed to be higher in parts of the developing world where hygiene standards are lower.

Children under 5 are most at risk for the simple reason that they are more likely to encounter the infection through playing outside and have lower standards of personal hygiene.

The infection is not transmitted from person to person. Always try to wash your hands after contact with sand, soil, or after stroking dogs and cats (and encourage your children to do the same).

SYMPTOMS

Once the eggs have been ingested, the larvae are released in the gut, penetrate through the gut wall and into the circulation. Via the circulation, the larvae are able to migrate to other organs in the body. This migration might last for up to 2 years, and the symptoms caused by the illness are dependent on where the larvae end up. Most commonly affected sites are the liver and the lungs, causing **fever, muscle pains, liver enlargement, cough** and **wheeze**. The worm can also find its way to the eye where it causes local damage, which can lead to blindness or a squint.

DIAGNOSIS AND TREATMENT

The larvae can sometimes be identified in **organ biopsies**, and **blood tests** may pick up antibodies to the worms. The illness is usually mild and **self-limiting**. Anti-worm treatments such as thiabendazole and albendazole can be tried but results are often disappointing. Laser surgery can be used to treat subsequent eye damage.

Trachoma

The WHO has mounted a global campaign to reduce the incidence and the risk of long-term eye damage caused by **trachoma**, the commonest cause of blindness worldwide, affecting up to 400 million people. It is particularly prevalent in the tropics, Central America, the Middle East and some Mediterranean countries. The disease is linked to poor personal hygiene, overcrowding and limited access to water and proper sanitation. The infection is transmitted to the eyes by contaminated hands or towels, and mainly affects children who are less diligent about hand-washing. Flies also play a significant part in the infective chain. There is no vaccination available, so vigilance in personal hygiene is important in areas where trachoma occurs.

SYMPTOMS

After an incubation period of about a week, early symptoms include irritation and **inflammation of the eye** with excessive tear production and discharge. Tiny grey lumps form on the inside of the upper eyelids about a month after the initial infection. Later on scarring of the **cornea** (the clear part of the eye, in front of the pupil) may occur, causing visual disturbance and even blindness.

DIAGNOSIS AND TREATMENT

Lab examination of cells scraped from the eye reveals evidence of the infection.

Used early, **antibiotic ointment** (chlortetracycline) applied for 2–3 months is a very effective treatment, as is oral **tetracycline**. Scarring to the eyelids can cause serious deformity and require surgery.

Tropical sprue

Tropical sprue occurs throughout most of Asia, some Caribbean islands, certain areas of Africa and India, Puerto Rico and parts of South America, although outbreaks have also been reported in northern Australia, Fiji, the Middle East and Central America. It causes interference in the absorption of some chemicals and nutrients from the small intestine (known as "malabsorption"). The specific cause is uncertain but likely to be infective (probably bacterial) because of its tendency to occur in epidemics in endemic areas and because it frequently responds to antibiotic treatment. It may be related to infection with certain types of **e-coli** bacteria.

SYMPTOMS

The symptoms may occur months or even years after returning from the tropics and vary in intensity but usually include diarrhoea (typically the stool floats and is difficult to flush away), abdominal bloating, loss of appetite and weight loss.

Diagnosis is often suspected after first excluding other possible causes of the diarrhoea (such as giardia), after which signs of malabsorption can be detected by lab tests. Abnormalities of the gut lining can be found in biopsies (taken via endoscopy – a fibro-optic "telescope" which allows doctors to examine the gastro-intestinal tract).

Vitamin supplements can improve the malabsorption

but a course of **antibiotics** (usually a tetracycline, for up to 6 months) may also be necessary for complete recovery. The long-term outcome is generally very good.

Tuberculosis

Despite a major decline in the incidence of **tuberculosis** (**TB**) in developed countries in the twentieth century, between 8 and 10 million new cases occur worldwide each year, with up to 3 million deaths from the disease annually. The WHO estimates that up to a third of the world's population is infected with TB.

Despite the generally declining trend over the past hundred years, the current incidence of TB is actually rising worldwide due mainly to the prevalence of HIV infection, which greatly increases the risk of catching TB. The bulk of TB infections occur in the tropics and subtropics, with the overall risk in the developing world between 20 and 50 times that of the industrialized countries.

TB can affect any part of the body but the bacteria responsible for causing the disease are spread by droplets coughed up by victims of active pulmonary (lung) TB. The germ is not very virulent and prolonged exposure is usually necessary for it to be transmitted. That said, exposure to the disease doesn't automatically mean you'll develop the disease – it's estimated only up to 15% of infected people will develop signs of the infection, 5% within 2 years, 5% within 5 years and the rest at some time in the remainder of their lifetime.

The disease occurs more commonly in overcrowded conditions, in the very young, the elderly, and those who have compromised immunity such as the malnourished and HIV sufferers.

From the initial infection of the lungs, the TB bacteria migrate to local lymph nodes, after which spread to the rest of the body may occur.

A vaccination against the disease is available (BCG) and a skin sensitivity test (the "Heaf" test) can identify those with natural immunity and those requiring vaccination (see p.21). In the UK, the routine testing for TB exposure in school-aged children and consequent immunization of those at risk is being phased out gradually, with high-prevalence areas being targeted. TB vaccination is not routinely given in the US, and Australia targets specific risk areas only.

SYMPTOMS

TB can remain latent, with no apparent symptoms, for many years. **Pulmonary TB** causes **shortness of breath** and a **cough** which often produces **blood-stained sputum. Weight loss, poor appetite, fevers** and **night sweats** also occur.

TB that has spread beyond the lungs, termed **miliary TB**, can cause a variety of problems depending on the exact location of the disease. More often than not, the symptoms are non-specific, with intermittent fever, weight loss, lethargy and general malaise. Common sites of spread include the brain (causing meningitis – see p.295), the bones and joints, the kidneys, bladder and genital tract, the heart and the intestines and abdominal organs.

DIAGNOSIS AND TREATMENT

The diagnosis of pulmonary TB can be made by microscopic examination of the **sputum**. TB elsewhere can usually be diagnosed by culture of **tissue biopsies**. A **chest x-ray** often shows distinctive signs of infection as well.

Although a serious illness, particularly in anyone with low immunity, TB is treatable and survival rates are good with timely therapy. Treatment should only be undertaken once a firm diagnosis is made, however, and always under medical supervision. There are a number of potent **antibiotics** and varying regimes possible, although bacterial resistance is a growing problem, particularly in China and eastern Europe.

Tularaemia

Tularaemia in animals can be found anywhere in the world but is particularly common in the southeastern and midwestern states of the USA (particularly Arkansas, Illinois, Missouri, Oklahoma, Tennessee, Texas, Utah and Virginia). The name is derived from Tulare County in California, where there was a significant outbreak in 1911.

The bacteria causing tularaemia are primarily found in wild animals (especially rabbits, hares, beavers and lemmings) and are usually transmitted to humans via contact with contaminated faeces or fur, or intermediate insect hosts. It may also be acquired by handling infected animal carcasses – hunters and children are most at risk. Incidence of the disease, although rare, is more common in summer.

SYMPTOMS

The incubation period is between 1 and 14 days and the symptoms depend on whether the bacteria entered the body through a wound or bite, or were inhaled or ingested. If the bacteria gain access to the body **via damaged skin** or a tick or insect bite (up to 80% of cases), an **ulcer** usually forms and local lymph glands enlarge after a few days. This phase is usually accompanied by a high fever and can progress into more widespread symptoms. **Inhalation** of the bacteria can cause pneumonia and **ingesting** them (for example by eating undercooked, contaminated meat) may cause tonsillitis, pharyngitis, vomiting, diarrhoea, abdominal pain and gastrointestinal bleeding. A less common mode of entry into the body is through the conjunctiva of the eye (by direct contact with infected blood). Common features of the illness regardless of mode of infection include **fever, tender swollen glands** (including liver and spleen), **generalized aches and pains** and a **rash**.

Untreated, the disease may develop serious complications such as septicaemia, meningitis, peritonitis, osteomyelitis (infection of the bones) and heart complications. With adequate antibiotic treatment, however, fatalities are very low (1% of cases).

DIAGNOSIS AND TREATMENT

A specialized **blood test** is the best method of detecting the infection – standard means of blood testing, ulcer swabbing and sputum or blood cultures rarely identify the organism.

Severe infections are best treated with intravenous streptomycin, requiring hospital admission. Less severe infections may be treated under close medical supervision with oral tetracycline.

Tungiasis

(Jiggers, Chiggers, Chigoes)

Tungiasis occurs throughout Central and South America, Africa and the west coast of India. The disease is caused by a pregnant female flea (a chigger), which penetrates the skin (commonly the side or overhang of your toenail) to lay her eggs. Tungiasis tends to be seasonal, when vegetation is at its thickest and the fleas are most abundant and active.

Avoid walking barefoot in endemic areas, and don't sit or

lie directly on the ground. Use insect repellents liberally where the risk is high. Bathing your feet in hot water after walking in chigger-infested country usually removes the fleas before they have the chance to become firmly attached, although isn't as reliable as wearing sturdy boots.

SYMPTOMS

The flea penetrates the skin not by burrowing but by injecting enzymes that cause it to break down. This digestive fluid causes **local pain and swelling** and looks like a **blister**. Intense itching can continue for several days after the flea has detached itself. Secondary infection can ensue and, left untreated, gangrene and septicaemia are dangers.

DIAGNOSIS AND TREATMENT

The condition is usually diagnosed by the characteristic nature and location of the **lesions** and confirmed when the skin is surgically removed revealing the flea and her eggs. This **minor surgical treatment** is the only way to remove the flea, and although many of the locals may have the skill to perform such surgery, equipment and conditions might not be sterile, so seek a doctor and a proper sterile environment. Apply sterile dressings to the wound afterwards and treat any signs of secondary infection aggressively with antibiotics (flucloxacillin, co-amoxiclav or erythromycin).

Typhoid

Typhoid is uncommon in developed nations where the standards of hygiene and sewerage disposal are adequate. The majority of cases in these countries are in returning travellers from the developing world where standards are less stringent. Worldwide it is estimated there may be as

many as 17 million cases of typhoid fever each year, accounting for 600,000 deaths.

Typhoid is a bacterial illness spread by ingesting contaminated food or water. The bacteria live only in humans and are passed in the faeces of an affected person or a carrier.

The likelihood of contracting typhoid from contaminated water tends to be "dose related" – the more bacteria you ingest the more likely you are of contracting the infection and the worse the symptoms will be. The risk of serious illness is increased in people with poor immunity or who are taking medications to suppress gastric acid secretion (eg for the treatment of a stomach ulcer), which acts as the body's first line of defence.

Typhoid **vaccines** are available and are recommended for anyone planning to travel to areas with poor standards of sanitation (see p.22). However, it's not totally effective (probably around 80% depending on conditions of exposure; less so in circumstances where contamination is heavy), so be vigilant with personal hygiene and when eating and drinking in high-risk areas.

▷▷See Food and drink, pp.40–43.

SYMPTOMS

The average incubation period is 2 weeks but varies depending on dose of bacteria ingested. The symptoms may be relatively mild initially, again dependent on the degree of exposure, but untreated, steady deterioration over a 2-week period occurs during which you can become extremely ill. Common symptoms are **high fever, headache, stomach pains, weakness, lethargy, loss of appetite, constipation** (although diarrhoea can occur), **coughing** and **deafness**. The fever tends to increase day by day for the first week, often worsening in the evening. Sometimes "rose-pink" **spots** develop on the trunk in the second week.

◁ Tokyo park massage, Mftaka Park, Tokyo. Photo © Kevin R.Morris/Corbis

Diarrhoea more commonly occurs in week 2 of the illness and may lead to significant dehydration. In severe cases the central nervous system can be affected, causing a meningitis-type illness and coma.

Complications of typhoid fever can affect the body in many different ways including perforation of the gut, increased bleeding tendency, pneumonia, kidney failure, DVT, meningitis, joint pains and infection of the bones. Mortality rate is approximately 10% for untreated cases, reduced to 1% with appropriate treatment. Up to 3% of cases become carriers.

DIAGNOSIS AND TREATMENT

Blood tests can show the presence of the bacteria in the first week; in the second week, the bacteria can usually be microscopically identified in a stool sample.

Throughout treatment, it's vital to ensure you drink plenty of **fluids**. Symptoms usually abate within 2 to 3 days of starting the treatment with **antibiotics** – usually amoxycillin, trimethoprim or ciprofloxacin. During treatment, be particularly diligent about hand-washing after going to the toilet and avoid preparing food for others.

Even when your symptoms disappear you may still be a **carrier** of the disease and risk infecting others. You should have at least one (preferably more) follow-up stool sample tested to detect whether or not the bacteria is still present in your gut.

Typhus

Typhus is the collective name for several different diseases. Common features are the causative organisms (*rickettsiae* bacteria), the mode of transmission to humans (via a tick, louse or flea bite) and the symptoms of a high fever followed by a rash. It occurs throughout the world in some or other form. There are **4 main types** of typhus infection: **epidemic louse-borne typhus, endemic flea-borne typhus, Rocky Mountain spotted fever** (see p.323) and **scrub typhus.** No vaccination is currently available against any form of typhus, and although risk to the traveller is small, it's essential that you take steps to avoid being bitten by the insect vectors in endemic areas.

▷▷ See Bite prevention, p.259.

DIAGNOSIS AND TREATMENT

Diagnosis of typhus can be confirmed by blood tests. Tetracycline (500mg 4 times a day for 7 days) or doxycycline (a single dose of 200mg may be enough or the standard course is 100mg twice daily for 7 days) will **treat** all types of the illness but cases of resistance have been reported (in Thailand), in which case ciprofloxacin (500mg for 7 days) is an alternative.

Epidemic louse-borne typhus

Epidemic louse-borne typhus occurs in the cool, mountainous areas of Africa, Central and South America, Asia, eastern Europe and Mexico. It can occur in explosive epidemics, particularly at times of famine or war when large numbers of people live in close proximity and in unsanitary conditions (for example in refugee camps). Over the past 50 years, the majority of outbreaks have occurred in Africa with Burundi, Ethiopia and Rwanda particularly affected. The microbe is passed to humans by **body lice**, which live in clothing and feed on the blood. The faeces of the infectious body lice enter the body via flea bite sites, abrasions or through the eyes. It's also possible to inhale the contaminated faeces. The disease does not spread directly from person to person.

High fever, **headache**, **dry cough**, **rigors**, **muscle pains**, **nausea** and **vomiting** usually occur within 2 weeks of being bitten, after which a **rash** appears on the torso, spreading to the rest of the body. The fever remains constant at around 40°C for a few days, and the headache can be severe. If the disease progresses, it can affect the central nervous system, causing permanent damage. There are many complications that can arise from epidemic typhus and without treatment, it can be fatal, although it may also resolve spontaneously. Recurrences many years after the original illness are possible.

Endemic flea-borne typhus

Endemic flea-borne typhus (also known as **murine typhus**) occurs worldwide but prevails around ports and coastal areas. Although rare in developed countries, intermittent outbreaks do occur. The disease-causing microbe is carried by rats and transmitted to humans by the bite of a **flea**. The faeces of the infectious flea usually contaminates the bite site, although it may also be contracted by inhaling the flea's dried faeces. In the USA (particularly central and south-central parts of Texas), the disease can be carried by fleas on dogs, cats and opossums.

SYMPTOMS
Typically, the onset is gradual over a period of 2 weeks following contact. The symptoms are similar to epidemic typhus only much milder, consisting of **high fever** (sometimes lasting up to 2 weeks), **headache**, **muscle pains** and a **rash**. Full recovery usually occurs, even without treatment, and fatalities are very rare indeed.

Scrub typhus

Scrub typhus occurs sporadically in parts of Southeast Asia, Australia, India and western Pacific Rim. It was responsible for the deaths of thousands of troops fighting in the Pacific in World War II. The illness is transmitted to humans by the bite of infectious mites – today you're most at risk hiking in cleared areas of jungle or forest.

SYMPTOMS

Close examination of the skin sometimes reveals tiny darkened scabs where the mites have bitten. Initial symptoms usually occur within 5 to 10 days of being bitten and manifest as a **sudden fever** and **severe headache** accompanied by **muscle pains**, a **dry cough** and **swollen lymph nodes**. A **rash** develops over the torso and limbs and the central nervous system can be affected, sometimes causing permanent damage. The illness can recur despite treatment with antibiotics.

Undulant fever

▷▷See Brucellosis, p.167.

Urinary tract infections

(Cystitis)

Urinary tract infections (**cystitis**) are far more common in women than men. Generally, they are easy to treat but if ignored, they can develop into more serious kidney infections. Episodes are often related to sexual activity.

   Symptoms include increased frequency in passing urine, often with sudden urgency; also pain on urinating, difficulty initiating it or a weak stream, foul-smelling or blood-stained urine. Fever, lower abdominal pain and pains in the small of the back, suggesting the infection has spread to the kidneys, can also occur.

Doctors often treat UTIs without laboratory testing, making the **diagnosis** solely from the reported symptoms, but a culture of a urine sample can confirm the diagnosis if necessary. To **treat** cystitis, first increase your fluid intake, in effect flushing the infection out. You'll also need a course of antibiotics: if you are not pregnant, trimethoprim is a good first choice, but amoxycillin or co-amoxiclav can also be used (and should be first choice if back pain suggests the kidneys are affected). Symptoms should settle fairly quickly with treatment but if they don't or if any deterioration is noted, seek medical advice, bearing in mind that the symptoms of some **sexually transmitted diseases** (see p.344) share similarities with those of cystitis, as does **schistosomiasis** (see p.337).

Preparations that can be bought over the counter for the treatment of cystitis do not contain antibiotics and opinion seems to be divided as to their relative merits.

Cantharis (30c every 2 hours for up to 6 doses) can be used to treat cystitis in cases where the urine is burning and passed in small quantities. You'll feel a constant urge to go and may have strong sexual urges, feeling that vigorous sex will alleviate the pain (although in fact it will only aggravate it). In addition to drinking plenty of **water** during an attack, brew your own **parsley tea** by pouring boiling water on a teaspoon of fresh or dried parsley and steeping for 5 minutes, or try chewing fresh parsley. Drinking **cranberry** or **blueberry juice** can also help – they work by preventing the adhesion of bacteria to the bladder walls.

Venezuelan equine encephalitis

Venezuelan equine encephalitis is a mosquito-borne viral disease carried by horses, rodents and humans and occurring in epidemics during the rainy seasons in Trinidad, Central America (Panama in particular) and northern South America. Outbreaks have also been reported in Florida and other parts of the USA. A **vaccination** has been developed but is not generally available, being reserved instead for lab staff working with the virus. Generally speaking, the infection is very rare and only likely to be a worry to travellers in the above areas during an epidemic and in close proximity to horses. This being the case, exercise the normal measures for insect bite avoidance.

▷▷See Bite prevention, p.259.

SYMPTOMS

After an incubation period of less than a week, the disease usually manifests as a **flu-like illness** with fever, rigors, severe headache, nausea, vomiting, diarrhoea and muscle pains. The fever normally lasts no longer than 4 days but can be followed by a period of weakness and depression lasting several weeks. A small minority of cases (less than 15% and usually under-15 year olds) develop encephalitis, which can be fatal.

DIAGNOSIS AND TREATMENT

Antibodies against the virus can be identified in the **blood**, confirming the diagnosis. There is no specific treatment other than **symptomatic relief** and, in more severe cases, intensive supportive care.

Viral haemorrhagic fever

Viral haemorrhagic fever is the collective name for a group of illnesses caused by different viruses but which have the common features of high fever and disturbance of the normal blood-clotting mechanisms. This can result in excessive, potentially life-threatening bleeding.

Signs to look out for are:

+ A dark, purplish ("purpuric") rash which doesn't blanch under pressure (see p.297)
+ Nose bleeds or bleeding gums
+ Sub-conjunctival haemorrhage (see p.212)
+ Bleeding from the bowel, either black tarry stools or bright red blood in the motions

Of the many kinds of haemorrhagic fever, only yellow fever has a preventative **vaccination**, and none is directly treatable other than symptom relief and supportive care for

Notable viral haemorrhagic fevers

+ Dengue haemorrhagic fever	p.197
+ Chikungunya fever	p.169
+ Crimean-Congo haemorrhagic fever	p.189
+ Ebola virus	p.208
+ Hantavirus infections	p.326
+ Lassa fever	p.264
+ Marburg virus	p.293
+ Rift Valley fever	p.322
+ Yellow fever	p.405

the body's normal functions. If there are signs of an increased tendency to bleed following a high fever, seek medical help urgently.

Viral haemorrhagic fevers rarely cause major epidemics (with the exception of yellow fever) but sporadic local outbreaks occur with devastating effect.

Weil's disease

▷▷See Leptospirosis, p.275.

West Nile fever

Outbreaks of **West Nile fever** occur in Egypt, Israel, India, Pakistan, France, parts of eastern Europe (there was a large outbreak in Bucharest in 1996) and the northern Mediterranean. Media interest in the illness escalated after outbreaks in New York City in summer 1999 and 2000.

This viral illness is transmitted to humans via mosquitoes and ticks. It is often carried by birds and may follow migratory patterns. It is not spread from person to person. There is no vaccination against the disease so you should avoid contact with birds in areas where there has been an outbreak and observe the usual anti-insect-bite measures (see p.259).

SYMPTOMS

After an incubation period of between 5 and 15 days, West Nile fever generally takes the form of a mild illness, with **headache**, **fever**, **weakness**, **swollen lymph glands**, **nausea**, **vomiting** and **skin rashes** common features. Rarely, **meningitis** can occur. The elderly are most vulnerable to the illness and the most seriously affected, with fatality rates of up to 15%.

DIAGNOSIS AND TREATMENT

The diagnosis can be made by a **blood test**. As with most viral illnesses, there is no specific treatment beyond symptom relief; **supportive care** may be necessary in severe cases. The illness is usually self-resolving, however, and leaves no long-term complications.

Worms

All manner of **worm** species can affect your health by gaining entry to your body in one of two ways: either burrowing directly through the skin (eg hookworms and threadworms) or by ingestion (eg tapeworms and roundworms). With the possible exception of tapeworms, worm infections are more common in hotter climates. There is no vaccination available against worm infections and avoidance measures include strict personal and food hygiene and not walking barefoot in endemic areas.

▷▷ See Staying well, pp.45.

Mebendazole is a very useful drug in treating a range of worm infections; however, it's not suitable for pregnant or breast-feeding women or children under 2. Although generally well tolerated it can occasionally cause abdominal discomfort and conditions such as diarrhoea and allergic reactions (rash, itching and swelling).

▷▷ See also Dracunculiasis, p.202; and Gnathostomiasis, p.236.

Ancyclostomiasis (hookworms)

Ancyclostomiasis, or **hookworm** infections, are common in the tropics and sub-tropics but also exist in more temperate climates in certain conditions (eg mines, and where agricultural methods involve human waste as fertilizer). The CDC estimates that up to 1 billion people worldwide may be infected by hookworms.

The hookworm's eggs, which are passed in the faeces of a carrier, hatch into larvae in the moist, warm soil, where they can remain for months before infecting another host by direct penetration through the skin. Avoidance of hookworms is fairly simple – don't walk barefoot in endemic areas.

Having penetrated the skin, the larvae migrate in a matter of days via the blood and lymphatic system to the lungs, from where they move up into the throat and are swallowed down into the intestine. Once in the gut, the worms mature into adults of about 1cm long, and are capable of producing eggs in about 5 weeks.

SYMPTOMS

An **itchy lump** can develop over the entry site, usually on the sole of the foot and called "**ground itch**". Secondary bacterial infections can occur around the area.

Infection with some subgroups of hookworm (usually those affecting dogs and cats) cause **cutaneous larva migrans**, or "creeping eruption", which is an itchy, linear skin eruption caused by the erratic progress of the larvae – a red line can often be seen to advance by a few millimetres every day.

Having migrated to the lungs, the larvae cause minimal symptoms; an irritable cough or wheezing occur in some cases. Once in the gut, the worms can cause **nausea, vomiting, diarrhoea** (sometimes bloody) and **abdominal pain**. Over a few weeks or months, the blood loss caused by the worms can lead to significant **anaemia**, with symptoms of tiredness, dizzyness and shortness of breath. The loss of protein from the gut caused by the feeding worms can lead to **oedema** (fluid accumulation in the tissues resulting from a low protein concentration in the blood).

WORMS

DIAGNOSIS AND TREATMENT

The eggs can usually be identified by examination of a **stool sample**. If anaemia is confirmed by a **blood test**, it's important to supplement the lost iron by taking oral **iron tablets**. A number of different drugs can be used to eliminate the worms themselves, among them **mebendazole** (see p.396) at a dosage of 100mg twice daily for 3 days (this cannot be used in pregnancy).

Strongyloidiasis (threadworms in the US)

Like hookworms, **strongyloidiasis** infection is more common in the tropics and sub-tropics but can occur in specific conditions elsewhere. Infection can persist for many years – it's still being picked up in veterans of the Vietnam and Second World wars.

Strongyloidiasis affects only humans, with the adult worms lodging in the small intestine. Their eggs escape in the faeces, after which the next generation of non-parasitic worms hatch within a week, mature and produce offspring. This generation of larvae reinfect humans by direct penetration of the skin. Like hookworm larvae, they make their way to the lungs before eventually settling in the gut.

SYMPTOMS

It takes about 4 weeks from initial penetration for the worm to mature. The vast majority of strongyloidiasis infections show no symptoms, but sometimes there is an **itchy lesion** at the point of entry and a meandering, intensely **itchy rash** occurs transiently as the larvae migrate through the skin. Occasionally **cough** and **wheeze** occur as the larvae pass through the lungs, after which **upper abdominal pain** and **diarrhoea** can occur as the adult worms mature in the gut. There may also be **weight loss**.

DIAGNOSIS AND TREATMENT

Larvae can be seen in the **stool** under a microscope. There are several suitable **drugs** to eradicate the worms, such as tiabendazole (25mg/kg body weight twice daily for 3 days) and albendazole (400mg twice daily for 3 days), neither of which should be taken in pregnancy.

Enterobiasis (threadworms, pinworms or seat worms in the US)

Occurring worldwide, **threadworms** are the most common of the worm infections to affect humans. It is particularly common in young boys living in cooler, temperate climates.

The eggs of this thread-like worm can survive for a long time outside the body, but their true home is the human gut, which they reach by the faecal–oral route – usually the unwashed fingers of little children handling food. They can also be transferred via bed linen, clothing, toys and the like. The adult worms survive in the gut for only 6 weeks and therefore ongoing enterobiasis tends to be a cyclical self-reinfection via fingernails.

SYMPTOMS

Symptoms are usually mild and restricted to **anal itching**, most prominently at night when the female worm is laying eggs. The vagina can also be affected.

DIAGNOSIS AND TREATMENT

The worms and their eggs can often be seen around the anus. **Mebendazole** (a single 100mg dose) is the preferred option for adults and children aged over 2 years (not recommended for under 2 – seek advice from your doctor). As reinfection is common, a further dose 2 to 3 weeks later is often necessary. All members of a household should take a

WORMS

course of medication regardless of whether or not they are experiencing symptoms, and all clothes and bedding should be washed in tandem with the drug treatment. Regular bathing and scrubbing of fingernails (particularly first thing in the morning) is an essential element in preventing re-infection during treatment.

Ascariasis (roundworms)

The **roundworm** is found worldwide but is particularly common in poor, rural communities where local faecal contamination of the soil is highest, perhaps through agri-cultural methods. It's estimated that around a quarter of the world's population is affected by roundworms, with a pre-ponderance of cases among children.

The roundworm itself is large (between 15 to 40cm long), and looks very like the common earthworm. They inhabit the human small intestine, feeding from its contents, only rarely causing blood loss or damage to the bowel.

The worm eggs pass out of the body via the stool and can remain infective outside the body for months or even years. After eggs are swallowed (on soily fingers or unwashed, raw vegetables), they hatch larvae into the small intestine. The larvae migrate through the gut wall, into the bloodstream and lodge in the lungs to mature further. They then move out of the lungs into the gullet where they are swallowed, ultimately lodging themselves in the small intestine.

SYMPTOMS

It takes between 60 and 75 days for a worm to mature after an egg is swallowed. Often the infection is entirely without symptoms, although heavy infestation can cause **nausea, vomiting, loss of appetite**, crampy **abdominal pain** and, in extreme circumstances, an **obstructed bowel**

WORMS

which in turn leads to complications such as appendicitis and liver and pancreatic damage. In the longer term, untreated, significant worm infection can lead to **malnourishment**. Occasionally, if numerous larvae are involved, the lung phase of the disease can cause cough, wheeze, shortness of breath and fever.

DIAGNOSIS AND TREATMENT

The eggs are usually identifiable in the **stool**. **Mebendazole** (100mg twice daily for 3 days) or piperazine (75mg/kg body weight as a single dose on 2 consecutive days) are effective treatments.

Trichuriasis (whipworms)

Whipworms have a worldwide distribution but predominate in poor communities with inadequate sanitation in warm, humid climates. The infection commonly co-exists with ascariasis. The worms embed themselves directly in the lining of the lower gut, causing ulceration and leading to significant **blood** and **protein loss** from the body. They reach maturity about 3 months later, growing to lengths of up to 5cm. Their eggs are released in the stools and mature in the soil before being ingested.

Like ascariasis, trichuriasis is spread by ingesting the worm eggs in contaminated soil. Self-reinfection through inadequate hand-washing is common. Always wash earth-soiled hands before you eat and avoid raw fruit or vegetables that haven't been thoroughly washed.

▷▷See Food and drink, pp.40–43.

SYMPTOMS

Symptoms are uncommon and usually only apparent in children. Heavy infestation can lead to **diarrhoea**, which

WORMS

may contain **blood and mucus**. Other symptoms can include abdominal cramp-like **pain**, **loss of appetite** and **weight loss**. In cases of long-standing infection, **anaemia** may develop.

DIAGNOSIS AND TREATMENT

Microscopic **stool** examination reveals the worm eggs. **Mebendazole** (100mg twice daily for 3 days) is an effective treatment but it is probably not worth treating light infections.

Trichinosis

Cases of **trichinosis** have been reported throughout the world but are particularly common in Europe and the USA (also in the hill tribes of northern Thailand). Cysts containing the infective larvae are ingested via under-cooked, contaminated meat (usually pork). The stomach's digestive juices dissolve the cysts and release the larvae into the intestine, where they mature into adult worms and reproduce, discharging larvae into the blood. This generation of larvae form cysts in the muscles and are responsible for most of the symptoms.

The cysts are killed by cooking (all parts of the meat above 65°C), freezing to −27°C for 36 hours, or microwaving. They are unaffected by pickling, smoking, salting or other methods of preserving meat.

SYMPTOMS

The large majority of infections show no signs of illness. **Abdominal pain** and **vomiting** may occur within 72 hours after eating the contaminated meat. The illness is not usually severe, although the release of the larvae into the blood circulation between 2 and 8 weeks after initial infec-

WORMS

tion can cause a number of symptoms: **fever with rigors**, **conjunctivitis**, **sensitivity to light** and **swelling around the eyes**, an itchy **rash**, **diarrhoea**, **shortness of breath**, **chest pain**, and **muscular pain** and **spasm**. Although rare, involvement of the heart or central nervous system can be fatal.

The symptoms gradually resolve spontaneously but the muscle pain, weakness and spasms can continue for several months.

DIAGNOSIS AND TREATMENT

Diagnosis can usually be made from a **blood test**, but sometimes a muscle biopsy is required.

Pain relief, antihistamines for the itch, muscle pain and spasm and bed rest are the basis of treatment. Severe symptoms involving the heart or brain may require high-dose steroids. Treatment against the worms themselves is only useful in the first few weeks to prevent them from multiplying and producing the migratory larvae. Tiabendazole (see strongyloidiasis) can be used to eliminate the adult worms from the intestine (25mg/kg body weight twice daily for 7 days).

Tapeworms

There are 3 common types of **tapeworm** affecting humans – the beef tapeworm, pork tapeworm and fish tapeworm – all of which are related to the worm causing hydatid disease (see p.250). **Beef** tapeworm is common in Mexico, South America, eastern Europe, the Middle East and Africa (Ethiopia has the highest infection rate in the world). **Pork** tapeworm is common in South America, Africa, Asia, the NIS and eastern Europe. **Fish** tapeworm infection (called **diphyllobothriasis**) can occur worldwide but tends to be more common in Scandinavia, the Baltic countries, lake-land regions of Switzerland and the Far East.

The cow, pig or fish ingests the worm eggs during feeding. The eggs hatch in the gut and migrate to the muscles, forming cysts (see trichinosis, p.402). If inadequately cooked, the cysts in the meat remain viable and mature into adult worms in the human gut, where they produce more eggs. There is no migration outside the human gut in tapeworm infections except rarely in the pork variety when the eggs (eg from poorly washed vegetables) rather than the larval cysts in meat are eaten (see below).

SYMPTOMS

Beef tapeworms are caught by eating raw, undercooked or smoked beef, and inhabit the upper gut of humans, where they can grow up to 10m long. Symptoms, if any, are usually mild with **vague abdominal discomfort** being the most common. Occasionally **diarrhoea, vomiting** and **weight loss** can occur, while rarely more serious problems can arise as a result of the physical obstruction caused by the growing worm (eg appendicitis or liver and pancreas inflammation).

Pork tapeworm infections are much less common than beef and often go unnoticed. Symptoms, if they occur, are mild and similar to those of beef tapeworm. A more serious illness called **human cysticercosis** can result from swallowing the eggs of the worm (as opposed to the larvae in raw meat), which behave as in trichinosis (see p.402): the hatching larvae invade the gut wall, gain access to the blood and are transported to other parts of the body, where they form cysts. The effects of cysticercosis may not become apparent for many years – the most commonly affected parts of the body are the brain (where the cysts can cause serious complications such as fits, paralysis and behavioural changes), the eye (causing local inflammation, sometimes leading to blindness) and the skin (with the formation of small, hard, pea-sized nodules).

Fish tapeworm infection results from eating raw fresh-water fish and usually causes only mild symptoms similar to those caused by beef and pork tapeworms. Because the worm interferes with the body's absorption of vitamin B12, a condition known as **pernicious anaemia** can develop, with symptoms similar to that of ordinary anaemia: tired-ness, lethargy, easy fatiguability.

DIAGNOSIS AND TREATMENT

Segments of beef and pork tapeworms are often visible to the naked eye in the stool, although microscopic examina-tion of the stools will confirm the presence of eggs. Biopsy of skin nodules, x-rays and blood tests can all help to diag-nose cysticercosis caused by pork tapeworm. Eggs of the fish tapeworm can usually be found by microscopic exam-ination of the stool.

Niclosinamide is effective against the gut-stage of all tapeworm infections, although the drug's side effects include nausea, vomiting, abdominal pain, itching and lightheadedness. A dose of niclosinamide is usually followed by a strong laxative to expel the worms from the gut.

Yellow fever

Ninety-one percent of reported cases of **yellow fever** occur in Africa, although the disease is also endemic in South and Central America. Hotspots of the illness are between the latitudes 15° north and 15° south of the equa-tor, with recent epidemics in Senegal, Liberia, Ghana, Benin, Cameroon, Gabon and Kenya. In South America,

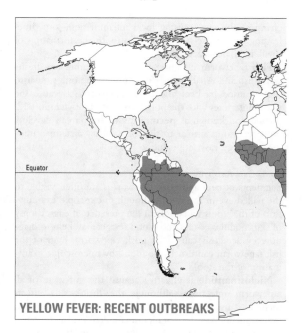

Equator

YELLOW FEVER: RECENT OUTBREAKS

the majority of cases occur in the Amazon region. Official figures on the reported number of cases and fatalities accountable to yellow fever are likely to significantly under-estimate the extent of the disease. It is principally a disease of tropical, forested areas but sporadic urban outbreaks do occur.

The virus causing yellow fever is related to dengue fever and Japanese encephalitis. Its natural host is the monkey but is spread to humans by mosquito bite. The disease can reach

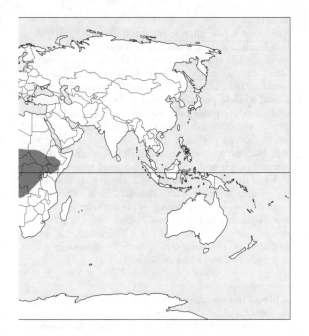

epidemic proportions in a relatively short space of time and the past 20 years has seen a rise in the number of reported epidemics and the countries affected. Urban outbreaks can be dealt with successfully by public health measures including insecticide fogging to kill the adult mosquitoes and the elimination of breeding sites such as water butts.

A live **vaccination** is compulsory when entering some endemic areas and some countries following a visit to endemic areas (see p.23).

SYMPTOMS

Symptoms appear after an incubation period of 3–6 days, but are often mild, self-limiting and unrecognizable as yellow fever. The classical picture of yellow fever is of a severe illness with an **initial sudden high fever** and disabling weakness and lethargy, accompanied by **headache**, **generalized muscle pains**, **abdominal pain** and **vomiting**. A relatively **slow pulse rate** may be present from the second day of the illness. The majority of those affected will improve over a period of about a week and the symptoms will disappear without treatment. However, around 15% of infected people will develop a second and more dangerous phase of the illness after a lull of a day or two. The vomiting returns together with **jaundice** (thus the name), a reduced flow of urine (a sign of failing kidneys), convulsions, signs of bleeding (eg nose bleeds, bruising under the skin, bleeding gums, etc) and shock. The fatality rate is high in those with complications (up to 50%) and usually occurs as a result of liver or kidney failure.

DIAGNOSIS AND TREATMENT

A **blood test** can identify the virus itself in the early stages, or antibodies to the virus later on.

There is no specific treatment other than **life support**, **symptomatic measures** and **nursing care**. But the majority of those infected will recover spontaneously with no long-term effects. Given that the illness is potentially fatal and the vaccine produces a high level of immunity, it would be very unwise to enter a yellow fever zone without being immunized.

YELLOW FEVER

First aid

The nature of the problem requiring **first aid**, almost by definition, cannot be foreseen. If you do find yourself in an emergency situation that requires first aid, a first step to take is to call for properly trained, **medical help**. The first-aid instructions on the next few pages should be regarded as **urgent temporary measures** while you wait for medical help to arrive.

A book can provide only basic guidelines, and there is no substitute for the hands-on experience of a **first-aid course** before you leave, especially if you're planning outdoor pursuits or you are going to be a long way from medical help for any period.

Unconsciousness

▷▷See also Fainting and shock, p.417.

Before diving in with a heroic flurry of resuscitation, it's worth remembering that the majority of unrousable people have simply fainted. Look for clues as to why the person may be **unconscious**:

+ Signs of trauma, eg head injury, electric shock, snake or insect bite, etc.
+ Medicalert bracelets or medallions worn by diabetics, epileptics, etc.
+ Signs of illness such as high fever, meningitis, convulsions, etc.
+ Signs of drug or alcohol use (opiate overdose is a common cause of respiratory arrest).

Once you're satisfied that there is no personal danger, shake or call to the patient to see if you are able to rouse them. If not, you'll need to check the casualty's airway, breathing and circulation (**ABC**).

Check the casualty's **airway** is not blocked (eg by dentures or their tongue). Look for signs of obstruction or a bluish tinge to the skin indicative of oxygen starvation (cyanosis). You may need to physically clear the obstruction from the mouth or throat. If the patient is lying on their back, then holding their jaw forward and tilting their head backwards will clear their airway, but if you suspect a neck injury, avoid the head tilt, simply support their jaw forward. Once you are happy that there is nothing preventing air from reaching their lungs, check for **breathing** by watching for chest movement and listening or feeling inhaled breath from their mouth. (If they're not breathing you will need to give mouth-to-mouth resuscitation – see opposite.) Check the casualty's **circulation** by feeling for a pulse. The easiest place to feel for a pulse is 2–3cm on either side of their windpipe (feel for the notch halfway down their neck, on either side of their oesophagus – the Adam's apple in men). Do not feel both sides together or else you may restrict the blood flow to the brain. If no pulse is felt you will need to start cardiac massage (**CPR**).

Only after you're satisfied the patient's airway is clear and their breathing and circulation are normal, put them in the **recovery position** (see p.412) and stay with them until they regain consciousness. If after 5 minutes they show no signs of recovery, reassess and call for help.

In the heat of the moment there is likely to be a good deal of panic and it helps to keep a cool head.

CARDIOPULMONARY RESUSCITATION (CPR)

CPR is a temporary measure to maintain oxygen flow to the brain (avoiding brain damage) until medical help arrives. *Never* practise these procedures on anyone whose heart is beating or who is breathing spontaneously.

If the casualty shows no signs of breathing or circulation, roll them on their back and **call for help**. It is usually necessary to perform mouth-to-mouth resuscitation and cardiac massage consecutively, and although this is possible to do on your own, it's much easier with two people. To perform **mouth–to–mouth resuscitation**, first tilt the head backwards. Using one hand to support the jaw and maintain the airway, with the other squeeze the nostrils to prevent air leaking when you breathe into the mouth. Take a normal breath and blow firmly (not too hard) and steadily into the casualty's mouth while forming an airtight seal with your lips. Watch for the rise and fall in the patient's chest to ensure that the air is reaching their lungs. You should aim for approximately **10 breaths a minute**. If the patient's mouth or jaw is damaged, it is also possible to give mouth to nose ventilation.

To perform **external heart massage**, kneel beside the casualty and place the heel of your left hand on the lower third of their breastbone. Cover this hand with the heel of your other hand and lock your fingers together. Lean over the patient, with your shoulders positioned directly over their breastbone (sternum). With straight arms, depress the sternum about 4 to 5cm with each movement before releasing the pressure (don't remove your hands). Try to achieve a steady swaying rhythm. If you press too hard, you risk breaking their ribs, too softly and you will not maintain circulation. Give **15 compressions before 2 breaths of mouth-to-mouth ventilation**, as a recurring cycle, aiming at a rate of 60 compressions a minute. If the patient is showing signs of recovery, check their ABC again. Keep going until help arrives.

The casualty who is unconscious but breathing and maintaining circulation should be put in the **recovery position**. This protects their airway and prevents them from choking in the event they vomit.

Kneeling beside the patient who is lying on his or her back, place the hand nearest to you palm upwards under the thigh nearest to you. This will, in effect act as a pivot for rotation. Bring their far hand across their chest and hold it palm outwards against their near cheek as you draw the thigh farthest from you towards you, bending the leg at the knee. This has the effect of rotating the patient towards you. Tilt their head backwards to maintain the airway and bend the knee that was previously farthest from you (now the top leg) to an angle of 90° to stabilize the position.

Head injury

If the casualty is unconscious, follow the recommendations above under "Unconsciousness". Before placing them in the recovery position, remember that if someone has suffered a head injury and is unconscious, it is possible that their neck may also have been injured.

Concussion is caused by the shake-up of the brain inside the skull. It can occur with or without a period of unconsciousness and the signs are confusion, bewilderment, nausea, vomiting and short-term memory-loss. Concussion may last for a few hours but is usually followed by complete recovery. However, any head injury must be closely observed for signs of deterioration over the subsequent 24 hours.

In any of the following situations, seek urgent medical help:

+ If the casualty is unconscious after the initial injury or lapses into delayed unconsciousness.
+ If blood or blood-stained fluid runs from their nose or ears.
+ If double vision or speech difficulties become apparent after the first 5 minutes.
+ If the patient continues to vomit after the first 2 hours (vomiting is not uncommon within the first 2 hours, especially in children).
+ If the casualty becomes confused or disoriented after having apparently recovered from the initial trauma.
+ If any weakness or numbness occurs.
+ If convulsions (fits) occur.
+ If the pupils become unequal, breathing becomes noisy, body temperature rises or the pulse becomes abnormally slow.
+ If a fractured skull is suspected.

Neck and spinal injuries

A **neck or spinal injury** should be suspected in anyone who has fallen awkwardly or from a height. If conscious, they may complain of numbness, pins and needles, or the inability to move.

Don't move the casualty unless you absolutely have to; it's imperative that their neck and spine are not bent or twisted. You will need to enlist several helpers and plan carefully before attempting to move them.

Support their head and neck in the so-called "neutral position" (looking straight ahead). Use clothing or towels as splinting support for their head and neck. If the casualty is unconscious, their airway can be protected by lifting and

413

supporting their jaw. Only attempt to turn the casualty once you are confident of keeping their neck and spine aligned.

Broken bones

Sometimes the diagnosis of **broken bones** (fractures) is obvious, with visible deformity, or even bones protruding through the skin (known as a **compound fracture**). More often than not, however, the damage is less easy to assess. Sometimes the casualty will report hearing or feeling a crack, but pain, bruising, swelling and loss of limb function can also occur with soft-tissue injuries (see opposite). It is not only damage to the bone itself that needs to be assessed but also the surrounding structures, such as blood vessels and nerves. Check for pulses beyond the suspected fracture on the limbs.

If a fracture is suspected, always seek **medical advice**. The diagnosis and the further treatment of a broken bone is dependent on X-ray findings and a thorough examination.

First-aid treatment of a suspected broken bone

Do not attempt to move the casualty unless they are in immediate danger. Check their pulse and more generally for other signs of shock (fracture of a large bone like the femur or pelvis can result in significant blood loss). If a limb is affected, support and cushion the area, taking care to keep the bone in a fixed position to avoid further damage. Only attempt to move the casualty when you are confident the fracture is sufficiently immobilized.

For open, or compound, fractures, cover the area with a sterile dressing to minimize the risk of infection. These types of injuries need urgent medical attention.

Soft-tissue injuries

Soft-tissue injuries are those affecting muscles, tendons and ligaments. Bruising follows damage to the blood vessels in the skin and underlying tissues usually as a result of direct trauma. The leakage of blood causes pain, swelling and dis-colouration.

In treating a soft-tissue injury, your aim is to limit the swelling and relieve the associated pain. Raise and support the affected area and apply ice or a cold compress as soon as possible. For pain relief, take paracetamol or ibuprofen as required. Bruising may be a sign of underlying bone damage, and if this is suspected, you will need an X-ray.

There's a range of homeopathic remedies you can use to treat soft-tissue injuries. **Arnica** is great in cases of overexertion, such as walking too far or carrying a heavy pack, when muscles feel sore and bruised, and for surface bruising (take 3 30c tablets for 1 or 2 days). If the soreness focuses on one particular area, for example the legs, resist the urge to rub or massage. Arnica ointment is also widely available and is an excellent treatment for bruising – don't apply it to broken skin, as it can cause a rash. **Hypericum** (dosage as for Arnica) is the best remedy for jolting of the spine – backache after horse or camel riding, bumpy road journeys and the like. **Rhus tox** (1 30c tablet at the end of the day for the first few days, followed up with Arnica shortly afterwards) helps stiffness the day after overexertion – typically you'll benefit from this remedy if you feel very stiff when getting up in the morning but loosen up as you get going. If, for example, you are going on a trekking holiday, and you know you're not in as good a shape as you should be, pack Rhus tox. **Ruta grav** is good for sprained wrists and ankles, torn ligaments and tendons and for sports injuries as a whole. Choose this remedy if the soreness and pain are no better after mobilizing – this distinguishes it from requiring Rhus tox. Sprains and torn ligaments can take a long while to heal – try taking 30c twice daily for 7 days, or a lower potency more often for the same period. A **combined ointment** containing Arnica, Rhus tox and Ruta grav is particularly useful on any activity holiday, while **cabbage** or **dark lettuce** leaves applied to local inflammations can be soothing and reduce redness and swelling – hold them in place with a sock, scarf or elasticated bandage.

SPRAINS

Sprains usually describe a strained or **over-stretched** muscle, tendon or ligament, and are a frequent problem among travellers carrying heavy luggage. Ankles, wrists, knees, the groin, the back and the neck are the most commonly affected areas – sprains can result from a definite injury or may creep up on you. Signs are pain that tends to be dull or throbbing and worse on movement, local swelling and, occasionally, bruising. Rest, followed by gentle mobilization, is the best treatment, while ice or a cold compress will help to relieve pain. If possible, raise the affected area to reduce swelling. NSAIDs (ibuprofen, etc) may be used to reduce inflammation and for pain relief (see p.52). Sprained ligaments can take up to 2 weeks to heal, and a previously injured ligament is likely to be weakened and therefore easily sprained again. Elasticated bandages can help as a physical support.

Choking

Choking is caused by an object lodging itself in the windpipe and obstructing the airway. The person affected experiences sudden difficulty in breathing, is unable to talk and becomes red in the face. Prompt action is needed to prevent them from suffocating. Sometimes it is enough to bend the casualty forward and slap them sharply between their shoulder blades – children can literally be tipped upside down. If this fails, then perform the **Heimlich Manoeuvre**: stand behind the casualty and place your right fist in the solar plexus (the top part of the abdomen in the inverted "V" of the ribs). With your other hand, grasp your fist and sharply thrust inwards and upwards 5 times. This should be enough to dislodge the blockage from the windpipe but if it fails first time, repeat the procedure or, with help, tip the casualty upside down holding them by the legs, and let gravity do the work.

Fainting and shock

Fainting is caused by a sudden drop in blood pressure, usually brought about by stress, emotion, fear, pain or overheating. If suspected, check their airway and breathing, loosen tight clothing and raise their legs. The drop is transient and recovery is usually quick.

Shock, in the medical sense, also occurs when the blood pressure drops significantly. Common causes are blood loss, septicaemia, heart failure, severe vomiting or diarrhoea, anaphylaxis and burns. The **signs** of shock are feeling faint or loss of consciousness; pale, cold, clammy skin; nausea; a rapid, weak pulse; and involuntary shaking. The danger of shock is that the drop in blood pressure can impair blood supply to vital organs such as the brain and heart. If shock is suspected, call for help and try to treat the underlying cause if it is obvious. Maximize the blood pressure to the brain by lying the casualty down and raising the legs. Keep the casualty warm by covering their body with a blanket. Closely monitor their airway, breathing and pulse rate and start CPR if necessary.

Fits

▷▷For first-aid measures, see under Epilepsy, p.91.

Bleeding

In most wounds, the **bleeding** comes from tiny capillary **vessels** which link the arterial system (carrying blood away from the heart) to the venous system (carrying blood towards the heart). The blood tends to ooze and loss is self-limiting. Bleeding from a **vein** tends to flow, the blood is darker and loss can be significant but is rarely life-threatening (depending on the size of the vein). **Arterial bleeding** is the most dangerous and even if a relatively small artery is damaged, blood loss can be serious. The blood in an artery is pumped at high pressure and tends to spurt in pulses with each contraction of the heart.

When someone is losing blood:

+ Lie them down and assess the degree of bleeding. If significant, call for help immediately.
+ If you have gloves or other means of protecting yourself from direct blood contact, use them.
+ If there is an obvious foreign body in the wound, do not try and remove it because it might be acting as a plug, and removal will cause further bleeding.
+ Apply direct pressure to the wound site, preferably using sterile gauze or a dressing of some kind. (Apply pressure to either side of a wound with a foreign body.)
+ If the wound is to a limb, raise and support it above the level of the heart. This reduces the blood pressure at the wound site and aids the body's clotting system. In an emergency when blood loss from a limb wound is severe,

applying pressure to the arterial pressure points at the groin or elbow may slow down the blood loss. Tourniquets should be avoided unless the situation is life-threatening. If required, apply the tourniquet as close to the wound as possible and tighten using a twisting motion – you must loosen the tourniquet every 20 minutes to allow blood flow to the limb beyond and to assess whether it's still needed.

✚ Once the bleeding has settled, clean the wound using antiseptic, apply a sterile dressing and, if possible, keep the limb raised.

✚ Seek help if bleeding continues, if the casualty becomes shocked or if a foreign body is present in the wound.

Bleeding from a **head injury** tends to be heavy, even if the wound is relatively small, because of the copious network of blood vessels covering the scalp. If the casualty is conscious and lucid, sit them down (don't lie them down) and apply direct pressure to the wound (do not apply pressure if a skull fracture is suspected). An ice pack or anything cold applied to the wound site may slow the bleeding. If bleeding continues unabated, it may be necessary to suture the wound – you'll need to seek medical help for this. Tape, sticking plaster or, better still, steristrips may be used as a temporary means of drawing the wound together. Do not attempt to suture a dirty wound, one that has been caused by a bite or any wound in which foreign material is visible but cannot be removed.

It's difficult to give specific advice for **superficial cuts and lacerations** because much depends on the nature and situation of the injury. Here are a few guidelines.

✚ Ensure that your tetanus cover is up-to-date. A booster currently lasts for 10 years, although for dirty wounds or high-risk situations, one after 5 years is recommended.

✚ Cuts and abrasions in tropical climates or which involve foreign bodies (splinters, coral), deep, penetrating injuries or animal bites (cats and humans in particular) are more likely to become infected. Cleanse the wound thoroughly as soon as possible using lots of clean water or weak antiseptic solution. Alcohol can be used in emergencies. If foreign material is evident in the wound, try to remove it (unless it is large and preventing heavier bleeding) prior to dressing because it will otherwise act as a focus for infection. Cover the wound with a sterile dressing and watch for signs of infection (see p.352). In cases of deep, penetrating wounds, a prophylactic course of antibiotics – flucloxacillin, co-amoxiclav, amoxycillin or erythromycin (see p.53) – will be necessary.

✚ For animal bites, consider the possibility of rabies (see p.316) and, if in doubt, seek urgent medical advice.

 Calendula, widely available as a cream, ointment, tincture, tea and oil, is an excellent natural antiseptic which heals cuts and grazes, soothes chafing, and helps eczema, nappy rash and the like. Use the tincture or lotion (both of which can be diluted in clean water) or the cream externally as a dressing on wounds, infections, ulcers and septic bites. Avoid calendula for deep or penetrating wounds, as it tends to heal things over quickly and could "seal" infection into the wound. However, used in combination with Hypericum tincture or lotion, its action is retarded slightly, making it more suitable for deep or dirty wounds. **Hypericum** is useful for injuries to areas rich in nerves – fingers, toes, lips, tongue, genitals. This remedy is ideal after cutting the sole of your foot or tip of your finger, after dental work where nerve pain remains, after falling over and putting your teeth through your lip. It's also good for what used to be called "railway spine" – the effects of a very jolting journey – or after landing on your tailbone in a fall. It can also help stave off sciatica and neuralgia. Characteristically, pains are sharp and electric, and extend along nerve pathways from the site of the injury (start with a 30c taken hourly for 3 or 4hr and then twice a day for a couple more days, as needed).

NOSEBLEEDS

Nosebleeds affecting young, fit people usually come from a part of the nose with a high concentration of blood vessels, located at the front and called "Little's Area". The cause is usually direct trauma or nasal congestion after a cold. The dry air at high altitude also desiccates the nasal lining, which often leads to bleeding. Older people can suffer from heavier bleeds from the large blood vessels at the back of the nose – "posterior bleeds" – and these are more difficult to control.

Bleeding from Little's Area is usually identifiable as dripping or a steady flow from one nostril. The bleeding is usually light and easily quelled by direct pressure over the area for 5 to 10 minutes. Applying pressure over the lower part of the nose compresses the offending vessel against the nasal septum and stems the blood flow. Pressure over the upper, bony part (bridge) of the nose is totally ineffective, although an ice pack over the bridge causes contraction of the vessels and may reduce or stop bleeding. Bleeding from Little's Area often recurs, and if frequent nosebleeds are a problem, it may be worth having the area cauterized by a doctor.

Bleeding from the back of the nose is rare in young people. Blood flows heavily, or even gushes, from one or both nostrils. This type of bleed is difficult to stop, and pressure to the front of the nose will only result in the blood pouring backwards and being swallowed. Don't underestimate these posterior nosebleeds – fatalities can occur through blood loss. Furthermore, without the right equipment, they can be difficult to treat and may need referral to a hospital with a specialist department. In the meantime, keep calm, sit forward and apply pressure to the front of the nose and ice packs to the bridge. (Some blood will be swallowed but the flow will be slowed.) Watch for signs of shock (see p.417). Bed rest is recommended for 24 to 48 hours after a posterior bleed.

Burns

From a medical perspective, **burns** are divided into superficial (first degree), partial thickness (second degree) and full thickness (third degree), depending on the depth of the tissue layers affected. Superficial burns affect only the outer skin layer. Pain, swelling and redness occur, but with prompt and adequate treatment the burn will heal within a few days without scarring. Partial thickness burns result in the formation of blisters, which, when extensive, may result in shock and a loss of blood plasma. Small areas of partial-thickness burns, however, respond well to first-aid measures, and scarring is rare.

Full-thickness burns affect all layers of the skin and sometimes the tissues underneath. The burn may be pale or charred and hard to the touch. Full-thickness burns may be painless because of damage to the nerves. Urgent medical assessment is required, and scarring is likely.

Drowning

Drowning occurs when the lungs are flooded with water leading to asphyxiation and subsequent respiratory and

First aid of a burn

+ Cool the burn as quickly as possible under cold running water. This reduces pain and swelling and minimizes tissue damage; if the burn is caused by contact with a chemical, the water washes the substance away. Remove similarly affected clothing promptly.

+ Assess the severity and extent of the burns. Smoke inhalation and toxic fumes can lead to respiratory failure, so check the casualty's airway, breathing and circulation (ABC). Resuscitate, treat shock (see p.417), and call for help as necessary.

+ Cover the burn with a sterile dressing. Infection is a real danger because the body's main defence – the skin – has been compromised. Do not use lotions or ointments on the affected area and do not dress with fluffy dressings – a clean polythene bag or kitchen film can be used instead.

+ Burns can be very painful, so always give the casualty adequate pain relief. Calamine lotion may be soothing for superficial burns.

+ Do not burst blisters; allow them to heal by themselves.

+ Antibiotics (flucloxacillin, co-amoxiclav or erythromycin) may be required to stave off infection.

cardiac arrest. In the event, it is important to check the victim's ABC (see p.410) and start resuscitation as soon as possible, even before you're out of the water.

Resuscitation has been successful with people who, having been pulled from the water, show no initial signs of life. This is because the cold water slows the body's metabolic rate, prolonging survival. The effect is particularly pronounced in children. For this reason, even if initial signs are pessimistic, you should continue resuscitation for up to 45 minutes after a drowning accident.

Once the casualty starts to breathe again, they should be placed in the recovery position (see p.412). Even after apparently successful resuscitation, the lungs may become swollen and cause delayed breathing difficulties. Remember that **hypothermia** (see p.174) is also a real danger. Medical assessment after a near-drowning is therefore important.

3

where
in the world?

Aspirin. Photo © Randy Faris/Corbis

"Risk" is a difficult concept to quantify in terms of travel health, as there are so many variables. Obviously you are less likely to come into contact with many infectious diseases if you are staying in five-star hotels and spending your days lounging by the pool than if you're backpacking on a tight budget off the beaten track. However, remember that it only takes one infected mosquito bite to give you malaria and one bad prawn to contract dysentery.

The purpose of this section is to give you some guidance on the sorts of health risks you may encounter at your destination. In order to do this, we've subdivided the world into **9 different parts**, each with a **generalized introduction** to the key risks you might face there. **Country-by-country listings** follow each introduction and are out of necessity selective – we've concentrated on the incidence of major diseases (yellow fever, malaria and the like) where relevant, as well as including some perhaps lesser-known health risks which may have made the news recently. **To get the full picture** of what risks await, it's important that you read the subsection introductions as well as the individual country listing.

Finally, every effort has been made to provide up-to-date information at the time of writing, but **things change** – sometimes quite rapidly – in response to extremes of climate, political unrest or epidemic outbreaks. It is strongly recommended that you contact your **doctor** or **travel clinic** for the most current advice before departure. There are also some very useful and accurate sources of information on the **Internet**, for more on which see Part 4. See also Part 1 for considerations to take into account before you set out – check out especially the information on **immunizations**, **insurance**, **insect-bite avoidance** and **food- and drink-hygiene**.

Africa

Of all the continents, Africa is perhaps the one that presents the most health hazards to the traveller. **Malaria**, **yellow fever**, **schistosomiasis**, **meningitis** and **African trypanosomiasis** are common in sub-Saharan regions, and incidence of **HIV** infection and AIDS are rising to alarming levels. Rates of **sexually transmitted diseases** and **hepatitis B** infection are high throughout the continent. Health risks are usually highest in the countries where there has been recent political unrest and fighting, leading to a breakdown in immunization campaigns and public-health measures. **Violence** is common in some countries, particularly in the sub-Saharan belt, and it is worth finding out the latest situation if you are planning to travel to anywhere there is unrest.

Longer-term travellers or those travelling into rural areas should ensure that their **normal childhood vaccinations** (particularly polio, tetanus and diphtheria) are up-to-date, consider **hepatitis B** vaccination, immunization against **meningococcal meningitis** (especially sub-Saharan regions), and check their **BCG** (TB) status. Carrying a sterilized pack of syringes, needles, drip sets, etc is also a good idea to avoid the need for local equipment in the event you require a blood transfusion. **Wounds** can become **infected** quickly because of the hot climate and need to be cleansed and dressed with particular care.

AFRICA

North Africa

Algeria, Egypt, Libya, Morocco, Tunisia

The type and extent of diseases found in North Africa differ from the rest of Africa mainly because it is geographically separated by the Sahara desert. **Diarrhoeal illnesses** are very common throughout the area, with high prevalence of **intestinal worm infections** and **giardia**. **Malaria** risk in North Africa is generally limited and neglible in the main tourist areas. Low risk exists in certain parts of Algeria, Egypt (El Faiyum area only), Libya, Western Sahara and Morocco. There is no risk in the Canary Islands or Tunisia. There is no risk of **yellow fever** in North Africa itself, but vaccination will be required if you are planning to enter Algeria, Egypt, Libya and Tunisia from an infected country. **Dengue fever** occurs in epidemics in Algeria, Egypt and Libya. **Schistosomiasis** occurs throughout Algeria, Libya, Morocco and Egypt, especially the Nile area. **Rabies** risk exists throughout. The incidence of **typhoid fever** is relatively high, especially in rural areas. **Influenza** epidemics occur between November and April. **Filariasis**, **onchocerciasis** and **leishmaniasis** all occur throughout the area, especially in the Nile Delta, although risk to the average tourist is low. **Brucellosis** and **hepatitis A** are common. **Trachoma**, **relapsing fever**, **Rift Valley fever**, **sandfly fever**, **typhus**, **West Nile fever**, **tungiasis**, **chikungunya fever**, **plague** and **echinococcosis** occur sporadically, although rarely pose a significant threat to tourists. **Snakes** and **scorpions** may be a hazard in rural areas. **Sandstorms** in rural areas can make walking and driving treacherous.

Algeria

Malaria prophylaxis is unnecessary in Algeria – although vivax malaria occurs in Ihrir in the Illizi Department, this is a geographically isolated area that rarely sees tourists. **Tungiasis** is prevalent, while **Lassa fever** occurs rarely in some rural areas. **Yellow fever vaccination** is required for all travellers over the age of 1 entering from an infected area.

Egypt

Travellers between June and October to the El Faiyum area need to consider **malaria** prophylaxis. The commonest type of malaria is vivax, which is chloroquine sensitive, although the falciparum variety has been reported. If you travel to this area, chloroquine alone is adequate prophylaxis, elsewhere none is necessary. **Cholera** is a risk in Egypt and while vaccination is no longer an entry requirement, food- and drink-hygiene **must be taken seriously**. **Yellow fever vaccination** is required for travellers aged 1 and over entering from an infected area (this also applies to travellers in transit from countries where yellow fever is endemic). A list of countries deemed "infected" is available from the embassy. A **HIV test** is required if you are applying for a work permit. Foreign tests are acceptable under certain circumstances (contact embassy for details).

Libya

There may be limited **malaria** risk in the southwest of the country from February to August, but there have been no reported cases since the 1980s. Outbreaks of **meningococcal meningitis** have occured in the Sebha region (the Fezzan) in the southeast. **Cholera** is a low risk. Libya **is reportedly rabies-free**. **Yellow fever vaccination** is required for travellers over 1 year of age coming from an infected area. A **HIV test** is required of anyone applying for residency.

Morocco

A minimal **malaria** risk (vivax only) exists between May and October in small pockets in the provinces of Al Hoceima, Taounate and Taza. Prophylaxis isn't strictly necessary, although if you're planning to travel to the risk areas in summer, consider chloroquine. **Tungiasis** is prevalent and **Lassa fever** occurs in some rural areas, but neither are likely to pose a significant threat to the average tourist.

Tunisia

Tungiasis is prevalent, Lassa **fever** occurs in some rural areas and **Mediterranean spotted fever** has been reported. However, none is likely to be a significant risk to the traveller. **Yellow fever vaccination** is required for travellers aged 1 and over entering from an infected area.

West Africa

Benin, Burkina Faso, Cape Verde Islands, Côte d'Ivoire, Gambia, Ghana, Guinea Republic, Guinea-Bissau, Liberia, Mali, Mauritania, Niger, Nigeria, Sao Tome and Principe, Senegal, Sierra Leone, Togo

Diarrhoeal illnesses are common, with high rates of **intestinal worm infections** and **giardia**. A high risk of **falciparum malaria** exists all year round in areas under 2600m in Benin, Burkina Faso, Côte d'Ivoire, Gambia,

Ghana, Guinea, Guinea-Bissau, Liberia, Mali, Mauritania, Niger, Nigeria, Sao Tome and Principe, Senegal, Sierra Leone and Togo. There is no risk of malaria on the Cape Verde islands, except on Sao Tiago. The incidence of chloroquine resistance is high throughout the area, and mefloquine is the recommended prophylaxis (except in the Cape Verde Islands and Mauritania). Although not always active, **yellow fever** poses a significant risk in Burkina Faso, Côte d'Ivoire, Gambia, Ghana, Mali, Mauritania, Nigeria, Senegal, Sierra Leone and Togo, particularly in rural areas – vaccination (with due certification) is sensible for all West African countries and is an entry requirement for many. **Dengue fever** occurs in epidemics throughout the region, most recently affecting Burkina Faso, Côte d'Ivoire, Guinea, Nigeria and Senegal. **Schistosomiasis** is common throughout the region but especially so in the savanna regions of Burkina Faso, Mali, Niger and Nigeria. **Rabies** is a ubiquitous risk. **Typhoid fever** is common in the region, particularly in rural areas. **Influenza** risk extends throughout the year. **Cholera** outbreaks have been reported from every country – although certification of immunization against cholera is no longer an international requirement, you may be asked for it in some remote border outposts. **Hepatitis A and E** are common in the area, while high rates of **hepatitis B** infection exist in the native population. **Meningococcal meningitis** is a risk (and immunization duly recommended) during the dry season from December to June in most West African countries but particularly Benin, Burkina Faso, Mali, Niger and Nigeria. **Lymphatic filariasis**, **chikungunya fever**, **cutaneous** and **visceral leishmaniasis** (mostly in the dry season), **onchocerciasis** (except Gambia and Mauritania), **African trypanosomiasis** (occurring in all countries except Gambia and Mauritania in isolated pockets),

Crimean-Congo haemorrhagic fever, **typhus** (louse-, flea- and tick-borne), **tungiasis**, **loasis**, **trachoma**, **dracunculiasis** (isolated pockets), **paragonimiasis** (mainly Liberia), **relapsing fever**, **echinococcosis** (mainly animal breeding areas), **Lassa fever** (significant rural reservoirs in West Africa), **Ebola** and **Marburg viruses** (rare) and **plague** all occur, to varying degrees, in the region, although the risks are generally small to tourists. **Myiasis** (mainly tumbu fly) is common in many rural areas. The dry, dusty climate can exacerbate **skin** and **respiratory problems**, and **snakes** and **scorpions** may be a hazard throughout the region.

Benin

Malaria risk is high throughout the year. The falciparum variety predominates and chloroquine resistance is common, so mefloquine is the recommended prophylaxis. **Yellow fever** risk occurs in all rural areas but especially in Atakora and Borgou, and **vaccination** is required for all travellers over 1 year of age. The hot, dusty, windy environmental conditions in November and December may exacerbate **respiratory problems**. With the exception of La Crique beach, west of Cotonou, the **sea currents** are strong and treacherous.

Burkina Faso

Malaria risk is high throughout the year. The falciparum variety predominates and chloroquine resistance is common, so mefloquine is the recommended prophylaxis. **Yellow fever** risk occurs in all rural areas, particularly the Poni Province; **vaccination** is required for all travellers over 1 year of age. The hot, dusty environment can exacerbate **breathing problems**.

Cape Verde Islands

There is limited **malaria** risk on Sao Tiago Island only between September and November, and malaria prophylaxis is not generally necessary. **Yellow fever vaccination** is required for all travellers over 1 year of age coming from either a currently infected country or countries that have officially reported yellow fever cases in the past 6 years (Kenya and Mali, at time of writing).

Côte d'Ivoire

Malaria risk is high throughout the year. The falciparum variety predominates and chloroquine resistance is common, so mefloquine is the recommended prophylaxis. **Yellow fever vaccination** is required for all travellers over 1 year of age.

Gambia

Malaria risk is high throughout the year across the country. The falciparum variety predominates and chloroquine resistance is common; mefloquine is the recommended prophylaxis. **Skin infections** are common countrywide in the rainy season. **Rift Valley fever** occurs in the Farafeni region. **Yellow fever** is endemic, but a particularly high-risk area is the Upper River Division; **vaccination** is required for travellers over 1 year of age entering from endemic or infected countries.

Ghana

Malaria risk is high throughout the year across the country. The falciparum variety predominates and chloroquine resistance is common; mefloquine is the recommended prophylaxis. A **cholera** epidemic occurred in the Builsa district of the Upper East Region in 1999. **Yellow fever** is considered endemic throughout the country, but particularly high risk in the Upper East **and Upper West Regions**. **Yellow fever vaccination** is necessary for all travellers entering the country.

Guinea Republic

Malaria risk is high throughout the year. The falciparum variety predominates and chloroquine resistance is common; mefloquine is the recommended prophylaxis. **Yellow fever** risk exists in all rural areas, particularly in the Siguiri Region. It's wise for all travellers over the age of 1 to be **vaccinated** against yellow fever, even though officially it's required only for those entering from infected countries.

Guinea-Bissau

Malaria risk is high throughout the year. The falciparum variety predominates and chloroquine resistance is common. Mefloquine is the recommended prophylaxis. Officially, **yellow fever vaccination** is only required of travellers over 1 entering from infected countries and some other specified countries (contact embassy for latest details), but because of the high risk in rural areas, immunization is recommended for all visitors.

Liberia

Malaria risk is high throughout the year. The falciparum variety predominates and chloroquine resistance is common. **Yellow fever** risk exists in all rural areas, especially Bomi, Bong, Grand Bassa, Lofa and Sino counties; **vaccination** is required of all travellers above 1 year of age.

Mali

Malaria risk is high year-round. The falciparum variety predominates and chloroquine resistance is common; mefloquine is the recommended prophylaxis. Risk of **yel-**

low fever exists throughout rural areas; **vaccination** is required for all travellers over the age of 1.

Mauritania

Malaria risk exists everywhere except for Dakhlet-Nouadhibou and Tiris-Zemour provinces, while in Adrar and Inchiri provinces it exists in the rainy season only (usually July–Oct). The recommended prophylaxis is a combination of chloroquine and proguanil. **Rift Valley fever** occurs in the southwest Trarza Region (mainly in the departments of Rosso and Keur Macene). Excepting travellers entering from non-infected areas and staying for less than 2 weeks, **yellow fever vaccination** is required for everyone over 1 year of age.

Niger

Malaria risk is high throughout the year. The falciparum variety predominates and chloroquine resistance is common. Mefloquine is the recommended prophylaxis. The risk of **yellow fever** infection exists in all rural areas; **vaccination** is required for all travellers above 1 year of age and is also recommended for those leaving the country. A **cholera** epidemic was reported in 1999, centred on Boboyé District east of Niamey. Medical facilities are generally poor and unable to cope with significant emergencies.

Nigeria

Malaria risk is high year-round across the country. The falciparum variety predominates and chloroquine resistance is common. **Yellow fever** risk occurs in all rural areas, especially the states of Anambra, Bauchi, Bendel, Benue, Cross River, Ekiti, Imo, Kaduna, Kano (outbreak in 2000), Kwara, Lagos, Niger, Ogun, Ondo, Oyo, Plateau; **yellow fever vaccination** is a requirement for travellers over 1 year of age coming from infected areas, but it's recommended for anyone over 9 months entering the country. A large **cholera** outbreak occurred in Kano State (mainly) in 1999.

Sao Tome and Principe

Malaria risk is high all year. The falciparum variety predominates and chloroquine resistance is common; mefloquine is the recommended prophylaxis. **Yellow fever vaccination** is required for all travellers of above 1 year of age.

Senegal

Malaria risk is high year-round across the country. The falciparum variety predominates and chloroquine resistance is common. Mefloquine is the recommended prophylaxis. **Yellow fever** risk exists in all rural areas and **vaccination** is required for travellers coming from endemic areas. **Rift Valley fever** occurs in the northwest.

Sierra Leone

Malaria risk is high throughout the year. The falciparum variety predominates and chloroquine resistance is common; mefloquine is recommended. Outbreaks of **yellow fever** occur in rural areas, particularly in the Eastern Province; **vaccination** is a requirement for anyone entering the country from infected areas, although it's advisable for all travellers. An outbreak of **Lassa fever** was responsible for several fatalities in Freetown in 2000.

Togo

Malaria risk is high throughout the year. The falciparum variety predominates and chloroquine resistance is common; mefloquine is the recommended prophylaxis. The risk of infection with **yellow fever** exists in all rural areas; **vaccination** is required from all travellers over 1 year of age.

Dracunculiasis is common in the indigenous population, but unlikely to pose a significant threat to travellers.

Central Africa

Angola, Cameroon, Central African Republic, Chad, Congo, Democratic Republic of the Congo (Zaire), Equatorial Guinea, Gabon, Sudan, Zambia

Diarrhoeal illness is common throughout the area. There is a high risk of chloroquine-resistant falciparum **malaria** year-round in all countries, including urban areas. Mefloquine is the recommended prophylaxis. Regardless of official requirements, you would be sensible to have a **yellow fever** vaccination, especially if travelling into rural areas, as substantial risk exists. Epidemics of **dengue fever** occur sporadically in the region. **Schistosomiasis** is widespread and common in all Central African countries. **Rabies** risk exists throughout. **Typhoid fever** is common, particularly in rural areas. **Influenza** risk exists year-long. **Cholera** outbreaks are common throughout the area. Outbreaks of **meningococcal meningitis** occur in the dry season (Dec–June), during which time **vaccination** is recommended for visitors to the northern regions of Angola, Cameroon, the Central African Republic, Chad and Sudan. Cutaneous and visceral **leishmaniasis** occur in drier areas of all countries of the region. **Hepatitis A and E** are common regionwide, but particularly in rural areas. High rates of **hepatitis B** infection exist in the native population. **African trypanosomiasis** can occur in all Central African countries, but transmission rates are particularly high (and a significant risk to travellers) in northern Angola and the Democratic Republic of Congo (mainly in the Equateur and Bandadu provinces) and southern Sudan. **Filariasis**, **loasis** (in Cameroon and Sudan particularly), **relapsing fever**, **tungiasis**, **myiasis** and **typhus** (flea-, louse- or tick-borne) occur in all countries. **Dracunculiasis** occurs in isolated pockets, and **echinococcosis** is widespread in animal breeding areas. **Paragonimiasis** has been reported in Cameroon, Equatorial Guinea, Gabon and Liberia. Trachoma and **onchocerciasis** are widespread (low risk in Zambia). **Plague** has been reported in Angola, the Democratic Republic of Congo and Zambia. **Lassa fever** and **Marburg** and **Ebola viruses** occur in rare outbreaks in rural areas. Adverse climatic conditions such as heat, dust and temperature fluctuations lead to a high incidence of **respiratory infections** and may exacerbate existing chest illness. Snakes, scorpions and spiders can be a hazard in some areas.

Angola

Malaria risk exists year-round throughout the country. The predominant strain is falciparum and chloroquine resistance is common. Mefloquine is the recommended prophylaxis. **Yellow fever** risk exists in all rural areas but is particularly high in Bengo and Luanda provinces; a **vaccination** certificate is required from travellers over 1 year of age coming from infected areas.

Cameroon

Malaria risk exists all year, predominantly the falciparum strain, and chloroquine resistance is common. Mefloquine is the recommended prophylaxis. **Yellow fever** risk exists everywhere except urban centres; **vaccination** is required for all visitors over the age of 1.

Central African Republic

Malaria risk exists year-long in all areas, is predominantly falciparum and commonly chloroquine resistant. Mefloquine is the recommended prophylaxis. The risk of **yellow fever** exists everywhere except urban centres, and **vaccination** is required for all visitors over the age of 1. An epidemic of **meningococcal meningitis** in 2000 affected a number of areas: Vakaga, Bamingui-Bangoran, Haute Katto and Ouham Pend.

Chad

Malaria risk exists year-round, predominantly the falciparum form and chloroquine resistant. Mefloquine is the recommended prophylaxis. The risk of **yellow fever** exists in all areas other than the urban centres; **vaccination** is required for all visitors over 1 year old.

Congo

Malaria risk exists throughout the year and across the country, is predominantly the falciparum form and chloroquine resistant. Mefloquine is the recommended prophylaxis. The risk of **yellow fever** exists everywhere except urban centres; **vaccination** is required for all visitors over the age of 1. **Onchocerciasis** is prevalent, with the greatest risk around the Djoue River basin and the River Congo downstream from Brazzaville.

Democratic Republic of the Congo (Zaire)

Malaria risk exists throughout the country all year. It is predominantly the falciparum form and chloroquine resistant; mefloquine is the recommended prophylaxis. The risk of **yellow fever** exists everywhere except urban centres; **vaccination** is required for all visitors over the age of 1. **Ebola**

virus outbreaks have occurred in Zaire, though the risk to ordinary tourists is very low. In 1999 and 2000, there were a number of cases of **Marburg virus** infection in Durba. A **cholera** outbreak occurred in Kinshasa in 1999 following flooding of the Congo. **Plague** has been reported from the Haut Zaire province. The population has been badly hit by **HIV** – infection rates are particularly high in Kinshasa.

Equatorial Guinea

Malaria risk exists throughout the country all year, predominantly the falciparum form, and chloroquine resistance is reported. Mefloquine is the recommended prophylaxis. The risk of **yellow fever** exists everywhere except in urban centres; **vaccination** is required for all travellers entering the country from infected areas.

Gabon

Malaria risk exists year-round, is predominantly the falciparum form and chloroquine resistant. Mefloquine is the recommended prophylaxis. **Yellow fever** risk exists everywhere except the urban centres – it's particularly high in Ogooue-Ivindo Province – and **vaccination** is required for all visitors over the age of 1.

Sudan

Malaria risk exists throughout the country all year, is predominantly the falciparum form and chloroquine resistant. Mefloquine is the recommended prophylaxis. The risk is low and seasonal in the north and along the Red Sea coast, and higher along the River Nile south of Lake Nasser and in central southern areas. The risk of **yellow fever** exists everywhere except urban centres; **vaccination** is required for all travellers over 1 entering the country from infected areas. A large outbreak of **meningococcal meningitis**

occurred in 2000, mainly affecting the states of Bahar aj Jabal, White Nile, South Kordofan and Sennar. **Visceral leishmaniasis** is epidemic in southern and eastern areas. **Dracunculiasis** is particularly prevalent in southern areas.

Zambia

Countrywide, the risks of **malaria** are highest between November and June (except in the Zambezi Valley, where high risk exists all year). It is predominantly the falciparum form and chloroquine resistant. Although there are no official entry requirements for **yellow fever immunization**, potential risk exists in the northwestern forest areas and vaccination should be considered by all travellers to rural areas. An outbreak of **cholera** occurred in Lusaka District in 1999. **Plague** has been reported in the Southern Province.

East Africa

Burundi, The Comoros, Djibouti, Eritrea, Ethiopia, Kenya, Madagascar, Malawi, Mauritius, Mayotte, Mozambique, Reunion, Rwanda, Seychelles, Somalia, Uganda, United Republic of Tanzania

Diarrhoeal disease, **giardiasis**, **dysentery**, **typhoid fever** and **hepatitis A and E** are widespread throughout the region. There is a high risk of **malaria** throughout the year in Burundi, Comoros, Djibouti, Eritrea, Ethiopia, Madagascar (especially coastal areas), Malawi, Mayotte, Mozambique, Rwanda, Somalia, Tanzania and Uganda. The predominant form is falciparum and chloroquine resistance is common. Mefloquine is the recommended prophylaxis. There is no malaria in Reunion or the Seychelles, and the risk in Mauritius is small and prophylaxis unnecessary. Outbreaks of **yellow fever** can occur in any of the mainland countries and, regardless of official requirements, immunization is recommended, particularly for travel outside urban centres. There is no risk of yellow fever on the Comoros and Seychelles. Epidemics of **dengue fever** occur sporadically in all countries (most recently in Djibouti, Kenya, Mozambique and Somalia). Significant **schistosomiasis** risk exists in Burundi, Eritrea, Ethiopia, Kenya, Madagascar, Malawi, Mauritius, Mozambique, Rwanda, Somalia and Tanzania. There is none reported in Comoros, Djibouti, Reunion and the Seychelles. Lake Malawi is a risk area for schistosomiasis despite local reassurances to the contrary. **Rabies** risk exists throughout the region, although there are no recent reports of the disease in Mauritius and the Seychelles. **Influenza** risk extends throughout the year. Outbreaks of **cholera** are common in East Africa, and some customs officials may ask for proof of immunization against it even though this is no longer required. **Meningococcal meningitis** tends to be a seasonal risk, occurring primarily in the dry season (Dec–June), although the risk is year-long in Burundi, Kenya and Tanzania. **Vaccination** is recommended when visiting high-risk (rural) areas, particularly in the dry season. High rates of **hepatitis B** infection exist in the native population. **Cutaneous** and **visceral leishmaniasis** may occur in dry areas. **Filariasis**, **trachoma tungiasis** and **worm infections** are common throughout the region although pose little threat to the average traveller. **Chikungunya fever**, **myiasis**, **onchocerciasis**, **African trypanosomiasis** (no reports in Djibouti, Somalia and the Indian Ocean islands), **Crimean-Congo haemorrhagic fever**, **typhus** (louse-, flea- or tick-borne types) and **relapsing fever** all occur to varying degrees throughout the region. **Plague** risk exists in pockets in Kenya, Madagascar, Malawi, Mozambique, Uganda and the United Republic of Tanzania. **Echinococcosis** is common in animal-breeding areas. **Dracunculosis** has been reported from most countries in the region. Sporadic outbreaks of **Rift Valley fever** and **Lassa fever** occur. **Marburg** and **Ebola viruses** occur in very rare and usually isolated instances. **Snakes**, **spiders** and **scorpions** can present a hazard throughout the region. The dusty, dry climate may cause **respiratory problems** to susceptible individuals.

Burundi

Malaria risk exists year-round, is predominantly the falciparum form and chloroquine resistant. Mefloquine is the recommended prophylaxis. The country is officially considered endemic for **yellow fever**, and risk exists in all but urban centres; **vaccination** is required from travellers over 1 year of age coming from infected areas. An outbreak of **cholera** occurred in the Rumonge District in 1999; although there is no official requirement for certification of **cholera vaccination**, there are reports that certification is required for visa purposes and even entry through customs. Proof of **vaccination against meningococcal meningitis** is an entry requirement.

The Comoros

Malaria risk exists all year, is predominantly the falciparum form and chloroquine resistant. Mefloquine is the recommended prophylaxis. There are no official entry requirements although some travellers from infected areas have

been asked to provide a **yellow fever immunization** certificate. An outbreak of **cholera** occurred on Anjouan Island in 1999.

Djibouti

Malaria risk exists throughout the year, is predominantly the falciparum form and chloroquine resistant. Mefloquine is the recommended prophylaxis. **Yellow fever vaccination** is required from travellers over 1 year of age coming from infected areas.

Eritrea

Malaria risk exists in all lowland areas below 2000m. The predominant form is falciparum and chloroquine resistance is common. Mefloquine is the recommended prophylaxis. **Yellow fever vaccination** is required from travellers coming from infected areas. **Altitude** may cause health problems in some areas.

Ethiopia

Malaria risk exists in all lowland areas (below 2000m) throughout the year. There is no risk in Addis Ababa. The predominant form is falciparum and chloroquine resistance is common. A large outbreak of **meningococcal meningitis** occurred in Addis Ababa and the regions of Amhara, Gambella and Tigray in 2000, as well as an **anthrax** outbreak in the Afar region. High rates of **relapsing fever**, **onchocerciasis** and **leishmaniasis** (cutaneous and visceral) have been reported; cutaneous leishmaniasis is particularly prevalent in high-altitude areas (over 4000m) in the west whereas the visceral form has high prevalence in the south, southwestern and northwestern areas. **African trypanosomiasis** is endemic in the western lowlands. **Schistosomiasis** is common with an estimated

2.5 million Ethiopians affected. **Altitude** may cause problems in Addis Ababa. **Yellow fever vaccination** is required from travellers over 1 year of age coming from infected areas.

Kenya

Malaria risk exists throughout the country year-round (although the risk is low in Nairobi). The most severely affected districts are Buret, Gucha, Kisii, Mount Elgon, Narok, Nyamira, Trans Mara, Trans Nzoia and West Pokot. The predominant form is falciparum and chloroquine resistance is common. Mefloquine is the recommended prophylaxis. **Yellow fever** risk exists in all rural areas; **vaccination** is required for anyone over 1 year old entering from endemic areas. **Cholera** has been reported in recent years from Nyanza, Eastern, Rift Valley and Nairobi provinces, and proof of **vaccination** may be required from some travellers arriving from cholera-infected areas, even though it's no longer an international requirement. Outbreaks of **Marburg virus** have been reported in Kenya, but are likely to be an insignificant risk to the average traveller. **Plague** has been reported in some remote rural areas.

Madagascar

Malaria risk exists year-round all over the country but is particularly high in coastal areas. The prevalent variety is chloroquine-resistant falciparum, and mefloquine is the recommended prophylaxis. A large outbreak of **cholera** occurred in the provinces of Antananarivo, Antsiranana, Fianarantsoa, Mahajanga, Toamasina and Toliary in 1999 and 2000, resulting in a large number of fatalities. **Plague** occurs in parts of Antananarivo, Antsiranana, Fianarantsoa, Mahajanga and Toamasina provinces. **Yellow fever vacci-**

nation is required for all travellers coming from, or having passed through, infected areas.

Malawi

Malaria risk exists all year, is predominantly the falciparum form and chloroquine resistant. Mefloquine is the recommended prophylaxis. A number of cases of **plague** were reported in 1999 from the Nsanje District. **Yellow fever vaccination** is required of travellers arriving from infected areas.

Mauritius

Malaria risk (predominantly vivax) exists in localized rural areas only and is greatest in the north. Chloroquine alone is sufficient prophylaxis, although no prophylaxis is needed if your stay is restricted to urban areas. There is no risk at all on Rodriguez Island. **Yellow fever vaccination** is required for travellers over 1 year of age coming from infected areas. A **HIV test** is required of all foreigners applying for a working visa or permanent residence (foreign tests may be accepted – contact the embassy for further details).

Mayotte

Malaria risk exists all year, is predominantly the falciparum form and chloroquine resistant. Mefloquine is the recommended prophylaxis.

Mozambique

Malaria risk exists year-round, is predominantly the falciparum form and chloroquine resistant. A large **cholera** epidemic has been ongoing since 1997. **Plague** has been reported from Tete and Zambezia provinces. **Yellow fever vaccination** is required from travellers over 1 year of age entering from infected areas.

EAST AFRICA

Reunion

Yellow fever vaccination is required for anyone over 1 year of age coming from infected areas.

Rwanda

Malaria risk exists throughout the country all year, is predominantly the falciparum form and chloroquine resistant. Mefloquine is the recommended prophylaxis. The recent civil war has resulted in an increase in the incidence of diseases in general, particularly those associated with contaminated water supplies. **Yellow fever** risk exists in all but urban centres; **vaccination** is required for anyone over the age of 1. Outbreaks of **cholera** are frequent, and customs officials may demand proof of immunization against it.

Seychelles

Yellow fever vaccination is required from travellers over 1 year of age coming from infected areas. Certification is also required from travellers who have passed through areas in the endemic zones within the preceding 6 days.

Somalia

Malaria risk exists year-round, is predominantly the falciparum form and chloroquine resistant. Mefloquine is the recommended prophylaxis. The war has caused an increase in incidence of many diseases, particularly **cholera** – a large epidemic in 2000 resulted in many deaths, principally in Bay, Lower Juba, Lower Shabelle, Mogadishu and Madug. **Yellow fever vaccination** is required of travellers coming from infected areas.

Uganda

Malaria risk exists throughout the country including some of the larger regional towns (Fort Portal, Jinja, Kampala,

Mbale and parts of Kigezi). **Yellow fever** risk exists in all but urban areas. Internal reports identify high rates of **HIV** infection in several areas (Kampala and the eastern towns of Malaba and Busia). **African trypanosomiasis** is common in two geographical belts, one heading northeast from the northern shores of Lake Victoria, and the other extending north from Lake Edward affecting the entire Uganda/Sudan border. **Plague** has been reported in the Arua and Nebbi districts. **Yellow fever vaccination** is required from travellers over 1 year of age coming from endemic areas.

United Republic of Tanzania

Malaria risk exists in all lowland areas including Pemba and Zanzibar islands. Risk of **yellow fever** is reportedly highest in the northwestern forest areas (low throughout the rest of the country). Yellow fever **vaccination** is required from travellers over 1 year of age coming from infected and endemic areas. Risk of **schistosomiasis** is particularly high in Lake Malawi. Outbreaks of **plague** have been reported in the Tanga Region.

Southern Africa

Botswana, Lesotho, Namibia, St Helena, South Africa, Swaziland, Zimbabwe

Diarrhoeal disease from a variety of causes is common, particularly in rural areas. Risk of **malaria** exists all year in certain regions. Chloroquine resistance is common. **Dengue fever** occurs in epidemics in the region, particularly South Africa, Swaziland and Zimbabwe. **Schistosomiasis** risk exists in Botswana, Namibia, South Africa (especially northern and eastern regions) and Swaziland (prevalent in all streams and lakes below 1200m) and to a lesser extent in Zimbabwe. **Rabies** occurs throughout the region with the exception of St Helena and, reportedly, Lesotho. Risk of **typhoid fever** exists throughout the region especially when travelling outside the cities. **Hepatitis A** and **B** infection are common. **Influenza** risk exists throughout the year in Botswana, and from May to October in Lesotho, Namibia south of the Tropic of Capricorn, South Africa and Swaziland. **Cholera** outbreaks occur throughout the region, but risk is low provided the usual food- and drink-hygiene measures are observed. **Crimean–Congo haemorrhagic fever**, **relapsing fever**, **Rift Valley fever**, **typhus** (mainly tick-borne), **African trypanosomiasis** (Botswana and Namibia only), **leishmaniasis**, **trachoma**, **onchocerciasis**, **chikungunya fever**, **plague** (sporadic, isolated pockets) and **echinococcosis** all occur to varying degrees. **Worm infections** are common, and **snakes** and **scorpions** are a risk in some areas. The dry and dusty climate of some parts of the region increases the risk of **respiratory problems** in susceptible individuals.

Botswana

Malaria risk exists in the northern part of the country and is highest from November to June. A combination of chloroquine and proguanil, or mefloquine are the suggested prophylaxis. **African trypanosomiasis** occurs in the Moremi Wildlife Reserve and western areas of the Chobe National Park.

Lesotho

There is no reported risk of malaria, schistosomiasis or rabies in Lesotho. **Yellow fever vaccination** is required from travellers entering from infected areas.

Namibia

Malaria risk is highest between November and June in northern regions and Omaheke and Otjozondjupa, and throughout the year along the Kavango and Kunene rivers. Chloroquine resistance has been reported and a combination of chloroquine and proguanil is the suggested prophylaxis. Rare outbreaks of **plague** have been reported in the Ohangwena region. Sporadic cases of **meningococcal meningitis** occur in Windhoek and in the north. **Yellow fever vaccination** is required from travellers entering from infected and endemic areas.

St Helena

There is no reported malaria risk on St Helena, and risk of other diseases is low compared to other African countries. **Yellow fever vaccination** is required from travellers over 1 year old entering from infected areas.

South Africa

Malaria risk (predominantly falciparum) exists in Mpumalanga Province (including the Kruger National Park), Northern Province and the KwaZulu-Natal coastal areas north of the Tugela River throughout the year but is highest between October and May. Chloroquine resistance is reported from the Venda and KwaZulu areas, and the recommended prophylaxis is either a combination of chloroquine and proguanil or mefloquine alone. Animal cases of **rabies** are particularly common in KwaZulu-Natal, Eastern Cape and Eastern Transvaal. **Yellow fever vaccination** is required from travellers over the age of 1 entering from infected or endemic areas.

Swaziland

Malaria risk (mainly falciparum) in all non-mountainous areas of the country exists year-round but is particularly high in the rainy season (Nov–Feb) and in the areas of Big Bend, Mhlume, Simunye and Tshaneni. Chloroquine resistance is widespread and mefloquine is the recommended prophylaxis. Damp weather conditions in the high veld can aggravate **asthma** and other **respiratory problems**.

Zimbabwe

With the exceptions of Bulawayo and Harare, **malaria** risk (predominantly falciparum) exists countrywide below 1200m. The risks are particularly high between November and June, with the exception of the Zambezi Valley where the risk is high all year. Chloroquine resistance is common and mefloquine is the recommended prophylaxis. Anyone travelling to Victoria Falls should take malaria prophylaxis. **Plague** occurs in isolated pockets of Matabeleland North Province, with the highest risk between September and February.

SOUTHERN AFRICA

Australia and the South Pacific

American Samoa, Australia, Christmas Island, Cook Islands, Federated States of Micronesia, Fiji, French Polynesia, Guam, Kiribati, Marshall Islands, Nauru, New Caledonia, New Zealand, Niue, Northern Mariana Islands, Palau, Papua New Guinea, Pitcairn Island, Samoa, Solomon Islands, Tokelau, Tonga, Tuvalu, Vanuatu, Wake Island, Wallis and Futuna

Diarrhoeal diseases of a variety of causes are not uncommon in the South Pacific islands. Falciparum **malaria** risk exists in Papua New Guinea, Vanuatu and the Solomon Islands – infection rates in the Solomon Islands are among the highest in the world. There is no risk of contracting **yellow fever** in any of the countries in this region, but many require proof of immunization if you are travelling from an infected country. **Dengue fever** occurs sporadically throughout the region, except New Zealand and only rarely in northern Australia. Dengue haemorrhagic fever has also been reported. **Typhoid fever** is prevalent throughout the South Pacific, particularly in less developed rural areas. With the exception of southern temperate regions of Australia, New Zealand and Pitcairn Island (risk from May–Oct), **influenza** risk exists throughout the year in all other countries of the region. Sporadic outbreaks of

hepatitis A and **cholera** occur on some islands of the South Pacific. **Filariasis** occurs rarely throughout the South Pacific and **worm infections** are common. Periodic outbreaks of **Japanese encephalitis** have been reported from a number of South Pacific islands but they are rare and the risk to travellers is very low. Prevalence of **hepatitis B** is high in the South Pacific islands but low in Australia and New Zealand. **Trachoma** occurs in some parts of Micronesia. The hot, tropical climate apparent throughout much of the area leads to an increased incidence of **skin** and **wound infections**. All cuts should be cleaned thoroughly. **Sharks** are present off many of the coastlines and, although attacks are rare, they do occur. Other **maritime hazards** include sea snakes, jellyfish, poisonous fish and coral. **Ciguatera** (and scombrotoxic poisoning) has been reported from many parts of the region although is rare.

American Samoa

Rare outbreaks of **Japanese encephalitis** have been reported and outbreaks of **dengue fever** occur sporadically. **Yellow fever vaccination** is required for travellers over 1 year of age coming from infected areas.

Australia

A variety of **mosquito-borne viral illnesses** (Barmah Forest virus, Murray Valley virus and Ross River fever) occur in epidemics mainly in Queensland, New South Wales, Western Australia and the Northern Territory. **Dengue fever** occurs sporadically mainly in northern Queensland. **Japanese encephalitis** has been reported on Badu Island (Torres Strait) and on the northern tip of the Cape York Peninsula between March and April, but risk to travellers is very low. **Tick-borne rickettsial spotted fevers** occur although outbreaks are rare. **Melioidosis** occurs rarely in tropical northern areas. **Giardia** and **cryptosporidium** may contaminate the water supplies from time to time. Australia is free of rabies but a rabies-like illness has been reported in fruit bats (**lyssa virus**). An outbreak of **legionnaires' disease** in Melbourne in early 2000 was traced to the aquarium. **Snakes** are found throughout Australia and are some of the most venomous in the world. Venomous **spiders** are also ubiquitous. Deadly box **jellyfish** are a hazard when swimming off the beaches of the north and the northeast between September and April. **Crocodiles** are found in many freshwater lakes and rivers of the north. **HIV testing** is required for all applicants for permanent residency over 15; others may be tested if there are grounds for clinical suspicion after a medical examination. Foreign tests may be accepted. **Yellow fever vaccination** is required from travellers over 1 year old if they have departed from an infected country having stayed overnight within the previous 6 days.

Christmas Island

Yellow fever vaccination is required for anyone over the age of 1 if they have travelled from an infected country having stayed overnight within the previous 6 days.

Federated States of Micronesia

Rare outbreaks of **cholera** and **Japanese encephalitis** have been reported from some islands. An outbreak of **cholera** on Pohnpei Island in 2000 resulted in a number of fatalities. A **HIV test** is required for work-permit applicants and anyone staying longer than 90 days.

Fiji

Yellow fever vaccination is required for visitors over 1 year old entering the country within 10 days of departing from an infected area.

French Polynesia

Yellow fever vaccination is required for all travellers over 1 year old entering from an infected country.

Guam

Japanese encephalitis has been reported in rare outbreaks between September and January (likely to have been imported).

Kiribati

Periodic outbreaks of **typhoid** occur. The lagoon in South Tarawa is highly polluted and swimming should be avoided there. **Yellow fever vaccination** is required from travellers over 1 year of age coming from infected areas.

Marshall Islands

Rare outbreaks of **cholera** occur. **HIV testing** is required for travellers planning to stay longer than 30 days and for those applying for work or residency visas. Foreign tests may be accepted.

Nauru

Outbreaks of **Japanese encephalitis** have been reported in the past. **Yellow fever vaccination** is required from travellers over 1 year of age coming from infected areas.

New Caledonia

Yellow fever vaccination is required from travellers over 1 year of age coming from infected areas.

New Zealand

A recent increase in the incidence of **cryptosporidiosis** has been reported from the Hawkes Bay area.

Niue

Yellow fever vaccination is required from travellers over 1 year of age coming from infected areas.

Northern Mariana Islands

Rare outbreaks of **Japanese encephalitis** (probably imported) have been reported, with the risk highest between September and January.

Palau

Yellow fever vaccination is required from all travellers over 1 year of age coming from infected areas or from countries where yellow fever is endemic.

Papua New Guinea

Malaria risk exists countrywide below 1800m (predominantly falciparum, vivax to a lesser extent) all year. Chloroquine resistance is very common and doxycycline is the antimalarial of choice. **TB** is common in the indigenous population. **Hepatitis A**, **typhoid**, **Japanese encephalitis** and **mite-borne typhus** occur sporadically. **HIV testing** is required for most people seeking a work or residency permit – aid workers and diplomatic staff are exempt. **Yellow fever vaccination** is required from travellers over 1 year of age coming from infected areas.

Pitcairn Island

Yellow fever vaccination is required for travellers over 1 year of age coming from infected areas.

Samoa

Yellow fever vaccination is required for anyone over 1 year old coming from infected areas.

Solomon Islands

Malaria risk is high across the islands (except southern and eastern outlying islets) all year, and incidence is rising. The predominant form is falciparum and chloroquine resistance is common. Doxycycline is the first-choice antimalarial. Rare outbreaks of **Japanese encephalitis** have been reported. **Yellow fever vaccination** is required of all travellers coming from infected areas.

Tonga

Sporadic outbreaks of **Japanese encephalitis occur**. **Yellow fever vaccination** is required from travellers over 1 year of age coming from infected areas.

Tuvalu

Rare outbreaks of **cholera** and **Japanese encephalitis** have been reported.

Vanuatu

Moderate **malaria** risk (predominantly falciparum) exists year-round. Chloroquine resistance is widespread and doxycycline is the recommended antimalarial. Rare outbreaks of **Japanese encephalitis** and **typhus** (mite- and tick-borne) occur.

Wake Island

There are no specific vaccination requirements for international travellers.

AUSTRALIA AND THE SOUTH PACIFIC

Eastern Europe and the NIS

Albania, Armenia, Azerbaijan, Belarus, Bosnia/Herzegovina, Bulgaria, Croatia, Czech Republic, Estonia, Georgia, Hungary, Kazakhstan, Kyrgyzstan, Latvia, Lithuania, Moldova, Poland, Romania, Russia, Serbia/Montenegro, Slovak Republic, Slovenia, Tajikistan, Turkmenistan, Ukraine, Uzbekistan

Health risks have become more common since the collapse of the former Soviet Union because of a deterioration in sanitary standards, the dysfunction of normal public-health measures and the short supply of drugs and immunizations. In particular there is a high risk of **water-borne infection** throughout the NIS and outbreaks of **diphtheria** became commonplace in the 1990s due to the breakdown of the standard childhood immunization programmes. Incidence has fallen since their reintroduction in the latter part of the decade. Travellers to this region should be particularly diligent in ensuring that their **normal childhood vaccinations** (particularly polio, tetanus and diphtheria) are up-to-date (boosters are recommended every 10 years). Longer-term travellers should check their **BCG** (TB) status and consider vaccination against **hepatitis B**.

Trichinellosis is relatively common in the region. Risk of **malaria** is restricted only to the Ararat Valley of

Armenia, isolated parts of Turkmenistan and the southern borders Azerbaijan, Tajikistan and Uzbekistan. There is a moderate risk of **hepatitis A** and **typhoid** throughout the area (particularly rural areas). **Respiratory tract infections** are prevalent in autumn and winter, whereas **gastrointestinal infections** are common in spring and summer. **Influenza** epidemics occur between November and April. Infrequent outbreaks of **cholera** have been reported from some countries. **Rabies** is found throughout the area (carried mainly by foxes). **Tick-borne encephalitis** and **Lyme disease** occur in rural forested areas of Central and Eastern Europe during summer. **Crimean-Congo haemorrhagic fever**, **tulareamia** and **rodent-borne hantavirus infection** occur in rare outbreaks.

Albania

Leishmaniasis (cutaneous and visceral), **sand-fly fever**, **West Nile fever**, **echinococcosis**, **brucellosis** and **typhus** (murine and tick-borne) have been reported, although all are rare. A **yellow fever vaccination** certificate is required from travellers over 1 year of age coming from infected areas.

Armenia

Vivax **malaria** risk exists, although low, between June and October in the Ararat Valley (Ararat, Artashat and Masis). Chloroquine alone is adequate prophylaxis. **Leishmaniasis** (cutaneous), **hepatitis E**, **echinococcosis** and **brucellosis** have been reported.

Azerbaijan

Vivax **malaria** risk exists between June and October in the southern lowland areas, the Baku suburbs, and the

Khachmas region on the northeast coast. Chloroquine alone is adequate prophylaxis. **Leishmaniasis** (cutaneous and visceral), **trachoma**, **echinococcosis** and **brucellosis** have been reported although are rare. **Plague** occurs in sporadic outbreaks in the south.

Belarus
Leishmaniasis has been reported in rare outbreaks. A **HIV test** is required of anyone staying more than 3 months.

Bosnia/Herzegovina
Dysentery and other gastrointestinal infections are particularly rife because of the disruption to water supplies and sanitation caused by fighting in the region. **Typhus** (murine and tick-borne) and **leptospirosis** occur though rarely.

Bulgaria
All foreigners planning to stay longer than 1 month for work or study are required to undergo an **HIV test**. Foreign tests may be acceptable – contact the embassy for further information.

Croatia
Typhus (murine and tick-borne) has been reported in rare outbreaks.

Czech Republic
Rocky Mountain spotted fever, as well as **tick-borne encephalitis** and **Lyme disease** occur in rare outbreaks in rural, forested areas.

Estonia
HIV testing is required for foreigners requesting work

permits or residency, and foreign tests may be acceptable – contact the embassy for further details.

Georgia

Vivax **malaria** exists in pockets in the southeastern part of the country between July and October; however, risk to travellers is low and chloroquine alone is suitable prophylaxis. **Leishmaniasis** (cutaneous and visceral), **Crimean-Congo haemorrhagic fever**, **echinococcosis** and **brucellosis** occur. An outbreak of **anthrax** occurred in Tbilisi in 1999, and rare outbreaks of **plague** have been reported from the south. A **HIV test** is required from all foreigners staying longer than 1 month. Foreign tests may be acceptable provided they are performed within the last 30 days.

Hungary

An outbreak of **meningococcal meningitis** occurred in 1999. **HIV testing** is required for anyone intending to stay more than 1 year. Foreign tests may be acceptable – contact the embassy for details.

Kazakhstan

Typhus (tick-borne), **leishmaniasis**, **Crimean-Congo haemorrhagic fever**, **brucellosis**, **trichinellosis** and isolated occurrences of **plague** have been reported although all are rare. **HIV testing** is required for visitors staying more than 3 months and must be undertaken within the month prior to arrival. **Yellow fever vaccination** is required from travellers coming from infected areas.

Kyrgyzstan

Typhus (tick-borne) and isolated foci of **plague** have been reported, although both are rare. Excluding diplomatic staff, **HIV testing** is required for visits longer than 1 month.

Latvia

Plague has been reported in the south. A **HIV test** is required for anyone over 15 applying for a residency permit.

Lithuania

Plague has been reported but is very rare. **Crimean-Congo haemorrhagic fever** occurs similarly in rare outbreaks. **HIV testing** is required for anyone applying for a permanent residency permit, and foreign tests may be accepted – check with the embassy.

Moldova

Brucellosis, **leishmaniasis** and **typhus** (tick-borne) occur although all are rare. **Plague** has been reported in the south. **HIV testing** is required for any visitors staying longer than 3 months. Foreign tests may be accepted – contact the embassy.

Poland

Air pollution, particularly in the Krakow area, may cause exacerbation of **respiratory conditions**.

Romania

Rare **West Nile fever** outbreaks have been reported in the southeast. **Brucellosis** occurs sporadically although risk to the traveller is low. An outbreak of viral **meningitis** occurred in the northern and eastern areas of the country in 1999.

Russia

Outbreaks of **Japanese encephalitis** have been reported from the southeast. **Leishmaniasis** occurs in the south, and in 1999 an outbreak of **Crimean-Congo haemorrhagic**

fever occurred in the area north of Stavropol. Outbreaks of **meningitis** have been reported from Volgograd. **Tick-borne typhus** occurs in central and eastern Siberia. Contaminated tap water causes a high prevalence of **gastrointestinal infections**. The water supply in St Petersburg especially has been linked to **giardiasis** (also common in the western regions). **Dysentery** is common throughout the country.

A negative **HIV test** is necessary for anyone applying for a visa to stay longer than 3 months, and the certification requirements are exacting and detailed. A medical examination may also be required. Foreign tests may be acceptable under certain conditions – check details with the embassy.

Serbia/Montenegro

Recent hostilities in the area have increased the risk of **water-borne illnesses** as well as rendering drugs and medical equipment in short supply. **Tick-borne encephalitis** occurs in rare outbreaks in forested areas and **leishmaniasis** is rare along the coastal areas. An outbreak of **tularaemia** occurred in western Kosovo in 2000. Murine and tick-borne **typhus** occur but again are rare.

Slovak Republic

Rocky Mountain spotted fever, **tick-borne encephalitis** and **Lyme disease** occur (though rarely) in rural, forested areas. **HIV testing** is required for long-term or permanent residency visas, and foreign tests may be accepted.

Slovenia

Murine and tick-borne **typhus** occur in rare outbreaks.

Tajikistan

Malaria (principally chloroquine-sensitive vivax) risk

exists between June and October, particularly in southern border areas (Khatlon region), and in some central (Dushanbe), western (Gorno-Badakhshan) and northern (Leninobod region) areas. Chloroquine alone is sufficient prophylaxis. **Trachoma** is common, while **Crimean-Congo haemorrhagic fever**, **typhus**, **leishmaniasis**, **sand-fly fever**, **tick-borne relapsing fever**, **brucellosis** and **echinococcosis** all occur but risks to the traveller are low. Rare occurrences of **plague** have been reported. A **HIV test** is required for all foreigners planning to stay longer than 90 days. Foreign tests may be acceptable.

Turkmenistan

Malaria (exclusively vivax) risk exists in the southeast of the country (mainly the Mary district) between June and October. Chloroquine alone is recommended as the most suitable prophylaxis. **Crimean-Congo haemorrhagic fever**, **typhus**, **visceral leishmaniasis**, **sand-fly fever**, **tick-borne relapsing fever**, **brucellosis** and **echinococcosis** all occur, but risks to the traveller are low. Epidemics of **hepatitis E** occur, and **trachoma** is common. **Plague** has been reported. A **yellow fever vaccination** certificate is required from all travellers arriving from infected areas. **HIV testing** may also be required.

Ukraine

Leishmaniasis, **sand-fly fever** and **plague** are all rare but have been reported. A **HIV test** is required for all applications for residency and for stays longer than 6 months. Foreign tests are accepted under certain conditions.

Uzbekistan

Crimean-Congo haemorrhagic fever, **typhus**, **leishmaniasis**, **sand-fly fever**, **tick-borne relapsing fever**,

brucellosis and **echinococcosis** have been reported. **Trachoma** is relatively common. **HIV testing** is required for anyone staying more than 15 days (organized tours may be exempt). Longer-term travellers are required to have their certification renewed after 3 months and annually thereafter. Foreign tests are accepted in certain conditions.

EASTERN EUROPE AND THE NIS

The Far East

Brunei Darussalam, Cambodia, China, Hong Kong, Indonesia, Japan, Laos, Macau, Malaysia, Mongolia, Myanmar (Burma), North Korea, the Philippines, Singapore, South Korea, Taiwan, Thailand, Vietnam

Diarrhoeal disease from a variety of causes is common throughout the Far East. **Giardiasis**, **dysentery**, **typhoid fever** and **hepatitis A** are widespread throughout the region (though Japan is relatively low risk). **Cholera** is also a risk in some areas. Significant **malaria** risk exists in Cambodia, southern China, Indonesia, Laos, Malaysia, Myanmar, the Philippines, Thailand and Vietnam. In some countries there is urban as well as rural risk. Mefloquine is the recommended malaria prophylaxis in the Far East, although mefloquine resistance has been reported in parts of Thailand. Chloroquine is still useful in parts of the Philippines. Risk is small, and very geographically limited, in Hong Kong and South Korea. There is no risk of malaria in Brunei Darussalam, Japan, North Korea, Macau, Mongolia, Singapore and Taiwan. Although there is no risk of contracting **yellow fever** in any of these countries, some may require proof of vaccination if you are travelling from an infected or endemic area. Epidemics of **dengue fever** are common in all countries, but particularly southern China and Taiwan. **Schistosomiasis** occurs along the Mekong delta in Cambodia and Vietnam with specific, localized areas of potential risk existing in China (eastern and southeastern regions), Indonesia, Laos and the Philippines. It is endemic in

THE FAR EAST

the southern Philippines and central Sulawesi. Risk of **rabies** exists in the area although is reportedly low in Singapore, the Malaysian islands and parts of Indonesia. (Taiwan and Japan are rabies-free.) **Typhoid** risk exists in all of these countries (low in Japan) especially in rural areas. **Influenza** risk extends throughout the year in Brunei Darussalam, Cambodia, Hong Kong, Indonesia, Laos, Macau, Malaysia, Myanmar, the Philippines, Singapore, Thailand and Vietnam, and from November to April in China, Japan, Mongolia, North Korea, South Korea and Taiwan. Risk of contracting **Japanese encephalitis** is slight but nevertheless exists in rural areas of most countries in the Far East – peak incidence is during the rainy season (April–Oct). If you plan to stay in rural areas, especially for more than a month, consider vaccination. **Filariasis** is prevalent in rural areas and **chikungunya fever**, **leishmaniasis** (visceral and cutaneous), **Crimean-Congo haemorrhagic fever** and **typhus** (mite-borne, mainly in deforested areas) all occur to varying degrees in the region although the risks to travellers are small. Rates of **hepatitis B** are high throughout the region. Rare outbreaks of **plague** occur in China, Mongolia, Myanmar and Vietnam. Fasciolopsiasis, paragonimiasis and clonorchiasis occur in most countries and **worm infections** as a whole are common throughout the area. **Hepatitis C and E**, **melioidosis**, **leptospirosis**, **Korean haemorrhagic fever**, **gnathostomiasis**, **echinococcosis** and **brucellosis** occur sporadically. **Trachoma** is present in some countries (most notably China). **Rhesus negative blood type** is rare in the Far East.

Longer-term travellers should check their **BCG** (TB) status, ensure all standard **childhood immunizations** (particularly polio, tetanus and diphtheria) are up-to-date and consider vaccination against **hepatitis B** and **Japanese encephalitis**.

Brunei Darussalam

A **cholera** outbreak was reported from the Muara District in 1999. **Yellow fever vaccination** is required from travellers over 1 year of age coming from, or having passed through in the preceding 6 days, infected or endemic areas. There may be a slight **malaria** risk along border areas.

Cambodia

Malaria risk (mainly falciparum) exists throughout the year except for in Phnom Penh and the vicinity of Tonle Sap. This includes Angkor Wat. Chloroquine resistance is common and mefloquine resistance has been reported from western provinces. Except for the western provinces where doxycycline is the preferred choice, mefloquine is the recommended prophylaxis. A **cholera** epidemic recently occurred in the Rottanakiri province in the northeast. **Japanese encephalitis** occurs in rural areas May to October and is relatively common. **Yellow fever vaccination** is required from travellers coming from infected areas.

China

Two varieties of **malaria** predominate in China: vivax and falciparum. Risks are very low in tourist areas, the main cities and all areas above 1500m. Where transmission exists, it tends to be seasonal, occurring from July to November north of latitude 33°N, from May to December between 33°N and 25°N, and throughout the year south of 25°N. Falciparum predominates in Hainan and Yunnan and, in these areas, mefloquine is the recommended prophylaxis. Vivax malaria has been reported from the following provinces: Anhui, Fujian, Guangdong, Guangxi, Guizhou, Hainan, Hubei, Hunan, Jiangsu, Jiangxi, Shandong, Shanghai, Sichuan, Xinjiang (only along the valley of the Yili River), Xizang (only along the valley of Zangbo River in the extreme southeast), Yunnan and Zhejiang. In these areas, chloroquine alone is considered adequate prophylaxis.

Japanese encephalitis is a risk in rural areas of the north between May and September and in the south from April to October. **Hepatitis B** rates are high in China and **hepatitis E** is prevalent in northeastern and northwestern areas. **Tuberculosis** is common in the native population. **Schistosomiasis** is found in many rivers and lakes of south-eastern and eastern regions along the valley of Chang Jiang (Yangtze) River and its tributaries. It is estimated that 1 million Chinese are affected by the disease. **Filariasis** occurs in south China and **cutaneous leishmaniasis** has been recently reported from Xinjiang (Tibetan Auto-nomous Region). A new strain of **cholera** (Bengal cholera) has appeared in western areas. **Rabid dogs** present a problem in China with estimates quoting up to 1 million people being bitten each year. Dust in Tibet and pollution elsewhere in the large cities may exacerbate **respiratory conditions**. **Altitude sickness** is a risk in the Tibetan Auto-nomous Region, Qinghai, Xinjiang, and parts of Sichuan, Yannan and Gansu. It can be difficult to find Western brand-name, non-prescription drugs throughout China.

Yellow fever vaccination is required from travellers coming from infected areas.

Hong Kong

There may also be slight **malaria** risk in some border and rural areas (Mirs Bay, Sai Kung and Yuen Long) although prophylaxis is not considered necessary. There is low risk of **Japanese encephalitis** in the New Territories between April and October.

Indonesia

Malaria risk is mainly restricted to rural areas and exists throughout the year. Around 75,000 cases of malaria are reported each year in Indonesia with the falciparum type accounting for roughly half. For most of the country, a combination of chloroquine and proguanil is adequate prophylaxis. However, there is particularly high risk in Irian Jaya where there is chloroquine resistance and here mefloquine is recommended. There is low (probably neglible) risk in the cities and in the resort areas of Bali and Java. There is low risk of **Japanese encephalitis** in rural areas year round (higher risk Nov–March). **Trachoma** has been reported although risk to travellers is very low. **Yellow fever vaccination** is required from travellers coming from infected and endemic areas.

Japan

Compared to the other countries in the region, health risks in Japan are low. **Japanese encephalitis** risk, although slight, exists from June to September in rural areas (April–Oct in Okinawa/Ryukyu islands). There is no risk in the major cities and urban areas. Pollution in Tokyo and some other large cities may exacerbate **respiratory problems**. **Filariasis** has been reported. Tap water is safe to drink. **Paragonamiasis** is a risk from eating raw fish.

Laos

Malaria risk exists in all areas throughout the year except the city of Vientiane. The majority of cases are caused by the falciparum type and chloroquine resistance is common. Mefloquine is the recommended prophylaxis. The low risk of **Japanese encephalitis** is greatest in rural areas from May to October. **Schistosomiasis** occurs in the Khong district of the south. **Yellow fever vaccination** is required from travellers coming from infected areas.

Macau

Rare cases of **Japanese encephalitis** have been reported.

Malaysia

Malaria risk (predominantly falciparum) is minimal in the towns and coastal areas of Peninsular Malaysia and Sarawak and is mainly restricted to the more remote, inland, rural, forested areas. Prophylaxis is only recommended if you are venturing deep into the rural forested areas and a combination of chloroquine and proguanil is considered adequate. There is a high malaria risk throughout the year in Sabah where chloroquine resistance is common and mefloquine is the recommended prophylaxis. A new and virulent strain of **cholera** has been reported in some areas. It is resistant to the normal cholera vaccination. Infection has been reported from Kuala Lumpur and Selangor states. Low risk of **Japanese encephalitis** exists in some rural areas with the majority of cases previously reported from Johor, Penang, Perak, Sarawak and Selangor. Travellers to the Taman Negara National Park should be particularly alert to the risks of **insect**, **leech** and **snake bites**. **Yellow fever vaccination** is required from travellers over 1 year of age coming from infected and endemic areas.

Mongolia

Meningococcal meningitis outbreaks occur in Mongolia (the 1994 epidemic was the B strain for which the standard vaccination is ineffective). **Plague** has been reported from the provinces of Uvs and Uvuhangai. A HIV test may be required for those staying longer than 3 months.

Myanmar (Burma)

Malaria risk (primarily falciparum) exists mainly in rural areas below 1000m and tends to be seasonal: throughout

the year in Karen State; from March to December in Chin, Kachin, Kayah, Mon, Rakhine and Shan states, Pegu Division, and the Hlegu, Hmawbi and Taikkyi townships of Yangon (formerly Rangoon) Division; from April to December in the rural areas of Tenasserim Division; from May to December in Irrawaddy Division and the rural areas of Mandalay Division; and from June to November in the rural areas of Magwe Division, and in Sagaing Division. Risks are minimal for visitors to the cities of Yangon (Rangoon) and Mandalay. Chloroquine resistance is common and mefloquine is the recommended prophylaxis although resistance is reported along border areas with Thailand. Risks from **Japanese encephalitis**, although low, are highest in rural areas between May and October. Outbreaks are particularly common in Shan State in the Chiang Mai Valley. **Visceral leishmaniasis** is prevalent and **trachoma** is reported. Cases of Bengal **cholera** have been reported. **Yellow fever vaccination** is required from travellers coming from infected areas. Nationals and residents are required to be appropriately immunized before departing to an infected area.

North Korea

Low **malaria** risk (predominantly vivax) exists in southern areas. No prophylaxis is necessary. Infection rates for **Japanese encephalitis** are unavailable but consider immunization if you are planning to visit a rural area between May and October. **Hantavirus** infection has been reported but is very rare.

The Philippines

Malaria risk (predominantly falciparum) exists mainly in rural areas below 600 metres throughout the year although there is no risk in Manila City and in the islands of Bohol,

◁ Medicinal herbs, China. Photo © Adam Woolfitt/Corbis

Catanduanes and Cebu. Low risk exists in the provinces Aklan, Biliran, Camiguin, Capiz, Guimaras, Iloilo, Leyte del Sur, Northern Samar and Sequijor. Highest risk exists in the Palawan group and the northern central provinces of Luzon and Mindanao. Generally a combination of chloroquine and proguanil is the recommended prophylaxis although chloroquine resistance is reported from islands of Basilan, Luzon, Mindanao, Mindoro, Palawan and the Sulu Archipelago, where mefloquine is the alternative. **Japanese encephalitis** occurs rarely in western Luzon, Mindoro and Palawan from April to November and throughout the year in other areas, with highest risk from April to January. **Chikungunya fever** is particularly common in urban areas of the central islands (eg Manila). **Gonorrhoea** resistant to penicillin is common in the Philippines, particularly in Manila and Cebu City. **Yellow fever vaccination** is required from travellers over 1 year of age coming from infected areas. All applicants for a permanent residency visa are required to undergo a medical examination which includes a **HIV test**.

Singapore

HIV testing is required for workers who earn less than $1250 per month and for applicants for permanent resident status. Foreign test results are not accepted. **Yellow fever vaccination** is required from travellers over 1 year of age coming from, or having passed through in the preceding 6 days, infected or endemic areas.

South Korea

Malaria risk exists in the northern part of Kyonggi-Do Province (vivax type) although this does not present a risk to the average traveller as it is a demilitarized zone. No prophylaxis is necessary. **Japanese encephalitis** occurs sporadically in rural areas between July and October. **Lymphatic filariasis** and **typhus** (mite- and tick-borne) occur although pose little risk to the traveller. **HIV tests** are required for some long-stay visitors – contact the embassy for further details.

Taiwan

Japanese encephalitis occurs sporadically in some rural areas between April and October, although rare cases have been reported around the Taipei area. **Filariasis** and **visceral leishmaniasis** occur although are unlikely to pose a significant risk to travellers. **Yellow fever vaccination** is required from travellers coming from infected areas. **HIV testing** is required for applicants for residency and work permits, and for anyone staying longer than 90 days. Foreign test results are accepted under certain conditions; contact the embassy for details. A **cholera vaccination certificate** is required if you arrive from, or passed through, an infected area.

Thailand

Malaria risk (commonly the falciparum variety) is highest in the hilly, forested areas bordering Myanmar and Cambodia (Tak Province in the west and Trat Province in the southeast), although these are areas that are infrequently visited by tourists. Risk exists throughout the year and the majority of cases in the high-risk areas are the falciparum type with both chloroquine and mefloquine resistance reported. If you are going to these high-risk areas, doxycycline is the suggested prophylaxis. Transmission rates are reportedly low in the interior of the country and on the Malay peninsula with little, if any, risk in established tourist areas such as Bangkok, Chiang Mai, Pattaya, Phuket, Songhkla and Ko Samui. For the majority of areas frequented by tourists, no prophylaxis is necessary although awareness of the risks is important.

Japanese encephalitis risk, although low, is highest between May and October in rural areas. Outbreaks are common in the Chiang Mai valley and have been reported in the suburbs of Bangkok. Rare cases of Bengal **cholera** have been reported and an outbreak of **leptospirosis** in the northeast of the country following flooding in 1999 caused a number of deaths. **Trachoma** occurs although poses little threat to travellers. **HIV infection** is rife in Thailand, especially among prostitutes in Bangkok and Chiang Mai.

Yellow fever vaccination is required from travellers over 1 year of age coming from infected and endemic areas.

Vietnam

Malaria risk (usually the falciparum variety) exists throughout the year in rural areas with highest risk in the southern provinces of Ca Man and Bac Lieu and the highland areas below 1500 metres. The falciparum variety predominates and chloroquine resistance is common. Mefloquine is the recommended prophylaxis. There is little risk in the Red and Mekong deltas and on the coastal plains north of Nha Trang. The WHO estimates that there are around 1.5 million cases of malaria in Vietnam each year. **Japanese encephalitis** risk is highest between May and October, especially in and around Hanoi. **Trachoma** occurs although poses little threat to travellers. Rare cases of **plague** have been reported from Gia-Lai-Cong Tum, Lam Dong and Phu Khan provinces. **Yellow fever vaccination** is required from travellers over 1 year of age coming from infected areas.

The Indian Subcontinent

Afghanistan, Bangladesh, Bhutan, India, the Maldives, Nepal, Pakistan, Sri Lanka

Diarrhoeal disease, **giardiasis**, **dysentery**, **typhoid fever** and **hepatitis A** and **E** are widespread. The risk of **malaria** is present throughout the region (with the exception of the Maldives) although is higher in some areas than others. The falciparum variety is present and chloroquine resistance is common. There is no risk of malaria in the Maldives. **Dengue fever** occurs sporadically throughout Bangladesh, India, the Maldives, Pakistan and Sri Lanka. There has been increasing prevalence in Sri Lanka in recent years. **Rabies** risk exists throughout the area except the Maldives. There is a risk of **typhoid fever** throughout the region, especially in rural areas. **Influenza** epidemics occur between November and April in Afghanistan, Bhutan, India in areas north of the Tropic of Cancer, Nepal and Pakistan and throughout the year in Bangladesh, India in areas south of the Tropic of Cancer, the Maldives and Sri Lanka. **Cholera** outbreaks have been reported from most of these countries with cases of the new, virulent Bengal strain occurring in Bangladesh, India, Nepal, Pakistan and Sri Lanka. Outbreaks of **Japanese encephalitis** occur seasonally (rainy season) in rural areas of Bangladesh, India, southern Nepal and Sri Lanka. Risk from **meningococcal**

meningitis exists throughout the year in India and Nepal. Risks are higher in situations of close contact with the locals. **Filariasis** is common in Bangladesh, India and the southwestern coastal belt of Sri Lanka. The incidence of **visceral leishmaniasis** has increased significantly in Bangladesh, India, Nepal and northern Pakistan (Baltisan). **Cutaneous leishmaniasis** occurs in Afghanistan, India (Rajasthan) and Pakistan. **Chikungunya fever**, **Crimean-Congo haemorrhagic fever**, **typhus**, **brucellosis**, **echinococcosis** and **sandfly fever** occur throughout the region although risks are low. **Tick-borne relapsing fever** and **typhus** occur in India and Afghanistan. A **tick-borne haemorrhagic fever** has been reported in forest areas of Karnataka State in India and in a rural area of Rawalpindi District in Pakistan. **Trachoma** occurs in Afghanistan, parts of India, Nepal and Pakistan. Rates of **hepatitis B** infection are high throughout the region. Altitude can lead to problems with **altitude sickness** and **sunburn** in the Himalayas. Venomous **snakes** and **scorpions** may be hazards throughout the region.

Longer-term travellers should check their **BCG** (TB) status, ensure all standard childhood immunizations (particularly **polio**, **tetanus** and **diphtheria**) are up-to-date and consider vaccination against **hepatitis B** and **Japanese encephalitis**.

Afghanistan

Malaria risk exists in all areas below 2000m with the highest incidence between May and November. The predominant type is vivax although falciparum has been reported and chloroquine resistance exists, particularly in the southern areas bordering Iran. A combination of chloroquine and proguanil is the recommended prophylaxis. In 1999, outbreaks of **cholera** occurred in the central (Kabul Province) and southeastern regions and **polio** in the northern Kunduz Province. **Visceral leishmaniasis** is prevalent. **Crimean-Congo haemorrhagic fever** occurs in rare sporadic outbreaks. **Sandfly fever** is prevalent and **tick-borne relapsing fever** common. A **yellow fever vaccination** certificate is required from travellers coming from infected areas.

Bangladesh

Malaria risk exists across the country (excluding Dhaka City) throughout the year. Chloroquine resistance is widespread along northern and eastern borders (the Chittagong Hill Tracts) and in the southeast of the country where mefloquine is the recommended prophylaxis. Elsewhere a combination of chloroquine and proguanil is considered sufficient. **Japanese encephalitis** occurs in rural areas between July and December. Outbreaks of Bengal **cholera** have been reported. Well water in the Ishwardi District and, to a lesser extent, Dhaka is contaminated with arsenic and should be avoided. It is estimated that nearly 60% of the native population are infected with **TB**. Those arriving within 6 days of passing through or departing from a yellow fever-infected area are detained in isolation for a period up to 6 days if they are not in possession of a **yellow fever vaccination** certificate.

Bhutan

Malaria risk exists throughout the year in the south of the country (the districts of Chirang, Gaylegphug, Samchi, Samdrupjongkhar and Shemgang). Chloroquine resistance has been reported in the falciparum variety. A combination of chloroquine and proguanil is the recommended prophylaxis. **Visceral leishmaniasis** is prevalent (although risk to the average traveller is small) and **meningococcal meningitis** is a sporadic risk. **Japanese encephalitis** risk is small although exists in southern lowland rural areas between July and December. The country's high altitude may cause problems with **altitude sickness**. A **yellow fever vaccination certificate** is required from all travellers entering from infected areas.

India

Malaria occurs throughout urban (including large cities such as Bombay and Delhi) and rural areas of India, except the highland areas of Himachal Pradesh, Kashmir, Sikkim and Jammu. Chloroquine resistance is confirmed throughout the country and is widespread in the east. More than 2 million cases are reported each year with the highest levels of transmission occurring in Gujarat, Tamil Nadu, Uttar Pradesh, Rajasthan, Haryana, Punjab, and Delhi. The dominant type is vivax but falciparum still accounts for over 40% of cases. In most areas a combination of chloroquine and proguanil is adequate prophylaxis. Risk of **Japanese encephalitis** exists particularly in eastern, coastal areas. In North India the period of highest risk is between July and December. In Andhra Pradesh it is between September and December (significant outbreak in 1999). In South India, the periods of highest risk are between May and October in Goa, October and January in Tamil Nadu, and August to December in Karnataka (with a second April–June peak in Mandya District). Urban cases have been reported. **Meningococcal meningitis** is a risk in Delhi and the northern areas, particularly to backpackers travelling between November and May. **Rabies** causes around 2000 deaths in India each year. **Visceral leishmaniasis** occurs in rural areas of eastern India. India may have one of the highest **AIDS** incidences in the world. A high percentage of prostitutes are infected with the virus and blood for transfusions is inadequately screened. **Tick-borne relapsing**

fever, **sandfly fever** and **typhus** are all common. Outbreaks of **chikungunya fever**, **Crimean–Congo haemorrhagic fever**, and **leptospirosis** occur but are rare. **Dracunculiasis** and **plague** occur in rare sporadic foci. Cases of **tick-borne haemorrhagic fever** have been reported in Karnataka. **Schistosomiasis** has been confirmed in Gimvi Village, Ratnagiri District, Maharashtra State but has also been reported from other locations. The chemical **arsenic** pollutes well water along the Ganges in West Bengal State. **Scorpions** and venomous **snakes** are found across the country but are particularly prevalent around the Madras area.

Anyone over the age of 6 months arriving by air or sea without a **yellow fever vaccination** certificate will be detained in isolation for a period up to 6 days if they arrive within 6 days of departing or passing through an infected area by air, or 30 days by sea. **AIDS testing** is required for all students over 18 years of age, anyone between 18 and 70 years of age with a visa valid for 1 year or more, and anyone extending a stay to 1 year or more, excluding accredited journalists and those working in foreign missions. The test must be performed within 30 days of arrival.

The Maldives

A **yellow fever vaccination** certificate is required from travellers coming from infected areas. **AIDS testing** is required for long-term visitors and foreign testing is not accepted.

Nepal

Malaria risk (predominantly vivax) exists in rural areas below 1200m, especially along the border with India and the Tarai districts of Bara, Dhanukha, Kapilvastu Mahotari, Parsa, Rautahat, Rupendehi and Sarlahi. There is no risk in

Kathmandu and in areas above 1200 metres. Chloroquine resistance has been reported and a combination of chloroquine and proguanil is regarded as adequate prophylaxis. **Meningococcal meningitis** is a risk in rural areas, particularly to backpackers along the Himalayan trails. Rare outbreaks of **Japanese encephalitis** occur in southern lowland rural areas (the Tarai) with the highest risk occurring between July and December. In 1999, outbreaks occurred in the districts of Banke, Dang, Jhapa and Kailali. Cases of Bengal **cholera** have been reported. **Altitude** can be a significant health risk in some areas. A **yellow fever vaccination** certificate is required from travellers coming from infected areas.

Pakistan

Malaria risk exists across the whole country and is highest in areas below 2000m. Chloroquine resistance occurs and around 40% of cases are attributable to the falciparum type. A combination of chloroquine and proguanil is regarded as adequate prophylaxis. Risk of **Japanese encephalitis** exists in rural areas between June and January. The risk is highest around the central river deltas and the area around Karachi. **Tick-borne haemorrhagic fever** occurs in rural Rawalpindi. **Trachoma** is common. Cases of **Crimean–Congo haemorrhagic fever** and Bengal **cholera** have been reported. A **yellow fever vaccination** certificate is required from travellers coming from any part of a country in which yellow fever is endemic (infants under 6 months exempt if mother has a valid certificate predating the birth of the child).

Sri Lanka

Malaria risk (predominantly vivax-type) exists throughout the year for travellers outside of Colombo, Kalutara and

THE INDIAN SUBCONTINENT

Nuwara Eliya. Chloroquine-resistance is widespread and a combination of chloroquine with proguanil is the recommended prophylaxis. Risk of **Japanese encephalitis** is highest in lowland rural areas between October and January with a smaller peak in May to June. Rare outbreaks of **chikungunya fever** and cases of **Bengal cholera** have been reported. A **yellow fever vaccination** certificate is required from travellers over 1 year of age coming from infected areas.

THE INDIAN SUBCONTINENT

The Middle East

Abu Dhabi, Bahrain, Cyprus, Iran, Iraq, Israel, Jordan, Kuwait, Lebanon, Oman, Qatar, Saudi Arabia, Syrian Arab Republic, Turkey, United Arab Emirates, Yemen

Diarrhoeal disease, **giardiasis**, **dysentery**, **typhoid fever** and **hepatitis A** are widespread and common throughout the region. **Cholera** is also a risk in some areas. **Malaria** risk exists in Iran, Iraq, Oman, Saudi Arabia, Syrian Arab Republic, Turkey, United Arab Emirates and Yemen. Sporadic outbreaks of **dengue fever** occur in Yemen. **Schistosomiasis** is found in parts of Iran, Iraq, Saudi Arabia, Syrian Arabic Republic and Yemen. **Rabies** risk exists throughout the area (although risks are low in Bahrain and Cyprus) and its prevalence is increasing in some areas. **Hepatitis B** is endemic throughout the region. **Influenza epidemics** occur between November and April (Bahrain, Cyprus, Iraq, Israel, Jordan, Kuwait, Qatar, Saudi Arabia (north of the Tropic of Cancer), Syrian Arab Republic, Turkey and the United Arab Emirates, and throughout the year in Iran, Oman, Saudi Arabia (south of the Tropic of Cancer) and Yemen. **Cutaneous leishmaniasis** is common throughout the area whereas **visceral leishmaniasis** occurs commonly only in central Iraq, the southwest of Saudi Arabia, the northwest of the Syrian Arab Republic, the west of Yemen and in southeast Anatolia in Turkey. **Filariasis**, **tick-borne relapsing fever**, **sandfly fever**, **typhus** (murine and tick-borne), **Crimean-Congo**

haemorrhagic fever and **plague** occur sporadically throughout the area, although all are rare. **Brucellosis**, **echinococcosis**, **Q fever** and **trachoma** are found to varying degrees throughout the region. **Snakes** and **scorpions** may be a hazard in some rural areas. Dry and dusty conditions may exacerbate **respiratory** and **sinus** problems as well as causing problems to contact-lens wearers.

Longer-term travellers should check their **BCG** (TB) status, ensure all standard childhood immunizations (particularly **polio**, **tetanus** and **diphtheria**) are up-to-date and consider vaccination against **hepatitis B**. There is no risk of contracting yellow fever from any of the countries of the Middle East.

Bahrain

Beach **pollution** can lead to infections of the ears, eyes, skin and gastrointestinal tract after swimming. **HIV testing** is required for any individual employed in health care, childcare and food handling. Foreign tests are not accepted.

Cyprus

Outbreaks of **legionnaires' disease** have occurred on the island although ongoing risk is negligible. **HIV testing** is required for all foreigners working or studying in Cyprus. Foreign tests are not accepted.

Iran

Malaria (vivax form) risk exists between March and November in areas north of the Zagros Mountains and in western and southwestern regions. In these areas chloroquine alone is sufficient prophylaxis. Chloroquine-resistant falciparum variety is reported in rural areas of the provinces of Hormozgan, Kerman and Sistan-Buluchestan and the recommended prophylaxis in these areas is a chloroquine/proguanil combination. **Schistosomiasis** occurs in the southwest of the country. **Tick-borne relapsing fever** has been reported. Air pollution can be a problem in Tehran and may exacerbate **respiratory problems**. A **yellow fever vaccination** certificate is required from all travellers coming from infected areas.

Iraq

Malaria (vivax type only) exists below 1500m (greatest risk between May and November) in the following provinces: Basrah, Duhok, Erbil, Ninawa, Sulaimaniya and Ta'mim. Chloroquine alone is the recommended prophylaxis. **Crimean-Congo haemorrhagic fever**, **visceral leishmaniasis** (common in central Iraq), and **schistosomiasis** have all been reported. A **cholera** outbreak in 1999 caused a number of deaths (Sulaimaniya particularly badly affected). **Polio** broke out in a small epidemic in southern Iraq in 1999. Sanctions against Iraq following the Gulf War have affected the availability of basic medical supplies. A **yellow fever vaccination** certificate is required from travellers coming from infected areas.

Israel

Risk of contracting infectious illness is generally less in Israel than for the rest of the Middle East. Air **pollution** along the industrialized coastal strip may cause **respiratory problems** (Haifa particularly badly affected). Although tap water is generally considered safe there have been outbreaks of dysentery in Haifa and Western Galilee in recent years.

Jordan

Hepatitis A infection is common. A **yellow fever vaccination** certificate is required from travellers over 1 year of age coming from infected areas. A **HIV test** is mandatory for anyone planning to stay longer than 3 months.

Kuwait

HIV testing is required for anyone applying for residency and foreign tests are not accepted.

Lebanon

Hepatitis A is common. A **yellow fever vaccination** certificate is required from travellers coming from infected areas. **HIV testing** is required for those planning to live and work in the country. Foreign tests may be acceptable under certain conditions and further advice should be obtained from the embassy.

Oman

Falciparum malaria risk exists all year round in limited geographical foci in the provinces of Musandam and North Batinah. In these areas, a combination of chloroquine and proguanil is the recommended prophylaxis; elsewhere no prophylaxis is necessary. A **yellow fever vaccination** certificate is required from travellers coming from infected areas. **HIV testing** is required for newly appointed employees of private sector companies or upon the renewal of work permits. Foreign tests are not accepted.

Qatar

HIV testing is required if you are seeking a residency or work visa, or if you are planning a stay of longer than 1 month.

Saudi Arabia

With the exception of the high-altitude areas of the Asir province, year-long **malaria** risk exists in the Southern

Region and localized rural areas of the Western Region. The predominant type is falciparum and chloroquine resistance is reported. A combination of chloroquine and proguanil is the recommended prophylaxis. **Hepatitis A** is common.

The risk of **meningococcal meningitis** in the Middle East is low but vaccination against the disease is a statutory requirement for the hajj pilgrimage to Mecca. The vaccination must have been administered not more than 3 years, and not less than 10 days, before arrival.

Pilgrims applying for a visa for the hajj festival may also be asked for proof of immunization against **cholera**. All pilgrims are also required to carry a card stating their name, nationality, the name of the guide in charge of the rites performed and any relevant medical details (eg chronic illnesses, allergies, medications). All travellers arriving from a country where **yellow fever** is active are required to be vaccinated. **HIV testing** is required for all applications for residency and work permits.

Syrian Arab Republic

There is a low risk of **malaria** (vivax) in rural foci along the northern border (especially the northeast). The risk is highest between May and October. Chloroquine alone is regarded as adequate prophylaxis. **Hepatitis A** is common throughout the country and **visceral leishmaniasis** occurs in the northwest. A **yellow fever vaccination** certificate is required from travellers entering from infected areas. **HIV testing** is required for anyone between 15 and 50 planning to stay for longer than 15 days or marry a Syrian national in Syria.

Turkey

Malaria of the vivax variety occurs between March and October in the area between southeast Anatolia and the

Iraqi border (rarely frequented by tourists). In this area chloroquine alone is adequate prophylaxis. There is no malaria risk in the main tourist areas of the west and south-west. Diyarkabir has been the centre of a number of recurring outbreaks of **dysentery**, **typhoid** and **meningitis**. **Cutaneous** (mainly in Anatolia) and **visceral leishmaniasis** (in the southeast) occur in geographically limited foci. **Pollution** in Ankara, notably the sulphur dioxide levels in winter, can cause **respiratory** problems.

United Arab Emirates

Malaria risk is limited to the rural foothill areas and valleys in the mountainous regions of the northern Emirates. Chloroquine resistance is reported in this area and a combination of chloroquine with proguanil is the recommended prophylaxis. There is no risk in Ajmin, Dubai, Sharjah, Umm al Qaiwan and in the Emirate of Abu Dhabi. Anyone over 18 applying for a work or residency visa is required to undergo a **HIV test**. The test is performed on arrival.

Yemen

Malaria risk exists throughout the country, excluding Aden (and its airport perimeter) and Sana'a. The risk is highest from September to February. Chloroquine resistance is reported and a combination of chloroquine with proguanil is the recommended prophylaxis. Limited foci of **onchocerciasis** and **dracunculiasis** are reported but are very little risk to tourists. **Altitude** may cause health problems in Sana'a. A **yellow fever vaccination** certificate is required from travellers over 1 year of age coming from infected areas.

THE MIDDLE EAST

North America, Central America and the Caribbean

North America

Canada, Greenland, St Pierre and Miquelon, USA (including Hawaii)

Generally speaking the risk of contracting a significant infectious disease in North America is low. **Dengue fever** occurs in isolated outbreaks in the southern states of the USA. **Rabies** is on the increase in some areas (US mid-Atlantic states). Avoid direct contact with raccoons, foxes, skunks, groundhogs and bats. **Influenza** epidemics occur between November and April. Rare outbreaks of **tick-borne diseases** such as Lyme disease, Rocky Mountain spotted fever, ehrlichiosis and human babesiosis, and a variety of mosquito-borne **encephalitis infections** such as St Louis virus, West Nile virus, Eastern and Western equine encephalitis, etc occur in all countries but mainly in the southern and western states of the US. **Plague**, rodent-borne hantavirus and tularaemia are very rare but have been reported particularly in the southern states of the US. Poison ivy and poison oak occur in Canada and the USA.

Encephalitis caused by a variety of different viruses can occur in sporadic outbreaks in all of the countries (see St Louis virus, West Nile virus, etc).

Air pollution in the large cities and heavily industrialized areas may cause **repiratory problems** in susceptible individuals. **Street crime** is common and tourists have been particularly targeted in some areas (eg Florida).

Canada

Rodent-borne hantavirus has been reported in the southwestern provinces. **Lyme disease** has been reported from southern Manitoba, Ontario, Alberta, British Columbia and Quebec provinces with a concentration of cases in the Muskoka region and the Long Point wildlife area on Lake Erie. Risk appears to be highest in the summer months. **Hepatitis B** is endemic. Toronto has the highest pollen count of any North American city in the summer which may cause problems to sufferers of **hay fever** and **asthma**. **HIV testing** may be required of any visitor suspected of being HIV positive and foreign tests may be acceptable. Contact the embassy for details.

Greenland

Hepatitis B is endemic. The greatest health hazard to the visitor is extremely **cold** temperatures in the winter months so go well prepared. Medical facilities are limited in Greenland and if a serious medical problem is encountered, evacuation is likely to be necessary.

St Pierre and Miquelon

Rocky Mountain spotted fever and **tularaemia** occur in rare, sporadic outbreaks.

USA

Outbreaks of **Lyme disease** have occurred in all but 6 states (Alaska, Arizona, Hawaii, Mississippi, Montana and North Dakota) and continue to occur in isolated pockets of the northeastern, mid-Atlantic and upper Midwestern states (May–Aug) and the Pacific northwest (Jan–May). **Rodent-borne hantavirus** occurs mainly in the western states but is very rare. Rare incidence of **ehrlichiosis** has been reported in northwestern Wisconsin, northeastern Minnesota, Connecticut and New York. There has been a recent epidemic of **dengue fever** in southern Texas. **Plague** occurs very rarely in isolated pockets of the southwest. An outbreak of **West Nile fever** in the New York City vicinity in 1999 and 2000 caused much media interest and was believed to have been spread by migratory birds. **Poisonous snakes** and **scorpions** can be found in most rural areas, more commonly in the south and the desert states. There may be restrictions on **HIV-positive travellers** (seek further advice from the embassy) and residency is refused to those who are HIV positive.

Mexico and Central America

Belize, Costa Rica, El Salvador, Guatemala, Honduras, Mexico, Nicaragua, Panama

Diarrhoeal diseases are common throughout Central American countries. **Malaria** risk tends to be confined to the low-lying, rural areas. Generally speaking, chloroquine alone provides adequate prophylaxis. In Panama to the east of the canal there is evidence of chloroquine resistance, where either chloroquine with proguanil or mefloquine should be used. **Yellow fever** vaccination is a requirement of most of the Central American countries if you are travelling from a yellow fever endemic area. There is a risk of contracting yellow fever in the rural regions of Panama. Frequent epidemics of **dengue fever** occur throughout the region. **Rabies** is widespread throughout the area and usually carried by domestic dogs or bats. Epidemics of **cholera** occur infrequently in all countries of the region. The risk of **influenza** occurs throughout the year in all Central American countries (not in Mexico north of the Tropic of Cancer when it occurs between November and April). **Typhoid fever**, **amoebic** and **bacillary dysenteries** and **hepatitis A** (high risk especially backpacking through rural areas) occur throughout the region. **Cutaneous leishmaniasis** occurs in all countries, with **visceral leishmaniasis** found in all but Belize, Costa Rica and Panama. **American trypanosomiasis** is found in localized, rural pockets throughout the 8 countries. **Onchocerciasis** is found in localized areas of Guatemala and south Mexico. **Paragonimiasis** occurs in Costa Rica, Honduras and Panama and **schistosomiasis** occurs in Guatemala and Panama. **Brucellosis** has been reported in Belize, El Salvador, Guatemala, Honduras and Nicaragua. **Typhus**, **Venezuelan equine encephalitis** and **plague** have been reported but outbreaks are rare. **Worm infections** are relatively common. **Snakes** and **scorpions** may be hazards in rural areas.

Longer-term travellers should check their **BCG** (TB) status, consider immunization against **hepatitis B** and check that their **normal childhood immunizations** are all up-to-date before departure.

Belize

Malaria risk (predominantly the chloroquine-sensitive vivax form) exists in all rural areas (including islands and resorts) and is particularly high in western and southern regions. A **yellow fever certificate** is required for all travellers entering the country from infected areas. **HIV testing** is required for application for residency and foreign tests may not be acceptable.

Costa Rica

Health care and standards of hygiene are reputedly the best in Central America. **Malaria** risk (mostly the chloroquine-sensitive vivax form) exists throughout the year in rural areas below 700m and is highest in the central forested areas (Alajuela, Guanacaste, Heredia and Limón provinces). **Lymphatic filiariasis** occurs, particularly in rural areas. An epidemic of **dengue fever** occurred in 1999 predominantly in the Limón province.

El Salvador

Malaria risk (mostly chloroquine-sensitive vivax), although small, exists throughout the year mainly in the rural areas of the north around Santa Ana below 600m. Outbreaks are more common in the rainy season (May–October). There has been an increase in the number of reported cases of **dengue fever**, including **dengue haemorrhagic fever**, in 2000. **Rabies** is a significant risk. A **yellow fever certificate** is required for all travellers over the age of 6 months entering the country from infected areas. Applicants for permanent residency over the age of 15 will be required to undergo **HIV testing** and foreign tests may not be accepted.

Guatemala

Malaria risk (chloroquine-sensitive) is present throughout the year in rural areas below 1500m with high risk in some regions (the departments of Alta Verapaz, Baja Verapaz, Ixcan, Petén – including the Tikal ruins - and San Marcos) and moderate risk in others (the departments of Escuintla, Huehuetenango, Izabal, Quiché, Retalhuleu, Suchitepequez and Zacapa). **Oropouche virus** infection occurs rarely. **Snakes** and **scorpions** can present a risk, mainly in rural areas. The pollution in Guatemala City may cause **respiratory problems**. A **yellow fever certificate** is required for all travellers over the age of 1 year entering the country from infected areas.

Honduras

Malaria risk (chloroquine-sensitive vivax) exists throughout the year in many departments, especially in the rural areas of Atlantida, Choluteca, Colon, Cortes, Gracias a Dios, the Bay Islands, Olancho, Valle and Yoro. There was a large epidemic of **dengue fever** and a **cholera** outbreak along the Nicaraguan and Guatemalan borders in 1999. A **yellow fever certificate** is required for all travellers entering the country from infected areas.

Mexico

Malaria risk (nearly always the chloroquine-sensitive vivax) is confined to certain areas. High risk exists in the states of Campeche, Chiapas, Guerrero, Michoacán, Oaxaca, Quintana Roo, Sinaloa and Tabasco, with lower risk in the states of Chihuahua, Durango, Hidalgo, Jalisco, Nayarit, Sonora and Veracruz. Chloroquine alone is sufficient prophylaxis although no prophylaxis is required for the main tourist areas on the Pacific and Gulf coasts. **Dengue fever** is particularly predominant in the northern border states where an epidemic occurred in 1999. **Cholera** presents a serious risk in some areas and food and water hygiene measures are essential. **Hepatitis E** has been reported in Mexico although risks of **hepatitis B** are relatively low compared to the rest of Central America. **Onchocerciasis** has been reported in the states of Chiapas and Oaxaca. During the 1990s, a number of cases of **gnathostomiasis** were reported in Acapulco believed to have been contracted by eating raw fish (in ceviche). Each year there are a considerable number of fatalities attributable to **scorpion stings**. **Pollution** levels in Mexico City are high and may cause **respiratory problems**, especially in those with asthma or cardiovascular illness. The altitude of Mexico City may give rise to mild symptoms of **altitude sickness**. A **yellow fever certificate** is required for all travellers over the age of 6 months entering the country from infected and endemic areas.

Nicaragua

Malaria risk (mostly chloroquine-sensitive vivax) exists throughout the country in rural areas and in the outskirts of some towns. Highest risk exists in Chinandega, Jinotega, Nueva Segovia, RAAN, RAAS and Rio San Juan. An outbreak of **cholera** in 1999 mainly affected the Jinotega, Managua, Nueva Segovia and RAAN . **Flooding** can cause serious problems in Nicaragua, especially along the east coast between May and November. A **yellow fever certificate** is required for all travellers over the age of 1 year entering the country from infected areas.

Panama

Malaria risk is low but exists throughout the year in Bocas de Toro province in the west and San Blas and Darien provinces in the east. There is no risk in the Canal Zone, Panama City and its environs. The predominant form is chloroquine-sensitive vivax although chloroquine-resistant falciparum has been reported in areas to the east of the canal (Darien and San Blas provinces). **Oropouche virus** infection is rare but occurs sporadically in some areas. In March 2000, **rodent-borne hantavirus** infection was reported from Los Santos Province. **Respiratory problems** may be exacerbated by the humid climate. **Yellow fever vaccination** certification is required for entry into the Darien Province. Yellow fever vaccination is strongly recommended for those travelling into rural areas (especially the Chepo, Darien and San Blas provinces). **HIV testing** is a requirement for anyone who applies to extend their visa once in Panama. Foreign test results may be acceptable in certain circumstances but contact the embassy for further details.

The Caribbean

Anguilla, Antigua and Barbuda, Aruba, The Bahamas, Barbados, Bermuda, Bonaire, The Caicos and Turks Islands, The Cayman Islands, Cuba, Curacao, Dominica, The Dominican Republic, Grenada, Guadeloupe, Haiti, Jamaica, Martinique, Montserrat, Puerto Rico, Saba, St Christopher (St Kitts) and Nevis, St Eustatius, St Lucia, St Maarten, St Vincent and the Grenadines, Trinidad and Tobago, The Virgin Islands

Diarrhoeal illnesses occur throughout the Caribbean but are more common on some islands than others. There is a **malaria** risk throughout the year in parts of the Dominican Republic and Haiti. The falciparum variety has been confirmed in both although no chloroquine resistance has yet been identified. Chloroquine alone is therefore regarded as sufficient prophylaxis although it is only necessary in these countries. Rare outbreaks of **yellow fever** have been reported in Trinidad and Tobago. A low level of risk of **dengue fever** exists throughout the year in most Caribbean islands and localized epidemics occur frequently. **Schistosomiasis** is rare but found in some parts of the Dominican Republic, Guadeloupe, Martinique, Puerto Rico and St Lucia. It has also been reported sporadically in Anguilla, Antigua, Bonaire, the British Virgin Islands, Dominica, Grenada, Montserrat, St Maarten and the US Virgin Islands. The risks on some of these islands are very low but exercise due precautions. **Rabies** risk exists in Cuba, Dominican Republic, Grenada, Haiti, Puerto Rico, and Trinidad and Tobago (particularly spread by the mongooses and bats). There have been no recent reports of rabies on Anguilla, Antigua and Barbuda, Aruba, Bahamas, Barbados, Bermuda, Bonaire, the Caicos and Turks Islands, the Cayman Islands, Curacao, Dominica, Guadeloupe, Jamaica, Martinique, Montserrat, St Christopher and Nevis, St Lucia, St Maartin, St Vincent and the Grenadines and the Virgin Islands. There is a small risk of **typhoid** in most rural areas on the majority of the islands. **Influenza** risk extends throughout the year on all Caribbean islands with the exception of the Bahamas and Bermuda when epidemics tend to occur between November and April.

Hepatitis A occurs throughout the Caribbean, especially in rural areas on the northern islands. **TB** and **hepatitis B** infection are relatively common in the indigenous populations of most Caribbean islands and longer-term travellers should check their **BCG status** before departure and consider immunization against **hepatitis B**. **Filariasis** and **leishmaniasis** occur on some islands but the risks are low to the average traveller. There are a variety of potential hazards in the sea including **spiny sea urchins**, **jellyfish** and coral. **Snakes**, **poisonous spiders** and **scorpions** may be a hazard in some areas. **Ciguatera** occurs sporadically throughout the Caribbean.

Anguilla

Yellow fever vaccination is required for those over 1 year of age travelling from infected areas.

Antigua and Barbuda

American trypanosomiasis has been reported in rural areas (risk is very low). **Yellow fever vaccination** is required for those over 1 year of age travelling from infected areas.

Aruba

American trypanosomiasis has been reported in rural areas, though the risk is very low. **Yellow fever vaccination** is required for those over 6 months of age travelling from infected areas. **HIV testing** is required of all intended immigrants and foreign tests may be acceptable under certain conditions. Check with the Netherlands Antilles' embassy before departure.

The Bahamas

Yellow fever vaccination is required for those over 1 year of age who have visited an infected area in the last 6 months.

Barbados

Leptospirosis occurs towards the end of the rainy season (Oct/Nov). **Hay fever** and **asthma** may be exacerbated during the sugar cane harvesting season. Local fruit which grow near beaches and resemble crab apples (machineel trees) are poisonous and the trees themselves emit an irritant juice in rain storms. **Centipedes** on the island can give a painful bite. Heavy surf and undercurrents make **swimming** dangerous off the east and southeast coasts. **Yellow fever vaccination** is required for those over 1 year of age travelling from infected countries.

Bermuda

The humid climate may exacerbate **respiratory** problems. Portuguese man-of-war **jellyfish** are commonly found around the island.

Bonaire

Intermittent cases of **cutaneous leishmaniasis** and **lymphatic filariasis** have been reported. **Yellow fever requirements** and **HIV testing** for prospective immigrants are the same as for Aruba.

The British Virgin Islands

Long-stay workers or immigrants to the British Virgin Islands may be asked to produce a negative **HIV test** result.

The Caicos and Turks Islands

Scorpions and **black widows** occur. **HIV testing** is required as part of a medical examination for all foreign workers applying for a work permit and foreign tests are not accepted (contact British Embassy for details).

Cuba

Human **fascioliasis** is endemic.

Curacao

Yellow fever requirements and **HIV testing** for prospective immigrants are the same as for Aruba.

Dominica

Diarrhoeal illness and **hepatitis A** are common. **Yellow fever vaccination** is required for those over 1 year of age travelling from infected areas.

The Dominican Republic

Malaria risk exists throughout the year in all rural areas (predominantly chloroquine-sensitive falciparum). More recent outbreaks have been reported from the tourist areas of Altagracia Province (mainly the area around Bavaro Beach). **Cutaneous leishmaniasis** has been reported. There has been a recent epidemic of **leptospirosis** in Santiago. Those seeking residency will be required to undertake a **HIV test** (foreign tests may not be acceptable).

Grenada

High humidity throughout the year (worse in June to Nov) may cause respiratory problems and predispose to fungal skin infections. **Yellow fever vaccination** is required for those over 1 year of age travelling from infected areas.

Guadeloupe

High humidity throughout the year may cause respiratory problems and predispose to fungal skin infections. **Cutaneous leishmaniasis** has been reported and **American trypanosomiasis** may be a risk in rural areas. **Yellow fever vaccination** is required for those over 1 year of age travelling from infected areas.

Haiti

Malaria risk (mainly chloroquine-sensitive falciparum variety) exists throughout the year in all areas below 300m.

It is particularly prevalent in coastal areas. **Hepatitis A** is common. **Meningococcal meningitis** (seasonal), **lymphatic filariasis** and **tularaemia** have been reported. **Yellow fever vaccination** is required from all travellers arriving from infected areas.

Jamaica

Diarrhoeal illnesses and **hepatitis A** are common. **American trypanosomiasis** occurs in some rural areas. **Black widow spiders** and **scorpions** are found but are rare. **Leptospirosis** outbreaks have been reported mainly during the mango season. A recent outbreak of **meningitis** in a group of American travellers was linked to a salad contaminated with eggs from a freshwater fluke. Pollen counts can be high on the island precipitating **hay fever** and exacerbating **asthma**. **Yellow fever vaccination** is required for those over 1 year of age travelling from infected areas.

Martinique

Cutaneous leishmaniasis is present although rare.

Montserrat

Frequent **volcanic eruptions** may pose a physical threat. The ash-laden air can cause **respiratory problems**. A **HIV test** is required for all long-stay visitors. Foreign tests may be acceptable under certain conditions but contact the embassy for further details.

Puerto Rico

"**La manga**" is a common flu-like illness which requires no treatment and settles after a few days. Incidence of **dengue fever** has been on the increase over recent years. **Lymphatic filariasis** occurs sporadically.

Saba

Yellow fever requirements and **HIV testing** for prospective immigrants are the same as for Aruba.

St Christopher (St Kitts) and Nevis

Yellow fever vaccination is required for those over 1 year of age travelling from infected areas. A **HIV test** is required for all long-stay visitors. Foreign tests may be acceptable under certain conditions but contact the embassy for further details.

St Eustatius

Yellow fever requirements and **HIV testing** for prospective immigrants are the same as for Aruba.

St Lucia

Cutaneous leishmaniasis and **lymphatic filariasis** have been reported. **Yellow fever vaccination** is required for those over 1 year of age travelling from infected areas.

St Maarten

Cutaneous leishmaniasis and **lymphatic filariasis** occur sporadically. **Yellow fever requirements** and **HIV testing** for prospective immigrants are the same as for Aruba.

St Vincent and the Grenadines

Lymphatic filariasis occurs sporadically. **Yellow fever vaccination** is required for those over 1 year of age travelling from infected areas. A **HIV test** is required for all temporary or permanent visa applications.

Trinidad and Tobago

The humid climate predisposes to heat rash and exacerbates **asthma** and **hay fever**. Avoid the local oysters as their habitat is polluted. There have been no outbreaks of yellow fever in recent years. **Yellow fever vaccination** is required for those over 1 year of age travelling from infected areas. Travellers planning a trip to the southeastern forested areas of Trinidad should consider immunization anyway and may require certification for onward travel. **HIV testing** is required for all applicants for residence or citizenship.

South America

Argentina, Bolivia, Brazil, Chile, Colombia, Ecuador, the Falkland Islands (Islas Malvinas), French Guiana, Guyana, Paraguay, Peru, Surinam, Uruguay, Venezuela

In terms of health hazards, South America can be divided into the northern tropical countries (Bolivia, Brazil, Colombia, Ecuador, French Guiana, Guyana, Paraguay, Peru, Surinam, Venezuela) where many diseases are endemic, and indeed common, and the southern temperate countries (Argentina, Chile, the Falkland Islands, Uruguay) where risks to the traveller are less in multitude and variety.

Travellers' diarrhoea is very common throughout South America, especially so in the tropical region. **Malaria**, mainly the vivax variety, occurs throughout the year in parts of Argentina, Bolivia, Brazil, Colombia, Ecuador, French Guiana, Guyana, Paraguay, Peru, Surinam and Venezuela. Falciparum has been reported in most of these countries (none in Argentina and less so in Peru and Paraguay) and chloroquine resistance is rife in some areas. **Yellow Fever** may occur in epidemics in the forested areas in Argentina (rare and northeast only), Bolivia, Brazil, Colombia, Ecuador, French Guiana, Guyana, Surinam and Venezuela. There is no risk of yellow fever in Chile, the Falkland Islands or Uruguay. Vaccination is recommended for travel to all of the tropical countries although risk areas are usually localized foci and epidemics are sporadic. Vaccination is mandatory for entry into French Guiana.

Hepatitis A is common throughout South America and epidemics of **dengue fever** occur throughout the northern, tropical countries and in northern urban areas of Argentina. **Schistosomiasis** is found in Brazil, Guyana, Surinam and north central Venezuela. A **rabies** risk exists throughout the region although it is low in Uruguay and the Falkland Islands. There is a moderate to high risk of **typhoid** throughout South America, especially in the northern countries when travelling outside the cities or main tourist areas. In tropical areas the risk of **influenza** may occur at any time of year. South of the Tropic of Capricorn the influenza season runs from May to October. **Cholera** outbreaks in the northern countries are frequent, particularly in Bolivia, Brazil, Colombia, Ecuador and Peru although risks to the tourist observing sensible food- and drink-hygiene measures are small. **Cutaneous leishmaniasis** and **mucocutaneous leishmaniasis** (increasing in prevalence in Brazil and Paraguay) occur in all 10 countries of the northern, tropical group. **Visceral leishmaniasis** is endemic in the northeast of Brazil and is found in pockets elsewhere in Brazil, occasionally in Colombia and Venezuela and rarely in Bolivia and Paraguay. **American trypanosomiasis** is found throughout South America except for the southern parts of Argentina and Chile. **Onchocerciasis** occurs in isolated foci in rural areas of northern Brazil, Ecuador and Venezuela. **Lymphatic filariasis** occurs in parts of Brazil, Guyana and Surinam. **Bartonellosis** (Oroya fever) is found in the valleys of the western slopes of the Andes up to 3000m. **Oropouche virus** infection occurs in parts of Brazil and Peru. **Plague** occurs in focused epidemics in parts of Bolivia, Brazil, Ecuador and Peru. **Trachoma** exists in Brazil, Bolivia and Peru. **Louse-borne typhus** occurs in mountainous areas of Peru and Colombia. **Paragonimiasis** has been reported in Ecuador, Peru and Venezuela and **gnathostomiasis** sporadically occurs in Peru and Ecuador. **Brucellosis** is common throughout the northern countries and **echinococcosis** occurs in most of the countries, particularly Peru. **Anthrax** may be a hazard to anyone in close contact with animals in Argentina, Chile and Uruguay. **Rodent–borne hantavirus** infection has occurred in rare outbreaks in the north-central and southwestern regions of Argentina and in Chile. Infection rates of **hepatitis B** and **D** are particularly high in the Amazon Basin although both occur elsewhere in the region. **Snakes** and **poisonous spiders** can be a hazard, particularly in jungle areas. **Worm infections** occur commonly throughout the continent. Long-term visitors should consider immunization against **diphtheria**, **hepatitis B** and check their **BCG** (TB) status.

Argentina

Malaria risk is low, exclusively vivax and confined geographically to the rural borders with Bolivia (lowlands of Jujay and Salta provinces) and with Paraguay (lowlands of Corrientes and Misiones provinces). The risk is highest between October and May. Chloroquine resistance has not, as yet, been reported and chloroquine alone is adequate prophylaxis. **Yellow fever outbreaks** and **cutaneous leishmaniasis** occur in the northeast although are rare. Reports of **rabies** have increased over the past decade, particularly in urban and suburban areas. There is a very small risk of **rodent–borne hantavirus** infection in the pampas and the centre of the country.

Bolivia

Malaria risk exists throughout the year in rural areas below 2500m in the departments of Beni, Pando, Santa Cruz and Tarija and the provinces of Lacareja, Rurenabaque, and

North and South Yungas in La Paz Department. Lesser risk exists in Cochabamba and Chuquisaca. The falciparum variety is common in the northern departments (Beni and Pando – especially around Guayaramerin, Puerto Rico and Riberalta) bordering Brazil. Mefloquine is recommended as the first line antimalarial in the Amazon Basin although elsewhere in the country chloroquine and proguanil are adequate. The departments of Beni, Chuquisaca, Cochabamba, Pando, Santa Cruz (all of the yellow fever cases in Bolivia in 1999), Tarija, and the subtropical part of La Paz are particularly prone to **yellow fever** epidemics. Yellow fever **vaccination** is recommended for all travellers to Bolivia although it is a requirement for all travellers over 1 year old entering from infected countries. **American trypanosomiasis** is particularly prevalent in provinces of Chuquisaca, Cochabamba, Santa Cruz and Tarija. Outbreaks of **visceral leishmaniasis** occur in the northeast of the country and in pockets elsewhere in the country. **Rodent–borne hantavirus** occurs sporadically. Flying straight into La Paz (nearly 4000m above sea level) can present problems with **altitude sickness** especially for those with pre-existing heart or lung problems.

Brazil

There is a high **malaria** risk below 900m throughout the year in the states of Acre, Amapá, Amazonas Maranhão (western part), Mato Grosso (northern part), Pará (except Belém City), Rondônia, Roraima and Tocantins). Risk is less in urban areas such as, Boa Vista, Macapá, Manaus, Maraba, Pôrto Velho and Santarém. Mefloquine is the suggested prophylaxis as chloroquine resistance is high. Elsewhere, no prophylaxis is required. There is no current malaria risk in the major tourist areas such as the Iguaçu Falls and major cities such as Fortaleza, Recife, Rio de

Janeiro, Salvador and Sao Paulo. **Yellow fever** is regarded as endemic for most rural areas, especially in the northern and western states. Most of the recent cases have occurred in the states of Goiás, Rio de Janeiro, Sao Paulo and Para. Yellow fever **vaccination** is recommended for all travellers to rural areas of Brazil although it is a requirement for all travellers over the age of 3 months entering from infected countries. An outbreak of **cholera** recently occurred in the Paranagua district of Parana State. **Mucocutaneous leishmaniasis** is increasing in frequency and the **visceral** form is endemic in the northeast with foci in other parts. Epidemics of **meningococcal meningitis** occur mainly in and around the Rio de Janeiro area although other parts of the country have been affected. **Brazilian purpuric fever** occurs rarely in Parana and Sao Paulo states. Air pollution in Sao Paulo City can be particularly severe and may cause problems if you suffer from **asthma**, **chest** or **heart problems**.

Chile

Meningococcal meningitis occurs in epidemic outbreaks. **American trypanosomiasis** has been reported in rural areas but is rare. **Hookworm** and **tapeworm** infestations are more common in rural areas. **Rodent-borne haemorrhagic fever** occurs rarely in the centre of Chile. **Anthrax** is an occupational hazard in Chile. **Echinococcosis** occurs in rural areas. Cases of **trichinosis** have recently been reported in the south of the country. Smog in the cities (especially Santiago) and extreme swings in temperature may exacerbate **respiratory illness**. The immediate area surrounding the Lonquimay volcano may be polluted (air and water) by a number of toxic chemicals as a result of its activity and is best avoided.

Colombia

There is a **malaria** risk in all rural areas below 800m throughout the year, although none in Bogota and its immediate vicinity. High-risk areas include Urabá (Antioquia and Chocó departments), Bajo Cauca-Nechi (Antioquia and Córdoba departments), the middle valley of the Magdalena River, Catatumbo (Norte de Santander Department), the whole Pacific coast area, the eastern plains (Orinoquia) and Amazonia. Whilst the majority of cases are caused by vivax, chloroquine-resistant falciparum malaria is common in some areas and mefloquine is the recommended prophylaxis. **Visceral leishmaniasis** occurs rarely. **Myiasis** (botfly and screwworm flies) is common in some rural areas. **Altitude sickness** is a risk when flying directly into Bogota (altitude 2600m). The US State Department states that there is a higher risk of being **kidnapped** in Colombia than anywhere else in the world. **Yellow fever vaccination** is recommended for the middle valley of the Magdalena River, eastern and western foothills of the Cordillera Oriental from the border with Ecuador to that with Venezuela, Urabá, the foothills of the Sierra Nevada, eastern plains (Orinoquia) and Amazonia although no certification is required for entry into the country.

Ecuador

Malaria risk exists in all areas below 1500m throughout the year with the highest risk found in El Oro, Esmeraldas and Manabi. Quito and its immediate vicinity, the central highland tourist areas and the Galapagos Islands are regarded as safe from malaria. Chloroquine resistant falciparum variety is common in Esmeraldas province and there mefloquine is the recommended prophylaxis. Elsewhere chloroquine alone is sufficient. Areas of particular risk for **yellow fever** are the provinces of Morona-Santiago, Napo,

Pastaza, Sucumbios and Zamora-Chinchipe. Yellow fever **vaccination** is a requirement for all travellers over 1 year-old travelling from infected countries and highly recommended for all of those travelling to rural areas over the age of 9 months. There have been a few reports of **diphtheria** in Quito over the past few years. **Altitude sickness** is a risk flying directly into Quito (2850m). Quito is situated close to an active volcano, Guagua Pichincha, and the threat of eruption in the near future is real.

The Falkland Islands

Water supplies and blood products are considered safe. **Echinococcosis** (rare) and **hepatitis A** occur.

French Guiana

There is a high **malaria** risk (predominantly falciparum) throughout the year in all areas of the southern interior along the borders with Brazil and Surinam and the north-west coast. Chloroquine resistance is common and mefloquine is the recommended prophylaxis although in other parts of the country malaria risk is low. **Myiasis** occurs in rural areas. **Yellow fever vaccination** is mandatory for all visitors over age 1.

Guyana

Malaria risk (predominantly falciparum) is high throughout the year in all rural areas and sporadic outbreaks occur in the more densely populated coastal belt. High levels of chloroquine resistance exist and mefloquine is the recommended prophylaxis. **High humidity** may cause breathing difficulties in susceptible people and makes fungal skin infections more likely to occur. A local drainage problem in the Georgetown area increases the risk of **hookworm infections**. There has been an outbreak of **plague** recently in the northeastern region of Tanga. **Yellow fever vaccination** is required for all travellers entering from infected countries and is recommended for anyone travelling outside of urban areas.

Paraguay

Malaria risk (almost exclusively chloroquine-sensitive vivax) tends to be seasonal (greatest risk from October to May) in some rural areas (Alto Paraná, Caaguazú and Canendiyú Departments) where chloroquine alone is the recommended prophylaxis. Elsewhere the risks are minimal. A large epidemic of **dengue fever** has been apparent throughout 1999 and 2000 with an estimated total of 100,000 cases across Paraguay. The worst affected area is Cuidad del Este on the Brazilian border. **Visceral leishmaniasis** is rare but reported. **Rats**, **scorpions**, **spiders** (eg tarantulas) and **snakes** may be found even in urban areas. Temperature swings in winter lead to a high incidence of **respiratory tract infections**. **Hookworm** infection is endemic so sandals must always be worn. A **yellow fever certificate** is required for travellers leaving the country travelling to endemic countries and all travellers entering from endemic countries.

Peru

Malaria risk exists throughout the year below 1500m in the following rural regions: Ayacucho, Cajamarca, Cerro de Pasco, Chachapoyas, Chanca-Andahuaylas, Cutervo, Cuzco, Huancavelica, Jaen, Junín, La Libertad, Lambayeque, Loreto, Luciano Castillo, Madre de Dios, Piura, San Martín, Tumbes and Ucayali with chloroquine-resistant falciparum reported from Jaen, Lambayeque, Loreto, Luciano Castillo, Piura, San Martín, Tumbes and Ucayali. Chloroquine and proguanil combined are considered adequate prophylaxis except in the areas where falciparum is reported where mefloquine is preferred. There is no risk for visitors to Lima, the coastal areas south of Lima and the highland tourist areas of Cuzco (city), Machu Picchu and Lake Titicaca. In 1999 cases of **yellow fever** were reported from the departments of Ayacucho, Huanuco, Junín, Loreto and San Martin. Yellow fever **vaccination** is required for all travellers over 6 months of age travelling from infected countries and recommended for anyone entering the country, particularly bound for jungle areas below 2300m.

Dengue fever outbreaks are particularly frequent in the Amazon Basin. Peru has the highest rate of **typhoid fever** in South America and the Amazon Basin in Peru has the highest levels of **hepatitis A**. Bites from **rabid bats** in the southeastern jungle areas and the Condorcanqui province in particular have caused a number of deaths. **Altitude sickness** can be a problem if you fly into the Andes (eg Cuzco or around the Titicaca area from the coast). High humidity in summer may lead to **respiratory difficulties** in susceptible individuals and **fungal skin infections**.

Surinam

Malaria risk in rural areas throughout the year with low risk in the Paramaribo District and the coastal area north of 5 degrees northern latitude. The predominant strain is falciparum and chloroquine resistance is common. Mefloquine is therefore the recommended prophylaxis. **Myiasis** (botfly and screwworm) occurs in rural areas. **Yellow fever vaccination** is recommended for all travellers over 1 year-old and required from those travelling from infected countries.

Uruguay

Typhoid fever occurs but is uncommon. The damp climate of Montevideo may exacerbate **respiratory illness-**

es. There have been no cases of rabies in recent years. A **HIV test** is required for anyone applying for residency. Foreign tests may not be accepted.

Venezuela

In 1999, over 20,000 cases of **malaria** were reported throughout the country. Risk exists throughout the year in all rural areas of Amazonas, Apure, Barinas, Bolívar, Sucre and Táchira states. Falciparum risk is restricted to municipalities in the jungle areas of Amazonas (Atabapo), Bolívar, (Cedeno, Gran Sabana, Raul Leoni, Sifontes and Sucre) and Delta Amacuro (Antonia Diaz, Casacoima and Pedernales). Chloroquine resistance is reported and mefloquine is recommended for prophylaxis in the Amazon Basin whereas the combination of chloroquine and proguanil is effective elsewhere. There is no significant risk in Caracas or Margarita. **Visceral leishmaniasis** occurs although is rare. **Schistosomiasis** is present in north central Venezuela. River water polluted with **mercury** in the southeastern region bordering Brazil has caused a number of deaths. The altitude and climate of Caracas may exacerbate **asthma** and other **respiratory problems**. Although a valid **yellow fever certificate** is not a prerequisite for entry, anyone planning to travel to rural areas (particularly Amazonas State) should be vaccinated.

Western Europe

Andorra, Austria, Azores, Belgium, Canary Islands, Denmark (including the Faroe Islands), Finland, France, Germany, Gibraltar, Greece, Iceland, Ireland, Italy, Liechtenstein, Luxembourg, Madeira, Malta, Monaco, Netherlands, Norway, Portugal, San Marino, Spain, Sweden, Switzerland, United Kingdom

Generally, specific health risks are rare in Western Europe. **Tick-borne encephalitis** occurs in forested areas of Western and Central Europe (from Scandinavia to the Mediterranean) and **Lyme disease** has been reported throughout Western Europe. The risk of contracting both of these diseases is very low but increases if you are camping or hiking in areas inhabited by deer in the summer months. Take suitable precautions against tick bites. The cold and damp climate in northern and central lowlands leads to a high incidence of **respiratory tract infections**, particularly in winter. Eating undercooked meat or fish as is the fashion in some European countries increases the risk of **worm infections**. **Rabies** risk exists in Western Europe (not in the UK and mainland Norway), principally in the fox population (bats in Greenland), although is very rare and unlikely to pose risk to the traveller. Whilst sporadic outbreaks may occur, especially in the rural areas of the hotter, southern countries of the region, the risk of **typhoid fever** is very low. **Influenza** epidemics occur between November and April in Western Europe. The risk of contracting **hepatitis A** is slightly increased in the Mediterranean countries and Portugal. The prevalence of **hepatitis B** is very low in the region. Murine and tick-borne **typhus**, **leishmaniasis** (cutaneous and visceral), **sandfly fever** and **West Nile fever** occur in sporadic outbreaks in Mediterranean countries. The increase in **leishmaniasis** incidence in Mediterranean countries is linked to the rise in prevalence of HIV infection. Outbreaks of **brucellosis** occur in the southern areas and **echinococcosis** in the southeast. **Crimean–Congo haemorrhagic fever** and **rodent-borne haemorrhagic fever** occur in very rare outbreaks. **Fasciola hepatica** has been reported in some countries. **Mediterranean spotted fever** occurs in rare outbreaks along the Mediterranean coast. **Diphyllobothriasis** is found in countries surrounding the Baltic Sea. There is no risk of malaria, yellow fever or schistosomiasis in Western Europe. High altitude in the Alps may cause **altitude sickness**. **Weever fish** can be a hazard off some beaches.

Austria

Lyme disease and **tick-borne encephalitis** are relatively common.

Azores

A **yellow fever vaccination** certificate is required from travellers over 1 year of age coming from infected areas (unless in transit at the airport).

Belgium

Because of **pollution**, swimming in the canals and rivers is ill-advised. **Lyme disease** may be a risk in the summer in the Ardennes area. An outbreak of legionnaires' disease occurred in Kapellen in the late autumn of 1999.

Denmark (including the Faroe Islands)

Diphyllobothriasis occurs rarely along the Baltic coast.

Finland

The winters are very **cold** and days can be very short. Vitamin D supplements may be a good idea for prolonged stays in the winter months (deprivation of sunlight).

France

Leishmaniasis (cutaneous and visceral), **sandfly fever**, **West Nile virus** and **typhus** (murine and tick-borne) occur very rarely along the Mediterranean coast. Air pollution in the large cities (particularly Paris and Lyon) may cause **respiratory problems**.

Germany

HIV testing is required for any foreigner staying more than 180 days in Bavaria. Foreign tests are not accepted.

Gibraltar

Leishmaniasis (cutaneous and visceral), **sandfly fever, West Nile virus** and **typhus** (murine and tick-borne) and **brucellosis** occur very rarely.

Greece

Leishmaniasis (cutaneous and visceral) (especially in Crete), **sandfly fever, West Nile virus** and **typhus** (murine and tick-borne) occur very rarely along the Mediterranean coast. **Echinococcosis** and **brucellosis** also occur with a higher incidence among those in close animal contact. Air pollution in Athens may cause **respiratory problems**.

A **yellow fever vaccination** certificate is required from travellers over 6 months of age coming from infected areas.

WESTERN EUROPE

519

HIV testing is required for women intending to work in entertainment centres. Foreign tests may be acceptable.

Ireland
A **measles** outbreak occurred in 2000, focused principally around north Dublin.

Italy
Leishmaniasis (cutaneous and visceral), **sandfly fever, West Nile virus** and **typhus** (murine and tick-borne) occur if only very rarely along the Mediterranean coast. **Echinococcosis** and **brucellosis** also occur rarely. Air pollution in the large cities (particularly Milan) may cause **respiratory problems**.

Luxembourg
The waterways are heavily **polluted** and swimming in them should be avoided.

Madeira
Entry requirements for Madeira are the same as for Portugal.

Malta
Leishmaniasis (cutaneous and visceral), **sandfly fever**, **West Nile virus** and **typhus** (murine and tick-borne) occur rarely along the Mediterranean coast. **Echinococcosis** and **brucellosis** also occur rarely. A **yellow fever vaccination** certificate is required from travellers over 9 months of age coming from infected areas, although under certain conditions those under 9 months may be subjected to a period of isolation.

Monaco

Leishmaniasis (cutaneous and visceral), **sandfly fever**, **West Nile virus** and **typhus** (murine and tick-borne) have been reported along the Mediterranean coast although outbreaks are very rare.

Portugal

Brucellosis, **leishmaniasis** (cutaneous and visceral), and **tick-borne illnesses** have been reported although incidence is very low. A **yellow fever certificate** is required from travellers over 1 year of age arriving from infected areas bound for the Azores or Madeira unless they are in transit through Funchal, Porto Santo or Santa Maria.

San Marino

Rare outbreaks of **leishmaniasis** (cutaneous and visceral) and **tick-borne illnesses** occur.

Spain

Leishmaniasis (cutaneous and visceral), **sandfly fever, West Nile virus** and **typhus** (murine and tick-borne) occur very rarely along the Mediterranean coast. **Brucellosis** also occurs rarely. Air pollution in the large cities may cause **respiratory problems**. A **medical examination** is required of anyone applying for residency, or work or student permits. This may involve a **HIV test** and foreign tests are accepted under certain circumstances. Contact the embassy for further details.

Sweden

Lyme disease is relatively common in the south of the country, especially during the summer months. **Diphyllobothriasis** occurs rarely along the Baltic coast.

United Kingdom

Incidence of **Bovine spongiform encephalitis** (BSE) in the UK has received much media attention and is an ongoing issue. Although the full extent of the disease and how it is spread are not yet known, it remains very rare. Stringent European regulations have probably rendered British beef to be some of the safest in Europe – however, you might ask if the beef you're eating is in fact British.

Lyme disease may be a small risk in the summer in the New Forest area. An increase in the incidence of **cryptosporidiosis** has been reported over recent months in the south Midlands. Most cases have been contracted from poorly maintained swimming pools. Air pollution can be a significant risk in the big cities causing **respiratory problems**.

Anyone requesting entry to the UK may be required to undergo a **HIV test**. Entry may be denied if the result is positive.

4

Directory

Aspirin. Photo © Randy Faris/Corbis

It's a good idea to discuss your travel plans face to face with a health professional, but there is much that you can do yourself in terms of preparation. These days often the most accessible and up-to-date information source by far is the Internet, with a huge number of websites dedicated to health in general and travel health in particular. There are also a great many books and telephone helplines which can be invaluable resources.

Below are some recommended starting points – out of necessity, the list is selective. General resources have been grouped under three headings – **General travel resources**, **General medical resources** and **Travel health resources** – after which recommendations targeting more specific interests are listed under headings that loosely reflect those used in Part 1 of this guide (Insurance, Medical kits, Travelling with children and the like).

General travel resources

Travel Advice Unit
Consular Division Foreign & Commonwealth Office,
1 Palace Street, London SW1E 5HE
☏ 020/7238 4503 & 7238 4504
🖷 020/7238 4545
Ⓦ *www.fco.gov.uk/travel/*
The British Foriegn Office website contains good individual country data, including information on political unrest, natural disasters, epidemics and aircraft safety.

Ⓦ *www.travel.state.gov/*
The US State Department Bureau of Consular Affairs' homepage, which contains a full list of US embassies abroad and many

interesting links. In particular check out Ⓦ *travel.state.gov/travel_ warnings.html* and Ⓦ *travel.state.gov/foreignentryreqs.html*.

Ⓦ *www.travel.roughguides.com*
We provide detailed country-by-country information as well as a complete listing of all our travel books, plus newsletters, talk rooms and more.

Ⓦ *www.odci.gov/cia/publications/factbook/*
Not for the paranoid, this fascinating and incredibly detailed directory compiled by the CIA provides political, economic and geographical facts on a country-by-country basis.

Ⓦ *www.roadnews.com/*
A good all round webpage – go to "Resources for the Frequent Traveler" for information on web-based fax and email services, exchange rates, world weather, travel warnings and, of course, travel health.

Ⓦ *www.britannica.com/*
A brilliant search engine, whether you want to know more about schistosomiasis or Singapore, it's all there and in impressive detail.

General medical resources

Medical websites

Ⓦ *www.vnh.org/*
The US Virtual Naval Hospital offers a wealth of advice on a broad spectrum of health problems. A bit short on specific advice for travellers, but if you have the time to wander, you're bound to find some health topics of interest, whether it's "Anthrax Prevention" or "Stress Management". Click the "For Patients" icon on the homepage.

Ⓦ *www.merck.com/*

Sponsored by the Merck drug company, this site has a mass of general health-related information under "Health Infopark" and via the online version of the Merck Manual ("Search the Book"). It's a bit cumbersome to use and it can be difficult to find specific information, but persistence will be rewarded.

Ⓦ *www.healthtouch.com/*

American website providing information on a broad range of health-related issues – just click the "Health Information" icon. "Drug Information" is also useful, with an A–Z of available medicines (American names), their uses, cautions, side effects, interactions and the like.

Ⓦ *www.drkoop.com/*

A well-established American site providing information on a wide variety of health-related subjects in addition to drug information, chatrooms, message boards and an "Ask the Experts" Q-and-A feature.

On-line consultations

There are a number of companies offering **virtual consultations**, enabling you to seek reliable, personalized advice 24 hours a day via the Net. Most require you to register then pay for each subsequent consultation. They usually reply to your query within 48 hours. This is a fast-growing area, but here are a few current options:

Ⓦ *www.britmed.com*

UK-based, so will not accept clients from the US or Canada.

Ⓦ *www.doctorglobal.com/*

New Zealand-based site offering specialized clinics over the Internet.

ⓦ www.thetraveldoctor.com/

US-based and specializing in travel medicine, the site offers nothing in the way of personalized consultations but for a fee will produce a detailed report on your destination, including disease risks, safety of drinking water, medicine availability, areas to avoid, etc.

ⓦ www.e-med.co.uk/

This British company offers private medical consultations via email, telephone and even in person. There is an initial membership fee and a further fee payable for each consultation.

Travel health resources

MASTA (Medical Advisory Services for Travellers Abroad) was set up by the London School of Hygiene and Tropical Medicine in 1984 with the aim of increasing awareness about travel health. They offer a MASTA Traveller's Healthline (pre-recorded: in the UK, ⓣ 0906/822 4100) which you phone up and leave details of your trip (dates, regions, types of accommodation you'll be staying in, whether you are pregnant, etc). They'll send a list of recommended vaccinations within a few days (payment is through your phonebill).

ProMED

307 Massachusetts Avenue NE, Washington, DC 20002
ⓣ 202/546-3300 (Voicemail)
ⓕ 202/675-1010
The ProMED, or Program for Monitoring Emerging Diseases, website is updated daily with reports of disease outbreaks. A little unwieldy (the information extends to plant and animal disease outbreaks as well as human), but very informed nevertheless.

The London School of Hygiene and Tropical Medicine

The malaria reference laboratory here offers a 24-hour phone

helpline advising on risk and preventative measures at your
destination: ℡ 0891/600350 (calls charged at £0.60 per minute).

British Airways Travel Clinics
115 Buckingham Palace Road, London SW1 (appointments only)
℡ 020/7233 6661; 30 Oxford St, Brighton (appointments only)
℡ 01273/606 636; or 156 Regent St, London W1 ℡ 020/439 9584
(drop in Mon–Fri 9.30am–5.15pm, Sat 10am–3.30pm)
A £10 consultation fee includes a MASTA list. Fees vary for
individual vaccinations.

Travel health websites

See the box overleaf for the top travel health sites. Others include:

Ⓦ *www.hc-sc.gc.ca/hpb/lcdc/*
Like the US CDC site (see box overleaf), the Canadian Laboratory
Centre for Disease Control's site offers a broad range of useful,
accurate and detailed advice – simply click on the "Travel Health"
icon. The website is available in both French and English.

Ⓦ *www.tmvc.com.au/*
The Australian version of the CDC travel website.

Ⓦ *www.fitfortravel.scot.nhs.uk/*
A neat and easily navigable travel-health site compiled and
maintained by the Scottish Centre for Infection and Environmental
Health. It's organized along similar lines to the CDC site although
the individual country data is refreshingly concise. Good links,
too.

Ⓦ *www.healthlink.mcw.edu/travel-medicine/*
A good, clear guide to travel-related medical topics from the
Medical College of Wisconsin. Written in an easy style, free from
medical jargon.

Top 5 travel health sites

ⓦ *www.cdc.gov*

Comprehensive website run by the American Centers for Disease Control and Prevention, packed with advice and links for both the traveller and those at home. Particularly useful are the "Traveler's Health" section, which provides excellent up-to-date outbreak and immunization advice, as well as specific sections for travel-related diseases, travelling with children, travellers with special needs, etc, and "Health Topics A–Z", an alphabetical listing of a large number of diseases. The whole of the site is accessible in both English and Spanish. If you can't find it here, you won't find it anywhere.

CDC also offer a travel health helpline (toll-free in the US): ⓣ 877/FYI-TRIP.

ⓦ *www.tripprep.com*

Superb site run by Shoreland Inc, packed with information on travel-related diseases in its "Traveler Information" section while serving up detailed, country-by-country commentary of health risks in its "Destination Information" section.

ⓦ *www.medicineplanet.com/*

It's hard to fault a website that has thought of everything: apart from providing information on immunizations, diseases, country-by-country risks plus a series of well-written articles, this California-based site has a couple of fascinating extras. A truly winning touch is the "Personal Travel History", in which you can enter your personal details (including whether you're

ⓦ *www.masta.org*

A good website from a reputable source (see p.528), although it doesn't quite match up to the CDC in terms of coverage and detail.

epileptic, pregnant, elderly, etc), along with your intended destination and within seconds you receive a customized, succinct resume of the risks involved in travelling to your destination, along with the suggested immunizations. Another clever idea, which will doubtlessly become increasingly important, is the "m-Health" feature, through which you can dial up the website via a mobile telephone and access the "International Medicine Translator" (eg to find out the various different names for paracetamol in Thailand), global disease outbreak updates and even on-call medical consultations.

Ⓦ *www.who.int/*
The World Health Organisation compiles invaluable global data on disease prevalence and trends, as well as designing and implementing eradication programmes. Their expansive website has excellent disease fact sheets (click the "Health Topics" icon on the homepage), the very latest on disease outbreaks and up-to-date advice on malaria prophylaxis and yellow fever vaccinations.

Ⓦ *www.wtgonline.com/*
Produced by the American Columbus Publishing Company, this site is the Internet version of their *World Travel Guide*, and offers both excellent coverage and ease of negotiability. Click "Region", then "Country" and then the arrow on the "Travel Information" window to reach health advice. The site is also accessible in German and Spanish.

Ⓦ *www.medteams.com*
Although strictly speaking designed for medical professionals, this site has a great deal of useful information for the non-medically

minded traveller in its "Country Facts" section. Subheadings of particular interest include "Diseases by World Region" (although a little out of date), "Other Insect Diseases", "Food, Water and Travelers Diarrhea" and "Blue Sheet, Summary/Disease", the last of which details countries currently regarded as "infected" with cholera, yellow fever and plague (again this needs some updating).

Ⓦ *www.doh.gov.uk/traveladvice/*
This website from the UK Department of Health is a pretty good "before you go site" with up-to-date advice on recommended immunizations and disease outbreaks as well as suggested medical kits.

Publications

Where There is No Doctor,
edited by David Werner (Macmillan).
Regarded as something of a bible for missionary and relief workers over the years, and fair to say that the book is very much focused on more general health-related issues of the developing world rather than those directly affecting the traveller. Nevertheless it offers a simple, practical, hands-on approach to all sorts of medical problems for the non-medically minded and is worth seeking out if you're planning a prolonged trip off the beaten track.

Travellers' Health: How to Stay Healthy Abroad,
Dr Richard Dawood (OUP; out of print).
First published in 1986, this well-respected book has long been regarded as the last word in travel health. Thoroughly researched and boasting a number of eminent contributors, it's less handy if you're intent on travelling light.

Health Advice for Travellers,
known as the "T6" leaflet (UK Department of Health).
Published annually, this booklet contains general information on

vaccinations, travel insurance and reciprocal healthcare arrangements between countries. Considering it's free, it's a great resource, available from UK post offices.

The returning traveller

If you suspect a travel-related illness, then your first stop is your family doctor or a speciality travel clinic. A number of websites provide the addresses of travel clinics, notably Medicineplanet (US; see p.530), British Airways (UK and South Africa: Ⓦ *www.british-airways.com*) and TMVC (Australia, New Zealand, Southeast Asia; see p.529).

Also worth checking out are:

The London Hospital for Tropical Diseases
4 St Pancras Way, London NW1 0PE
Ⓣ 020/7387 4411;
Ⓣ 0839/337733 (Travel Clinic healthline)
Ⓕ 0991/991992
Ⓦ *www.uclh.org/htd*

Ⓦ *www.istm.org*
A really useful site produced by the International Society of Tropical Medicine giving contact addresses, telephone numbers and email addresses of travel clinics in 39 different countries.

Travel Screening Services (London)
Ⓣ 020/7830 9683|
Ⓦ *www.tropicalscreening.com*

Insurance

ⓦ *www.abi.org.uk/*

Good basic, independent advice from the Association of British
Insurers. Click on "Consumer Advice and Information", then
"Holiday", then "Holiday Insurance and Motoring Abroad".

ⓦ *www.armchair.com/*

Armchair World offers an interesting website with everything from

Rough Guides Travel Insurance

Rough Guides offer their own travel insurance, customized for
our readers by a leading UK broker and backed by a Lloyds
underwriter. It's available for anyone, of any nationality, travelling anywhere in the world, for those aged over 65 aswell.

There are two main Rough Guide insurance plans:
Essential, for effective, no-frills cover, starting at £11.75 for 2
weeks; and Premier – more expensive but with more generous
and extensive benefits. Each offers European or Worldwide
cover, and can be supplemented with a "Hazardous Activities
Premium" if you plan to indulge in sports considered dangerous, such as scuba-diving or trekking. Unlike many policies,
the Rough Guides schemes are calculated by the day, so if
you're travelling for 27 days rather than a month, that's all you
pay for. You can alternatively take out annual multi-trip insurance, which covers you for all your travel throughout the year
(with a maximum of 60 days for any one trip).

For a policy quote, call the Rough Guides Insurance Line on
UK freefone ℡ 0 800/0150906, or, if you're calling from outside Britain on ℡ (44)1243/621 046. Alternatively, get an
online quote at www.roughguides.com/insurance.

resources for the traveller to food and wine information. An odd mixture, but the article under "Travel-Related Insurances" is particularly worth a read.

Ⓦ *www.travelassist.com/mag/a64.html*
A short but useful appraisal from the American TravelASSIST magazine.

Travel by air

Disinsectization
More information on disinsectization can be obtained from the CDC website (Ⓦ *www.cdc.gov/travel/sprayair.htm*), or for quite detailed explanation and country specifics, check out Ⓦ *ostpxweb.dot.gov/policy/safety/disin.htm*

Aerophobia
Check Ⓦ *www.fearofflying.com/*, a commercial US-based website run by Tom Bunn, an ex-airline pilot and, handily enough, trained therapist. The site endeavours to get you to enroll on their course – there again, that might be just what you need. It's a bit short on advice unless you enroll.

Another commercial site which doesn't give too much away unless you enroll is Ⓦ *www.flywithconfidence.com/*.

Melatonin
There's a great deal of information about melatonin at Ⓦ *www.pricespower.com/power* but bear in mind the idea is to get you to buy the product, which they'll deliver to your door.

Another commercially sponsored site, but with some interesting links to newsgroups, FAQs, articles and studies, is Ⓦ *www.melatonin.com/*

Medical kits

You can order travel health products online from the MASTA and Armchair World websites (see pp.530 & 534). Otherwise try the following commercial websites, which offer a broad range of kits at various prices:

Harris International Healthcare Ltd
10115 Towhee Ave, Adelphi, MD 20783-1209
ⓣ 301/422-2706 or 800/577-0955
ⓦ www.safetravel.com/

Travel Healthy
349 East Las Colinas Blvd, Suite C, Irving, TX 75039
ⓣ 972/401-1331
ⓕ 972/739-2806
ⓦ www.travelhealthy.net/

Alternative kits

See ⓦ www.homeopathyhome.com (opposite) and
ⓦ www.redmtremedies.com/ (p.538) websites. Also:

Ainsworth Homoeopathic Pharmacy
36 New Cavendish Street, London W1
ⓣ 020/7935 5330 or 7486 4313
They sell a travel kit containing 10 of the most useful homeopathic remedies.

Helios Homoeopathic Pharmacy and Clinic
ⓣ 01892/536393 or 537254
ⓔ info@medicalert.co.uk
ⓦ www.helios.co.uk
Offer a travel kit of homeopathic remedies, as well as supply individual mail-order remedies and books.

Medical emergency ID

Medicalert
1 Bridge Wharf, 156 Caledonian Rd, London N1 9UU
ⓣ 020/7833 3034
ⓕ 020/7278 0647
ⓔ info@medicalert.co.uk
ⓦ www.medicalalert.co.uk
Also try ⓦ www.medicalert.com.au and ⓦ www.medicalert.org,
Australian and US sites respectively.

Homeopathy and alternative medicine

The Society of Homoeopaths in the UK (ⓣ 01604/621 400) will
provide details of your nearest practitioner and answer any
queries. You can also contact:

The Homoeopathic Information Service
23 Berkeley Road, Bishopston, Bristol BS7 8HF
ⓣ 0117/944 5147
ⓔ info@HomInf.org.uk
ⓦ www.hominf.org.uk/
See opposite for suppliers of homeopathic travel kits in the UK.

Websites

ⓦ *www.homoeopathyhome.com*
you're searching for anything remotely homeopathic, this site holds
a wealth of US and UK homeopathy contacts, interesting articles,
chat rooms, discussion groups and addresses of suppliers of
homeopathic goods. Check the "Directory", "Reference" and
"WWW" icons.

ⓦ *www.classicalhomoeopathy.com/*
A very detailed site with a multitude of generalized articles on homeopathy although specific advice is difficult to find. Perhaps the most
useful resource is the ability to consult a homeopath online (for a fee).

ⓦ *www.create.org/elchai/*
A good introduction to herbal remedies including advice on
preparation of herbal teas (click on "Herbs for Healthy Balance").

ⓦ *www.picoftheweb.com/healing/herbs/*
A useful, non-commercial information site which offers similar
options to the above elchai site.

ⓦ *www.redmtremedies.com/*
A commercial site from Red Mountain Remedies selling herbal
products as well as a herbal health kit for travellers.

Publications
The World Traveller's Manual of Homoeopathy, by
Colin B. Lessell (C.W.Daniel Co. Ltd).
Very detailed for the long-haul traveller.

The Traveller's Guide to Homoeopathy, by Phyllis
Speight (Beekman).
A small, light and economical guide for beginners.

Natural Healing for Women, by Susan Curtis and Romy
Fraser (HarperCollins).

The traveller with asthma

All the sites listed under "Medical websites" above contain
information on asthma; ⓦ*www.merck.com/disease/*, in particular,

holds a massive amount of information under the "Asthma " icon.

The traveller with diabetes

Diabetes is well represented on the Internet, and most countries have a diabetic association. The sites listed above under "General medical resources" will all have information but below are a few more specific contact addresses, phone numbers and websites.

Diabetes UK (formerly the British Diabetic Association)
10 Queen Anne St, London W1M 0BD
℡ 020/7323 1531
⨏ 020/7637 3644
Ⓦ www.diabetes.org.uk/

The Canadian Diabetes Association
15 Toronto St, Ste #800, Toronto, ON, M5C 2E3
℡ 416/363-3373 or 800/BANTING
Ⓔ info@diabetes.ca
Ⓦ www.diabetes.ca/

American Diabetic Association
ADA National Service Center,
1660 Duke Street, Alexandria, VA 22314
℡ 703/549-1500 or 800/DIABETES
Ⓦ www.diabetes.org/
There's a wealth of information on this site, so it takes a bit of finding the few useful bits for the diabetic traveller: add "ada/c60e.asp" to the above stem.

Australian Diabetes Society
145 Macquarie St, Sydney, NSW 2000

ⓣ 612/9256 5462
ⓕ 612/9241 4083
ⓦ www.racp.edu.au/ads/

International Diabetes Federation
1 rue Defacqz, B-1000 Brussels, Belgium
ⓣ (32) 2/538-5511
ⓕ (32) 2/538-5114
ⓔ idf@idf.org
ⓦ www.idf.org/eng/
Go to "Links" for the best worldwide diabetic links page you'll find.

Diabetes New Zealand
P.O.Box 54, Oamaru
ⓣ (64) 3/434-8110 or 0800/DIABETES
ⓕ (64) 3/434-5281
ⓔ info@diabetes.org.nz
ⓦ www.diabetes.org.nz/

ⓦ www.umassmed.edu/diabeteshandbook/
An online "handbook" of everything you need to know as a
diabetic provided by the University of Massachusetts Medical
School. Chapter 14 deals with travel. The site is also available in
Spanish.

The traveller with epilepsy

British Epilepsy Association
New Anstey House, Gate Way Drive, Yeadon, Leeds LS19 7XY
ⓣ 0113/210 8800
ⓕ 0113/391 0300
ⓔ epilepsy@bea.org.uk
ⓦ www.epilepsy.org.uk/

Epilepsy Foundation of America
4351 Garden City Drive, Landover, MD 20785
℡ 301/459-3700 or 800/EFA-1000
🅕 301/577-4941
🅔 webmaster@efa.org
🅦 www.efa.org/

Epilepsy Canada
1470 Peel St, Ste 745, Montréal,
QUÉ H3A 1T1
℡ 514/845-7855 or 800/860-5499
🅕 514/845-7866
🅔 epilepsy@epilepsy.ca
🅦 www.epilepsy.ca/

Epilepsy Queensland Inc
PO Box 459, Brisbane, Albert St 4002, Queensland, Australia
℡ 07/3404 3131
🅕 07/3404 3125
🅦 www.eqi.org.au/

Travelling with HIV

The **CDC** (see p.530) has useful information under the heading of
"Special Needs Travelers", but the Internet is not short of
dedicated HIV/AIDS sites so a little surfing will pay off. Here are
but a few worthy sites:

🅦 www.aegis.com/topics/travel.html
Aegis claims to be the largest HIV/AIDS website in the world and
this link into their "Traveling with HIV" section is invaluable.

ⓦ *www.thebody.com/*

An excellent US-based website offering a great deal of information on HIV and AIDS. Articles from their monthly magazine, "Body Positive", which frequently cover travel health issues, can be accessed through the website. Check out the article by Ronald Russo in the June 1999 edition, "On the Road with HIV... or, How to Have a Healthy, Fun Vacation".

ⓦ *www.infoweb.org/*

HIV Infoweb has a vast amount of information and links. Click the "Travel-Related" icon.

ⓦ *www.outandabout.com/*

Offering a large amount of information under the "Gay Travel Health" icon.

ⓦ *www.aidsnet.ch/*

Advice on HIV and AIDS in French, German, Italian and English, also providing up-to-date visa and entry restrictions on an individual country basis for HIV. Click on the flag for the language you wish to use, scroll down to "Thematic Information" and click on "Tourism and Travel".

ⓦ *www-hsl.mcmaster.ca/tomflem/std.html*

A useful Internet link resource for HIV, AIDS and other sexually transmitted diseases.

The elderly traveller

There's useful advice for the elderly traveller on the **Medicineplanet** and **Shoreland's Tripprep** (under "Special Needs") websites (see p.530). More tailored sources of information include:

Age Concern
1268 London Rd, London SW16 4EJ
Ⓣ 020/8679 8000
Ⓕ 020/8679 6069
Ⓔ *infodep@ace.org.uk*
Ⓦ *www.ace.org.uk*

Help the Aged
St James's Walk, Clerkenwell Green, London EC1R 0BE
Ⓣ 020/7253 0253
Ⓕ 020/7250 4474
Ⓔ *info@helptheaged.org.uk*
Ⓦ *www.helptheaged.org.uk/*
You have to look quite hard for practical holiday information on
their site, but it's worth the search. Go to "Advice and Info" then
"Info Point". Scroll down the list of PDF files to "Holidays" and
you'll find 13 pages of useful information. The "Useful Links" under
"Advice and Info" are also good.

American Association of Retired Persons
601 E St. NW, Washington, DC 20049
Ⓣ 800/424-3410
Ⓔ *member@aarp.org*
Ⓦ *www.aarp.org/*
The AARP website has a wealth of information on many issues,
plus travel reviews, anecdotes and special-offer holidays found
under "Trips 'n' Travel".

Council on the Aging (Australia)
Level 2, 3 Bowen Crescent, Melbourne, Victoria 3004
Ⓣ 03/9820 2655
Ⓕ 03/9820 9886
Ⓔ *cota@cota.org.au*
Ⓦ *www.cota.org.au/*

Look for a great many links under "Information Sheets" as well as "Links to the Web".

The disabled traveller

The Disabled Traveller, by Alison Walsh (BBC Books), is an excellent general resource packed full of further information sources and contacts (order it from Disabled Traveller, PO Box 7, London W12 8UD).

The **CDC** and **Medicineplanet** websites (see p.530) also provide useful advice specifically for disabled travellers. Recommended among the large number of dedicated websites dealing with disability issues are:

Ⓦ *www.eskimo.com/~jlubin/disabled/travel*
If you had but one website to visit, this should be the one. The site is maintained by Jim Lubin who is tetraplegic himself.

Ⓦ *www.disabilitynet.co.uk*
An excellent general reference resource with global, penpal and consultation links.

Ⓦ *www.access-able.com*
An invaluable resource with links to many other related sites, this site contains information on databases, tours, accommodation and local contacts.

Access-Able Travel Source
PO Box 1796, Wheat Ridge, CO 80214
Ⓣ 303/232 2979
Ⓕ 303/239 8486
Ⓔ *carol@access-able.com*

ⓦ *www.wheelabout.com/links*
Run by an Australian car-hire firm; the links page offers good
information for the disabled traveller in Australia and elswhere.

ⓦ *www.hicom.net/~oedipus*
Click on "Blindness-Related Resources on the Web and Beyond"
for international links for the visually and hearing impaired.

ⓦ *205.136.244.3/bistext/fsheets/19.stm*
A very useful webpage if you have special needs and you're
planning a trip in and around the UK.

ⓦ *www.ukstroke.com/holidaycare/*
This UK-based charity is a great source of information for the
disabled traveller. Although specific information is limited and it lacks
any links, a large number of publications are available to order.

Holiday Care Service
2nd Floor, Imperial Buildings, Victoria Rd,
Horley, Surrey RH6 7PZ
ⓣ 01293/774535
ⓕ 01293/784647

Travelling with children

CDC and **Medicineplanet** websites (see p.530) all provide good
information.

ⓦ *www.sleeptight.com/EncyMaster/*
The principle aim of this website is to get you to buy a copy of their
"Sleep Tight Video", but the encyclopedia of children's complaints
authored by Dr Jeffrey Hullis enough to keep any paranoid parent
awake for many a long hour.

Women travellers

ⓦ *www.dfait-maeci.gc.ca/*
The Canadian Department of Foreign Affairs and Trade's website
has a really good article for women travellers, in French or English.
Click on "Travel" then scroll down the options on the left to find
"Her Own Way – Advice for the Woman Traveller".

ⓦ *www.journeywoman.com/*
A little eccentric in places, but with a great deal of useful
information. The list ranges from altitude sickness to the 10 best
places in the world to meet single men (apparently). Enough said!

The active traveller

Altitude
Shoreland's Trippreps and **Medicineplanet** websites (see p.530)
have good advice on altitude sickness. Other useful contacts
include:

CIWEC Clinic Travel Medicine Center
Yak & Yeti Road, Durbar Marg, PO Box 12895, Kathmandu, Nepal
ⓣ (977) 1/228531or 241732
ⓕ (977) 1/224675
ⓔ *advice@ciwec-clinic.com*
ⓦ *www.ciwec-clinic.com/*
Kathmandu-based travel clinic offering advice about altitude
sickness as well as more general health information.

The British Mountaineering Council
177-179 Burton Rd, Manchester
ⓣ 0161/445 4747
ⓕ 0161/445 4500

Ⓔ office@thebmc.co.uk

Ⓦ www.thebmc.org/

Click on "The World", scroll down to "Mountain Medicine" for some very useful articles.

The Himalaya Rescue Association

Ⓦ www.nepalonline.net/hra/

Detailed medical advice, good mountaineering links.

Scuba diving

Ⓦ www.mtsinai.org/

The website of the Mt Sinai Hospital, Cleveland, USA. Scroll down the menu on the left, click "Pulmonary Medicine", then "Scuba Diving", and you'll find an amazingly detailed synopsis of the medical considerations surrounding diving. There are also an impressive number of useful diving links.

Scuba Diving Explained, Lawrence Martin.
Order from Best Publishing Co, PO Box 30100, Flagstaff, AZ 86003-0100.

Ⓦ www.scubadiving.com/

A great all-round site for divers run by Rodales Scuba Diving Magazine. Click on "Training and Safety", then "Dive Medicine" for a series of useful articles.

Ⓦ www.voicenet.co.jp/~jeanphi/dangeroussealife.htm

Clear and concise descriptions of the whole spectrum of marine hazards by a former Special Forces Commando.

Other interesting websites on diving include Ⓦ www.bsac.com/ (the British Sub Aqua Club), Ⓦ www.diving-uk.com/ and Ⓦ www.amazinscuba.com/

First aid

The **Virtual Naval Hospital Website** (see p.526) contains excellent first aid advice, covering everything from bites and stings, to fractures, to open abdominal wounds.

The Australian website Ⓦ *www.medicalonline.com.au/* Offers useful advice under "First Aid", with information also on the treatment of sports injuries (click the "Disease Index" icon, then "Sporting Injuries"). Links to an impressive variety of related resources by clicking "Other Med Sites".

For local first aid courses, contact your national Red Cross: Ⓦ *www.redcross.org/*.

Blood transfusions

The Blood Care Foundation

16 Lonsdale Gardens, Tunbridge Wells, Kent TN1 1NU

Ⓣ 01732/742 427

or

Chemin de la Petite-Fontaine

CH-1270 Trelex , Vaud, Switzerland

Ⓣ (41) 22/369 19 04

Ⓕ (41) 22/369 28 14

Glossary

abscess – a localized collection of pus

allopathic – reference to orthodox medical treatment

anaemia – a deficiency of haemoglobin in the blood

analgesics – pain killers

anaphylaxis – an extreme hypersensitivity reaction which can be life-threatening

antiemetics – drugs used to prevent vomiting

antivenin – an antitoxin which counteracts venom

asymptomatic – without symptoms

BCG Bacillus Calmette-Guérin: a vaccination against TB

biliary tract – common word for the liver, gall bladder and bile ducts

cardiac – pertaining to the heart

cardiovascular – pertaining to the heart and blood vessels

carrier – a person or animal harbouring disease-producing organisms without exhibiting symptoms

chancre – a red, hard, painless skin lesion associated with syphilis

CNS – Central Nervous System

conjunctiva – thin layer of cells covering the front of the eyeball and the inner surface of the lids

contra-indicated – a condition in which a drug must not be given

cyanosis – a blue tinge to the lips and skin resulting from lack of oxygen

cystitis – bladder inflammation

diagnosis – determination of a disease by assessment of the symptoms diuretic – a drug that promotes fluid loss through the kidneys causing increased urine output

DVT – Deep Vein Thrombosis – the formation of a blood clot in one of the deep veins of the leg, usually manifesting as a painful, swollen, hot, red calf

encephalitis – inflammation of the brain

endemic – prevalent, common or frequently occurring in a particular area

endoscopy – a flexible fibreoptic tube passed down the throat to examine the stomach

envenomation – the transfer of poisonous venom

enzymes – naturally-produced proteins which act as catalysts for chemical reactions between other substances

epidemic – a rapid, geographically localized, spread of infectious disease

faecal-oral – the method by which most gut microbes are passed on, ie faeces to hands to mouth

fluke – a flat-worm, usually parasitic

fracture – a broken bone

glaucoma – a build-up of pressure within the eye producing visual problems

haemoglobin – the oxygen-carrying molecule of the blood

haemorrhagic fever – a viral infection which results in increased bleeding tendency

hypoglycaemia – low blood sugar

immunoglobulins – antibodies, used by the body to fight infection

immunosuppressed – an inability to fight off infection

impetigo – a bacterial infection of the skin which results in honey-coloured crusting

intravenous – drugs or fluids given directly into a vein via a drip or injection

jaundice – yellow discolouration of the skin and conjunctiva resulting from a build-up of bile pigments in the blood and with a variety of causes

lumbar puncture – a large needle is passed into the space around the spinal cord to tap off cerebrospinal fluid for lab analysis

lymphangitis – inflammation of the lymphatic system

lymphatic system – the anatomical system connecting the lymph glands to the venous system of the blood

malaise – non-specifically unwell, "out of sorts"

meningism – the physical signs that suggest meningitis

meningitis – swelling of the meninges, the membranes covering the brain

microfilariae – embryos of filariae, a parasitic worm family transmitted to vertebrates by insects

morbidity – the state of being diseased

NIS – New Independent States: the former Soviet Union

nodule – a knob-like growth

NSAIDs – Non-Steroidal Anti-Inflamatory Drugs

oedemaoedema (edema in US) – swelling caused by accumulation of fluid in the tissues

pancreatitis – inflammation of the pancreas

perineum – the area of the body between the genitals and anus

peritonitis – inflammation of the peritoneum, the lining of the abdominal cavity

pessary – a drug placed in the vagina

photophobia – intolerance to bright light

pneumothorax – a punctured lung, causing air to escape into the chest cavity

porphyria – a rare, inherited disorder which affects the production of haemoglobin in the red blood cells

prognosis – the likely overall outcome of an illness

prophylactic – preventative

prostate gland – a gland surrounding the urethra (the bladder outflow) in men

pulmonary – pertaining to the lungs

purgative – a drug that promotes bowel clearance

purulent – the presence of pus

pyrexia – fever

renal – pertaining to the kidneys

reservoir – where disease-causing organisms are maintained in the wild

rickettsia – a virulent sub-group of bacteria responsible for a number of potentially serious illnesses, eg Rocky Mountain spotted fever, Q fever and typhus

RIG – Rabies Immunoglobulin; part of the post-exposure treatment for rabies

rigor – uncontrollable shaking and a sensation of cold caused by fever

sciatica – back pain which radiates down the back of the leg

septicaemia – blood poisoning

suppository – a drug in tablet form which is placed in the rectum

symptom – a departure of normal body function, appearance or sensation usually indicative of disease

topical – local, usually referring to the application of creams, etc, to the skin

tourniquet – a tight constriction wrapped around a limb to restrict blood flow

URTI – Upper Respiratory Tract Infection; medical speak for a "cold"

vesicles – a fluid-filled skin lesion; "water blisters"

WHO – World Health Organization

zoonosis – a disease acquired by contact with animals

Index